Cultural Atlas of
FRANCE

Project Manager Graham Bateman
Editor Michael March
Art Editor Steve McCurdy
Cartographic Manager Olive Pearson
Cartographic Editor Sarah Rhodes
Picture Researcher Linda Proud
Design Adrian Hodgkins
Index Angela Mackeith
Proof Readers Lin Thomas, Sue Phillips
Production Clive Sparling
Typesetting Reina Foster-de Wit, Niki Whale,
Peter MacDonald Associates

Advisory Editor Professor Jacques Le Goff

AN ANDROMEDA BOOK

Planned and produced by
Andromeda Oxford Ltd
11-15 The Vineyard, Abingdon
Oxfordshire, England OX14 3PX

Facts On File, Inc:
460 Park Avenue South
New York NY 10016
USA

Facts On File Limited
Collins Street
Oxford OX4 1XJ
United Kingdom

ISBN 0-8160-2619-X

U.S. CIP data available upon request
from the Publisher

A British CIP catalogue is available
from the British Library

Facts On File books are available at
special discounts when purchased in
bulk quantities for businesses,
associations, institutions or sales
promotions. Please call our Special
Sales Department in New York at
212/683-2244 (dial 800/322-8755
except in NY, AK or HI) or in Oxford
0865/728399.

Origination by Eray Scan Ltd,
Singapore; Daylight Colour Art Ltd,
Singapore.

Printed in Italy by G. Canale & Co,
Turin.

10 9 8 7 6 5 4 3 2 1

Frontispiece Scenes from the French
Revolution by Le Sueur, 18th century,
gouache. Musée Carnavalet, Paris
(photos Jean-Loup Charmet).

Cultural Atlas of
FRANCE

by John Ardagh
with Colin Jones

☑
Facts On File
New York • Oxford

CONTENTS

Special Features

All texts written by John Ardagh except * Colin Jones (with additional contributions by † Ann Hughes-Gilbey and †† Dorothy Erskine).

List of Maps

CHRONOLOGICAL TABLE

	500	700	900	1100	1200	1300	1400	1500
FRANCE AND THE OUTSIDE WORLD	481–c.560 Clovis and his successors spread Frankish powers throughout Gaul and beyond	From early 8th century Frankish expansion in Europe 768–814 Construction of Carolingian Empire c.800–911 Viking raids and settlement 838–42 Arab raids on Mediterranean coasts 843 Treaty of Verdun: partition of Carolingian Empire and establishment of West Francia	917–27 Magyar raids 1066 Conquest of England by the Normans: beginnings of Anglo–Norman empire 1096–1270 The Crusades	1154–1259 Angevin Empire of Henry III of England	1214 Battle of Bouvines 1259 Treaty of Paris: English holdings in France reduced to Guyenne	1337–1453 Hundred Years War against England 1346 Battle of Crécy 1356 Battle of Poitiers 1360 Treaty of Brétigny: massive English expansion in southern France	1415 Battle of Agincourt 1429 Joan of Arc's intervention in the Hundred Years War 1453 End of the Hundred Years War: only Calais still in English hands 1494–1559 Italian Wars	1515 Battle of Marignano 1525 Battle of Pavia 1534–5 Expeditions of Jacques Cartier in Canada 1559 Treaty of Cateau–Cambrésis ends Italian Wars
POLITICS AND CONSTITUTION	MEROVINGIANS 481–751 481–511 Clovis 481–c.560 Creation of the kingdom of the Franks 511–751 Kindgom continually subdivided among Merovingian dynasty 639–751 The *Rois fainéants* and the mayors of the palace 687 Pepin of Herstal mayor of the palace	CAROLINGIANS 751–987 751 Pepin the Short deposes the Merovingian Childeric III and establishes the Carolingian dynasty 768–814 Charlemagne 888 Election of a "Robertian", Eudes, as king	911 Normandy ceded to the Vikings ("Normans") 922–87 Political rivalry between the Carolingians and the Robertians ("Capetians") CAPETIANS 987–1328 987 Election of "Robertian" Hugh Capet as king	1108–37 Louis VI "the Fat" 1137–80 Louis VIII 1180–1223 Philip Augustus	1226–70 Louis IX (Saint Louis) c.1250 Parlement of Paris constituted 1285–1314 Philip IV "the Fair":growth of state bureaucracy	1302 First meeting of representative assemblies of the "estates" VALOIS 1328–1589 1337–1453 Hundred Years War with England 1358 Parisian uprising led by Etienne Marcel	1422–61 Charles VII 1429 Charles VII and Joan of Arc lift the siege of Orléans: Charles crowned at Reims 1477 Death of Charles the Bold, duke of Burgundy 1491 Charles VIII marries Anne of Brittany	Late 15th to 16th centuries Renaissance monarchy 1515–47 Francis I 1560–98 Wars of Religion BOURBONS 1589–1792 1589 Henri of Navarre succeeds Henri III and as Henri IV ends the Wars of Religion by 1598 1589–1610 Henri IV
RELIGION AND CULTURE	?496 Baptism of Clovis	716–54 Saint Boniface christianizes Germany 732 Charles Martel defeats the Arabs at Poitiers 754 Pepin II crowned by Pope Stephen III at Reims Mid 8th to early 10th centuries "Carolingian Renaissance" 779–801 Institution of the tithe 800 Coronation of Charlemagne as Holy Roman Emperor by Pope Leo III	910 Establishment of the Benedictine monastery of Cluny Late 10th to early 11th centuries Peace and Truce of God movements 1095 Council of Clermont: Pope Urban II proclaims a crusade 1096–9 First Crusade Late 10th to mid 12th centuries Romanesque art and architecture	c.1100 *Chanson de Roland* 1147–9 Second Crusade 1189–92 Third Crusade "12th Century Renaissance" Mid 12th to 16th centuries Gothic architecture	1202–4 Fourth Crusade 1209–29 Albigensian Crusade 1217–21 Fifth Crusade 1228–9 Sixth Crusade 1244 Fall of Monségur, last Albigensian stronghold 1248–54 Seventh Crusade 1270 Eighth Crusade: death of Saint Louis in Tunis 1297 Canonization of Louis IX	1307 Philip the Fair arrests the Knights Templar (trial 1310–14) 1309–78 Papacy resident in Avignon	1431 Joan of Arc burned at the stake in Rouen 1438 Pragmatic Sanction of Bourges Late 15th to 16th centuries Renaissance: Italian influences in art, music, architecture, etc	1516 Concordat of Bologna with the Pope 1520s–1530s Spread of Lutheranism in some cities 1539 Edict of Villers–Cotterets: French the official state language 1560–98 Wars of Religion 1572 Massacre of Saint Bartholomew 1598 Edict of Nantes establishing religious tolerance
SOCIETY AND ECONOMY	6th to 7th centuries Continuing breakdown of urban life following the fall of the Roman Empire and the barbarian invasions Early development of feudal ties	9th and 10th centuries Major economic disruption caused by Viking, Arab and Magyar raids Feudalism and serfdom established 877 Charles the Bald makes fiefs hereditary		c.1100–c.1300 Period of medieval prosperity: urban growth, population increase, economic diversification		1315–16 Major famine 1347–52 Black Death 1352–1720 Plague present in France 1358 Major peasant uprising in northern France (the "Jacquerie") 14th and 15th centuries Economic distress caused by population decline, and damage caused by wars and famines		16th century Urban growth, rise of capitalism, the "price revolution"

1600	1700		1800		1900		
1618–48 Thirty Years War: France actively involved from 1635	**1756–63** Seven Years War: France loses Canada		**1815** Congress of Vienna: France loses most of her colonies		**1914–18** World War I	**1956** Independence for Morocco and Tunisia	FRANCE AND THE OUTSIDE WORLD
1659 Treaty of the Pyrenees with Spain	**1778–83** French involvement in the American War of Independence		**1830** French involvement in Algeria begins: construction of a "second empire"		**1919** Treaty of Versailles: Alsace and Lorraine regained	**1956** Suez crisis	
1689–1851 "Second Hundred Years War" with England: a series of conflicts fought in Europe and the colonies	**1792–1815** French Revolutionary and Napoleonic Wars		**1859** Italian War: annexation of Savoy and Nice		**1939–45** World War II	**1958** Algerian crisis provokes the overthrow of the Fourth Republic and the establishment of the Fifth	
1689–1715 Wars of Louis XIV			**1870** Franco–Prussian War: loss of Alsace and Lorraine		**1940** France crushed by Germany: armistice: partition of France into occupied territory and Vichy regime	**1960** Decolonization of black Africa	
			Late 19th century Major colonial gains		**1954** Battle of Dien Bien Phu: France loses Indo China	**1962** Evian Agreements grant independence to Algeria	
					1954 Algerian uprising begins	**1966** Withdrawal from military involvement in NATO	

1600	1700		1800		1900		
1614 Last meeting of the Estates General before 1789	**1715–74** Louis XV		THE FIRST EMPIRE 1804–15	THE SECOND REPUBLIC, 1848–52	**1920** Congress of Tours: foundation of the French Communist Party	THE FOURTH REPUBLIC 1944–58	POLITICS AND CONSTITUTION
1624–43 Cardinal Richelieu principal minister	**1789** French Revolution: National Constituent Assembly		**1814** Overthrow of Napoleon	**1851** Louis Bonaparte president for life	**1936–8** The Popular Front	**1944–6** Provisional government	
1643–61 Cardinal Mazarin principal minister	**1791** Legislative Assembly		**1815** The "Hundred Days": final defeat of Napoleon	THE SECOND EMPIRE, 1852–70	THE ETAT FRANCAIS (VICHY GOVERNMENT) 1940–4	**1946** Fourth Republic instituted	
1648–53 The Fronde	FIRST REPUBLIC 1792–1802		THE RESTORATION 1815–30	**1852** Coup d'état of Louis Bonaparte: emperor as Napoleon III		THE FIFTH REPUBLIC 1958–	
1661–1715 Sole rule of Louis XIV (king since 1642)	**1792** Overthrow of Louis XVI: establishment of the First Republic		**1815–24** Louis XVIII	**1870** Overthrow of Napoleon III	**1940** Fall of the Third Republic after military defeat by Germany: Pétain head of state of the Vichy government	**1958** Overthrow of Fourth Republic: de Gaulle president of the Fifth Republic	
	1792–4 The Convention: the Terror		**1824–30** Charles X	THE THIRD REPUBLIC 1870–1940	**1944** Liberation: establishment of a provisional government	**1968** "May events"	
	1795–99 The Directory		THE "JULY MONARCHY" 1830–48	**1870–1** The Paris Commune		**1969** Pompidou replaces de Gaulle	
	1799–1804 The Consulate, under the control of Napoleon Bonaparte		**1830–1848** Louis–Philippe	**1875** Constitutional Law		**1974** Election of Giscard d'Estaing as president	
				1886–9 Boulangism		**1981** Election of Mitterrand as president	
				1894–1906 The Dreyfus affair			

1600	1700		1800		1900		
Late 16th to 17th centuries The Counter-Reformation	18th century The Enlightenment		**1801** Concordat between Napoleon and Pope Pius VII reestablishes Catholicism	Post **1882** Education reforms introduced by Jules Ferry	**1905** Separation of church and state		RELIGION AND CULTURE
1631 Establishment by Renaudot of the *Gazette*	**1791** Civil Constitution of the Clergy		**1804** Napoleonic Civil Code	**1895** Cinema performance by Lumière	Post **1918** Dada and Surrealism		
After **1640** Growth of Jansenism	**1793–4** "Dechristianization" movement under the Terror		Early 19th century Romanticism in literature, music, art		Post **1945** Existentialism		
1661–82 Construction of Versailles			**1881** Pasteur produces anthrax vaccine		**1960** onwards Structuralism and post–structuralism		
Late 17th century Triumph of Classicism					**1977** Opening of the Pompidou Center, Paris		
1685 Revocation of the Edict of Nantes							

1600	1700		1800		1900		
1620–70 Period of major provincial unrest caused by economic problems and the construction of the absolutist state	**1720** Last plague in France: at Marseille	**1789–99** Major social legislation introduced by the Revolutionary assemblies: abolition of feudalism, abolition of workers' associations, introduction of the metric system etc	**1806–14** Continental System	Late 19th to 20th centuries Growing anxiety about France's aging population	**1929–38** The Depression	**1948** Marshall Plan accepted	SOCIETY AND ECONOMY
1662–83 Colbert, Louis XIV's finance minister, introduces mercantilist economic policies	18th century Beginnings of the "Demographic Revolution": unprecedented and unchecked rates of population growth; fall in the death rate; beginnings of mass contraception	**1792–1815** Revolutionary and Napoleonic Wars seriously disrupt the economy and reorient it away from colonial and international trade toward the land	**1842** Major railroad construction begins		**1936–8** Major social reforms introduced under the Popular Front	**1951** Schuman plan for European coal and steel pooling	
			c.**1850**–c.**1870** Major economic growth		**1940–4** Reactionary social and anti-trade-union measures under Vichy	**1957** Treaty of Rome for Common Market	
			1864,1888 Workers' associations legalized		Post **1945** Baby boom	**1981–3** Under Mitterrand, radical social and economic reforms	
			1870s Economic depression: agricultural prices fall (to mid 1890s): acceleration of the "rural exodus"		**1945** Major nationalization program introduced	Post **1983** Mitterrand reduces social ambitions: growth of mass unemployment	
					1947 Monnet Plan adopted		

PREFACE

Every civilized person, it has been said, has two spiritual homelands, his or her own and France. Although this may be an exaggeration, certainly France for many centuries has played a central role in European civilization, and has exerted a unique fascination. The French may sometimes seem a difficult people, contentious and self-interested: but they have a remarkable sense of style, a taste for good living (the cooking and the wines are the world's best) and a passion for ideas. Their intellectual and artistic achievements have had the widest influence. For centuries a kingdom, then the center of a colonial empire and now a republic, France today plays a leading role in the European Community as it moves toward closer integration.

The *Cultural Atlas of France* endeavors to explore this heritage, alike in terms of the past and the present. Part One looks at the geography of France, a land of beautiful and varied scenery, and a land that belongs both to north and to south Europe. Its shape is harmonious and its climate mild, and its fertile soil has endowed it with an unusually rich and diverse agriculture. Part Two traces the history of France, from the cave-dwellers of prehistoric times, through the Roman colonization, the Hundred Years War with England, the reign of the "sun king" Louis XIV, the Revolution and Napoleon, and on via two world wars to the prosperous and stable 1990s. It shows how the disparate peoples that make up France were welded by the rulers in Paris into a highly centralized state; and it explores the background to France's long hostility with Britain and with Germany, and how this today has settled into close partnership. History is analyzed in terms of social, economic and cultural developments, as much as political ones.

Part Three first looks at French society today and the postwar conflicts between change and tradition. In some ways, economic modernization has transformed society; in other ways, old patterns and attitudes persist. The key role of the state is examined, and the recent decline in its power. Other themes explored are the bureaucratic system, the changing class structure, family ties, the emancipation of women, changes in the educational system and in the role of the Catholic Church, and the opening up of France to Europe and the world (despite a disturbing new backlash of racism). A section on life-styles deals with cuisine, holidays,

housing and the social impact of the postwar change from an agriculture-based to an industrial society, as millions of peasants migrated to the towns and faced up to the problems of modern suburban living. The second chapter of Part Three examines culture and intellectual life in France, historically and in today's context – the role of the state as patron of the arts, the recent spread of cultural activity from Paris to the regions, the blossoming of the performing arts despite the decline in creativity, the French attitudes to culture and the role of the intellectual, the musical renaissance, and why French television is so mediocre.

Part Four is concerned with the French regions. It traces their remarkable postwar economic revival; the growth of a new regional awareness, most notable in areas such as Brittany, Languedoc and Alsace; and the recent reforms giving more power to local government at the expense of the central state. The different regions are then explored one by one, in terms of their history, culture, economy and landscape.

Within each chapter, illustrated features bring special subjects into a closer focus, while the range of maps provide an extra background, physical, historical, economic and human.

The writing of the text has been divided between the two of us. Colin Jones was largely responsible for the historical section down to 1945 and John Ardagh for most of the remainder of the book. Colin Jones would like to thank Keith Cameron, John Critchley and Linda Hurcombe for their help in reading through the text, and Jonathan Barry, David and Susan Braund, Simon Burnell, Malcolm Cook, Nigel Mills and Malyn Newitt for their assistance with various knotty problems. Kelsey and Blanche Jones were a great help with the chronological table.

John Ardagh
Colin Jones

PART ONE
THE GEOGRAPHICAL BACKGROUND

LAND, CLIMATE, PEOPLES

Geographical features

Significantly, France is the only country in Europe to belong geographically to both north and south and to have both an Atlantic and a Mediterranean seaboard. Its situation explains a lot about its character, its history and its people. It has a wide variety of soil and scenery, climate and vegetation, which balance to create a certain harmony, a temperateness and mellowness that are the essence of France. Even its shape is pleasing, a neat hexagon (the French often refer to their country as *l'hexagone*); and all its borders are natural ones, either seas, high mountains or wide river (the Rhine), except on the northeast side, facing Belgium. By West European standards it is a fairly large country, nearly as big as Britain and the new Germany together. It is relatively thinly populated, especially relative to the Low Countries and Italy.

The north and west of the country are fairly flat; the east, center and south are mostly hill or mountain. The oldest mountains are not the very high ones, the Alps and Pyrenees, but the lower-lying Ardennes, Vosges and Massif Central, which date back some 250 million years. The forested Ardennes plateau, made of schistose rock, stretches on into Belgium. Also thickly wooded, the narrower Vosges range rises to 1424 meters, before falling rapidly toward the Rhine plain to the east; its southern end has rounded summits of

crystalline rock. The sprawling Massif Central, covering much of south-central France, is made up of plateaus of crystalline rock to the north, extinct volcanoes in the center, and limestone and granite massifs to the south. Its highest peaks are the volcanic *puys* south of Clermont-Ferrand, reaching 1886 meters at the Puy de Sancy. To their south is the wide limestone plateau of the Causses, cut by the Tarn gorge and other deep winding canyons, while to the southeast of the Causses is the wild granite-and-schist range of the Cévennes, its steep southern slopes covered with forests of pine and chestnut. Finally, the Armorican massif, mainly granite, runs through central Brittany and southern Normandy, where its highest hill, a mere 417 meters, is nonetheless the high point of the western French plains.

Of the much younger mountains, dating from the Tertiary and Quaternary periods (65 to 2 million years ago), the Pyrenees form a long natural barrier between France and Spain, rising to 3404 meters at the Aneto Peak, just beyond the Spanish border. The French Alps are only the western part of the great Alpine chain, but

Agricultural regions of France

France's agriculture is extremely rich and varied. In the northern areas are great plains given over to cereals and sugar beet; the farms are mainly large. Timber is produced in the forests of the Vosges, Les Landes and the Massif Central. Sheep also roam the uplands of the Massif Central, while dairy cattle and poultry are bred in Normandy, Brittany and elsewhere. In Provence, fruit and olives are cultivated. Vineyards are found over much of France.

Right View of Mont Blanc in the French Alps.

major fishing port

▲ mountain summit (height in meters)

agricultural zones

- arable
- fruit, vines, vegetables
- pasture
- rough grazing
- woods and forest
- nonagricultural land

scale 1 : 7 500 000

0 — 150km
0 — 100mi

Boulogne

Cherbourg · Dieppe

Port-en-Bessin

Brest

St Malo

Douarnenez

le Guilvinec · Lorient

Loire

Seine

Marne

Rhine

Saône

La Rochelle

Marennes

Dordogne

Garonne

Puy de Dôme
1463 ▲

Puy de Sancy
1886 ▲

MASSIF CENTRAL

Rhône

Mont Blanc
▲ 4807

ALPS

Sète

Vignemale Peak
▲ 3298

PYRENEES

Corsica

Mte Cinto
▲ 2710

they include its highest point, Mont Blanc (4807 meters), and Europe's two greatest regions of glaciers and all-year snow. The high central peaks of the Alps are crystalline, while the lower Jura Mountains along the Swiss border to the north are of folded limestone. They form a series of plateaus cut by deep valleys and rise to 1723 meters at the Crête de la Neige.

A number of plains lie between these various ranges and the coasts. The most important of them, the Paris Basin, consists of low fertile plateaus sloping toward the limestone depression where Paris lies. To the north and east are the chalky plains of eastern Normandy, Picardy and Champagne. The broad plain of the very fertile Loire river valley is backed by the low crystalline plateaus of Anjou and the limestone plateaus of Touraine. The Aquitaine Basin, to the south, is crossed by the river Garonne and its tributaries, flowing from the Massif Central; it includes the great flat sandy expanse of the Landes, artificially transformed into pine forest in the 19th century. To the east, the river Rhône, as it nears the sea, enters a broad plain cut by rocky limestone hills; the narrow vineclad Languedoc plain, between the Cévennes and the sea, is backed by stony scrub-covered foothills known as *garrigues*; and the fertile Roussillon plain is squeezed between the sea and the eastern Pyrenean foothills.

Four main rivers, and their tributaries, flow through these plains to the sea. The Rhône, rising in Switzerland, goes via Lake Geneva and Lyon to its delta near Marseille. It is fed by the Isère, Drôme and Durance rivers, which bring water from melted alpine snow, and by the Saône; in places it has been harnessed for hydroelectric plants and other industrial purposes. The Garonne rises in the Pyrenees and flows to the Atlantic by way of Toulouse and Bordeaux. Fed by the Tarn, Lot and Dordogne, it has rapid currents and is little used for navigation. The Loire, France's longest river (1020 kilometers), rises in the Massif Central and is joined by the Cher, Indre, Mayenne and other tributaries: depending on the rainfall upstream, it is sometimes slow and serene, sometimes swift and given to flooding. The Seine, which is excellent for navigation, is fed by the Yonne, Marne and Oise on its looping route through Paris to the sea at Le Havre. A fifth river, the mighty Rhine, does not flow through France, but forms its border with Germany for 200 kilometers, and is joined by other major rivers rising in France, the Meuse and Moselle.

The coastlines of France are varied. In the extreme north, Cap Griz Nez is the highest of a series of chalky cliffs that continue into eastern Normandy, alternating with sandy beaches. In western Normandy and Brittany the coast is more jagged, with wild headlands of granite rock: but again there are sandy coves. France's long western coast is mainly flat, marshy in places, with many offshore islands. The Landes coast west of Bordeaux has a wide unbroken beach of fine sand, backed by high dunes. Over on the Mediterranean, the Côte Vermeille by the Spanish border has rugged reddish rocks. The flat Languedoc coast is backed by lagoons that were once mosquito-infested: these have now been cleared, and big new resorts built. In the Rhône delta, the Camargue is a strange, appealing region of lagoons and marshes, full of birds and other animals. From Marseille to the Italian border, the hilly coast is extremely beautiful, covered with luxuriant foliage: but it has become heavily urbanized and swamped by tourism, especially along its eastern stretch, the famous Côte d'Azur (Riviera),

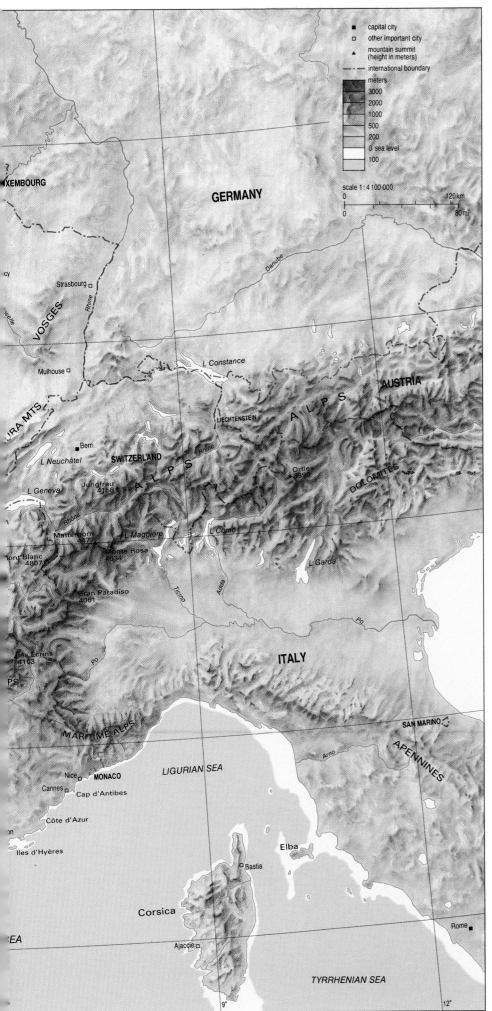

capital city
other important city
mountain summit
(height in meters)
international boundary

meters
3000
2000
1000
500
200
0 sea level
100

scale 1 : 4 100 000

0   120 km
0   80 mi

France: physical features
France has a neat hexagonal shape (the French often call it *"l' hexagone"*), and all its frontiers are natural ones of sea or mountain, except on the northeast. The highest mountain ranges are the Alps (along the Italian border), followed by the Pyrenees bordering Spain. Three main rivers flow westward: the Seine, Loire and Garonne; the Rhône flows to the Mediterranean, while the upper Rhine forms part of the Franco-German border.

Above top This flat landscape of arable fields is typical of the lowlands of the north and west. The fields used to be parceled into small bits, as here, but today in most areas they have been enlarged, so as to permit modern mechanized farming.

Above center Chalky cliffs and wide beaches are typical of the Normandy coast. In Brittany they are more rugged and indented, and down most of the west coast they are flat and smooth.

where mountains sweep majestically down to the sea.

In this nation with an unusually rich and diverse agriculture, the variation in farming landscapes are in part the result of soil and climate. In the rolling *bocage* country of the northwest, the small fields are divided by hedges and copses. Here, Brittany is devoted to pig-breeding, poultry and milk production, and vegetables; Normandy to cattle, rich dairy products and apple orchards. On the broad plains of the Paris Basin the fields are much larger and more open, given over to cereals and sugar beet. Fruit and vegetables are grown intensively in the middle Loire valley, on the lower Rhône plain, and in the Charentes by the west coast. The Massif Central, where the fields are divided by low stone walls, devotes itself to sheep-breeding. In the south, where summers are hot and the soil often dry, many slopes are terraced to avoid erosion. Wine is grown over most of France except the extreme north and northwest.

Climate and people

Situated at crossroads on the western edge of Europe, France is influenced by three different types of climate: Atlantic, Continental and Mediterranean. These combine to give a climate that is varied but mostly temperate, with sufficient rainfall for the farmers' needs. In Brittany, in particular, the westerly winds from the ocean bring much humidity but warm winters; these winds blow across most of France, which nearly all the year is subject to the cyclonic depressions from the Atlantic. But in the east, the continental influence brings greater extremes of temperature, with frosty but clear winters and hot but often stormy summers. Down by the Mediterranean,

summers are hot and dry for long periods, bringing the problem of forest fires; winters are fairly mild, but punctuated by a chill and violent wind from the north, the Mistral, which blows for several days at a time.

These variations in climate, in terrain and in farming activity, help to explain the differences of temperament in the French people: generally volatile and emotional in the hot south; cheerful and easy going on the temperate plains and in wine growing districts; more serious and reserved in mountain areas and in parts of the north. Racial variations are also significant, for although highly conscious of belonging to one nation, the French are of very diverse origins, in a land that has seen countless immigrations. In Roman times most of the inhabitants were Gauls, a race of Celtic origin who came from Central Europe. They intermarried with the Romans to produce a people who today are generally thought of as Latins, though in fact the pattern is more complex. On the periphery of France are many peoples who are totally non-Latin. The Basques, with their own strange language and living astride the border with Spain, were there long before the Gauls. The Bretons, also distinct from the Gauls, are Celts who arrived later from England and Ireland. The Normans derive from Scandinavian immigrations. The Flemish minority in the north is almost identical to the Flemish Belgians, while the Alsatians are an Allemanic people, close cousins to the Badeners and Swiss–Germans across their border. Except for the Normans, all these minorities have their own local language (as do Provençaux, Languedociens and Corsicans), even if in daily use it has now been largely replaced by French. In short, although centralizing pressures over the centuries have

Right These tidy vineyards are in Alsace; they produce fruity white wines of high quality. This is a fairly northerly region for good wines, but the vines are protected by the Vosges to their west. The champagne vineyards are even farther north. Most other French wine, including the vast output of cheap table wine, comes from the southern two-thirds of the country.

Climate of France
Through most of France, the all-year climate is temperate and sunny enough to sustain its exceptionally rich and varied agriculture. Rain and snow (*below*) do not fall excessively, but there are big regional variations. In the Pyrenees, Alps and other mountains, snow falls in winter, to the delight of skiers. Brittany, western Normandy and parts of the Massif Central also have wet winters; and in Brittany and the western Pyrenees, sudden showers are common in spring and autumn. In summer, rainfall is well above average in eastern France, to the dismay of holidaymakers in the Alpine and Vosges regions. Summers are hot and dry in the Mediterranean area, bringing the hazard of forest fires. The Loire valley, Paris basin and adjacent areas have only moderate rainfall all year, but enough to irrigate their very fertile farmlands.

The range of temperatures (*below right*) demonstrates clearly that the climate of France belongs both to northern and southern Europe, as well as to the mild-Atlantic seaboard and to the harsher Continental shelf. In

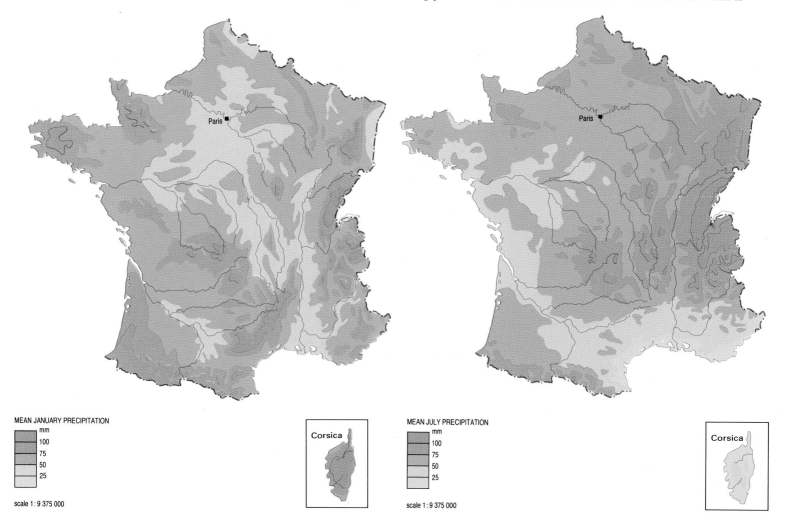

MEAN JANUARY PRECIPITATION

mm
100
75
50
25

scale 1 : 9 375 000

Corsica

MEAN JULY PRECIPITATION

mm
100
75
50
25

scale 1 : 9 375 000

Corsica

winter, the temperature falls sharply in the upland areas of eastern France while the Atlantic coast remains fairly warm. Temperatures stay quite high along the Mediterranean coast in winter despite the chill Mistral wind that blows from the north. In Marseille and Toulouse, the outdoor terrace-cafés are still full in November, when Paris is beginning to freeze. It was the Côte d'Azur's warm, sheltered winter climate that first brought it glory as a resort of the rich and leisured.

welded the French into one political nation with a strong sense of identity, the sense of local or regional identity also remains very much alive.

The location of the main urban population centers has related to local mineral resources or to trade routes, or both. Paris in early times was set up in a fertile basin, at a point where the Seine is easily navigable to the sea. Centrally placed on the northern plain, it has long been the magnet of hyper-centralized France and has grown steadily. With its suburbs, it is by far the largest urban center. The thickly populated

area around Lille, in the north, first developed because of its strategic trading position, near to England and the Low Countries, then grew into a major industrial center when its coal mines were exploited. Northern Lorraine, likewise, used its coal and iron-ore resources as the basis for its industry. Lyon became an important trading and industrial city because of its key position where the Rhône and Saône valleys meet; of the two big towns in nearby valleys, both well away from trade routes, St Etienne's heavy industry was based on its coal mines, while more recently Grenoble's amazing postwar growth has been helped by local hydroelectric power, and by the appeal of its Alpine touristic environment.

Even more so, a touristic appeal explains the urban growth of the Côte d'Azur, around Nice, a leading holiday and residential destination since the last century. Marseille, to the west, originally a Greek colony, is ideally placed near the mouth of the Rhône as France's major Mediterranean port. Some other larger towns have a mainly rural hinterland but have developed either as regional capitals or for trade reasons, or both – Toulouse on the Garonne, historic capital of Languedoc; Bordeaux near the mouth of that river, capital of Aquitaine; Nantes on the lower Loire, former capital of Brittany; and Strasbourg on the Rhine, Alsace's capital. Since World War II, France's population has tended to shift noticeably toward the coasts, mostly to the south, where climate and scenery are so attractive, while a broad swathe across the middle, from the Ardennes through the Massif Central to the central Pyrenees, traditionally always rather thinly populated, is now becoming increasingly more so.

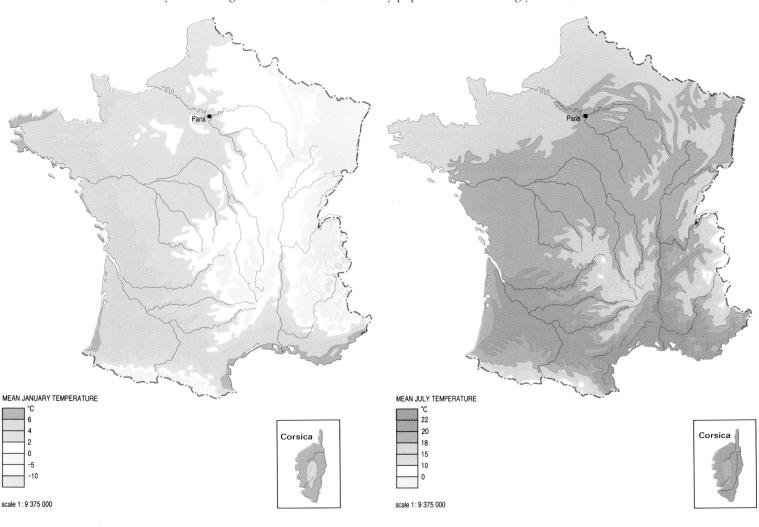

MEAN JANUARY TEMPERATURE

°C
6
4
2
0
-5
-10

scale 1: 9 375 000

Corsica

MEAN JULY TEMPERATURE

°C
22
20
18
15
10
0

scale 1: 9 375 000

Corsica

17

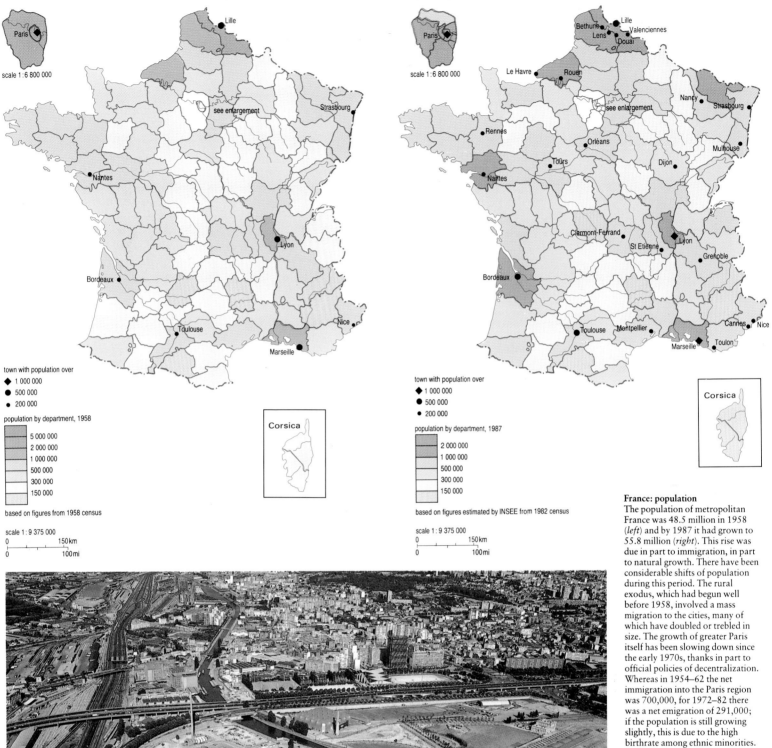

scale 1:6 800 000

Paris

Lille

see enlargement

Strasbourg

Lyon

Nantes

Bordeaux

Nice

Toulouse

Marseille

town with population over
◆ 1 000 000
● 500 000
• 200 000

population by department, 1958

5 000 000
2 000 000
1 000 000
500 000
300 000
150 000

based on figures from 1958 census

scale 1:9 375 000
0   150km
0   100mi

Corsica

scale 1:6 800 000

Paris

Bethune   Lille
Lens   Valenciennes
Douai

Le Havre   Rouen

Nancy
Strasbourg

see enlargement

Rennes
Orléans
Mulhouse

Tours   Dijon

Nantes

Clermont-Ferrand
St Etienne   Lyon

Bordeaux   Grenoble

Toulouse   Montpellier   Cannes Nice

Marseille   Toulon

town with population over
◆ 1 000 000
● 500 000
• 200 000

population by department, 1987

2 000 000
1 000 000
500 000
300 000
150 000

based on figures estimated by INSEE from 1982 census

scale 1:9 375 000
0   150km
0   100mi

Corsica

France: population

The population of metropolitan France was 48.5 million in 1958 (*left*) and by 1987 it had grown to 55.8 million (*right*). This rise was due in part to immigration, in part to natural growth. There have been considerable shifts of population during this period. The rural exodus, which had begun well before 1958, involved a mass migration to the cities, many of which have doubled or trebled in size. The growth of greater Paris itself has been slowing down since the early 1970s, thanks in part to official policies of decentralization. Whereas in 1954–62 the net immigration into the Paris region was 700,000, for 1972–82 there was a net emigration of 291,000; if the population is still growing slightly, this is due to the high birthrate among ethnic minorities. The main concentrations of population are around the periphery of France, whereas a large part of the center is thinly populated; this trend is continuing.

(Note that the black symbols on this map refer to conurbations, not *communes* (boroughs). The borough of Lyon, for example, has only 418,000 people, whereas the conurbation is some 1.2 million.)

Left The new science and museum complex of La Villette (foreground) located in the inner suburbs of Paris. The high-rise apartment blocks all round greater Paris bear witness to its rapid growth during the earlier postwar decades.

PART TWO
FRENCH HISTORY

FRANCE BEFORE THE FRANKS

France and the French

Where and how does the story of France and the French begin? Nationhood has been a recent growth in human history, and to focus solely on the emergence of the French nation-state would be misleading. Throughout history, a succession of peoples – Celts, Greeks, Romans, Franks, Scandinavians, Jews, Spaniards, Portuguese, Algerians and many others – have chosen to live within the roughly hexagonal area that is today called France and have contributed to the culture that is now characterized as French. Within the "hexagon", bounded by the Pyrenees, the Mediterranean, the Alps, the Rhine and the Atlantic, thriving local traditions have long acted as a brake on political and cultural unification. The history of France is thus the chronicle both of political centralization and of regionalism, local customs and cultural peculiarities.

The Neolithic Revolution

The earliest human inhabitants of France appeared during the Ice Age, probably somewhere between one million and 700,000 years ago. They were ancestors of *Homo sapiens sapiens*, who did not emerge until about 40,000 BC. Perhaps resembling "Cro-Magnon" man (whose heavy-jowled skull, dated to c. 30,000 BC, was discovered in 1868 in the Dordogne), *Homo sapiens sapiens* displayed a versatility and resilience that marked the species out for survival. They lived in caves and hunted in packs, arming themselves with stone axes and rocks to trap and kill the huge prehistoric animals (mammoth, rhinoceros and so on) that congregated in herds in the sub-Arctic tundra of northern Europe. In contrast to the simplicity of their way of life, these people produced a vivid and striking art, as is seen in the cave painting of Lascaux and other sites in the Dordogne and Pyrenees. As the Ice Age ended (c. 10,000 BC), more of the regions became inhabitable. The warming of the atmosphere accelerated the decline of the great European tundra, which became increasingly colonized by forest, and the wildlife that it supported also disappeared. Hunters who had been able to feast on wandering herds now turned their attention to the animals of the forest. The hunters of the Mesolithic period (10,000–6000 BC) could select their quarry from boar, deer, game birds and rabbits. The same range of animals, incidentally, was in the hunter's sights in the Sunday shooting parties of the Third Republic celebrated in Jean Renoir's classic film, *La Règle du jeu* (1939).

The change in France's animal populations made a hunter–gatherer existence more precarious, and perhaps instigated a move toward a more settled way of life. "The Neolithic (or Late Stone Age) Revolution" was a shift away from a nomadic form of existence to one of primitive farming communities, using stone tools and living off the land by cultivation and herding. Farming methods have, of course, changed drastically since those early days, but the intensely rural character of life within the "hexagon" has remained. As recently as 1945, a third of the working population of France was employed in agriculture, compared with only 5 percent in the UK, 20 percent in the Netherlands and 23 percent in West Germany. More than other nations, France has always had its feet in the soil.

Immigration and cultural diffusion from areas in the East, where the shift to farming had already begun, helped to accelerate the development in France. In about 6000 BC, an area on the coast of Provence became the first in France to adopt farming as a way of life. The people herded sheep, goats and pigs, grew cereals, employed a wide range of wooden and bone tools and produced a distinctive pottery. Then, from about 4500 BC, a quite separate current of change began to reach northern France from the East. Its influence owed as much to cultural imitation and adaptation as to military conquest. To the people of the postglacial age, farming and the settled way of life it brought with it made sense, and did not need to be imposed by force.

However, these changes occurred only slowly. It took two and a half millennia or more – from about 6000 BC to the Chasseyan civilization of 3800–2700 BC – before agriculture was the predominant way of life in France. Even then there was much regional and cultural variation, evident in different burial customs and pottery styles of the period. The inhabitants of the Armorican peninsula, for example, built characteristically vast stone graves and monuments. This Breton culture of dolmens, menhirs and stone alignments, which were constructed over a period of two millennia, has long evoked a sense of mystery and grandeur that has led later generations to ascribe these megaliths to the druids, the Romans, fairies and – most recently – to extraterrestrial beings.

Not only was the Neolithic Revolution in France protracted – it also remained incomplete. It did not spell the end of all hunting and gathering. What had once been a lifestyle, however, now became a *ressource d'appoint*, or useful adjunct. The proportion of wild game consumed round the hearths of the Neolithic farmers fell steadily – from perhaps 60 percent of all meat in 3500 BC to 10 percent or less by the 1st millennium BC – but it never disappeared altogether. Likewise, people continued to eat berries, mushrooms, hazelnuts and other plants gathered from the woods. Forest, cultivable land and pasture were the three structural components that made up the ecosystem of traditional French rural civilization.

A vital consequence of the Neolithic Revolution was population growth. In hunter–gatherer societies population density rarely exceeds two persons per square kilometer, much lower than among farming communities. Population expansion from the 5th to the 1st millennium BC was also due to migration from the East, where the farming revolution had already occurred, and where the resultant growth in population may have stretched economic resources to trigger the migration. The new arrivals brought with them new techniques and new cultural forms. The Beaker civilization, for example, which flourished from

Above A golden diadem from the tomb of an Iron Age princess at Vix in Burgundy. Measuring 27cm across and weighing 480g, it is the finest of a collection of artefacts discovered on this site since 1953. The piece is possibly of Scythian (south Russian) origin.

Right "The Laussel Venus". This stone relief figure, dating from around 19,000 BC, was discovered in a cave shelter at Laussel (Dordogne). The woman, who looks plump or possibly pregnant, raises the horn of a bison toward her face.

Below Around Carnac (Morbihan) in Brittany, a region of only 20 by 15km contains the greatest concentration of megalithic objects in Europe. The Carnac stone alignments situated at Kermario, dating from the late Neolithic period, cover an area of 1120 by 120m. Their original purpose is obscure. They were possibly used for astronomical sitings, but more likely for pagan rituals.

warrior caste or aristocracy, with levels of wealth that could not be attained by most members of the society. Bronze and Iron Age culture was built on war and conquest and the social hierarchy reflected these values. The Celtic Gauls, in particular, were fearsome warriors, equipped with a formidable iron-based weaponry from the 6th century BC. Exposing their tattooed bodies, they fought naked, often decapitating their war-victims and hanging the severed heads from their horses' manes, before taking them home to pickle them.

Besides the farmer and the warrior, Bronze and Iron Age civilization also included a class of artisans, who produced luxury items and were often found in the retinue of warrior chieftains. The Gauls became renowned for the quality of their artistry in decorative metalwork in particular. In about 600 BC a Greek colony was established at Massilia (Marseille), stimulating trade along a network of routes and making available the products of the more advanced societies of the Near East. Mediterranean luxury goods, such as jewels, decorative ware and wine, were exchanged for tin, copper, iron, cereals, salt, slaves and possibly sausages (already, the use of salting pork was earning the Gauls a reputation for fine charcuterie) from northern Europe.

Developments in trade and manufacturing helped trigger early urban development, as grouped settlements, in most cases too small and undifferentiated to classify as towns, made their appearance. In the south, from the 7th century BC, fortified settlements were built on high land, and some of these, such as Massilia and the towns at Entremont (near Aix-en-Provence) and Ensérune in the Béziers region became major centers. Yet, the vast majority of the population of Gaul still lived in villages or isolated rural dwellings and worked as farmers, though they too now enjoyed greater prosperity. Very probably, a large part of all the land ever cultivated in France (up to an altitude of 2,000 meters) was being farmed by the last centuries before Christ. Moreover, the population density of some – particularly upland – areas was probably as high as it is today. When later, in the 1st century AD, Gaul passed under Roman control, it may have been socially and economically backward compared with Greece and Rome, but it was not lacking in prosperity or cultural and demographic vitality.

The Gauls and religion

The Gauls attached great importance to religious and spiritual life. They worshiped an earth goddess and a number of other deities. They also made a cult of ancestors, whom they worshiped in sanctuaries, where they practiced ritual sacrifice of humans and animals. The sanctuaries were perceived as being on the fringe of another world, along with springs, wells and caves, to which the Gauls also attached religious importance.

The religious life of the Gauls was in the hands of druids. To a 20th-century mind it is difficult not to think of the folkloric images of these figures – part-priest, part-savant, part-philosopher – as presented in the French comic strip Astérix. Certainly, they seem to have played an important role in Gaulish society, defining and defending laws and customs and arbitrating in disputes as well as maintaining a religious role. Druids were recruited from all ranks of society and served long apprenticeships. The druids of Gaul were reputed to hold an annual convention in a

2000 BC, was famous for its pioneering use of copper – at first a luxury good used for decoration and some forms of armor. Around 1800 BC, the peoples of central Europe began to combine copper with tin to produce a tougher and more resistant alloy, namely bronze. These developments marked the beginning of the age of metal in Europe – the Bronze Age (1800–700 BC), which was followed by the Iron Age (700 BC to the end of the millennium).

The Bronze and Iron Ages

The societies of the Bronze and Iron Ages were more prosperous than their predecessors. This was particularly true of those peoples present from about 1250 BC (seemingly the ancestors of the Celts who established themselves throughout France from the 7th century BC). Originating in central Europe, they developed heavy plows with metal cutting-edges, which extended the amount of cultivable land and, with the introduction of course rotation, helped boost cereal productivity. They also practiced a distinctive form of burial by incineration in "urn-fields". Celtic tombs, in particular, show an impressive material culture. The tomb of an Iron Age princess discovered at Vix in Burgundy and dating from about 500 BC, for example, contained a four-wheeled chariot, many items of personal property and a superb golden diadem. Such costly possessions demonstrated the existence of a social hierarchy and the emergence of a

Cave Art

Below The most celebrated and majestic prehistoric cave art is located in the cave of Lascaux, near Montignac in the Dordogne. It was discovered accidentally in 1940 by four boys looking for a lost dog. As well as several steep galleries, the cave contains the now famous "Hall of Bulls", or "Rotunda", dating from about

It is little more than a century since prehistoric cave paintings and engravings were discovered. Dismissed initially as the idle doodlings of shepherds or as cunning forgeries, they are now acknowledged as an outstanding cultural form.

Cave art is found mostly in a Franco-Cantabrian area covering northeast Spain, the Pyrenees and the Dordogne, but extends as far as the Paris basin in the north, the Rhône in the east and Gibraltar in the south. It has been discovered in over a 100 caves and covers 20 millennia — between about 30,000 and 10,000 years ago. People of the 20th century are much closer in time to the last cave artists than those people were to their earliest forebears. The most famous art is found in the cave of Lascaux.

The content of cave art represents a kind of carnival of animals. Plant forms are rare and human figures are relatively few. As seems fitting for the hunter–gatherer societies that created these images, pride of place goes to the massive animals on which the people preyed: bison, aurochs, musk-ox, horse, deer, ibex, as well as reindeer, rhinoceros and mammoth.

The purpose of this extraordinary artistic achievement is difficult to ascertain. The images can hardly be considered hearthside decoration – many are far from the cave opening (in some cases well over a kilometer away), in places that are virtually inaccessible and in permanent darkness. The primitive animal-fat lamps used by the people of the time can have only dimly lit a few of the images. A religious explanation seems more likely. The places may have been used for a magic ritual before a hunt – many of the animal images show spears, lances and even hunters – or perhaps for some kind of initiation rites.

Bottom left Though hand prints are quite common in cave art, human figures are not numerous and are represented with far less realism and detail than animals. This representation seems to refer to the hunt: the bison's entrails are shown hanging out.

Bottom center Frieze of swimming stags. Cave images were painted using ochres, burned bone and oxides of manganese, and applied by hand as well as by primitive brushes. Scratched engravings are also very common. As is often the case with cave art, these images carelessly overlay even more ancient ones.

Bottom right Like the frieze of swimming stags, this superb Lascaux painting, known as the Great Black Cow, is about 3m above floor level, which suggests that crude scaffolding must have been erected to allow the artist or artists proper access. The painting shows evidence of remarkable technical ability as well as a steady hand.

17,000 years ago. This astonishing menagerie of prehistoric animals is depicted in characteristic yellows, browns, reds and blacks. Some images show a sense of movement and a degree of perspective. Lascaux subsequently fell victim to mass tourism. Intact for nearly 20 millennia, the caves were closed to the public in 1963 after two decades of exposure to the public led to severe pollution and degradation.

ritual location (possibly near to Orléans) in the middle of the forest of the Carnutes tribe – a striking example of Gaulish unity which was otherwise little in evidence.

At the time of the Roman invasion, Gaul appeared to enjoy a uniformly rural economy, with a common way of life and a shared religious world-view. Not far below the surface, however, there were major regional differences. "Gaul is divided into three parts," Julius Caesar remarked, but the great Roman general erred on the side of caution. He was referring only to what the Romans sniffily called "Hairy Gaul" (*Gallia Comata*) – the area to the north of "the Province" (*Gallia Narbonensis* as it became), the wide strip of coastline, formally under Roman control since 125–121 BC, that ran from Provence through Lower Languedoc to the Roussillon. This Mediterranean region, which Hannibal had crossed with his elephants when he attacked Rome in 218 BC, had long been linked to the Italian peninsula: the *Via Domitia* connecting with Roman Spain, became a major economic axis. Of the three northerly divisions referred to by Caesar, Celtic Gaul (*Gallia Celtica*) differed ethnically to some extent from the more Iberian-influenced Aquitaine (*Gallia Aquitania*) in the far southwest and from the more Germanic Belgic Gaul (*Gallia Belgica*) in the north east.

Each of the four areas itself formed a patchwork quilt of tribes, often further broken down into sub-groups inhabiting a smallish, "natural" geographic and ethnic region, or *pagus* (*pays*). The traditional form of political organization was hereditary monarchy, but in some southern and central tribes (notably the Arverni, the Aedui and the Helvetii) a powerful aristocracy had replaced kingship. Relations between tribes and within them were characterized by a system of dependency or clientage. Powerful, aggressive tribes such as the Arverni, centered in the Massif Central, imposed their will on smaller groups and subjected them to hostage-taking and the payment of tribute. Long before the Romans conquered Gaul, they sought friends and allies among these tribal groupings, exposing them to cultural influences and further political uncertainty.

When Gaul came under direct Roman control in the Gallic Wars (58–51 BC), Julius Caesar did not disrupt a stable "political" system, but one based on tribal feuding and rivalries. The great Arvernian warrior Vercingetorix, whose defeat at the siege of Alesia in 52 BC marked the effective end of the Gaulish tribes' resistance, appears to have had some sense of "national" unity, but this was probably the last throw of a desperate gambler rather than the program of an effective politician. From the moment Caesar intervened militarily in Gaul – allegedly to defend the Aedui, Rome's allies, from the aggression of their neighbors, the Helvetii – he was able to rule by playing one Gaulish tribe off against another. So far from spelling the end of Gaulish unity, Alesia merely highlighted the deep divisions that already existed.

Roman Gaul

The Roman conquest of Gaul introduced a degree of stability that had been lacking beforehand. From 31 BC Augustus Caesar fixed the frontiers of the three Gauls and in AD 43 Lugdunum (Lyon) was established as their effective capital. It became the home of a Gaulish assembly that met annually and the hub of an impressive road system. The Romans also erected a fortified frontier on the Rhine – the *limes* – which demarcated the boundary between the Roman and the Germanic, or "barbarian", world.

The Gauls began to prosper, because, in the words of the Greek writer Strabo, they "stopped fighting and started working". The *pax romana* allowed the economic potential of the Gaulish provinces to be realized. There were a few anti-Roman rebellions at first, but they were mainly local and isolated affairs. Generally, the Gauls, once free from the effects of internal disorder and tribal fighting, increased their material wealth dramatically. The transition to the status of Roman province took place without disturbing local power structures, as each province was split into *civitates*, geographical units that largely respected the main tribal groupings. New forms of local self-government – elected magistrates, assemblies, and so on – allowed the indigenous ruling classes, now in togas and following Roman religion (which from the 4th century AD was Christianity) rather than Gaulish druidism, to maintain their power and prestige. These local elites conscientiously paid taxes and tribute to Rome, and reaped considerable advantages from their place within its empire.

To a large extent, the Roman Empire in Gaul was governed by Gauls, not by Romans. Surprisingly few Italian administrators crossed the Alps, and those who did intermingled harmoniously with the local population. Thus, the *pax romana* was mostly maintained for Gauls by Gauls.

The urban way of life of the Romans was also adopted by the local elites, as towns emerged in Gaul for the first time. Julius Caesar had found Gaulish settlements made of wattle-and-daub: several centuries of Roman rule produced a huge spate of building in stone, brick and marble. Public buildings (forum, curia and so on) and leisure facilities (theaters and baths, for example) formed the architectural and social backbone of all cities. The scale of construction was unprecedented and would remain so for more than a millennium. The theater built at Autun could seat an audience of 33,000 and those of Arles and Nîmes over 20,000 each – in all cases, more than the populations of the cities themselves. The water supply that fed the public baths, prestige buildings and private households exceeded the demands of many modern cities; it required massive engineering works of which the Pont-du-Gard, near Nîmes, is an outstanding example.

It was a tribute to Gaul's agricultural efficiency that it could be rapidly urbanized and yet, at the same time, be self-sufficient in food. Roman Gaul was built on the backs of the peasantry. They lived in independent village communities or belonged to the villas of Gallo-Roman elites, and benefited from regional and international trading patterns and a superb distribution network. Fresh oysters from the North Sea were enjoyed in what is today the Paris region, while the *pâté de foie gras* served at the tables of wealthy imperial families in Rome came from geese that had been driven there, along Roman roads, from as far away as Boulogne.

The barbarian invaders

The security that Gaul enjoyed as part of the Roman Empire lasted till the 3rd century AD. From then on, Germanic tribes launched raids across the *limes* which, in time, became more widespread. In 275, Franks from the northeast and the Alamanni, who

Left Funerary monument from the second half of the 1st century AD. The dead man is shown standing between his mother and his father. Roman funerary art was highly expressive and aimed at evoking, and sometimes celebrating, the life of the deceased.

Below, left and right The two sides of a Roman coin from the imperial mint at Lyon (*Lugdunum*). One side shows the emperor Tiberius, dating from between AD 9 and 14.

The reverse side shows a Lyon altar dedicated to the imperial cult of Rome and Augustus (on the coin, ROMETAUG). The altar is flanked by flying victory figures.

attacked the Alsace region, sacked between 60 and 70 cities, triggering local unrest and riots.

The Roman emperor Diocletian (284–305) strengthened military defenses but could not resolve the problem. Indeed, the Empire faced economic difficulties, which forced the Romans to seek a compromise with the barbarian tribes. Basically, there were not enough men available to work in the fields and serve in the army. The authorities reacted by settling barbarians within the Empire. From the 3rd century they created *laeti* settlements of barbarian prisoners-of-war and refugees in depopulated areas. Later, they introduced a system of *foederati*, whereby whole tribes under their leaders were permitted to settle, in return for an obligation to perform military service. In 406 the barbarian influence on the Empire increased when tribal groups forcibly crossed the Rhine to settle, having made no prior agreement with the Gallo-Romans. "The whole of Gaul smoked in a single funeral pyre," was how a Gallo-Roman bishop described the carnage of that year. The Vandals and the Alans passed through French territory on their way to Spain and then Africa; the Alamanni moved into Alsace; the Burgundians settled more to the south; the Visigoths established the first barbarian kingdom in Aquitaine in 418.

Even the Roman army proved unable to resist the barbarian influence. Roman troops were themselves often of barbarian origin, and they cooperated with fellow barbarians: Attila and the Huns were defeated near Troyes in 451 by a Roman army that included Franks, Burgundians and Visigoths. By 476, when the Western Empire ended, Roman Gaul had been brutally parceled out among new barbarian kingdoms and the stage was set for a period of considerable turmoil.

tribal groupings of pre-Roman Gaul
- Armorican
- Belgian
- Celtic
- German
- Iberian

◯ tin deposit

◯ wine production

Osismi Coriosol

Veneti

DARIORITUM Vannes
Locmariaquer

Roman Gaul

Roman Gaul was like a patchwork quilt. Across and within the major administrative boundaries into which the Romans divided Gaul there were numerous local divisions and subgroups. Because of quasi-ethnic differences within the formal outline of Roman Gaul, German, Belgian, Iberian and Armorican (Breton) groupings were scattered around the Celtic core. But at another level, a dense tribal network continued to exist. Socio-economic differences were also important: some areas were less organized around the villa than others; some practiced a degree of specialized agricultural or industrial production, making wine or producing tin, for example. Another major distinction was between town and countryside: rural areas were often primitive compared with the culturally rich and sophisticated Roman towns, linked together by the excellent road network.

Roman Cities in Gaul

The most striking and enduring feature of the Roman colonization of Gaul was the urban framework established by the conquerors. However, by Roman standards Gaulish cities were not large. At the height of the Empire, Rome had a population of 700,000 and Alexandria, Antioch and Carthage about 200,000 each. Yet the biggest cities in Gaul – Autun, Lyon, Narbonne, Nîmes, Reims and Trier – had populations of only 20–30,000. Paris (*Lutetia*) had about 8,000 inhabitants, and most other cities 5–6,000.

Urban life was not spread evenly across Gaul. There were fewer and less impressive cities in the center, west and northwest of the country than in the heavily Romanized south and east. Nevertheless, this urban way of life, which was new to the Gauls, had considerable impact. Rome was the model on which city planners based urban design, so that Gaulish cities tended to have the classic mix of public buildings – forum, curia and basilica (the law and administration buildings), capitol, temples, baths, theaters, and so on – and private dwellings. Roman towns of this period represented a more epic material culture than that of any other epoch before the industrial age.

Left Head of Octavian (later Emperor Augustus) discovered at Arles (*Arelate*).

Below An artist's reconstruction of the great rural villa at Estrées-sur-Noye in the department of the Somme. A main residence is shown at the far end, with a courtyard lined with cottages and storehouses in front of it. Such villas were as typical of Roman Gaul's economic development as great cities like Nîmes and Arles. How many rural villas were inhabited at the same time is difficult to say, but it seems that rural areas of northern Gaul, in particular, were very highly populated.

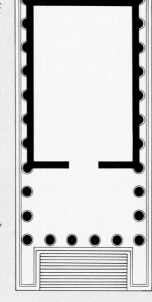

Above The famous Maison Carrée in Nîmes (*Nemausus*). Situated to the south on the forum, the temple was built in 16 BC and dedicated to Emperor Augustus. An adaptation of the temple of Apollo in Rome, it measures 26 by 13m in area and stands 15 m high. A plan is shown *center left*.

Top The Pont du Gard aqueduct over the river Gardon to the north of Nîmes in southern France was built in the 1st century AD. It remains one of the finest Roman engineering achievements still in existence. Measuring 49m high and 270m long, it carried water to the city from Uzès, some 24km away, supplying each citizen with 400 liters of water daily – much more than the present-day system provides.

Above A Roman mosaic from Nîmes. The artistic quality of Roman mosaics was very high.

Above The amphitheater at Arles, built in the 1st century AD, could seat over 20,000 people. Like its replica in nearby Nîmes (*right*), it doubtless hosted a variety of entertainments, including gladiatorial and animal fights (animal cages have been excavated under the central ring). The imperial cult was especially developed in Nîmes, as is shown by the central position accorded a statue of the emperor Augustus. Unmatched in size and technical sophistication for centuries, Roman buildings and monuments were designed to impress. Function took second place to symbolic grandeur with which successive generations identified. The Nîmes amphitheater has lasted so well partly because later generations found different uses for it. In the Middle Ages, the building was occupied by squatters and became a fortified apartment block, as the city shrank drastically with demographic decline and pressure of barbarian incursions.

Above This head of Venus (only discovered in 1835) is 37 centimeters tall and was probably a copy of the Venus of the Capitol in Rome.

THE DARK AGES TO THE REVOLUTION

The Merovingian dynasty

The *limes* that marked the boundaries of the Roman and barbarian worlds since the 1st century BC had come to have little significance as the protective isolation and segregation of the past gave way to more contact and communication between the two societies. Indeed, the Germanic tribes that invaded Gaul in the 5th century had already assimilated the Roman way of life into their culture long before their fateful incursions. In response to this looming threat, tribes formed confederations. One such grouping was the Franks, a "tribal swarm" which, by the mid 4th century, straddled the frontier. The dominant group, the Salian Franks, were ruled by the Merovingian dynasty, who derived from the half-mythical Merowech and wore their hair long. Merowech's grandson, Clovis, king from 481 to 511, laid the foundations of the Frankish state in a series of bloody campaigns and massive atrocities. In 486, he defeated Syagrius, king of Soissons and commander of the last outpost of the Roman Empire, and went on to defeat other barbarian rulers including the Burgundians in 500 and the Visigoths in 507. The expansion begun by Clovis was continued by his sons, who secured Burgundy in 536, won Provence from the Ostrogoths in 537, and campaigned in central Germany and on the Italian peninsula. In 507, while Clovis was in Toulouse, following his victory over the Visigoths he received a letter from Pope Anastasius conferring on him the titles "consul" and "Augustus". His imperial aspirations prompted him to choose a new capital, Paris, and it was there in 511 that he died, the first and best-known of the "long-haired kings".

Clovis died a Catholic Christian. He had been converted under the influence of his wife, the Burgundian princess Clotilda. Very probably the main reason for his change of faith was political, for Christianity constituted a bridge between the Merovingian dynasty and the Gallo-Roman population. The Franks owed much of their long-term success to such strategies of shrewd accommodation. As they themselves were a tiny minority – probably numbering only 150,000–200,000 – there was a limit to what they could achieve by force. Thus the Salic laws associated with Clovis were not imposed on Gallo-Romans, who were still judged under Roman law. The old *civitates* and *pagi* (plural of *pagus*) divisions were maintained, and posts of count at *civitas* (singular of *civitates*) level were frequently occupied by the local elites. The Franks also understood the need to have the church of the Gallo-Romans on their side. Bishops played a more important role in local government than most counts, to whom they were often related by ties of kinship. The existing diocesan framework was maintained, forming links with classical antiquity that would last until 1790, when the Revolutionaries reorganized France's ecclesiastical geography.

However, below the surface of the powerful Frankish empire, deep cracks were beginning to appear. Because of rivalries among heirs, the empire opened up by Clovis was only rarely and briefly united in the two centuries down to 687. For most of the 6th century, the lands were divided three ways between the Merovingian family: Austrasia in the northeast, including much west German territory; the central and western area of Neustria; and Burgundy in the southeast. Aquitaine and Provence gradually freed themselves from Frankish control, which had never been very strong. Fragmentation stimulated family quarrels and dynastic power-struggles. The rulers themselves remained increasingly on the periphery of

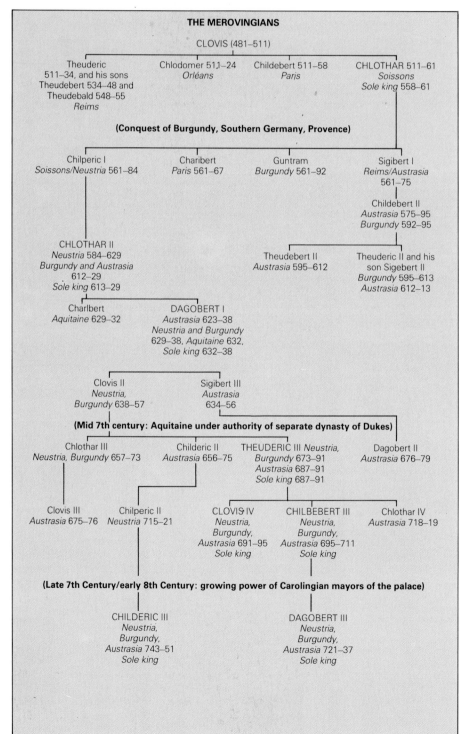

THE MEROVINGIANS

CLOVIS (481–511)

Theuderic 511–34, and his sons Theudebert 534–48 and Theudebald 548–55 Reims

Chlodomer 511–24 Orléans

Childebert 511–58 Paris

CHLOTHAR 511–61 Soissons Sole king 558–61

(Conquest of Burgundy, Southern Germany, Provence)

Chilperic I Soissons/Neustria 561–84

Charibert Paris 561–67

Guntram Burgundy 561–92

Sigibert I Reims/Austrasia 561–75

Childebert II Austrasia 575–95 Burgundy 592–95

CHLOTHAR II Neustria 584–629 Burgundy and Austrasia 612–29 Sole king 613–29

Theudebert II Austrasia 595–612

Theuderic II and his son Sigebert II Burgundy 595–613 Austrasia 612–13

Charlbert Aquitaine 629–32

DAGOBERT I Austrasia 623–38 Neustria and Burgundy 629–38, Aquitaine 632, Sole king 632–38

Clovis II Neustria, Burgundy 638–57

Sigibert III Austrasia 634–56

(Mid 7th century: Aquitaine under authority of separate dynasty of Dukes)

Chlothar III Neustria, Burgundy 657–73

Childeric II Austrasia 656–75

THEUDERIC III Neustria, Burgundy 673–91 Austrasia 687–91 Sole king 687–91

Dagobert II Austrasia 676–79

Clovis III Austrasia 675–76

Chilperic II Neustria 715–21

CLOVIS IV Neustria, Burgundy, Austrasia 691–95 Sole king

CHILBEBERT III Neustria, Burgundy, Austrasia 695–711 Sole king

Chlothar IV Austrasia 718–19

(Late 7th Century/early 8th Century: growing power of Carolingian mayors of the palace)

CHILDERIC III Neustria, Burgundy, Austrasia 743–51 Sole king

DAGOBERT III Neustria, Burgundy, Austrasia 721–37 Sole king

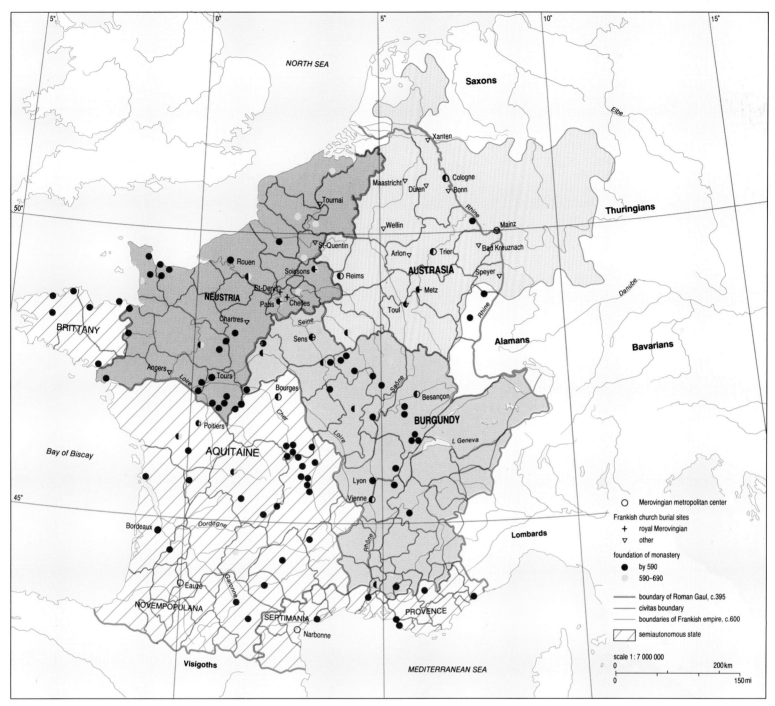

NORTH SEA

Saxons

Thuringians

Alamans

Bavarians

AUSTRASIA

NEUSTRIA

BRITTANY

BURGUNDY

AQUITAINE

Bay of Biscay

NOVEMPOPULANA

SEPTIMANIA

PROVENCE

Lombards

Visigoths

MEDITERRANEAN SEA

○ Merovingian metropolitan center

Frankish church burial sites
+ royal Merovingian
▽ other

foundation of monastery
● by 590
● 590–690

boundary of Roman Gaul, c.395
civitas boundary
boundaries of Frankish empire, c.600
semiautonomous state

scale 1 : 7 000 000
0   200km
0   150mi

The Christianization of France
The heartland of the Frankish empire built up by the Merovingian dynasty lay in the northeast, where most of the legacy of Clovis was divided and subdivided among the sub-kingdoms of Neustria, Austrasia and Burgundy. Aquitaine increasingly detached itself in the 7th century, while outlying areas in the south and the west habitually acknowledged only the overlordship of the Merovingian line. The old civitas boundaries of the Roman Empire provided the building blocks of which these changing political unities were composed. They often corresponded to diocesan boundaries, and ecclesiastical institutions, such as monasteries, were a key element of Merovingian power.

these conflicts, as power passed to the stewards of the royal household and estates. The post of "mayor of the palace" (*major domus*) was a crucial one, in that most of the rulers' income derived from their properties. From the ranks of the "mayors of the palace" of Austrasia came the wealthy and powerful Arnulfing family who, because of the frequency of the name Charles (*Carolus*) in the family, were also known as the Carolingians. In 687 the Carolingian Pepin of Herstal defeated Neustrian forces at the battle of Tertry, uniting the northern Frankish territories under his power as "mayor of the palace". Already the end of the Merovingian dynasty was in sight.

The Carolingians
Although they were written off as *rois fainéants* ("do–nothing kings") by their Carolingian successors, and indeed by most subsequent historians, the long-haired kings had, in very unfavorable economic and political circumstances, created the most powerful state in all western Europe. The breakdown of the Roman Empire had severely dislocated the western economy. There were recurring famines – the chronicler Gregory of Tours spoke of peasants in 585 reduced to making flour from grape-pips and hazel catkins – and frequent epidemics of plague and dysentery. The atmosphere of uncertainty and foreboding created severe problems for the exercise of authority. Only by repeated campaigning to provide their powerful followers with sufficient booty to keep them satisfied and retain their loyalty could the Carolingians of the early 8th century build on Merovingian achievements. The illegitimate son of Pepin of Herstal, Charles Martel, led campaigns against turbulent north Germanic groups and expanded Frankish power well into central Europe. In the late 720s, he marched south to subdue the Aquitanian duke, Eudes. There, he encountered Arab forces who had crossed the Pyrenees from Spain, which the militant troops of Islam had invaded in 711 and conquered. At the battle of Poitiers, in 732, Charles Martel inflicted a defeat on the Arabs which once and for all checked their advance in western Europe.

It was a tribute to the prestige that the Merovingians still enjoyed that Charles Martel's heir, Pepin the Short (741–68), installed the rather pitiful Merovingian prince, Childeric III, as king. Part of his prestige derived from the religious sense of awe that surrounded a dynasty allegedly descended from a deity (Merowech). This made usurpation difficult. Pepin's solution to the problem was significant for the history of the monarchy in France. In 751, after assembling the Frankish nobles to elect him king, he had himself and his sons Carloman and Charles (the future Charlemagne) consecrated in a religious ceremony, in which he was anointed by his friend, Saint Boniface. Some three years later, Pope Stephen repeated the ceremony, endorsing the deposition of Childeric who had his head shaved – quite a fate for a "long-haired king"! – and was banished to a monastery. The Carolingian usurper thus became God's elect, and in so doing established a tradition of divine-right kingship that lasted until the 19th century.

The church profited under the Carolingians. The latter maintained the role of bishops in local administration and generously supported the monasteries. They imposed a tithe, regulated between 779 and 801, which became one of the bulwarks of ecclesiastical power until the French Revolution of 1789. Wherever the Carolingians extended Frankish power, they established the authority of the church, notably in pagan Germany, whose conversion to Christianity was the special concern of Saint Boniface. Pepin the Short fought against heathen races too, expelling the Arabs from the Narbonne region in 759. He was also a staunch ally of the papacy, defeating the Lombards in northern Italy in the 750s, supporting the beleaguered Pope Stephen II and establishing new papal states around Rome.

Charlemagne and the Carolingian Renaissance
The alliance between the Carolingian dynasty and the papacy strengthened further under Pepin's son and successor, Charlemagne (768–814), who extended Frankish authority over most of the Christian west. On Christmas Day 800, Pope Leo III placed a crown on the head of Charlemagne, consecrating him Emperor – the first western emperor since 476. Imbued by his sense of charisma as an anointed monarch, Charlemagne took his religious responsibilities seriously, protecting both the church within his empire and the papacy. The Carolingian Renaissance, which Charlemagne helped to promote, was largely religious-inspired. There was renewed interest in classical antiquity among many clerics; an artistic revival that concentrated on ecclesiastical art and architecture, biblical exposition and manuscript illumination; and educational initiatives that were largely aimed at producing a better-instructed clergy. In many respects, however, Christianity among the Carolingian elite was little more than a veil covering more atavistic instincts. Charlemagne himself – a prodigious figure, standing over 1.8 meters tall, hugely energetic, and living to the age of 72 (longer than all but a handful of his subjects) – retained the instincts and demeanor of a warrior chief and led an aristocracy that preferred warfare and hunting to the civilization of antiquity.

The new Emperor was hardly very Roman. Although the title flattered his self-image, Charlemagne would have felt uncomfortable in a toga. His biographer Einhard recounts, he preferred the Frankish

Left Metal equestrian statuette of either Charlemagne (king of the Franks from 768, emperor 800–14) or possibly Charles the Bald (emperor 843–77). The figure, whose dress, moustache, sword and crown indicate imperial status, dates from the late 9th century, though the horse was extensively restored in the Renaissance period.

Below Signature of Charlemagne. The K, R, L and S of Karolus (Charlemagne's Latin name) are centered on the overlaid A and O. Charlemagne himself probably only managed the central brushstrokes as he could write very little.

"national dress" of tunic and leggings. The power of the Roman Empire had long been grounded in a centralized civil service, a professional army and uniform laws. Charlemagne had none of these. His numerous decrees, or "capitularies", are famous – and were famously ignored. He adapted the administration so as to produce a more uniform servant class, including bishops and counts (responsible to the emperor and bishops) in local government, supervised by roving emissaries (the *missi dominici*) who reported personally to the emperor. The highly decentralized system, however, could only be held together by Charlemagne's traveling the circuit and by continued warfare. There were military campaigns every year from the time of Charles Martel to the coronation of Charlemagne. After 800, as the more aggressive early years of his rule yielded to a more negative and defensive last phase, the problems of the Empire became more acute.

Breakup of the empire
The country faced not only internal problems in the years following the reign of Charlemagne, but also the renewal of threats from outside. Between 838 and 842, Saracens from north Africa launched raids into the Midi, and from the last years of the 8th century, Vikings from Scandinavia had begun plundering the west coast, a last wave of barbarian invasions of the kind that had been at the origins of Frankish power occurred. From the 830s, these attacks were extended to the north and from 859 the southwest was raided. The destruction and economic dislocation caused by these Norsemen (*normands* in French) were considerable, and spread to eastern France after attacks by Magyar raiders in the 10th century.

Above Jeweled talisman that reputedly belonged to Charlemagne (though the style may suggest a later 9th-century date). Worn on a chain round the neck, the brooch was constructed out of a vial in which a sacred relic could be kept.

The Normans

Around the year 800, there was an extraordinary diaspora of Viking freebooters. Massive migratory hordes from Denmark and Norway took to seaborne raiding, spreading fear from Kiev in the east to Greenland in the west. The coasts and river systems of western and southwestern France in the 9th century were often plundered by Viking longboats.

The Vikings eventually began to settle, at first in the Scottish islands and in Greenland, and then, by the early 10th century, in northern France. Following a major defeat in 911, the Viking chieftain Rollo made an agreement with Charles the Simple of France to settle his band in the region of Rouen. Rollo also agreed to adopt the Christian faith and to protect the area from attacks. By the second half of the century, the Vikings came to terms with the indigenous Frankish–Gallo-Roman population. Rollo's family married Frankish princesses, took Christian names, and started to offer patronage to the church. The Vikings, or Norsemen, became Normans.

In 1066, the duke of Normandy invaded England, defeated King Harold at the battle of Hastings and seized power. These descendants of Viking pirates who less than two centuries before had been raiding and pillaging the coasts of France, established a powerful Anglo-Norman state which for a long time threatened the authority of the French dynasty.

Below left The church of Saint-Germain-des-Prés, Paris. On Easter Day 845, a Viking fleet sacked Paris and refitted its vessels with timbers hacked from the beams of this, the city's oldest church. Further raids on the city followed in 856, 861 and 885–6. "There is not a road", recorded one local chronicler of the time, "that is not strewn with the bodies of slain Christians."

Below The fortified castles of the Normans permanently marked the landscape. The donjon, or central tower, of the castle at Falaise overlooking the river Aure dates from the early 11th century.

Above The Bayeux tapestry recording Duke William of Normandy's conquest of England was commissioned by Bishop Odo of Bayeux toward the end of the 11th century. This scene shows the kind of longboats which ferried his invasion force across the Channel in 1066.

Faced with these external threats, the Empire could not revert to the economy of plunder that had played a key role in Merovingian and early Carolingian kingship. Dynastic wranglings added to the problems. In 817, the announcement by Charlemagne's successor, Louis the Pious (814–40), that the empire would be subdivided on his death created turmoil among his children. They waged war against their father from 830 until his death, and then in 840 among themselves. Eventually, in 843, a tripartite division of the great Carolingian empire was agreed, by the Treaty of Verdun, whereby Charles "the Bald" (840–77) took "West Francia", his brother Louis "the German" an eastern bloc, and the third brother, Lothaire, the

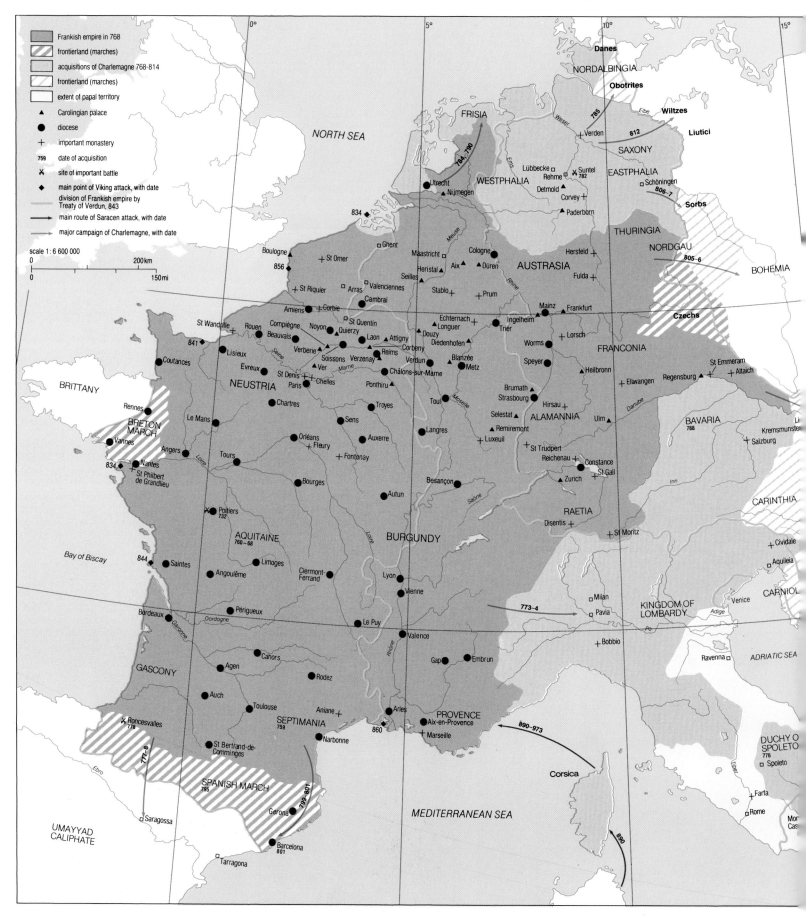

middle region and the imperial title. The death of Lothaire in 855 produced further subdivision.

By the Treaty of Verdun, the areas that were later to become, broadly speaking, France and Germany were definitively separated. Moreover, the middle territory contained Lorraine (Lotharingia), which would become a major bone of contention between them until the present century. Far from the Treaty of Verdun representing the "birth of a nation", however, the creation of West Francia, though based on the legacies of Celtic, Gallo-Roman and Merovingian Gaul, was essentially a makeshift solution to a family crisis. The lands formed a linguistic and ethnic patchwork: northern travelers to the Basque region claimed that the local inhabitants barked like dogs when they spoke. The river Rhône was still a frontier: Provence, the Dauphiné, the Franche-Comté, the Jura and the Lyonnais had their own rulers and were not part of West Francia. In the south, the spoken language was the romance-oriented *langue d'oc*, and Roman law still had great influence, while customary law based on Frankish traditions prevailed in the north, where a Germanic dialect, *langue d'oïl*, was spoken. At bottom, all that the inhabitants of West Francia had in common was a ruler to whom an oath of loyalty was due. Over the next century and a half down to the end of the Carolingian dynasty in 987, regional differences became even more pronounced, as central authority fragmented under new pressures.

The decline of central power was especially marked in the reign of Charles the Bald (840-77). The poor state of the economy, under constant siege from the Viking raids, made territorial expansion impossible, and virtually forced Charles to reward his followers by giving away his own lands, thereby reducing his own power and prosperity. The aristocracy benefited from Charles's embarrassment and from the inability of his successors to regain control. The system of *missi dominici* (roving emissaries) begun by Charlemagne broke down in the middle of the 9th century as his successors were less energetic in enforcing it than he had been. A tradition of the title of hereditary count grew up, and, from 877, when they began to halt the practice of submitting their finances for central government approval, all counts changed their status from one of state official to one of hereditary territorial prince.

Already, by 888, the Carolingian dynasty had lost a great deal of prestige over its failure to deal with the Viking menace. Consequently an assembly of nobles, recognizing the need for a ruler who could command a field army, determined in that year to elect one of their number as king. They chose Eudes, the son of one of Charles the Bald's henchmen, who had brilliantly defended Paris against the Vikings in 885. For the next century, power alternated between a line of "Robertians" (Eudes' father was Robert the Strong) and the last Carolingians, signaling the end of monarchical

Above Lothar, who reigned from 954 to 986, was one of the last Carolingian rulers of France. His reign was overshadowed by the rising power of the Robertians, or Capetians.

The Carolingian Empire
The Carolingian Empire represented the most ambitious and far-reaching transnational European state since the Roman Empire. Held together for four decades by the boundless and restless energy of Charlemagne, who from 800 enjoyed the prestige of the imperial title, it could not fail to crumble in time. The Treaty of Verdun of 843 split it into three constituent parts, but the periphery was already being lost to the eastern Empire (in Venice and southern Italy) and the Slavs. One of Charlemagne's key achievements was the spread of monastic discipline, educational reforms and Christianized piety: these proved a more lasting legacy.

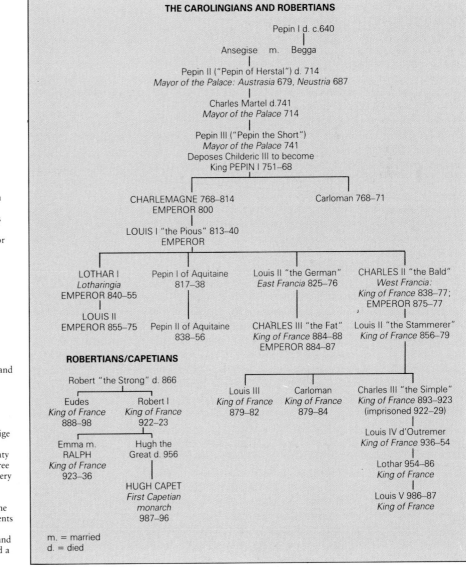

THE CAROLINGIANS AND ROBERTIANS

Pepin I d. c.640

Ansegise m. Begga

Pepin II ("Pepin of Herstal") d. 714
Mayor of the Palace: Austrasia 679, Neustria 687

Charles Martel d.741
Mayor of the Palace 714

Pepin III ("Pepin the Short")
Mayor of the Palace 741
Deposes Childeric III to become
King PEPIN I 751–68

CHARLEMAGNE 768–814   Carloman 768–71
EMPEROR 800

LOUIS I "the Pious" 813–40
EMPEROR

LOTHAR I   Pepin I of Aquitaine   Louis II "the German"   CHARLES II "the Bald"
Lotharingia   817–38   *East Francia 825–76*   *West Francia:*
EMPEROR 840–55   *King of France 838–77;*
                                                                         EMPEROR 875–77

LOUIS II   Pepin II of Aquitaine   CHARLES III "the Fat"   Louis II "the Stammerer"
EMPEROR 855–75   838–56   *King of France 884–88*   *King of France 856–79*
                                            EMPEROR 884–87

ROBERTIANS/CAPETIANS

Robert "the Strong" d. 866

Eudes   Robert I   Louis III   Carloman   Charles III "the Simple"
King of France   *King of France*   *King of France* *King of France* *King of France 893–923*
888–98   922–23   879–82   879–84   (imprisoned 922–29)

Emma m.   Hugh the   Louis IV d'Outremer
RALPH   Great d. 956   *King of France 936–54*
King of France
923–36

                  HUGH CAPET   Lothar 954–86
                  First Capetian   *King of France*
                  monarch
                  987–96   Louis V 986–87
                                                                       King of France

m. = married
d. = died

authority. "You have so many partners and equals in the kingdom," bishop Hincmar of Reims told his ruler in the late 9th century, "that you reign more in name than in reality." In the 10th century principalities emerged that were almost wholly outside monarchical control. These included Brittany and Viking Normandy in the west, Flanders in the north, and Aquitaine and Burgundy in the south. The fragmentation process spread to the traditional heartlands of Frankish power: Maine and Anjou, for example, achieved independent status between 940 and 970. By the time that Hugh Capet of the Robertian line was elected king in 987, France was effectively a patchwork of petty states, and the royal domain was restricted to a scrap of land, centered in the Ile de France, measuring only some 200 by 100 kilometers. The beginnings of the Capetian dynasty could scarcely have been more inauspicious.

The growth of feudalism

The transition from central to local authority was implicit within the emerging feudal system. At the heart of feudalism lay bonds of personal loyalty and dependence, onto which was grafted a landholding arrangement developed by Merovingian and Carolingian rulers. They had granted lands to followers in return for an oath of personal fealty (loyalty), whereby the inferior partner – later, vassal – owed service to his lord. Gradually, the land grant – or fief, as it came to be called – began to entail the additional transfer of judicial and political power in return for military service. The state of the European economy made such land grants a valuable means of rewarding followers. Changes in the conduct of war also played their part. The Muslim invasions of the 8th century had established armored heavy cavalry as the most powerful battleground weapon. However, maintaining a mounted warrior was so expensive that rulers had to make land grants to knights to help them to recover their costs. The dominant feudal class was thus the military elite (often descendants of Carolingian local officials), who exacted payments from the peasants living on their landed holdings. Frequently, this involved service and dependency, deliberately mimicking the feudal relationship between lord and vassal. Given the impotence of central power to protect them against external violence and faced with waves of barbarian invaders, the peasant populations were increasingly willing to turn for protection to their local warlord. From this arrangement the manorial system grew up. In it, lands owned by the nobles were worked by serfs (dependent peasants) who in their own right owned hereditary tenures, albeit under the judicial, political and military authority of their seigneurial lord (lord of the manor).

The oath of fealty by which individuals tied themselves as vassals to a lord took the form of an act of homage in which the vassal's hands were placed between those of the lord. At the height of the feudal system, vassals, in return for the protection and aid offered by their lord, bound themselves to follow him to war (and possibly to bring armed followers with them); to offer advice when consulted; to attend their lord's court of justice; and to pay a range of feudal aids, such as disbursing the lord's ransom if he was captured. Dependency chains ran throughout the whole of feudal society, so that a vassal's lord – a count, for instance – could himself be the vassal of another lord – a duke or perhaps even the king. This

made the exercise of central power very difficult. The monarch was afforded only limited access to the subjects of the major feudal blocs, which were controlled by powerful feudal lords. These territorial princes, however, could, in turn, find it difficult to impose their will on recalcitrant castellans shielding behind the fortified walls of medieval castles. This social pattern intensified so that, by the year 1000, there were very few free peasants in France, and little property without a feudal lord and feudal obligations vested within it. The customs that regulated the conduct of the feudal lords became increasingly complex, evolving into chivalry, an elaborate code of honor. But the distinction between honor and personal ambition was often blurred. Chivalrous disputes shaded imperceptibly into vicious private wars, plundering raids and the exercise of terror. When two knights fight, Saint Peter Damian (100–72) noted, "the poor man's thatch goes up in flames".

The role of the church

The belligerence and aggression that characterized the feudal order reflected the view, current from early in the 11th century, that society was the sum of three distinct estates: the First, prayers (*oratores*), the Second, fighters (*bellatores*), and the Third, workers (*laboratores*). This tripartite division, which remained intact until the French Revolution of 1789, highlights the role of the church as a feudal institution. The most powerful and prestigious ecclesiastical appointments went to noble families, and between one-fifth and one-third of feudal landed property was held by the church. Even ceremony and ritual bore the stamp of feudalism: the widespread practice of seeking intercession from saints paralleled the seeking of feudal protection; the holding together of hands in prayer replicated the gestures of the act of homage. The establishment of church autonomy was a slow and imperfect process, which occurred in stages. These included the monastic reform movement launched

Top A 15th-century manuscript illumination from the Chronicle of Saint-Denis, showing Hugh Capet with one of his bishops. Hugh (Hugues) Capet of the Robertian line, duke of France from 956, was the first Capetian monarch, elected in 987. Little is known of him except that he seems to have placed special emphasis on the sacred character of kingship.

Above Signature of Hugh Capet on a diploma dated 20 June 989.

Chivalry

Chivalry was the code of behavior of the *chevaliers* (knights), mounted cavalrymen who formed the backbone of the feudal system. The term is prescriptive, indicating how the knightly elite ought to act, according to an ethic of virtuous conduct. In practice, there was often little of virtue in what they did.

The chivalric code evolved over time, but one of its constant features was the importance of literary models. The *Song of Roland* (c. 1100), for example, described the conduct of Charlemagne's warrior Roland at the battle of Roncevalles fought against Spanish Muslims in 778. Roland provided a powerful and enormously influential example of courage and fidelity to his leader, to his fellow knights and to God. Loyalty to aristocratic ladies was an ingredient added by the troubadour literature of the 12th century, when courtly love conventions urged courtesy toward women as part of the chivalric ideal. Tales of King Arthur and the Round Table, notably from the work of Chrétien de Troyes (c. 1135–c. 1183), elaborated this tendency. Such literary models idealized a past to which the present failed to conform. Nostalgia for a golden age was a theme of chivalrous writings.

The church attempted to exploit the code of chivalry for its own advantage, promoting the idea of the Crusade, which laid down the framework for international relations and the repression of internal dissent from the 11th to the 14th century. The Crusades were occasions of much heroic and altruistic behavior as well as some appalling atrocities.

Left An illumination from *Le Livre des tournois du Roi René* (c. 1460) which shows a female audience joining in the admiration of the display of helmets and banners prior to a tournament. The tournament became a place for conspicuous and symbolic display.

Below right Jousting in tournaments represented a form of competitive and martial play which trained a knight in horsemanship and battle and brought him into contact with chivalric conventions and practices. It was dangerous, sometimes fatal. The knights' ladies awaited the fate of their champions from a grandstand position.

Below left King Arthur and the Knights of the Round Table receiving a vision of the Holy Grail. The quest for the Grail – allegedly the chalice used by Christ in the Last Supper – was one of the most potent symbols of the chivalric ideal, linked with the ideal of a knight's search for spiritual perfection. The Grail is first mentioned by Chrétien de Troyes (c. 1180) and is best known from the legendary tales of King Arthur.

from Cluny after 910; the "peace and truce of God" movement in the 10th and 11th centuries, which attempted to limit feudal violence and lawlessness; and the campaign launched in the late 11th century by Pope Gregory VII (1073–85) to reduce lay influence within the church.

The renewed spiritual prestige that the church enjoyed over lay society as a result of these reforms was shown in the Crusades, which lasted from the 11th to the 13th century. The crusading ideal was to a large extent a Christianized form of chivalry. Pilgrimages to the Holy Land had been interrupted from the 1070s by the forays of the Seljuk Turks in the Eastern Roman Empire. In 1095, at a Church council held at Clermont, Pope Urban II called for a Crusade against the infidel. The First Crusade was thus proclaimed from within France and, thanks to inspirational preaching in the Midi by Peter the Hermit (1050–1115) immediately won widespread support. When the Crusades were at their height, perhaps as much as half of the French nobility participated in them. Foremost among nations as a crusading power, the French were also in the vanguard of opposition to Muslim power in Spain and Portugal and prominent in the crushing of the Albigensian heresy in southern France in the early 13th century. This religious commitment on the part of the French nobility coincided with the material interests of successive Capetian rulers. Crusading accustomed the feudal lords to Capetian leadership and helped develop shared values and solidarity with the king. It enhanced the prestige of the dynasty that the most saintly of their number, Louis IX (1226–70) died while crusading in north Africa in 1270; he was canonized in 1297. The diversion of knightly energies away from France to the

struggle against the infidel also reduced levels of violence at home but allowed the nobility to pursue the economy of plunder that they found so congenial. "Before the Christians started for the lands beyond the sea," wrote Guibert de Nogent (1053–1130?), "the Kingdom of France was prey to perpetual disturbance and hostilities..."

Charismatic kings

The church, whose interests the Capetians so sternly defended, played a major part in the ascendancy of the Capetian dynasty, which placed great emphasis on the sacred character of kingship. As with the Carolingians, a Capetian coronation was a religious event. The king was anointed with holy oil, and so was said to rule "by the grace of God". In addition, since the reign of Robert the Pious (996–1031), Capetian kings were allegedly endowed with miraculous powers, in particular being able to cure scrofula ("the King's Evil") by the power of the royal touch.

The Capetians thus possessed charisma, in the true sense of the word, which no feudal lord could match. Yet an aura of sanctity did not amount to real temporal authority. Indeed, the survival of the Capetians after 987 probably owed more to weakness than to strength: no one, it seemed, could be bothered to replace them! The role that they played as overlord to the great territorial princes gave them some vestigial authority, but only as a kind of feudal umpire. However, in several respects, the dynasty enjoyed good fortune, which its potential rivals could not share. The situation of their territories at the hub of a major communications network in the center of northern France represented a considerable asset. The soils of those lands, moreover, were among the richest and most productive in the whole of France. Luck even accompanied the Capetians into the marriage bed: six successive rulers from Hugh Capet onward were able to provide a male heir. Hugh further initiated the practice of crowning the heir in the king's own lifetime, which helped to abolish the traditions of elective kingship and partible inheritance that had dominated the last century of the Carolingian dynasty.

In the reigns of Louis VI "the Fat" (1108–37), Louis VII (1137–80) and Philip II "Augustus"

Above The First Crusade sets sail under the leadership of Godefroy de Bouillon (c. 1061–1100). The French monarchy and nobility played a highly significant role in the Crusades between the 11th and the 13th century. Godefroy, who was elected king of the newly conquered Jerusalem in 1099, was an exemplary Crusader who upheld the chivalric code. Historians usually distinguish eight Crusades, though in reality they often overlapped: The First Crusade (1095–99); Second (1147–9); Third (1189–92), led jointly by Philip Augustus, the emperor Frederick Barbarossa and Richard "Coeur de Lion" of England; Fourth (1202–4), when Constantinople was sacked; Fifth (1217–21); Sixth (1228–9); Seventh (1248–54) and Eighth (1270), which were both led by Saint Louis, who died at Tunis in 1270.

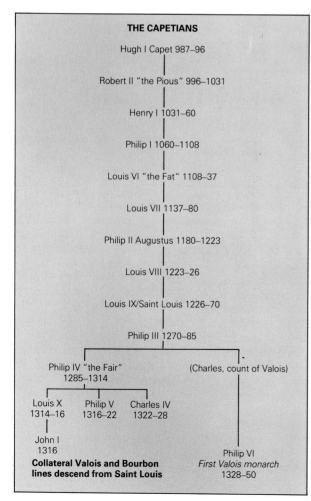

THE CAPETIANS

Hugh I Capet 987–96

Robert II "the Pious" 996–1031

Henry I 1031–60

Philip I 1060–1108

Louis VI "the Fat" 1108–37

Louis VII 1137–80

Philip II Augustus 1180–1223

Louis VIII 1223–26

Louis IX/Saint Louis 1226–70

Philip III 1270–85

Philip IV "the Fair" 1285–1314   (Charles, count of Valois)

Louis X 1314–16   Philip V 1316–22   Charles IV 1322–28

John I 1316

Collateral Valois and Bourbon lines descend from Saint Louis

Philip VI
First Valois monarch
1328–50

Capetian France
Originating in a tiny strip of land centered on Paris, the Capetian dynasty took time and persistent effort to develop. By the early 14th century, in face of the emergence of the threatening Anglo-Norman state, it had become one of the most powerful political systems in Europe. The church played a considerable part in this development. The geography of Capetian power was the geography of the Gothic style, which was particularly associated with the dynasty. Centralization was still a patchy and erratic process, and the apanages given by Louis VIII and Louis IX to their sons had the effect of countering much of the centralizing thrust.

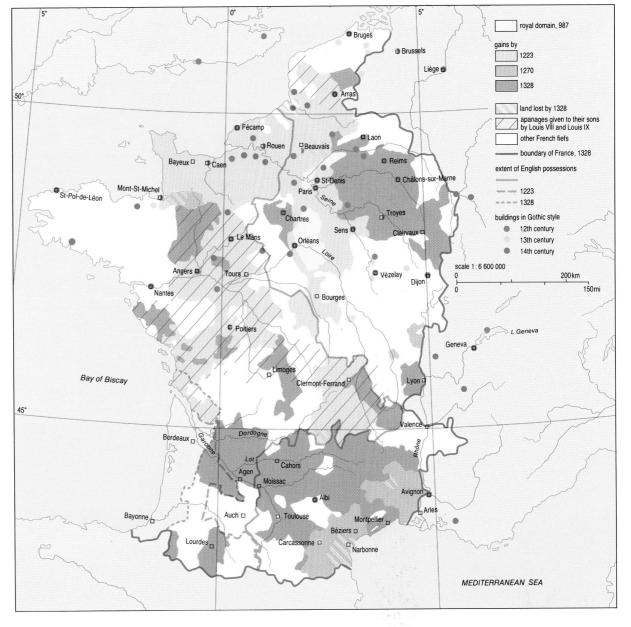

(1180–1223), the prestigious façade of Capetian kingship acquired more substance. In asserting their authority, these rulers behaved more like cunning peasants than oriental despots, husbanding their limited resources and carefully extending their control in stages, notably under the wise counsel of Abbot Suger of Saint Denis (c. 1080–1151). First, they strengthened their authority within their own lands over obdurate castellans and local vassals, and then strove to extend their control over the territorial princes. The greatest obstacle was presented by the dukes of Normandy, whose authority had swollen to cover the whole of England following the Norman invasion of 1066. From the middle of the 12th century, this problem became acute. In 1152, Louis VII rejected Eleanor of Aquitaine as his queen, who then married Henry Plantaganet, count of Anjou. He first became Duke of Normandy and, in 1154, following a period of anarchy within England, was crowned Henry II of England. Henry's Angevin empire ran down the western side of France from the Somme to the Pyrenees – an area far larger than the lands of the king of France.

It was principally Philip Augustus who undermined Angevin power on mainland France and reestablished Capetian supremacy by plotting against Henry's son

Richard I "Coeur de Lion" of England (1189–99), who had fought alongside him on the Third Crusade. In 1202, Philip invoked his authority as the suzerain (overlord) of Richard's successor, John, declaring him a "felonious vassal" for his failure to attend his court to answer charges. In moves against John, Philip captured Normandy and Poitou in 1204, and Touraine and Anjou in 1205. Capetian expansion in northern France in the 1190s, notably in Artois and in Picardy, provoked so much local hostility that the counts of Flanders and Boulogne joined with the king of England and the German emperor in an anti-Capetian coalition. In 1214, however, in the historic battle of Bouvines, Philip forced his rebellious vassals to cede. The pendulum continued to swing France's way in subsequent decades. By the Treaty of Paris in 1259, a compromise was reached whereby Henry III of England recognized as Capetian annexations all the former English possessions except the Guyenne, in exchange for several important concessions on the Capetians' side.

Using a mixture of force, trickery and diplomacy, Philip Augustus had vastly extended the Capetian sphere of influence. Besides campaigning against the English in the west and southwest, he and his successors Louis VIII (1223–6) and Saint Louis (Louis IX)

also pushed into southern areas where the Cathar (or Albigensian) heresy – a form of Manicheanism (which held that Satan was the equal of God) – had penetrated the Midi in the 12th century and taken root. In 1208, Pope Innocent III publicly called for a crusade against the Albigensians. Philip Augustus gave tacit support to Simon de Montfort (1150?–1218), who in 1209 led a band of nobles south against the count of Toulouse, the protector of Catharism. This internal crusade was conducted with extraordinary savagery, and resulted in de Montfort succeeding as count of Toulouse in 1215. Louis VIII reaped the fruits of this victory in 1226, as Toulouse came under his control. The Capetian dynasty had thus extended its power as far as the North Sea, the Atlantic seaboard and the Mediterranean coast.

Organs of state

Royal authority was considerably strengthened by the development of the administrative machinery of the state. Saint Louis and especially Philip IV "the Fair" (1285-1314) established an embryonic state bureaucracy. Organs of central control (an exchequer, a more rational household organization and council of advisers, a common currency and so on) were developed and salaried royal officials – the *baillis* (in the south, the *sénéchaux*) – were sent out to supervise local administration and legal process. In new royal courts of appeal, or *parlements*, university-trained "legists" (law specialists) offered standards of justice superior to those of the feudal lords. Renewed interest in classical antiquity led to the development of Roman law and, in particular, to a concept of sovereignty that made of the king not just a feudal overlord but also an heir of Roman *imperium*, an emperor in his own country, who legislated for the whole realm. This dizzying prospect perhaps went to the head of Philip the Fair, who attacked the authority of the church and supported the establishment of the papacy at Avignon.

In 1307 he arrested the leaders of the crusading order, the Templars, who had become powerful international bankers, and after a notorious show-trial executed them and expropriated their possessions.

Another major administrative innovation was Philip calling a meeting, in 1302, of representatives of the three estates – *oratores, bellatores,* and *laboratores* – to discuss matters of state. This body was essentially a sounding-board and intelligence network for the ruler, which foreshadowed the creation, in the 15th century, of the Estates General, a truly national representative body. It also testified to the existence of a crude "public opinion", which emerged as a sign of a more diversified and sophisticated economy.

Social and demographic changes

The period from the late 12th to the early 14th century was indeed one of brilliant social and economic advance. The ending of Viking and Hungarian raids helped to improve economic stability, as did a general improvement in Europe's physical climate. At the same time, the acquisition of precious metals from West Africa and the Near East stimulated the commercial sector of the European economy. Technological improvements also played their part. The introduction of the choke collar, iron horseshoes and heavier, wheeled plows improved the productivity of the soil, while watermills and windmills provided new mechanical sources of power.

One of the most outstanding features of the economic expansion of these years was a massive population rise. The number of people occupying the area of present-day France increased from 16 millions in the 9th century to 22 millions by 1328 – a level that was not surpassed until the 18th century. Extra mouths gave peasant farmers an incentive to produce more food; but extra hands also, in a labor-intensive economy, allowed more to be produced. Much more land was brought under cultivation, sometimes by

Above The royal seal of Philip Augustus (1180–1223). The fleur-de-lys, associated with the Capetian dynasty since 1147, was to remain a key royal emblem. At his coronation, Philip Augustus wore a gown with golden fleur-de-lys on a dark-blue background, called a "cosmic" mantle because it evoked the stars against the firmament.

Above The seal of the Knights Templar. A crusading order, the Templars took monastic vows but lived the life of soldiers, defending the holy places in the East and protecting pilgrims. In the late 12th century their growing wealth made them the target of Philip the Fair (1285–1314), who arrested the Parisian knights and seized their assets. After a show-trial in which they were charged with devil-worship and sodomy, 54 Templars were burned at the stake in 1310-14.

Left Montségur, 1200m above sea-level in the foothills of the Pyrenees, was the last major stronghold of the Albigensian heretics. The remote mountain fortress, now in ruins, fell to an extended siege in 1244. Two hundred Cathars were burned at the stake following its capture. The Albigensian crusade was part of a wider strategy by which southern France was brought under the control of the Capetians.

Above The Palace of the Popes in Avignon. The papacy was based in Avignon from 1309, under the influence of the powerful Philip the Fair. Until 1378, seven French Popes resided in the city, which they preferred to the marshy and malarial Rome. The Great Schism that split the church into rival papacies from 1378 to 1417 consolidated the papal status of the city. The photograph shows the second of the two adjacent papal palaces, built 1352–62. The city and adjacent region of Comtat Venaissin remained in papal hands until the French Revolution.

extending into forest or wasteland, sometimes as a result of massive land clearance and pastoral farming in which the Cistercian monks specialized. Entrepreneurs touted for colonizers for the new communities. In the Midi, heralds rode around blowing a trumpet to announce the new-found lands being made available to peasant families.

The beneficiaries of this wave of economic expansion were often the social elite, who creamed off a good part of the peasant surplus. Yet the boom benefited some peasants too, particularly those who escaped from their feudal lords into the new villages or who produced for the expanding grain-market. On the landed estates, peasant dues were increasingly paid in kind or in cash, as feudal labor services (*corvées*) went into decline. The feudal lord became less of an economic producer than a rentier – a mere receiver of rents and dues – albeit one with extensive powers over his peasants. These changes also affected the physical appearance of the countryside. In the north and northeast of France, the open-field system of cereal cultivation established itself and peasant life increasingly revolved around the village. The 30,000 villages then in existence provided the framework for French rural life from that time onward.

Economic expansion also produced growth in the urban sector. Between 1100 and 1300, French towns,

no longer under the threat of invasion, increased their populations to levels unknown since the Romans. Although still of a strongly rural flavor – green fields and farmyard aromas were never far away – the towns housed large concentrations of craft workers and members of the tertiary sector (professional people, domestic service workers and so on), who benefited from the increased opportunities for international trade. The circuit of fairs in Champagne, for example, covering four towns and lasting a period of six weeks, provided a center for the exchange of cloth from the two most advanced manufacturing regions of medieval Europe, northern Italy and Flanders, and a location for other regional specialities – Spanish leathers, Scandinavian timber goods and furs, eastern spices – and related services, such as banking.

The spectacular urban growth coincided with the high point of medieval feudalism. Often, towns grew up nestling against castle keeps and monastery walls. Many feudal lords were personally responsible for creating the towns and fairs because they attracted wealth and could be exploited for tolls and other dues. The revenue could then be spent on keeping them in their accustomed lifestyle which, with the pressures of fashion, hunting and tournaments, was becoming increasingly expensive. Soon, however, the towns were pressing for their independence. Associations of

Chartres

The Gothic cathedral at Chartres is one of France's most famous, most beautiful and most significant buildings. The pointed arch of the Gothic style made its earliest appearance in the rebuilding of the abbey church of Saint-Denis by abbot Suger, Louis VII's adviser, after 1132, but it was more strikingly employed on the west front of Chartres cathedral in 1145. The teams of builders who worked here moved on to Sens (whose cathedral, completed in 1170, was the first to be built wholly in the Gothic style) and other centers. A fire at Chartres in 1194 necessitated large-scale rebuilding which was completed in 1240. Of the original building only the crypt, the base of the towers and the west facade remain.

The architectural success of Chartres cathedral attracted widespread imitation. The Gothic style it embodied became an international byword until the 15th century. Gothic cathedrals were built throughout Europe, from Upsala to Famagusta, through northern Italy, the Rhineland, Bohemia and Hungary.

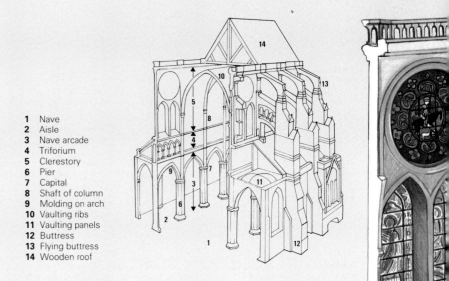

1 Nave
2 Aisle
3 Nave arcade
4 Triforium
5 Clerestory
6 Pier
7 Capital
8 Shaft of column
9 Molding on arch
10 Vaulting ribs
11 Vaulting panels
12 Buttress
13 Flying buttress
14 Wooden roof

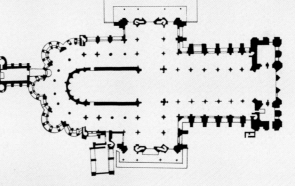

Left and Center Left Stained glass windows showing sculptors and stone masons (*center left*) and joiners, carpenters and cartwrights (*left*), in the Window of Saint Julian the Hospitaler. Chartres cathedral today has 173 stained-glass windows – including several that date from the first rebuilding in about 1150 – covering 2,500 square meters of glass, and justly renowned for their inimitable bluish hue. Many commemorate not only sacred scenes but also, as here, the city's shopkeepers and artisans. By financing many of the cathedral's stained-glass windows, the city's guilds and corporations showed their gratitude for the benefits that the building brought to the city. Its architectural renown and spiritual radiance made it a major pilgrimage site, which boosted the city's economy.

Above Cutaway view of Chartres cathedral. The use of pointed arch and ribbed vault represented a new flexibility in structure. It enabled the designer to go round corners more easily, reducing the amount of masonry necessary. Flying buttress supports further enabled the building to be reduced to a skeletal structure. The walls became glass, supported by fine clusters of shafts, and the height could be increased to impart greater elegance.

Below Sculpture from the left bay of the North Porch showing flax being carded. Gothic sculpture became freer and more expressive, with figures projected into space and sculpted in the round. They also became more naturalistic in form, often blending the secular with the sacred.

Below From the right bay of the North Porch, a homely allegorical sculpture (c. 1230) of February, one of the monthly labors, warming his feet by a fire. Altogether, the cathedral has 2,000 sculpted figures in its porches and portals.

41

town-dwellers, bound together by an oath of fraternity – a gesture that contrasted with the submissive act of feudal homage – sought rights of self-government and self-defence. As these were often at their lord's expense, bitter power-struggles ensued. The feudal class could no longer take its privileges for granted: the bourgeoisie was already presenting a challenge.

The familiar tripartite division of society was becoming dated. Although the military and ecclesiastical elites were still the dominant classes, the concept of the Third Estate that encompassed the rest of society was no longer appropriate to its constituent diverse groups. Increasingly, public law took account of the pluralistic fabric of medieval society. Individual provinces and towns had their own rights and privileges, including rights of self-regulation. There were independent guilds, in which urban manufacturing was organized, and similar bodies for professional workers, such as merchants and lawyers, as well as for ecclesiastical personnel — cathedral chapters, for example. France was becoming a "society of orders", composed of many different types of corporate-interest groups.

Culture and learning

The growing sophistication of French society was reflected in cultural developments. In architectural terms, the period was dominated by the cathedral and the castle, the buildings characteristic of the first and second estates. The classic stone-built castle, seigneurial residence and fortified seat of the nobility, became increasingly widespread from the late 12th century. From roughly the same time, Gothic cathedrals began to supersede churches built in the Romanesque style, which according to Raoul Glaber, the 11th-century monk, had ringed France "with a white robe of new churches". The Gothic church was a spectacular urban phenomenon. Its economic consequences were not always happy: attempts by the town of Beauvais to achieve the highest vaulted roof in Europe, for example, led to the celebrated building crash of 1284, and may have inhibited the economic development of the town. Probably no underdeveloped society in history has managed to construct so massive an institutional network of buildings of such little economic value.

The architectural glories of the Gothic style are the best known example of a cultural dynamism that is referred to as the "12th-Century Renaissance". Like the Carolingian Renaissance of the 9th century, it exemplified a revival of interest in the literature and culture of classical antiquity, and in particular a fascination with the lay learning of the ancient world. In the 13th century the works of Aristotle and the traces of ancient culture in Jewish and Arabic civilizations, to which Europe had been increasingly exposed since the Crusades, came to the fore. North of the Alps, loose associations of individuals formed around teachers, who were often linked with cathedral schools. In Paris and Chartres, among other cities, these acquired rights as centers of learning and gradually assumed corporate status as "universities".

The development of state bureaucracy opened up the law and royal service as alternative careers to the church and stimulated demand for university education. Attracted by teachers at the forefront of contemporary knowledge, the young men who formed the student population were a cosmopolitan, footloose, boisterous crowd, particularly in Paris, which had the

reputation for the most exciting teachers, such as the brilliant dialectician Pierre Abelard (1079–1142). At first, the church welcomed universities as potential scourges of heresy, but some churchmen were distrustful of this intellectual milieu, where "nothing is fully known until it has been torn to shreds in argument" (to quote Robert de Sorbon (1201–74), founder of the college for poor students that was later the Sorbonne). Partly to keep the intellectual movement within the bounds of orthodoxy, in the mid-13th century the church's greatest thinker Thomas Aquinas (1225–74), a member of the Dominican order, went to Paris. Aquinas's blend of Aristotle's philosophy and church dogma laid the foundation for religious orthodoxy down to the rise of modern science.

Aquinas's teachings at the University of Paris were the crowning glory of France's cultural achievements in the High Middle Ages. France's Gothic style had conquered Europe; its universities were the acknowledged European leaders; its wealth, fashions and political systems were much envied; and because of the size of France, its population far exceeded those of any rival states. Even a dynastic shift in 1328, when the last Capetian, Charles IV (1322–8), failed to produce an heir and the throne passed to the collateral Valois line, could not shake the kingdom. Indeed, the fact that the Valois claim prevailed over that of Edward III, king of England, revealed the beginnings of a nationalistic spirit among the social elite. "The French did not admit without emotion", a Parisian monk recorded, "the idea of being subject to England." At about the same time, an Italian observer noted, "In all of Christendom the king of France has no equal." In fact, signs of decline were visible.

Social and economic decline

"A fame, bello et peste, libera nos, Domine" ("From famine, war and plague, deliver us, O Lord"). The medieval litany lists the three social evils that halted France's economic expansion. Population growth depended on an increase in the food supply but this had its limits. In particular, new land that came under the plow failed to achieve the necessary high yields. Fragmentation of peasant holdings below viable levels of self-sufficiency also occurred. Local shortages, triggered by harvest failure, multiplied and grew into famines that affected all Europe, such as in 1315–16. High grain prices, caused by periodic harvest failures, affected in turn the commercial and manufacturing sectors of the economy, and from 1310 the Champagne fairs went into decline. Food shortages sparked off social unrest, such as the massive risings opposing feudal rule in Flanders between 1323 and 1328. The reappearance of plague in Europe in 1347 after a break of seven centuries dealt a further devastating blow to the old order. Originating in the late 1330s in central Asia, the Black Death followed silk routes westward before Genoese vessels carried it to southern France in late 1347. Few regions were unaffected by it. According to the contemporary chronicler Froissart, between 1347 and 1349 France lost about one-third of its population, and this estimate is probably no exaggeration. "The world is coming to an end," noted another chronicler of his troubled times, when attacks

Above Late 14th-century helmet.

Left In 1392, leading troops into Brittany, Charles VI (1380–1422) had a sudden fit of insanity and rode against his own men, waving a lance. This was the first bout of a mental illness that plagued him periodically to his death, and led to the weakening of France internally and internationally. There was a renewal of internecine strife, involving notably the Burgundian and Armagnac clans. Also, by the Treaty of Troyes (1420) Charles had to accept the virtual partition of his kingdom between Burgundy and England, with the English monarch Henry V marrying his daughter and becoming his heir.

Previous pages The lower chapel of the celebrated Sainte-Chapelle on the Ile de la Cité in Paris. It was built in 1248 as a private chapel for Saint Louis (Louis IX), before he went on a Crusade. The king's residence was adjacent to the chapel, which was designed to house the Crown of Thorns and other relics. Renovated in the 19th century, the chapel retains much of the original 13th-century stained glass for which it is famous.

The Hundred Years War
The economic and cultural strength of medieval France received a crushing blow with the appearance in 1347 of the Black Death in which perhaps as much as one third of the population died. The devastating impact of this epidemic disease was exacerbated by the disruptive effects of warfare. Although the size of armies was small, their destructive impact on a hard-hit rural economy was considerable, while the virtual breakdown of the political system produced much lawlessness. English power had expanded from its Gascon toehold in the southwest in 1377, so that the north was utterly dominated by Anglo-Burgundian power. The fortunes of the Valois dynasty were never lower than in 1429, on the eve of the appearance of Joan of Arc. Joan's triumphant progress temporarily rocked the English on their heels, and paved the way for the reconquests achieved by Charles VII. By the end of the 15th century, England's continental possessions had been confined to Calais, and Burgundian attempts to erect a buffer power between France and Germany had been thwarted.

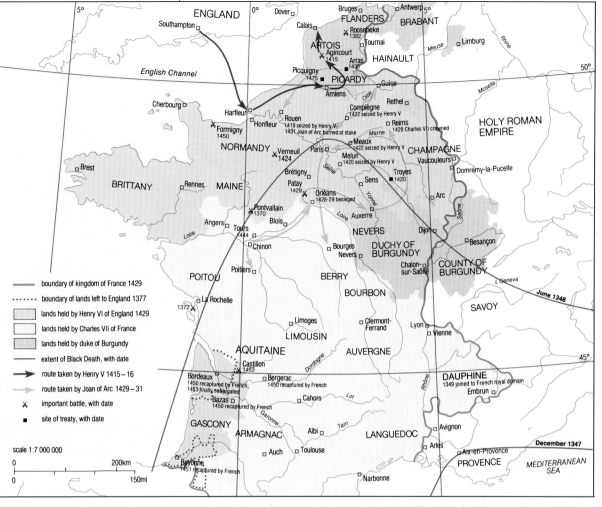

boundary of kingdom of France 1429
boundary of lands left to England 1377
lands held by Henry VI of England 1429
lands held by Charles VII of France
lands held by duke of Burgundy
extent of Black Death, with date
route taken by Henry V 1415–16
route taken by Joan of Arc 1429–31
✕ important battle, with date
■ site of treaty, with date

scale 1:7 000 000
0   200km
0   150mi

on Jews signaled a desperate search for human scapegoats. Until the 18th century, plague remained a threat that was always on the social horizon.

Population losses brought about further stagnation and decline in the economy. Labor had become a scarce and costly commodity, and the towns experienced mass poverty. It was said that in Metz, in 1419, a man could have four prostitutes for the price of an egg. On the land, attempts by seigneurs to make their peasants pay the cost of the crisis failed. Indeed, some of those peasants who survived were able to benefit from increased mobility and higher wages. The lords offset their losses as best they could, but overall the crisis weakened the land-owning class and spelt the end of manorial farming.

The Hundred Years War
To compensate for their losses, many of the nobility resorted to traditional methods of plunder. Consequently, from the early 14th to the mid 15th century, France was in a state of nearly continuous warfare, the so-called Hundred Years War against England. The war started in 1337 as a feudal dispute, when Philip VI (1328–50), the first Valois monarch, confiscated the duchy of Aquitaine, owned by Edward IV of England. Edward led an army across the Channel to defend his rights, and also as a claimant to the French throne to which, through his mother, he asserted a legal title. The following century of intermittent wars and uneasy peace was characterized by some of the better-known events in the national histories of England and France: the brilliant feats of arms of English bowmen at Crécy (1346), Poitiers (1356) and Agincourt (1415); and the subsequent French resistance, inspired by the charismatic figure of Joan of Arc (1412–31), notably in the siege of Orléans (1429).

The Hundred Years War, however, was more than one fought between fledgling nations; it was also a civil war of the most cynical kind, as feudal vassals sought personal advantage by supporting the king of England. The jockeying for power by Armagnac and Burgundian factions, particularly from the 1390s to the 1410s, was especially vicious. English armies together with their French allies were always comparatively small – 40,000 at the most – and caused relatively few deaths in battle. However, the relentless pillaging by armed bands of vigilantes, who created corridors of destruction wherever they passed, considerably aggravated the existing demographic and social problems.

In 1453, England conceded defeat in a peace that left only Calais in English hands. The Valois dynasty emerged much strengthened by the victory, after surviving some critical times. In the late 1350s, the call by a leading Paris merchant, Etienne Marcel, for representative government coincided with the Jacquerie (1358), a peasant rising in northern France that had been triggered by military depredations. The Jacquerie was bloodily put down, with over 20,000 deaths among the peasants.

France at this time was described by the Italian humanist poet Petrarch as "a heap of ruins". Following Agincourt (1415), French fortunes were at another low ebb, when Charles VI (1368–1422) was forced to accept the Englishman Henry V as his heir. Charles VII (1422–61), before Joan of Arc persuaded him otherwise, was neurotically uncertain of his own claims to the throne and was mockingly dubbed "King of

Joan of Arc

The extraordinary career of Joan of Arc has made her one of the best known, but perhaps least understood, figures of French history. Canonized as recently as 1920, it was only in the 19th century that the "Maid of Orléans" was adopted as a mascot of French right-wing nationalism. Earlier generations found her more difficult to fathom.

One of five children, Joan (*Jeanne*, or *Jehanne* in French) was born about 1412 to a moderately wealthy farmer in Domrémy in Lorraine. She was 13 when she started hearing the voices of Saints Michael, Catherine and Margaret, instructing her what to do. Her reputation preceded her appearance in Chinon, in February 1429, where Charles VII was ruing the possible loss of his kingdom to the English. Joan identified Charles from a group of courtiers and convinced him of her divine mission to drive the English out of France. She persuaded him to give her command of an army to lift the English siege of Orléans, which she accomplished. The English were driven north of the Loire and their aura of invincibility was severely damaged. Joan was instrumental in bringing Charles to Reims. His coronation in this traditional place made him king "by the grace of God" and fortified his prestige.

However, Joan's role at court became increasingly uncertain as those who urged negotiations with the English came to prevail over the pro-war group with which she was identified. Taken prisoner, she was handed over to the English by the Burgundians, who were still allies of the English. The English tried her as a witch in Rouen. Despite a heroic defence, she was sentenced at first to life imprisonment, then to be burned at the stake. The sentence was carried out in 1431, after Charles VII had failed to ransom her.

Joan's habit of dressing in men's clothes, plus her claims to divine guidance, helped to condemn her as a heretic and sorcerer – charges that were supported by false evidence. Her death exemplified a growing intolerance within late-medieval Europe toward unorthodox behavior and religious views. This tendency was particularly strong in France. The Knights Templar had been tried in 1310 for alleged sodomistic orgies and worship of the devil and unnatural behavior was also attributed to Jews and lepers. Similar charges and attacks were made against the Waldensian heretics in the Alps. The purge of such dissidents increased after Joan's death with growing numbers of trials for witchcraft.

Right Joan is one of a handful of great historical characters who is portrayed by each successive age in its own image. This martial, armored Joan, by an anonymous Franco-Flemish artist appears in a manuscript book of poems (c. 1455) by Charles of Orléans.

Below The Hundred Years War started as a war of knights, fought according to chivalric conventions. By the time of Joan of Arc, the conduct and nature of warfare was changing fast. English bowmen had laid low the flower of French knighthood. The discovery of gunpowder brought the appearance of heavy artillery on the field of battle, as shown in this 15th-century illumination.

Above The earliest portrait of Joan of Arc, and the only one made in her lifetime. It was penned into a register of the great law court, the Parlement of Paris, in May 1429, recording the relief of the siege of Orléans.

Right In this illumination from a Book of Hours representing a death vigil, the devils of hell mete out a gruesome fate to the souls of sinners. The late Middle Ages displayed a growing awareness of hell and the devil, and both were imaginatively portrayed by artists and theologians. Women were thought to be particularly vulnerable to the devil's blandishments, so Joan's judges found it easier to believe that her voices were diabolical in origin rather than divine.

Bourges". As it proved, he and his son, Louis XI (1461–83), were to be the architects of the recovery of France and the rebuilding of its government.

Reconstruction and expansion

Crucial in the reconstruction of France were military and financial reforms. The advantage that armed infantrymen enjoyed over cavalry on the field of battle highlighted the inadequacy of the old feudal levy, and obliged rulers to have recourse to paid mercenaries. Between 1439 and 1445 a rudimentary professional army was set up called the *compagnies d'ordonnance*. At the same time, Charles VII established the principle that the army should be maintained through direct taxation (the *taille*). A standing army financed by royal taxation and independent of any representative body such as the Estates General laid the foundation for the absolute monarchy throughout the early modern period, and would disappear only with the Revolution of 1789.

Other features of future absolutism were also put in place in the reigns of Charles VII and Louis XI. New tax areas, called *généralités*, were created, while the monarch gained extensive control over appointment to the higher clergy by the Pragmatic Sanction of Bourges (1438), later modified by the Concordat of Bologna (1516). A restructured royal council, dominated by secretaries of state and masters of requests (*maîtres des requêtes*) rather than feudal dignitaries, formulated state policy. To promote the ideology of royalty, the king indulged in elaborate ceremonial displays and tournaments and in patronage of the arts, which glorified the dynasty. The "Renaissance monarchy" of the early 16th century had its roots in this earlier period.

For more than a century, France had continued to expand. The acquisition of the Dauphiné in 1349 spread the kingdom significantly across the Rhône for the first time. The seizure of Guyenne in 1453 from the English was followed by the further annexations of Alençon (1456), the Armagnac lands (1473), Burgundy (1477), Provence (1481), the Anjou lands (1489) and Brittany (1491). One of the most striking features of the expansion was the balance achieved between centralized and decentralized power. Across Europe, the king of France had a reputation for absolute power: Louis XI, the Milanese ambassadors noted, did not want to "share his kingdom". Yet, the king did not rule uniformly throughout the realm. Some acquired territories were allowed to retain local institutions, while outlying provinces were given their own high courts, or *parlements* – Toulouse in 1443, Grenoble in 1453 and so on. Local estates (representative bodies) – more manageable than the national Estates General – were also permitted: Brittany, for example, kept its estates after it was incorporated in 1491. In practice, "absolutism" meant maintaining local forms of administration and incorporating these into the "fundamental laws of the kingdom", France's unwritten constitution.

Burgundy, the Italian Wars and the Renaissance

Only when perceived as a threat to the state, or as a rival to its power, was local government put down. One such case was the duchy of Burgundy, created as a semi-autonomous appanage by John II (1350–64) for his son Philip "the Bold". Under a succession of powerful dukes, the duchy developed administrative machinery as effective as that of the kings of France.

Above Illumination showing a witch on her broomstick. Fear of the devil and his works combined with a general misogyny among celibate male clerics to send to their deaths tens of thousands of women accused of witchcraft and of consorting with the devil.

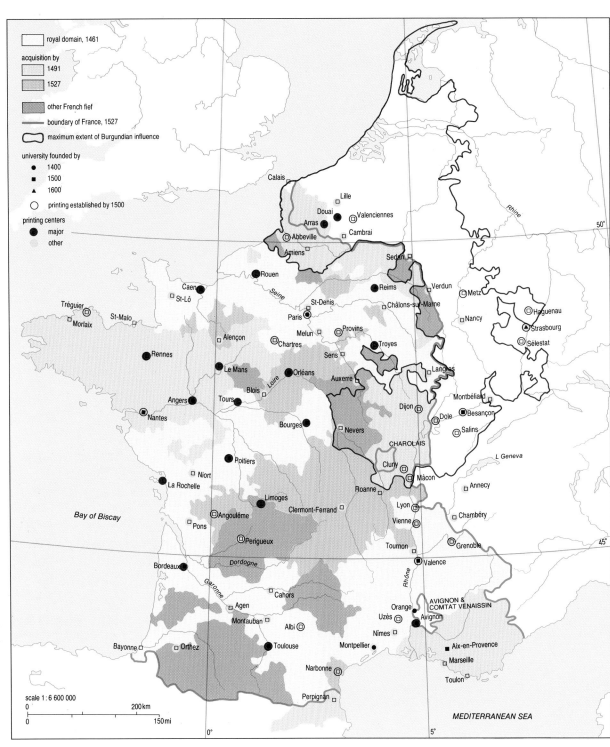

Map legend:
- royal domain, 1461
- acquisition by
  - 1491
  - 1527
- other French fief
- boundary of France, 1527
- maximum extent of Burgundian influence
- university founded by
  - 1400 (circle)
  - 1500 (square)
  - 1600 (triangle)
- printing established by 1500 (open circle)
- printing centers
  - major (filled circle)
  - other

scale 1 : 6 600 000
0 — 200 km
0 — 150 mi

Map labels:
Calais, Lille, Douai, Valenciennes, Arras, Cambrai, Abbeville, Amiens, Sedan, Rouen, Reims, Verdun, Metz, Caen, St-Lô, St-Denis, Châlons-sur-Marne, Nancy, Haguenau, Tréguier, Paris, Strasbourg, Morlaix, St-Malo, Melun, Provins, Sélestat, Alençon, Chartres, Rennes, Le Mans, Sens, Troyes, Blois, Orléans, Langres, Angers, Tours, Auxerre, Montbéliard, Nantes, Bourges, Nevers, Dijon, Dole, Besançon, CHAROLAIS, Salins, Poitiers, L. Geneva, Niort, Cluny, Mâcon, La Rochelle, Roanne, Annecy, Limoges, Lyon, Chambéry, Angoulême, Clermont-Ferrand, Vienne, Pons, Périgueux, Tournon, Grenoble, Bordeaux, Dordogne, Valence, Garonne, Cahors, Agen, Orange, AVIGNON & COMTAT VENAISSIN, Montauban, Uzès, Avignon, Albi, Nîmes, Bayonne, Orthez, Toulouse, Montpellier, Aix-en-Provence, Narbonne, Marseille, Perpignan, Toulon, Bay of Biscay, Seine, Loire, Rhine, Rhône, MEDITERRANEAN SEA

France and the Renaissance
After its success in the Hundred Years War, the French state had to reorganize its central power base, which had suffered from the Anglo-French conflict. By 1500, the threat of Burgundian power had been eliminated. War was conducted abroad, in Italy, rather than within France, allowing a flowering of culture. Art and architecture reflected Italian Renaissance styles, but perhaps the most powerful cultural influence was the rapid spread of the printing press.

Right John, duke of Berry (1340–1416) was the son of King John II "the Good" (1350–64). The duke commissioned the Limburg brothers to design the celebrated book of hours called *Très riches heures du duc de Berry*, from which this illumination is taken. The duke, in a fur cap and blue robe, is seen seated at the table.

Above center Peasant apple-picking. This illumination is from a manuscript version (c. 1460) of Pietro de Crescenzi's *Rusticon*, an agricultural manual composed in Italy in about 1305. The work was published for the first time in 1471 and reprinted many times.

Above Medal of Anne of Brittany (1477–1514). Duchess of Brittany from 1488, she married Maximilian of Austria, before Charles VIII forced her to annul the marriage and marry him instead in 1491. Brittany thus came under royal control for the first time. On Charles's death, Anne married his successor, Louis XII. Brittany became an integral part of the French kingdom in 1532.

Far right Portrait by Jean Fouquet of Guillaume Jouvenel des Ursins (1401–72), Chancellor of France in 1445.

At one stage, it seemed that the duchy, enlarged by the acquisition of Artois and Flanders, might constitute a "middle kingdom" between France and Germany on the lines of the Treaty of Verdun in 843. The defeat and death in battle in 1477 of Charles "the Bold" (1467–77) ended the Burgundian threat, but it did so at a price. Although the duchy of Burgundy was incorporated into the French kingdom, adjacent Franche-Comté remained in the family of Charles "the Bold" whose heir, Mary, married a Habsburg. This laid the foundations for the Valois–Habsburg – later, Bourbon–Habsburg – rivalry, which was the major axis of European international relations till the late 17th century.

The battlefield on which this rivalry was expressed in the 15th to 16th centuries was the Italian peninsula. French successes included the triumphant southward march of the young Charles VIII (1483–98) in 1494, his siege artillery piercing city walls that offered resistance; and the brilliant victory of Francis I (1515–47) at Marignano in 1515. Arguably, the French had to oppose Habsburg influence here in the early 16th century if they were to avoid encirclement by the Habsburg Emperor, Charles V, ruler of Austria, Spain, Franche-Comté and the Low Countries. Overall, the successes of the French troops in the peninsula, where they were a constant presence from 1494 to 1559, were offset by disasters, such as the defeat at Pavia in 1525, where Francis I was taken prisoner. Under the Treaty of Cateau-Cambrésis (1559), which ended the Italian Wars, France acquired Calais and the "Three Bishoprics" (Toul, Metz, Verdun), but lost any claim to a foothold on the Italian peninsula. Perhaps the significant point about the Italian Wars was that France had been able to have an aggressive foreign policy at all. The wars signaled the

end of a lengthy period of civil strife and political weakness. They also testified to the vigor of France's economic recovery.

France's improved economic performance formed part of a general European pattern of recovery from the disruptive effects of the Black Death and the feudal crises of the late Middle Ages. Population growth accelerated and began to approach pre-Black Death levels, causing housing problems in many cities and stimulating urban development. Urbanization, in its turn, acted as a stimulant to the economy, with agricultural production, for example, expanding in response to urban demand. Many towns developed a wider and more sophisticated industrial base – to include silk, leather, metalwork and glasswork, for example – and this was accompanied by the growth of guilds and corporations, each having its own location in the city, and the forging of further trading links within France and Europe.

The early 16th century also witnessed a communications revolution. The discovery of the New World was shifting the center of European economic and cultural life from the Mediterranean to the Atlantic. Besides more intensive economic exchange, there was a great dissemination of ideas. The advent of printing brought about a massive growth in the production and diffusion of texts of every sort – a process complemented by the development of a public postal system. Significantly, the French language was becoming the privileged language of communication. It made inroads on Latin, the medieval language of science and religion, and Provencal, whose formerly vigorous literature had declined in the 15th century. Among the great writers of the 16th century were the humanists Rabelais (1494–1553) and Montaigne (1533–92), who manipulated a French language

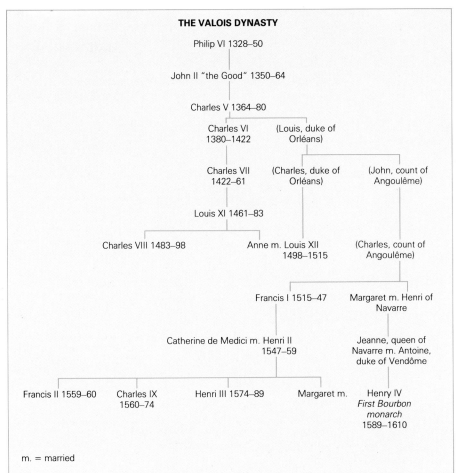

THE VALOIS DYNASTY

Philip VI 1328–50

John II "the Good" 1350–64

Charles V 1364–80

Charles VI 1380–1422 — (Louis, duke of Orléans)

Charles VII 1422–61 — (Charles, duke of Orléans) — (John, count of Angoulême)

Louis XI 1461–83

Charles VIII 1483–98 — Anne m. Louis XII 1498–1515 — (Charles, count of Angoulême)

Francis I 1515–47 — Margaret m. Henri of Navarre

Catherine de Medici m. Henri II 1547–59 — Jeanne, queen of Navarre m. Antoine, duke of Vendôme

Francis II 1559–60 — Charles IX 1560–74 — Henri III 1574–89 — Margaret m. — Henry IV *First Bourbon monarch* 1589–1610

m. = married

which, by the royal edict of Villers-Cotterets in 1539, became the official language for all legal documents. As a spoken language, French remained a minority tongue till 1789, overwhelmed as it was by other languages (German, Italian, Spanish, Breton and so on) and a plethora of local *patois*; it was in this Renaissance period, however, that the French language achieved the status of official written language of the French people.

The Renaissance also had its dark side. One of the most distinctive features of economic development was inflation. It was small by today's standards and, indeed, rising prices produced both positive and negative effects. Peasants and other landowners who could produce for the market benefited greatly, as food prices were among the most buoyant. People working for fixed wages or receiving fixed rents, however, suffered. The 16th century was a time of growing social division. Massive fortunes were made more massive at one end of the social spectrum, yet at the other, large numbers of people lived on the bread-line, faced starvation at times of harvest failure and posed a growing threat to public order, a situation with which governments found it difficult to deal.

Left Anonymous 17th-century portrait of François Rabelais (1494–1553), the great humanist and satirist. A Greek scholar, physician and polymath, Rabelais became curé of Meudon. Best known for his multivolumed satirical tales of Gargantua and Pantagruel, Rabelais was one of the most brilliant figures of the Renaissance in France.

Right Henry II, ruler since 1547, was fatally wounded in a jousting accident in Paris in 1559 when less than 40 years old. In this engraving, the famous royal surgeon Ambroise Paré (c. 1509–90) is shown preparing to tend the king, who has received a fragment of the lance of the count of Montgomery in the left eye.

Left A 15th-century tapestry depicting "the bath". One of a series illustrating seigneurial life, it was manufactured in the southern Netherlands and presently hangs in the Cluny Museum, Paris.

The Wars of Religion
The Reformation, which originated in 1517 in Martin Luther's stand against corruption in the Roman Church, spread throughout Europe in the following decades, shattering the religious unity of medieval christendom. Its impact on France – it perhaps divided the French more decisively than any other European state – was considerable. The religious divide that developed between Catholics and Calvinists (or Huguenots as they were called) soon passed from polemic to bloodletting. The St Bartholomew's Massacre in Paris and other cities in 1572 was only the most notorious episode in a bloody chronicle of religious struggle. The confessional divide between Catholics and Huguenots that had emerged by the end of the Wars of Religion in 1598 was highly complex. The inverted horseshoe of Huguenot strongholds – from the Rhône valley and the Cévennes in the southeast through Béarn, the Bordelais and Poitou into Normandy in the northwest – was to prove the basis of the religious geography of French Protestantism into the 20th century. The consequences of the confessional schism for the French polity were dire: France was eclipsed as a European power until the Thirty Years War (1618–48).

TOVRNELLES

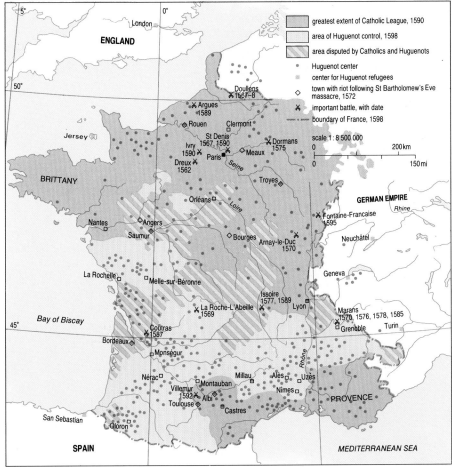

The Wars of Religion

Despite the ideological absolutism of the French state, central government was less powerful than its language and pretensions suggested. Its limitations became obvious from the middle of the 16th century, when there was a resurgence of civil strife, grounded in the social and ideological tensions produced by economic change. After sporadic attempts at repression, the government failed to prevent Protestantism from establishing itself as a powerful minority religion. The problem became pressing from the early 1550s, as Calvinist missionaries working out of Geneva spread the new faith among the nobles and bourgeoisie as well as the artisans and townspeople who had been among the relatively few supporters of French Lutheranism in the 1520s. By 1560, a distinctive religious geography of Protestantism was emerging in France, with some 2,150 so-called "Huguenot" communities. Perhaps as much as half of the nobility and a third of the bourgeoisie had become Protestant.

The Wars of Religion (1560–98), which at times threatened to tear the state apart, concerned not only religious dispute but also resistance by the nobles to centralized state power. The sudden weakening of the authority of the crown following the death of Henri II in a jousting accident in 1559 triggered the conflict. Two of Henri's successors – Francis II (1559–60) and Charles IX (1560–74) – were minors, and the third, Henri III (1574–89) was weak and ineffective. The dominant political personality till 1589 was their mother, Catherine de Medici, the widow of Henri II. In 1560, the Estates General were called for the first

The Huguenots

So strong was Protestantism in France around 1560, that its replacement of Catholicism as the state religion became a real possibility. Broad swathes of support at every level of society, from the lowest to the highest, meant that the French Protestants – or Huguenots, as they were (inexplicably) called – were rightly optimistic about their chances of success.

Religious questions were clouded, however, by the increasing involvement of political factions in the affairs of state during the regency of Catherine de Medici. A weak monarchy would have had problems with overly powerful subjects even at the best of times; those problems were compounded by religious rivalry and intolerance. The succession of religious wars that lasted until 1598 turned into a faction fight between the ultra-Catholic Guise family, who were particularly strong in eastern France, the Protestant Montmorency clan, based in the center, and the Huguenot Henri of Navarre (the future Henri IV) whose base was in the southwest. The issue was further complicated by the armed intervention of England, who sided with the Huguenots and Spain, a Catholic power.

In fact, the scale of actual fighting was fairly limited, but the economic disruption caused by political and military uncertainty was considerable. In time, there emerged a Catholic standpoint – that of the *politiques* – according to which some concessions to the Huguenots were acceptable in return for social and political harmony. This compromise made the task of Henri IV in bringing factions together easier.

The Counter-Reformation of the 17th century put the Huguenots under renewed pressure, even before Louis XIV formally abolished the Protestant church in France in 1685. Only on the very eve of the 1789 Revolution did French Protestants regain some measure of religious acceptance.

Right Miniature of Charles IX (1560–74). Born in 1550, Charles was still a child when he acceded to the throne on the death of his sickly brother Francis II (1559–60), and was completely dominated by his mother, Catherine de Medici.

Below The Edict of Nantes, 13 April 1598. By allowing Huguenots limited freedom of religion, Henri IV won their support, but also kept the Catholics on his side. The possibility of a confessional state had receded – at least for the time.

Left An engraving recording the massacre of several hundreds of Huguenots in the city of Tours in 1562. The thousands of Protestants murdered in Paris in the St Bartholomew's Eve Massacre of 1572 were only some of the many victims of religious intolerance during the Wars of Religion.

Below Catholics on the march in Paris. The attempt by Henri III (1574–89) to make concessions to the Huguenots prompted a massive Catholic backlash led by the powerful Guise family. They aimed to depose Henri as king so as to prevent the succession of the Huguenot Henri of Navarre (the future Henri IV). The Catholic League, organized by the Guises, won much support from religious fanatics in the capital.

Below Watercolor portrait of Catherine de Medici (1519–89). The unexpected death of her husband Henri II in 1559 brought this Italian princess into the limelight as the dominant political figure of her times. She is acknowledged to have ordered the St Bartholomew's Eve Massacre of 1572.

time since 1484, showing the need that Catherine felt, as regent, for some form of public legitimation. Appeals to national unity, however, went unheeded by a nation increasingly divided by rival faiths and soon by bloodshed. Between 1562 and 1598, eight religious wars were fought. Although the scale of military operations was relatively small, the disruption caused by the frequent breakdown of law and order was very considerable.

Religious intolerance exacerbated other conflicts: 3,000 followers of the tendency denounced as the Waldensian heresy were killed in mid-century in the Alps, but they were greatly outnumbered by those executed for witchcraft from the 1580s, when French witch-hunting was at its most virulent. The "Saint Bartholomew's Eve" massacre of leading Protestants in Paris (1572) was the most infamous example of the mood of religious intolerance: 2,700 Protestants were murdered in Paris, and more than 20,000 in the provincial cities. Such violence, however, only fortified Protestant resistance. The monarchy could not eradicate Protestantism, but neither could it implement a policy of religious tolerance, which was anathema to some influential subjects, notably the arch-Catholic Guise family. In 1588, Henri III had the Guises murdered. "Only now", he said, "am I king."

Henri III's triumph was short-lived: in 1589 he was himself assassinated by a Catholic extremist. As Henri was childless, the throne passed to Henri of Navarre (1589–1610), a descendant of the Bourbon line who, from the Béarn in southwestern France, led the Protestant community's resistance. In winning over France's Catholic heartlands, Henri IV combined coercion with political acumen. Above all, it was necessary to conquer Paris, the center of armed resistance and home of ultra-Catholic fanaticism since Saint Bartholomew's Eve. This was achieved in 1593–4 by a classic gesture: Henri abjured his Protestantism for the Catholic faith – he adjudged Paris, he said, "worth a mass". The move was well received by a broad spectrum of Catholic opinion. After the sectarian horrors through which the Catholics had lived, they prized social harmony above the establishment of a unitary confessional state. Henri followed this up by the Edict of Nantes of 1598, which introduced religious toleration. In the same year, he signed the Peace of Vervins with Philip II of Spain, who had earlier sought to profit from internal French weakness.

For the remainder of his reign, Henri IV displayed the combination of firmness and diplomacy that had won him power. His principal minister, Sully (1560–1641), worked to reestablish economic prosperity, following the disasters and destruction of the previous decades. Henri's legendary wish, however, that every peasant should have a "chicken in his pot" was royal propaganda rather than economic policy. The peasantry was, in fact, in dire straits, as was shown by a number of peasant uprisings – notably the Croquant (from the French *croc*, "bill hook") revolt in the southwest in 1595–6: and its situation was not improved by the burden of heavy taxes. To others, the idea that the monarch's task was to ensure community welfare seemed to make sense after the horrors of the Wars of Religion, and propagandists of absolutism, such as the great humanist thinker Jean Bodin (1530–96), presented the king as the only alternative to anarchy.

The assassination of Henri IV in 1610 upset the new order. Henri's successor, Louis XIII (1610–43) was

then merely nine years old, so that Henri's widow, Marie de Medici, initially acted as regent. As an adult, Louis proved weak and vacillating, while his son, Louis XIV (1643–1715), inherited the throne as an infant and came to full power only in 1661. The years from 1610 to 1661 were marked by consistent, if ultimately unavailing, efforts to reverse the centralizing tendencies established by the first Bourbon ruler, Henri IV. The scale of resistance was considerable. The Protestant community posed a threat to state unity until the late 1620s. Popular discontent seethed – there were riots and risings every year from the 1620s to 1648, including massive peasant revolts by the Croquants between the Loire and the Garonne in 1636–7, and the Nu-Pieds ("Bare Feet") in Normandy in 1639. These disturbances climaxed in the civil war known as the Fronde (1648–52), which saw political elites fighting among themselves for control of the state apparatus. If a state's strength is judged against the virulence of resistance within it, then France at this time was desperately weak. Beneath this surface instability, however, the foundations of French power in Europe were being laid.

State power and bureaucracy

The architects of the reconstruction of the bases of French absolutism were the "cardinal ministers" Richelieu (1585–1642), who controlled the royal council from 1624 to 1642, and his successor, the Italian Mazarin (1602–61). To combat Habsburg encirclement of France, Richelieu involved France in the Thirty Years War (1618–48) at first covertly, then, from 1635, in open warfare. The French army was greatly enlarged, particularly after defeat by the Spanish at Corbie (1636), when Paris was vulnerable to enemy seizure. In just a couple of decades the number of soldiers rose from twenty or thirty thousand to more than a quarter of a million. The maintenance of a larger army necessitated an unparalleled growth in royal taxation. Taxes increased threefold between 1630 and 1648, with a further 50 percent rise by the end of the century. State power also increased to contain the discontent that these changes produced.

A major factor in the strengthening of state power was the growth of ministerial government. Principal ministers like Richelieu and Mazarin, and effective bureaucrats such as Jean-Baptiste Colbert (1619–83), Louis XIV's great finance minister, made ambitious princelings politically unimportant. Already the king's council had become too much of a bureaucracy for the process to be reversed. The high nobility was compensated for its loss of political power by an affirmation of its social status. "Nothing is dearer to me" said Louis XIII, "than to do all I can to preserve my nobles." They included a growing number of "Robe" nobles, who served the state administratively, as well as the older, military "Sword" nobility. The nobility benefited from greater state patronage, and a rapid expansion in the number of state officials from perhaps 12,000 in the 16th century, to four times as many by the 1660s. As government offices were purchased, the increase also provided more revenue for the state. Between 1610 and 1630, state income from the sale of administative posts increased tenfold. This system of venality of offices became more controlled in a way that gave placemen a vested interest in the stability of the state. From the 1620s, Richelieu sent out to the provinces specially appointed officials to regulate the

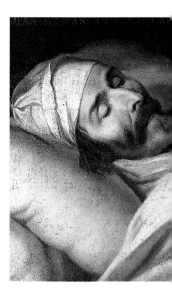

Above The death of Armand-Jean du Plessis, cardinal de Richelieu (1585–1642). The great "cardinal minister" was one of the principal architects of royal absolutism. He dominated the royal council from 1624 to his death, bringing the Huguenots to heel, centralizing the royal administration and crushing the political ambitions of the great feudal magnates. This painting is by Philippe de Champaigne (1602–74), one of the finest exponents of French classicism.

Top left Drawing by the Dauphin, the future Louis XIII, when he was only five years old. It was kept by the prince's personal physician, Jean Héroard, whose medical journal recounts, among other things, the child's upbringing and sex education.

Bottom left The Italian Jules Mazarin (1602–61) was a papal diplomat when Cardinal Richelieu took him into his service in the early 1630s. He made himself indispensable to his master and to Louis XIII. When Richelieu died, Mazarin became head of the royal council. On Louis's death, in 1643, he became the close confidant of Louis's widow, the queen regent Anne of Austria, who ruled France while Louis XIV (born in 1637) was a minor. But effectively Mazarin was the real ruler. Very unpopular at the time of the civil war, or Fronde (1648–52), he nevertheless survived and amassed a huge personal fortune.

The Ancien Régime
The Ancien Régime, covering the centuries leading up to the Revolution of 1789, was a period in which society and state were closely intertwined, at least in theory. The Bourbon dynasty developed the absolute monarchy into the most powerful and prestigious state in Europe. Louis XIV's palace at Versailles was widely admired and copied by aspiring autocrats throughout Europe. Administrative centralization through the system of intendants (state-appointed officials sent to the provinces to regulate local officials) was

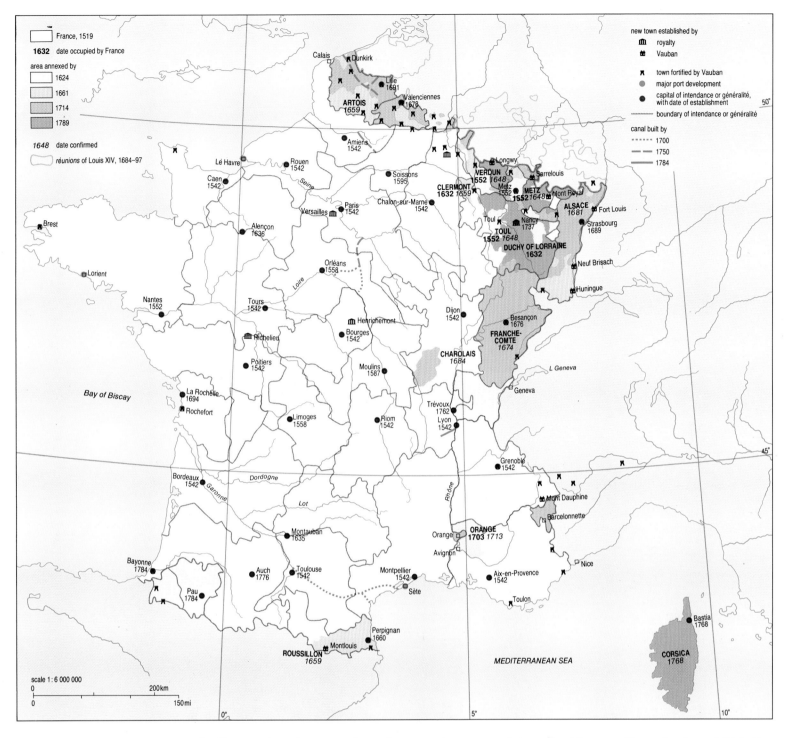

France, 1519
1632 date occupied by France
area annexed by
1624
1661
1714
1789

1648 date confirmed
réunions of Louis XIV, 1684–97

new town established by
🏛 royalty
⚜ Vauban

🏹 town fortified by Vauban
● major port development
● capital of intendance or généralité, with date of establishment
— boundary of intendance or généralité

canal built by
.... 1700
— — — 1750
——— 1784

scale 1 : 6 000 000
0   200 km
0   150 mi

accompanied by the acquisition of strong, defensible frontiers. Although not all Louis XIV's military plans bore fruit – the *réunions* of 1684–97 were lost in his later wars – land was won on all land frontiers, and was secured by massive military engineering works often planned and supervised by the military engineer Vauban, who constructed new towns at key defensive points and fortified other vulnerable places. Civil engineering works at the same time included road improvements, port development and impressive canal construction, which boosted France's economic infrastructure.

venal officers, who often saw themselves as private entrepreneurs as much as public officials. These special officials, called Intendants, were given more general powers from the mid 1630s, which later assumed almost vice-regal proportions. The Intendants were the fundamental agent of state centralization until the fall of the Ancien Régime in 1789.

The regulation of public taste and opinion
The centralized bureaucracy which developed in the 17th century had no place for consultation or representation. The Estates General went into abeyance and the expression of opinion came under tighter surveillance. Richelieu was a brutal censor, who incarcerated those with unacceptable views in the Bastille prison. To manipulate public opinion he introduced France's first newspaper, the *Gazette*, published from 1631 by his protégé Théophraste Renaudot.

In addition, he became very preoccupied with the regulation of public taste. From the time of Richelieu onward the absolute monarchy was closely associated with patronage of the arts. For example, Louis XIV's construction of the palace of Versailles was a brilliant effort at self-glorification for which the greatest contemporary talents were employed. They included the architect Louis Le Vau (1612–90), sculptor François Girardon (1628–1715), painter Charles Le Brun (1619–90), garden designer André Le Nôtre (1613–1700) and the Francine family of water engineers. The éclat of royal patronage coincided with one of the most outstanding periods in the history of French culture. Literary patronage, for example, extended to Corneille (1606–84), Racine (1639–99), Bossuet (1627–1704) and Molière (1622–73). Indeed, in all spheres – from cabinetmaking to tapestries, from sculpture to portraiture – royal patronage helped to make the French classical style the object of envy and emulation for the century to follow.

There was also state involvement in the formulation of religious policy. French Catholicism went onto the offensive. The reformers were no longer content just to eradicate Protestantism – they aimed to Christianize the whole of society. Education was one of the primary means of so doing. Besides the Jesuits who, by 1700, had 150 establishments within France containing 60,000 pupils, there were the Oratorians, established by Pierre Bérulle (1575–1629), the Ursulines, and a host of lesser-known teaching orders. Poor relief was another area of religious activity. The Company of the Holy Sacrament, a group of religious and lay activists, sought to revive the notions of Christian charity and mutual assistance. More prosaically, the Daughters of Charity, established by Vincent de Paul and Louise de Marillac in 1633, provided professional standards of nursing care and served as a model for others. In general, the contribution of women to the religious revival was considerable. Barbe Acarie founded the French Carmelites, Jeanne de Chantal was co-founder with François de Sales of the Visitandines and Angélique Arnaud established the Port-Royal convent. In addition, many of the reform endeavors received financial support from wealthy widows and spinsters.

The state also provided money and material support for such projects, as Christianity among the masses produced a more docile and obedient population. When ecclesiastical opinion threatened too much independence of mind, the state could be brutal. Jansenists were routinely persecuted for their rigorous adherence to Augustine's teaching in opposition to the Jesuits. Protestants too found themselves subjected to a crescendo of repression, and in 1685 Louis XIV revoked the Edict of Nantes, outlawing Protestantism and making Catholicism the monopoly religion.

Economic repercussions

The Revocation of the Edict of Nantes ran counter to the king's economic strategy. Under the ministry of Colbert, Louis XIV had followed mercantilist policies, whereby he sought to build up the economy through

Above Théophraste Renaudot (1586–1653), the founder and first editor of the *Gazette*. By profession a physician, he was one of Richelieu's most able propagandists.

Above left France's first newspaper, the *Gazette de France*, founded in 1631. It was an important organ of government and had no place for opinion or debate. It remained the official newspaper of the French state until the French Revolution and, with some changes, survived till 1914.

Below Collective portrait (c. 1670) of conventional characters of the Italian *Commedia dell'arte* and actors of French farce. On the far left is the great dramatist, actor and director Molière (1622–73), stage name Jean-Baptiste Poquelin. He is dressed as Arnolphè, the bourgeois character from his own great comedy, *L'Ecole des femmes*. Molière's comedies often satirized the good and the great, yet they won the support of the royal court as well as popular audiences in Paris.

state intervention. Trading companies were chartered and given extensive governmental subsidies; a strong navy was created; colonial penetration was encouraged – notably in India, Madagascar, North America and the Caribbean; state manufactures were subsidized; aggressive tariffs policies were introduced; and communications were improved – the Canal du Midi (1665–81), covering nearly 250 kilometers from Toulouse to Agde and linking the Mediterranean and

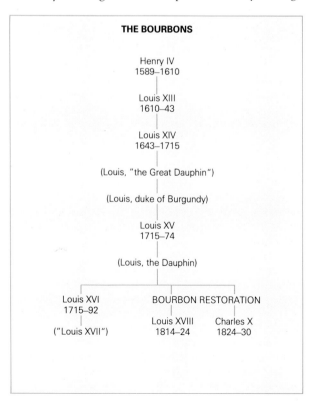

THE BOURBONS

Henry IV
1589–1610

Louis XIII
1610–43

Louis XIV
1643–1715

(Louis, "the Great Dauphin")

(Louis, duke of Burgundy)

Louis XV
1715–74

(Louis, the Dauphin)

Louis XVI
1715–92

("Louis XVII")

BOURBON RESTORATION

Louis XVIII
1814–24

Charles X
1824–30

Right Louis XIV visiting the Gobelin tapestry factory. In 1662 the king's prinicipal minister, Jean-Baptiste Colbert (1619–83), reorganized tapestry works in Paris as the Royal Factory of Tapestry and Carpet Weavers to the Crown. The artist Charles Le Brun (1619–90), who was responsible for this tapestry, was put in charge of the factory, which produced many of the finest works to be found at Versailles and in other royal palaces. Still in operation, the factory has produced more than 5,000 tapestries.

Below The siege of Namur, 1692, during the War of the League of Augsburg (1689–97), by Jean-Baptiste Martin. Colbert's policy of sound finance and state economic intervention allowed Louis XIV to wage wars that were ultimately his, and France's, ruin. State-sponsored artists, such as Martin, engaged in dynastic propaganda by portraying military successes.

Atlantic, was arguably the most outstanding work of civil engineering since Roman times. The Revocation caused the emigration of 200,000 Protestants – many of them prized skilled workers, who joined France's industrial and political rivals. The priority that Louis gave to dynastic and religious goals over economic objectives also reduced the likelihood of France winning a protracted war. The "Sun King" became repeatedly involved in costly foreign adventures, in particular the War of Devolution (1667–8), the Dutch War (1672–8), the War of the League of Augsburg (1689) and the War of Spanish Succession (1702–13). He did, however, make some important gains, including Roussillon and Artois in 1659, Flanders and Franche-Comté in 1678 and Strasbourg in 1681. Moreover, frontier defenses were now strengthened by the fortresses designed by Vauban (1633–1707), the brilliant military engineer. But all this had been achieved by the 1680s, and in Louis' final years there seemed little chance of success against a European coalition.

The 18th century thus started at a low ebb. When France's aging monarch died in 1715, there were few to mourn his passing. The economy was reeling and poverty was widespread. The attempts by Colbert and his ministers to build up the economy had been spoiled by an unfavorable economic climate and by reckless indulgence in war. Yet, from this unpromising start, the French economy made impressive progress over the course of the century. From the 1730s the population increased rapidly, rising from 21.5 millions in 1700, to an unprecedented 28.6 millions in 1789. The end of civil strife, protection from incursions by foreign troops and the disappearance of plague (the last outbreak of which was in Marseille in 1720) removed many of the barriers to population expansion. Furthermore, whereas in former times a significant population rise might have led to a subsistence

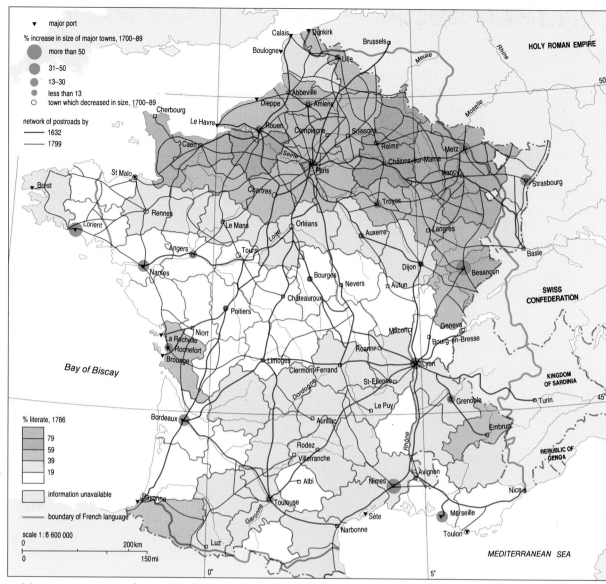

The Age of Enlightenment
The 18th century was a great period of communication and the spread of both material goods and ideas, as traditionalist society was increasingly penetrated by currents of commerce and exchange. The network of postroads thickened to allow quicker and easier communication while towns developed apace, especially those linked to the booming Atlantic trade. Vast differences across the country persisted, however, in levels of wealth and education. Literacy standards varied enormously, with people in the north and northeast – demarcated by a line roughly from St Malo to Geneva – better educated than the poorer, more illiterate south and southwest. In those areas, French was not the dominant language, and had to compete with Breton, Basque, Catalan, Occitan and a variety of patois as the first language spoken by the local people.

Above The French philosopher, physician and mathematician René Descartes (1596–1650) lived from 1629 in Holland, returning only occasionally to France. The philosophy that he developed became one of the foundations of modern science. His principle of "methodic doubt", as elaborated in his *Discourse on Method* (1637), challenged received knowledge and encouraged a more critical approach to truth which was highly influential in the 18th-century Enlightenment.

crisis, mass starvation became a thing of the past after the great crisis of 1709–10.

France had thus achieved the "vital revolution". Although periodic shortages continued to cause hunger and hardship, death from starvation was no longer a danger. In the 18th century, food production in France rose by about 40 percent. The increase was partly due to improved productivity through more scientific farming methods and partly to better marketing and distribution. Any farmer – peasant, bourgeois or noble – who had a food surplus benefited from the steady rise of prices caused by increased demand. Many consumers, however, were relatively worse off, as wages failed to keep pace with prices. A number of legal disputes arose when peasants challenged their lords' exploitation of seigneurial privileges for unfair commercial advantage and contested the worsening of the lot of the poorer peasants. Discontent was rumbling in the countryside long before the Revolution of 1789. Urban consumers, who also suffered in times of grain shortage, increasingly expressed their dissatisfaction by rioting.

For a minority, the upturn in the economy from the third and fourth decades of the 18th century produced prodigious benefits. Industrial production increased fourfold between then and the 1789 Revolution, as did trade with Europe, while colonial trade – benefiting particularly the Atlantic ports such as Bordeaux, Nantes and Saint-Malo – expanded by as much as

1,000 percent. France's growth equalled, and in many areas surpassed, those of contemporary Britain, which was on the eve of its Industrial Revolution. Most of those who profited from the developments were from the ranks of the French bourgeoisie, whose numbers had swelled from 700,000 in 1700 to 2.3 millions in 1789. They included members of the service sector – lawyers, doctors, officials and so on – who were prominent among the revolutionaries of 1789. Some aristocrats also benefited from the economic upturn: proprietors in mining and metallurgy were mostly from the nobility.

The Age of Enlightenment

Economic exchange encouraged cultural diversity. The leading intelligences of the day – the *philosophes* – preached rationalism and liberal tolerance. These thinkers of the Enlightenment, as the movement was called, attacked rigid dogmas and intolerance and, though their message was not entirely new, they reached a wider audience than any similar movement had done before. Sometimes to beat the censors, they dressed up their ideas in fiction spiced with humor – as in the stories (*contes*) of Voltaire (1694–1778) or as educational material, for example, the great multi-volumed *Encyclopédie* (1751–72) edited by Diderot (1713–84). By their efforts, the *philosophes* changed the atmosphere of intellectual debate: the principle of methodic doubt that had earlier been established by

Above Voltaire, pen name of François-Marie Arouet (1694–1778), the most celebrated and one of the most polemical of the *philosophes*. Multitalented, he wrote poetry, prose, history, plays, short stories and journalistic articles. His critical approach and acerbic wit alienated both church and state, and from 1759 he lived at Ferney on the Swiss frontier, so that he could leave France quickly if necessary. He made a triumphant visit to Paris in 1778, when he was feted by the public, the court and the literary establishment.

Center The Genevan Jean-Jacques Rousseau (1712–78), son of a watchmaker, was one of the most influential figures of the Enlightenment. Robespierre and other Revolutionaries later used his *Social Contract* (1762) as their blueprint for a new society. Before 1789 he was better known for his social comment and his novels than for his political writings. His view that human beings were naturally good, and that civilization could be a corrupting influence upon them was the theme of his best-selling novels such as *Emile* (1762). His *Confessions*, published posthumously, created a scandal because of the details of his private life, but fed the cult of Jean-Jacques as Enlightenment antihero.

Right Denis Diderot (1713–84), a witty, pugnacious intellect and gifted writer and dramatist, was perhaps best known for establishing and editing the multivolume *Encyclopédie* (1751–72). This "Bible of the Enlightenment", which contains articles by every major intellectual figure of the age was not only highly informative but also rich in social criticism.

Descartes (1596–1650) signaled a degree of detachment from theologically-circumscribed thought.

The prestige accorded to science – notably in the empirical method detected in the work of Isaac Newton – was a distinctive feature of Enlightenment thinking. Whereas, however, the science of the previous century had concentrated on the natural world (Galileo's astronomy, Harvey and the circulation of the blood, Newtonian mechanics and so on), the *philosophes* tried to tackle the science of human beings as social animals. Yet politically they were often very different one from another: the most influential political thinker, Montesquieu (1689–1755), was a provincial magistrate with vaguely Whiggish views; the Genevan Jean-Jacques Rousseau (1712–78), on the other hand, preached direct democracy in his *Social contract* (1762). The language of social and political engineering infected even the monarchy: although Louis XV (1715–74) and Louis XVI (1774–92), like good Capetians, followed the ritual touching to cure the "King's Evil" (scrofula), their edicts increasingly intoned the Enlightenment language of public welfare and communal liberties.

The end of the Ancien Régime

Despite the enlightened idiom that it affected, the government found it difficult to adapt to economic, social and cultural change. The conception of the state as the upholder of corporate "liberties" as rights was attacked by those who argued that these liberties were, in effect, unjustifiable privileges that were jealously guarded by the wealthiest and most powerful members of society and were therefore unjustified. These vested interests thwarted the government's attempts to solve a serious financial crisis in the last decade of the Ancien Régime, when faced with a soaring national debt caused by French involvement in the American War of Independence (1775–83). Ministers realized that the state could only emerge from its financial problems by reducing the tax privileges of the nobility and clergy. The great reforming minister Turgot (1727–81) attempted to introduce fundamental economic, social and political changes between 1774 and 1776, but was dismissed by the new, young

king Louis XVI. The privileged classes closed ranks to frustrate reform endeavors. The government finally convened the Estates General – a sure sign of desperation for an absolute monarchy – to try to sort out the financial mess.

As Chateaubriand (1768–1848) observed, the revolutionary crisis of 1789 was started "by the patricians"; it was to be finished "by the plebeians". So much change had occurred in society that the governmental crisis could not be contained within the elite. Elections to the Estates General included all social classes – even the humblest villages voted, voicing their complaints in "books of grievances" (*cahiers de doléances*). With censorship lifted, the leaders of the reform movement among the nobility were overtaken by a mobilized peasantry and a bourgeoisie that had found its voice. The idea of liberty as a proprietary right of the wealthy increasingly came under attack from those who saw it as something intrinsic to everyone, whatever their social or political status.

Hunger now fused with anger to create a revolutionary situation. The financial and political crises coincided with a grain shortage caused by harvest failures in 1787 and 1788. Hungry peasants and the urban bourgeoisie and petit-bourgeoisie became frustrated by aristocrats' squabbles and government vacillation, which, once the Estates General met in May 1789, caused social reform to be blocked. An ill-conceived plan by Louis XVI to stage a military coup and dissolve the Estates General spread panic and anxiety throughout the country. A massive, nationwide peasant revolt took place, characterized by attacks on seigneurial rights and personnel in the provinces. In Paris on 14 July 1789, when the price of bread was at its highest level since the reign of Louis XIV, a crowd stormed the Bastille, the royal prison and fortress, and symbol of state power. Louis XVI was forced to concede that the Estates General was a National Assembly that would introduce constitutional government for the first time, according to principles outlined in the new assembly's Declaration of the Rights of Man (26 August 1789). Some contemporary observers said that the revolution was now over: in fact it had only just begun.

Versailles

The palace of Versailles, 24 kilometers to the south-west of Paris, stands as a monument to absolute monarchy, and to Louis XIV in particular, who turned what had been little more than a royal hunting lodge into one of the masterpieces of French architecture.

From the start, Versailles was conceived as a massive prestige project, involving extensive state patronage of the arts. A team of the greatest talents of the day was assembled, including architect Louis Le Vau (1612–70), painter Charles Le Brun (1619–90), sculptor François Girardon (1628–1715), garden designer André Le Nôtre (1613–1700), and the Franchine family as water engineers for the palace's 1,400 fountains. Louis visited and often stayed at the palace, before finally establishing his court there in 1682. The building of Versailles accounted for 5 percent of the government's gross annual revenue.

The palace allowed Louis XIV freely to indulge his passion for hunting and other courtly pleasures, such as entertaining mistresses and staging concerts and ballet. The palace was also an exercise in power architecture, whereby Louis emphasized his social and political superiority. Basic amenities counted for less than conspicuous display: accommodation for courtiers was often cramped, and toilet facilities were few. Versailles became the center of power and court patronage, where sycophantic nobles vied with one another for the king's favors. The court also became a fashion center, imposing its own lavish styles on an aristocracy that was dependent on royal largesse.

Right Louis XIV's successor, Louis XV (1715–74), was notorious for the women he kept. The most famous of his mistresses was Jeanne-Antoinette Poisson, Madame de Pompadour (1721–64). The daughter of a financial clerk, she attracted the king's attention in 1745 and was soon installed as his official mistress, with the title of marquise. A keen patroness of the arts, she remained in favor despite the hatred of jealous courtiers until her death, in 1764.

Below Marie-Antoinette's little Trianon country-house, originally built for Madame de Pompadour. Finding official court life rather stuffy, the queen preferred to indulge in frivolous pastimes around the Versailles estate with a clique of favorites. She established an English-style garden and toy hamlet where she and her friends dressed up as shepherds and shepherdesses.

Below left Louis XV's grandson and successor, Louis XVI (1774–92), detested his grandfather's vices and all his life remained faithful to his Austrian wife, queen Marie-Antoinette. However, he maintained the pomp associated with the Versailles life-style.

Left The king's bedchamber. Court life at Versailles was so governed by ceremony that even this room was the focus of intense public activity. Each day, the monarch engaged in a complex semipublic ritual of getting up and, in the evening, retiring to this bed, hung with gold and silver embroidered brocade. For a courtier to be present was considered to be an honor; to be asked even to hold the king's shirt was an even greater one. Despite the ceremony and show, however, Louis XV was known to slip away most nights to a cosier room in his private suite.

Above Louis XIV dressed as Apollo, the sun god. Louis's Versailles was the home of a variety of aristocratic festivities and pastimes. A keen patron of ballet, the king was himself a considerable performer. The sun was Louis's personal symbol, which recurs time and again throughout Versailles.

Left As well as housing the royal court, Versailles also acted as the nerve-center of government. Ministerial offices existed side by side with buildings of the king's court, and clerks and officials even outnumbered courtiers. After the experience of the Fronde (1648–52), when Louis XIV was personally humiliated by a mob in the Tuileries palace in Paris, he sought a location for government where he could exercise his absolutism unchallenged from a safe distance. When, eventually, in 1789 the king's absolute power was challenged, one of the first moves of the National Assembly was to bring the royal family back to Paris.

THE MAKING OF MODERN FRANCE

The French Revolution

The Declaration of the Rights of Man adopted by the National Assembly of France forms a principal source of the United Nations' Universal Declaration on Human Rights in force today. Indeed, the French Revolution still provides the basic political agenda for contemporary liberal societies. It was a watershed in the history of humanity and much of our political vocabulary still derives from this time. "Liberty", "equality" and "fraternity" – that triad of values with which the Revolutionaries sought to build a new society and a new polity – have never quite lost their original emotional appeal. More mundane terms, such as political "left" and "right", "anarchist", "terrorist" and "bureaucrat" also originated in those years. The liberal phase of constitutional monarchy up till 1792 marks one of the most fertile and creative phases in French history, in which the political and social framework was totally transformed. Ancient provinces were abolished, and a system of departments (*départements*) was imposed. The department was – and largely still is – the unitary framework of state administration, and this was extended to cover finance, religion, the law and military organization. Major reforms were introduced, including equality before the law, which replaced the system of hierarchy and privilege formerly inherent in French society. Press freedom was permitted, and religious tolerance introduced. Economic freedoms were also established in a spirit of laissez-faire. The feudal regime was formally dissolved, to the delight of most peasants; internal tolls were abolished, opening up a truly national market; restrictions were placed on state intervention; the first moves were made toward establishing a metric system of weights and measures (implemented in the 1790s); guilds and workers' associations were abolished (notably through the Le Chapelier Law of 1791); and, at all levels, the principle of election based on property franchise was systematically followed.

Not surprisingly, the nobles who had suffered from the abolition of feudalism and privilege soon yearned for the old regime. Many of them emigrated and tried to persuade foreign rulers to intervene against the National Assembly. The economic disruption caused by the Revolution also caused difficulties for many peasants and wage-earners, while attempts to enforce religious reforms succeeded only in dividing the French clergy, half of whom refused to swear allegiance to the Civil Constitution of the Clergy introduced in 1790–1.

The religious issue proved fundamental to the Revolutionary experience. The nationalization of church lands in November 1789 allowed the National Assembly to circumvent the state bankruptcy that had precipitated the Revolution. It also won over much middle-class support for the new regime, as the lands were sold off to the highest bidders. But the move had its critics, who included some of the clergy. The ecclesiastical oath was a form of early opinion poll by which communities pressurized their priests to

support, or reject, the Revolution. The geography of opposition to the Revolution sketched out in 1791 formed the basis of a new political geography for the following centuries. The profiles of the "two Frances" appeared on the political map: one clericalist, traditionalist and pro-monarchical, the other anticlerical and vigorously republican. Certain clericalist areas, such as the Vendée department in the west, soon became engaged in open civil war against Paris.

The religious dispute also weakened the position of Louis XVI. The enactment of the Civil Constitution prompted his attempt, in June 1791, to flee Paris to Varennes in a bid to hold out for constitutional revision. The advent of war with Europe from 1792 cost him his throne and ultimately he lost his life. On

Below center Revolutionary propaganda in 1789 portrayed the Ancien Régime peasant as crushed by royal taxes (*tailles, impôts*), as well as by the tithes of the clergy and the seigneurial dues of the nobility.

Below bottom The Festival of the Supreme Being on 8 June 1794 (20 Prairial Year II under the new Revolutionary Calendar) celebrated the triumph of the radical left (the Montagnards) in the National Assembly with this specially constructed mountain (*montagne*).

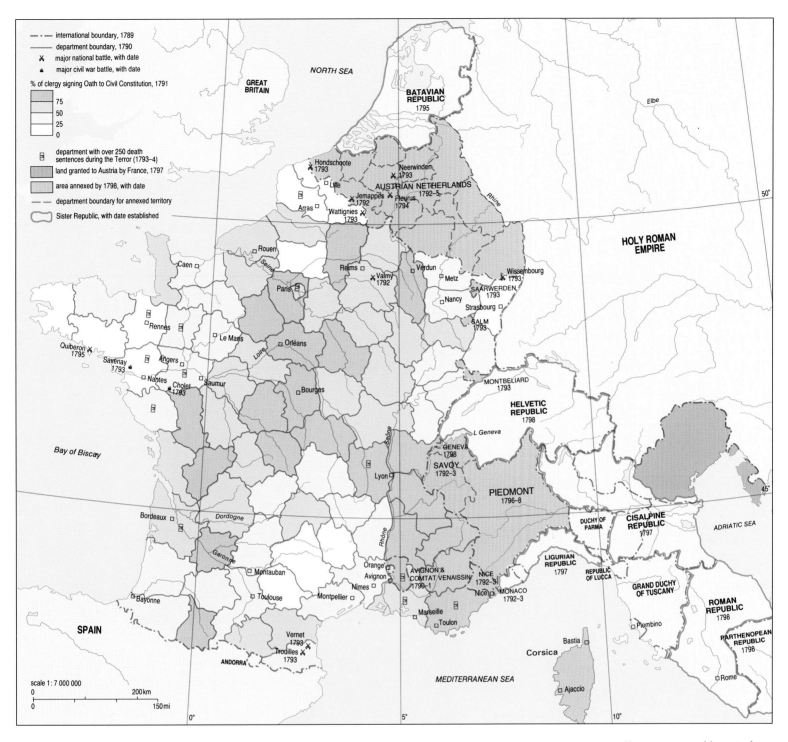

Map legend:

- - - - - international boundary, 1789
———— department boundary, 1790
✕ major national battle, with date
▲ major civil war battle, with date

% of clergy signing Oath to Civil Constitution, 1791
75
50
25
0

▣ department with over 250 death sentences during the Terror (1793–4)
land granted to Austria by France, 1797
area annexed by 1798, with date
- - - department boundary for annexed territory
Sister Republic, with date established

NORTH SEA
GREAT BRITAIN
BATAVIAN REPUBLIC 1795
Elbe
HOLY ROMAN EMPIRE

Hondschoote 1793
Neerwinden 1793
Lille
AUSTRIAN NETHERLANDS 1792–5
Jemappes 1792
Fleurus 1794
Rhine
Arras
Wattignies 1793
Rouen
Seine
Reims
Verdun
Valmy 1792
Metz
Wissembourg 1793
Caen
Nancy
SAARWERDEN 1793
Strasbourg
Paris
SALM 1793
Rennes
Le Mans
Orléans
Loire
Quiberon 1795
Savenay 1793
Angers
Nantes
Cholet 1793
Saumur
Bourges
MONTBÉLIARD 1793
HELVETIC REPUBLIC 1798
L. Geneva
GENEVA 1798
SAVOY 1792–3
Bay of Biscay
Lyon
Saône
PIEDMONT 1796–8
DUCHY OF PARMA
CISALPINE REPUBLIC 1797
ADRIATIC SEA
Bordeaux
Dordogne
Rhône
LIGURIAN REPUBLIC 1797
REPUBLIC OF LUCCA
Garonne
GRAND DUCHY OF TUSCANY
Montauban
Orange
Avignon
AVIGNON & COMTAT VENAISSIN 1790–1
NICE 1792–3
Nîmes
Nice 1792–3
MONACO 1792–3
ROMAN REPUBLIC 1798
Bayonne
Toulouse
Montpellier
Marseille
Toulon
Plombino
SPAIN
Vernet 1793
Trouilles 1793
Bastia
Corsica
PARTHENOPEAN REPUBLIC 1798
ANDORRA
MEDITERRANEAN SEA
Ajaccio
Rome

scale 1 : 7 000 000
0   200km
0   150mi

The French Revolution

Although it originally defined itself as pacifist and unifying, in fact the French Revolution proved both highly divisive and ultra-militaristic. Religion was a major source of conflict: the ecclesiastical reorganization introduced by the Civil Constitution of the Clergy divided French priests and believers into schismatic and non-schismatic camps, and sketched out a religious geography that would last into the 20th century. War, started in 1792 to defend the gains of the Revolution from European interference, similarly changed from being a war of national defence into a war of expansion. Civil war raged too, especially during the period of the Terror (1792–4). Death sentences were passed for counter-revolutionary offences. Republican puppet states (Sister Republics) were erected to shield France from foreign states.

10 August 1792, a mass rising of Parisians, resentful of his faint-heartedness at a time of national emergency, overthrew him. He was replaced by a Convention, elected by manhood suffrage for the first time in European history, which proclaimed a republic "one and indivisible".

War and the Terror

The First Republic remained undivided – but only just, and at enormous cost. Divisions of long-lasting significance in French political life opened up between right-wing supporters of decentralization (the Girondins), authoritarian supporters of centralization (the Jacobins, whose centralizing instincts were later adapted by Napoleon and the Third Republic), and a left-wing extremist group (the Cordeliers, Marat). By mid-1793, the regime faced foreign armies occupying French soil on every front, as well as open civil war in the west and on the Mediterranean seaboard. This massive crisis was eventually surmounted by reinforcing central authority on Jacobin lines. The Committee of Public Safety, created in April 1793 under the pressure of popular militants, or *sans culottes*, from the streets of Paris, acted decisively on all fronts. First, it launched a campaign known as the Terror against internal opponents including the Girondins on the right and the Cordeliers on the left. The Terror filled the political elites, who were its main targets, with an extreme and enduring revulsion. Second, the Committee instituted a package of radical social reforms, including price-fixing, land redistribution and a primitive form of welfare state, to win mass support for the Republic. Third, it pitted the masses against the armies of Europe: the so-called *levée en masse* instituted in August 1793 was tantamount to national conscription and was the first instance of a modern "nation in arms".

The military successes of the First Republic were

The French Revolution – Myth and Reality

Whereas there has been little argument as to the political importance of the French Revolution, the role of violence within it has always been hotly disputed. The image of the French as a violent and bloodthirsty nation (*buveurs de sang*) sending countless victims to the guillotine passed into the counterrevolutionary folklore of Europe during the Terror. In fact, the guillotine, though widely viewed as an instrument of oppression, was introduced in the 1790s as a more humane means of administering capital punishment. Executions under the Ancien Régime were far more brutal. Breaking on the wheel – the bones of victims were routinely broken before they were raised on a column to die – was a standard method. Bodily mutilation – the lopping off of limbs and the tearing out of tongues – was also widely practiced. By comparison, the speed, simplicity and decisiveness of the guillotine blade could be considered as having introduced an element of mercy into the procedure of execution.

The number of victims of the guillotine in the Revolution has also been greatly exaggerated. Executions in Paris totaled 2600 – a figure that is remarkably small compared with the massive body-counts of some repressive 20th-century regimes. Deaths under the Terror as a whole may have exceeded 200,000, of which three-quarters or more were by shooting in areas where civil war was raging. In the regions of Lyon, Marseille and Toulon in the Midi, and in western France, a royalist peasantry and disaffected townspeople waged a war to the death against the Republic, and could only be defeated by extreme force in return. Well over half of French departments lived through the Terror with fewer than 20 executions.

Above Sketch of Louis XVI in the Temple prison. The Revolution had transformed the portly cheerful figure of the last days of the Ancien Régime into a haggard, broken man awaiting his execution. Less than 40 years old, Louis was already an old man.

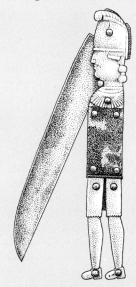

Above Penknife in the shape of a member of the French Guards. This military unit, stationed in Paris, came over to the side of the rebels in 1789, and their expertise in artillery assisted in the taking of the Bastille.

Below The storming of the Bastille in July 1789. This somber, massive and threatening 14th-century fortress served as state prison and arms dump at the heart of Paris. It had to be captured if Parisians were to prevent Louis XVI from launching a coup d'état to disperse the new National Assembly. On 14 July the king was forced to accept a constitutional monarchy. When he visited Paris several days later to show his goodwill, the tricolor flag was flown, incorporating the red and blue that symbolized Paris with the Bourbon white.

Above A counter-revolutionary. In March 1793, the Vendée department revolted against the National Assembly in Paris, and a full-scale civil war was soon in progress in western France. The military threat here was contained, but rebellions continued to flare up spasmodically here until the end of the decade. Most of the rebels were peasants, calling for the return of church and king, but their leaders were often drawn from the dandified ranks of the aristocracy, aping the styles of the Ancien Régime.

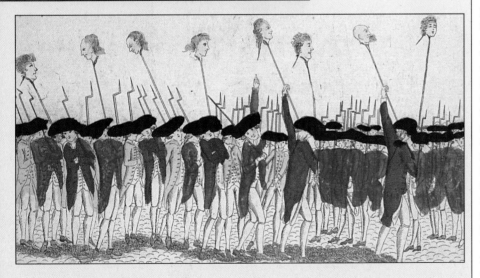

Left The execution of Louis XVI on 21 January 1793 on the Place de la Révolution (now Place de la Concorde). The king's refusal to throw in his lot with the revolutionaries made him vulnerable once war against Europe had begun in April 1792. A massive popular insurrection in Paris on 10 August 1792 ended his reign, and he was sentenced to death after a long and dramatic trial by the National Assembly. This anti-Revolutionary picture shows the guillotine surrounded by troops, allegedly there to hold back the crowds who wished to free their beloved monarch. In fact, there is no evidence that this was the case.

Above Severed heads mounted on pikes are paraded around Paris on 14 July 1789, the day of the storming of the Bastille. The sight became a regular feature of every popular insurrection in the capital until 1794.

indeed brilliant. Commanded by young officers who before 1789 would never have acceded to high posts, the army not only cleared French soil of foreign armies (by mid-1794) but also spread French power into central and southern Europe. Napoleon Bonaparte (1769–1821), a Corsican, first made his name in the Italian Campaigns of 1796–7. By the late 1790s, France was incorporating new territories into the Republic and setting up puppet regimes in neighboring states. France had become *"la grande nation"* whose power in Europe, after 1795, brooked no challenges.

One of the first casualties of the ending of the war emergency of 1793–4 was the radical social reform program advanced by the Committee of Public Safety. The fall and execution in July 1794 of Robespierre (1758–94), the Committee member most associated with the program, signaled a broad retreat from its democratic radicalism. The post-1795 regime, the Directory, endeavored to substitute the rule of law for the Terror, but proved weak and unconvincing. When the Republic met with new military difficulties in 1798–9, it spurned both a solution based on greater democracy (on the lines of 1793–4) and one based on Bourbon reaction, especially as the pretender, the would-be Louis XVIII, threatened a return to the old order. The Republic looked instead to a military dictator who would safeguard the gains of 1789 both on the field of battle and, through strong and determined autocracy, at home in France. Following a coup d'état in November 1799, Napoleon Bonaparte came to power.

The Napoleonic Empire

"From Clovis to the Committee of Public Safety, I embrace it all," Napoleon remarked, with a dictator's characteristic lack of modesty. Napoleon exemplified the tradition, in the history of France, of extending state power and centralizing government. He was less creative and original than is often claimed, and retained the major administrative reforms of the Constituent Assembly. He placed a state nominee, the prefect, at the head of each department, a centralizing refinement that looked back to the Intendants of the Ancien Régime. The Napoleonic Code of 1804 – whose influence on legal systems throughout the world has been immense – owed its inspiration to the lawyers of the revolutionary assemblies. Many of his economic policies would have pleased Colbert, though his creation of the Bank of France in 1800 was a significant innovation. His educational reforms – notably the establishment of *lycées* (grammar schools) and the Imperial University – were diluted versions of more ambitious plans mooted in the 1790s. His egalitarianism, particularly his maintenance of equality before the law and the "career open to talent" in state service, had Revolutionary roots too, as did much of his religious policy. By the Concordat of 1801 with the pope, he reestablished Catholicism as the majority religion of the French after a period of outright anticlericalism in the 1790s, but Protestantism and Judaism were also tolerated. Persuading the pope to legitimize the Revolution's reforms won Napoleon much support from the peasantry and middle classes, and even from exiled pro-clerical former aristocrats who were persuaded to return to France.

As an authoritarian, Napoleon opposed press freedom and prized hierarchy. His creation of the

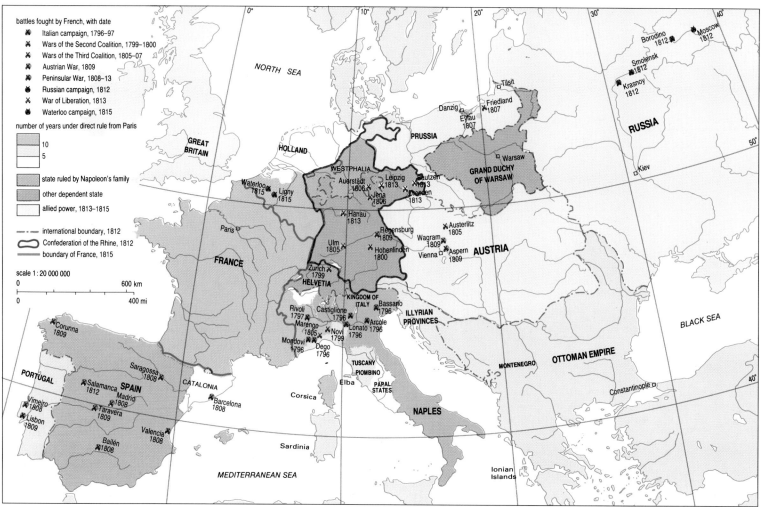

battles fought by French, with date

- ⚔ Italian campaign, 1796–97
- ⚔ Wars of the Second Coalition, 1799–1800
- ⚔ Wars of the Third Coalition, 1805–07
- ⚔ Austrian War, 1809
- ⚔ Peninsular War, 1808–13
- ⚔ Russian campaign, 1812
- ⚔ War of Liberation, 1813
- ⚔ Waterloo campaign, 1815

number of years under direct rule from Paris

- 10
- 5

state ruled by Napoleon's family

other dependent state

allied power, 1813–1815

— · — · international boundary, 1812

⟿ Confederation of the Rhine, 1812

— boundary of France, 1815

scale 1 : 20 000 000

0 — 600 km
0 — 400 mi

légion d'honneur, an award for service to the country, and his establishment of an ostentatious court society and imperial nobility had Bourbon echoes (rather ludicrously, he came to refer to Louis XVI as "my uncle"). Political life was reduced to a façade, particularly after his accession to the title of Emperor in 1804. These excesses were tolerated by the majority of the French people, however, so long as the country enjoyed material prosperity, religious harmony and protection of the fundamental gains of the Revolution.

Around 1810, the benefits of the Napoleonic regime began to dwindle. A quarrel with the pope undid most of the Emperor's earlier work and soured his clerical image. Napoleon's foreign policy ran into trouble as

well. After the 1790s, France continued with territorial expansion, and at its height the Empire contained 130 departments stretching from the Adriatic to the Baltic. The war strategy had been to extend French economic power at the same time as enlarging French political influence. By imposing French rule on new areas of Europe, Napoleon made them pay the price of war (through naked plunder, high taxes and military conscription) and was able to cushion the French from the economic burden. By 1810, however, Napoleon found that it was not possible to conquer more distant regions without overstretching his resources. His disastrous Moscow campaign of 1811–12 – in which he lost half a million

Napoleonic Europe
The Napoleonic Empire in 1812 showed French power in Europe at its greatest. France dominated Europe through the extension of its own direct rule, through client states (often ruled by members of the Bonaparte family) and through specially-constructed political systems, such as the Confederation of the Rhine. Established as a result of military victories in the field, the Empire never commanded the wholehearted support of the varied populations of its many constituent parts. Non-French men and women tended to resent France's political and economic policy, which was aimed at cutting off the European mainland from the burgeoning economic power of Britain. France was successful in fighting off the challenge of the other major powers who banded together in a succession of anti-French coalitions. There were already signs, however, that the Empire had overstretched itself, which was confirmed by the disastrous Russian campaign of 1812–13 and the consequent wars of liberation in Spain, Germany and elsewhere. By then, the powers that had managed to resist French military power – Britain, Austria, Prussia and Russia – were finally regrouping effectively and combining to register France's defeat.

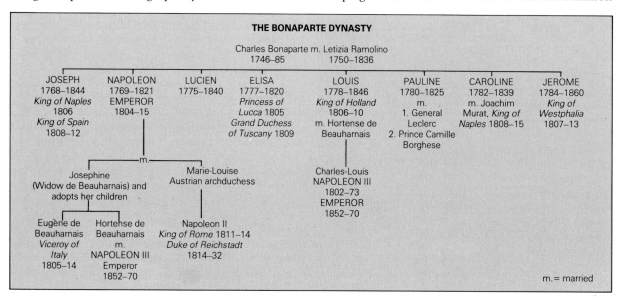

THE BONAPARTE DYNASTY

Charles Bonaparte m. Letizia Ramolino
1746–85 · 1750–1836

JOSEPH	NAPOLEON	LUCIEN	ELISA	LOUIS	PAULINE	CAROLINE	JEROME
1768–1844	1769–1821	1775–1840	1777–1820	1778–1846	1780–1825	1782–1839	1784–1860
King of Naples 1806	EMPEROR 1804–15		*Princess of Lucca* 1805	*King of Holland* 1806–10	m.	m. Joachim Murat, *King of Naples* 1808–15	*King of Westphalia* 1807–13
King of Spain 1808–12			*Grand Duchess of Tuscany* 1809	m. Hortense de Beauharnais	1. General Leclerc		
					2. Prince Camille Borghese		

— m. —

Josephine (Widow de Beauharnais) and adopts her children

Marie-Louise Austrian archduchess

Charles-Louis NAPOLEON III 1802–73 EMPEROR 1852–70

Eugène de Beauharnais *Viceroy of Italy* 1805–14

Hortense de Beauharnais m. NAPOLEON III Emperor 1852–70

Napoleon II *King of Rome* 1811–14 *Duke of Reichstadt* 1814–32

m. = married

Napoleon and
the Bonapartes

Napoleon's military successes, administrative creativity and international dominance overshadow one of the most distinctive features of his rule: the use of his family as a lever of international power. When his father, a lawyer, died his mother, Letizia, was left with a large family.

Napoleon's seizure of power in 1799 placed him in an undisputed position to do his family good. Until his overthrow in 1814–15, he acted as a kind of mafia godfather, making the extension of Napoleonic power coincidental with the influence of the Bonaparte clan. His elder brother Joseph (1778–1844) was made first king of Naples (1806), then of Spain (1808). The younger Louis (1778–1846) became king of Holland (1806), and Jérôme (1784–1806) king of Westphalia (1807). Only Lucien (1775–1840), who turned out to be the black sheep of the family, received no largesse. Of his sisters, Elisa (1777–1820) became grand Duchess of Tuscany (1809); Pauline (1780–1852) married an Italian prince (second marriage) and lived a wild, hedonistic life; and Caroline (1782–1839) married Murat, one of Napoleon's generals, and became queen of Naples (1808). Napoleon's protection extended outside his immediate kin. Eugène de Beauharnais, his stepson through empress Josephine, was appointed viceroy of the kingdom of Italy (1805); his uncle Joseph Fesch (1783–1839) was made a Cardinal; and the sister of Jérôme's wife married another of Napoleon's generals, Bernadotte, who became crown prince, and ultimately king of Sweden.

Left Louis Léopold Boilly's (1761–1845) famous portrait of the new First Consul captures the glint of ambition in Napoleon's eye.

Below This collective portrait of the Bonaparte clan in 1809 at a ball in honor of Frederick Augustus, King of Saxony, captures the family at the height of its success. "If it lasts..." was the apposite comment of Napoleon's mother at the remarkable rise in her family's fortunes. It did not.

Above A cartoon of 1814 showing Napoleon performing acrobatics to keep his home, the palace at Fontainebleau, unharmed. The attempt to straddle Europe between Madrid and Moscow failed: the Peninsula War in Spain and Portugal drained the Napoleonic Empire of much valuable manpower, while the Russian campaign of 1812–13 proved a costly fiasco which encouraged Napoleon's enemies to regroup. The Quadruple Alliance between Britain, Prussia, Austria and Russia worked in concert to crush Napoleon militarily, to eject him from France, and to go on to redraw the map of Europe, putting an end to France's imperial pretensions.

men – was a major setback for his strategy. For the first time, the cost of the war had to be borne by France itself. At home taxes rose and levels of conscription were boosted, just as a serious industrial and agricultural crisis occurred, causing an increase in unemployment. Napoleon was eventually dethroned following military defeat by the allied powers of Austria, Britain, Russia and Prussia; but as he made his way to the tiny island-prison of Elba in 1814, he was already virtually an outcast in his native France. After escaping from Elba, he enjoyed a brief flirtation with further glory in the "Hundred Days", when he seized power and formed a new army, but defeat at Waterloo in 1815 proved to be his final undoing.

Restoration of the monarchy

At its best the Napoleonic regime had offered the social groups who had benefited most from the Revolution – namely the liberal professions, landowning middle classes and peasantry – a political framework that avoided the extremes both of reactionary Bourbon absolutism and of full-bodied social radicalism. Essentially, the political history of the 19th century represented variations on this centrist theme. The restored Bourbon monarchy of Louis XVIII sensibly did not attempt to return to pre-1789 society. The new Constitutional Charter resembled the Constitution of 1791 rather than the political system of the Ancien Régime, and the government was initially dominated by liberal royalists. The bulk of Revolutionary and Napoleonic institutions – including the land settlement, the departments, the prefecture, the Civil Code and the Bank of France – were retained. This outraged the ultra-royalists such as Joseph de Maistre (1753–1821), who accused Louis XVIII of ascending "the throne of Bonaparte" but it was generally favored in the country as a whole.

The political balance achieved by Louis XVIII was a delicate one. Even before Louis' death in 1824, the regime was moving to the right, a trend that was forcefully continued by his brother and successor Charles X. He signaled his desire for an alliance of "throne and altar" by holding a traditional-style coronation at Reims, followed by a bout of touching to cure the "King's Evil" (scrofula). Charles saw himself as ruler "by the grace of God" rather than by the wish of the people, and had no compunction about increasing the power of the church or favoring legislation to return confiscated properties to émigré aristocrats. His attempt in 1829–30 to muzzle the press and rule independently of representative institutions coincided with a period of widespread economic distress and problems. The regime found few friends when three days of insurrection in Paris – the "Trois Glorieuses" (July 27–9, 1830) – led to the final overthrow of the Bourbon line.

Slightly surprisingly, perhaps, the beneficiary of the 1830 Revolution was the head of the collateral, Orleanist line, Louis-Philippe. He guaranteed the liberal freedoms that Charles X had sought to subvert, thereby signaling completely the liquidation of aristocratic influence at the heart of French politics, a process begun in 1789. The new "July Monarchy" inaugurated the supremacy of the bourgeoisie in French social and political life.

Paradoxically, despite France's turbulent political life since 1789 – the country has experienced two monarchical ruling houses, two empires, five republics and an interim autocracy (the *Etat français* of 1940–4) – change has been accompanied by a considerable degree of continuity and social stability. The legal and administrative framework instituted in the Revolutionary and Napoleonic eras has provided a stable backdrop against which political change has taken place.

The importance of agriculture to the French economy has also been a powerful force for stability. France has had a higher proportion of its population on the land than any contemporary industrializing state. In England, the urban population outnumbered country-dwellers by the 1830s, in Italy by the 1870s, in Germany by about 1900 and in the United States by about 1920. France did not achieve this demographic shift until the 1930s, and for most of the 19th century the rural population represented between two-thirds and three-quarters of the total population. The presence of a strong peasantry acted as a brake on rapid social transformation.

The bourgeoisie too had a strong interest in land. Between 1688 and 1815, France had lost a "Second Hundred Years' War" against Britain, and casualties included the French colonial empire and a booming world-trade sector. The country's economic geography underwent an enduring shift, with the center of gravity moving from the Atlantic seaboard to the land frontier: cities such as Lyon and Strasbourg benefited while Bordeaux, La Rochelle, Rouen and Le Havre suffered. Land continued to be a safe and solid investment, and landowners represented the most dominant sector of the post-Revolutionary bourgeoisie. The big landowners were better able to withstand the depression in agricultural prices, which lasted some 35 years from 1817 to 1851, and they, together with the most successful members of the industrial, commercial and financial sectors, formed the "grande bourgeoisie" who dominated and influenced the July Monarchy.

Above left Louis-Philippe (1830–48), the Duke of Orléans, was from a collateral branch of the Bourbon dynasty overthrown in the 1830 Revolution. As the young Duke of Chartres, he had been a revolutionary in 1789, but had defected from France at the beginning of the Terror in April 1793. His revolutionary past belied his general demeanor. Here shown mounting the Parisian barricades in 1830 with the Revolutionary tricolor, he was, in fact, the most staid of rulers.

Above When Charles X (1824–30) tried to rule like a Bourbon king of the Ancien Régime, the Restoration monarchy, set in place by the Allied conquerors of Napoleon, fell. Measures he introduced on 25 July to shackle press freedom and reduce the franchise provoked three "glorious" days of action (*Les Trois Glorieuses*) in Paris. From 27 to 29 July 1830, popular militancy behind hastily constructed barricades drove the royal army out of Paris and toppled the government. France was on the verge of a new Republic until the middle-class backers of the insurrection proclaimed as king Louis-Philippe, in early August.

The 1848 Revolution

The position held by the "grande bourgeoisie" under the July Monarchy became increasingly resented. "France is bored", quipped the liberal statesman Lamartine (1790–1869), whose analysis of the causes of the 1848 Revolution, which overthrew the July Monarchy, highlights the regime's inability to enlist enthusiasm or mass support. "Enrichissez-vous!", was the message of Guizot (1787–1874), a dominant politician of the France of the 1840s; it generally had little appeal, as wealth was concentrated within so few hands. Even the voting rights were confined to about a quarter of a million men, out of a total population of well over 30 millions. The regime had nothing to offer the impoverished working classes growing up in cities undergoing industrialization. A rising by the unemployed silk-workers in Lyon in 1831 was put down by force. The appearance of cholera in 1832 – over 100,000 deaths were caused by the first outbreak alone – created havoc among urban populations, with the government powerless to act. The lack of a social and welfare conscience helped to inspire a number of radical and socialist writers, including Fourier (1772–1837), Louis Blanc (1802–85), Cabet (1788–1856) and Blanqui (1805–81), who won a growing following among working-class activists. The drabness of the July Monarchy contrasted with the glamor of the Napoleonic legend. Middle-class intellectuals, in particular, admired the Emperor's cult of heroism, energy and individualism, as reflected in the writings of Victor Hugo (1802–85), Stendhal (1783–1842) and Balzac (1799–1851) and in the art of the Romantic movement. Discontent among all social groups grew after the bad harvests in 1846 and 1847. A political campaign in the major cities, using public banquets as a front, called for the extension of the franchise but resulted in the overthrow of Louis-Philippe in February 1848. This time, the leaders of revolution chose a Republic.

The Second Republic (1848–52) restored social radicalism, championed by the descendants of the Parisian *sans-culottes*, to the center stage of politics for the first time since the 1790s. The "bored" bourgeoisie of the July Monarchy took fright. However, a radical social program including universal manhood suffrage and the right to work proved double-edged when the new electorate – swollen from a quarter of a million to 9 million voters – returned a moderate and conservative majority. Calls to replay the Terror of 1792–4, by establishing a radical Parisian dictatorship over the backward provinces, foundered, and radical demonstrators were crushed on the streets of Paris in the June Days of 1848. A liberal republic headed by a president elected for a four-year spell was instituted, but there was a twist in the tail when, in the presidential elections, Louis Bonaparte (1808–73), Napoleon I's nephew, was returned with 5.5 million out of 7 million votes. The

Peasant Life

Bottom left and below The simple dignity of peasant life in the 19th century, as captured in the work of Jean-François Millet (1814–75). Rural life-styles were still highly resistant to change. The peasant holding was the basic unit of agricultural production, to which all members of the household were expected to contribute. Even quite young children could herd sheep or goats, or perform basic tasks such as winnowing (*bottom left*). School absenteeism was always at its most acute during the harvest. Women too (*below* seen gleaning) also had a key role to play in ensuring the subsistence of the peasant family. Marriage partners were mostly chosen locally.

Although the French Revolution brought massive political and cultural change, its impact on France's economy was far more muted. Often viewed as a "bourgeois revolution", it produced no major breakthrough toward a capitalist society. Indeed, in some respects, the Revolution marked a step backward, for the most buoyant sectors of the Ancien Régime's economy (notably foreign trade) were severely hit by the Revolutionary and Napoleonic wars.

On the land, peasants utilized their gains from the Revolution (notably the abolition of seigneurial dues and the church tithe) to resist the incursions of capitalism. Most seemed to prefer to settle back into time-honored routines, with life-styles set in a strongly traditionalist mold. The diet consisted still mainly of black bread, as it had done in the 13th century. Long after the Revolution had introduced the metric system, peasants persisted in reckoning in premetric units – in leagues, pounds, feet and so on.

The French language made only slow progress, and foreign tongues and patois were more widely heard on the land than the French of the Académie française. The Catholic church, more alive to its pastoral responsibilities in rural areas, fought against new secular philosophies. Society and culture remained highly regional and traditionalist. Not until the coming of the railroad and, especially from the 1880s, the introduction of obligatory primary schooling, did local barriers break down. For many French people of the time, the Ancien Régime, although formally abolished, lived on socially and economically.

Second Republic clasped a Napoleonic viper to its bosom as had the First, and the result was similarly terminal. On 2 December 1851, Louis Bonaparte organized a coup and had himself elected president for 10 years, and he followed this a year later by holding a plebiscite to have himself appointed Emperor.

The Second Empire

Napoleon III, as he called himself (Napoleon I's son, who had died childless in 1832, had, in fact, never ruled as Napoleon II), posed as the antithesis of social radicalism but distanced himself from the royalists. In so doing, he remained in the centrist (*juste milieu*) tradition between radicalism and reaction. He reassured the middle classes by promising social harmony – "The Empire means peace," he declared – and the preservation of Revolutionary institutions. He also had the support of the peasantry, who tended to remember not the harshness of his uncle's rule but rather that the First Empire had consolidated the Revolutionary land settlement and kept taxes low. Napoleon III offered a stimulating environment for entrepreneurs. The Second Empire saw a marked acceleration in economic activity, a fact that owed perhaps less to state intervention than to a coincidental upswing in the world economy. Between the late 1840s and the late 1860s, foreign trade tripled; the value of industrial production doubled; and mechanized power in industry increased fivefold, as did the railroad network. This business boom was grounded in new financial institutions offering credit – the Crédit Lyonnais was founded in 1863, for example, and the Sociéte ´Générale in 1864. To the economic achievements of the regime were added prestigious social projects. The construction of the Paris boulevards by Baron Haussman (1809–91), Prefect of the Seine from 1853 to 1869, made the capital, already renowned for its cultural and worldly pleasures, an international showcase.

In the 1860s, Napoleon increasingly sought to find allies on the left. An amnesty of political prisoners led to the gradual implementation of more liberal measures. These included a freer press, rights of workers' associations (1864), greater ministerial responsibility and even, in 1869–70, a liberal constitution. In foreign policy, Napoleon presented the Empire as peace-loving but he was frequently drawn to military glory and he worked hard to build up a "second colonial empire". Charles X had invaded Algeria, and Louis Philippe had expanded in Africa and the Pacific, but it was Napoleon III who established a French presence worldwide. By 1870, France was second only to Britain as a colonial power, and in a strong position to benefit from the "scramble for colonies" of the following decades. Napoleon also took France into the Crimean War (1854–6) and a war in Italy against Austria (1859), and in the 1860s attempted to intervene militarily in Mexico. It was, however, a disastrously ill-advised war with Prussia in 1870 that brought about his own downfall and cost France two of its most industrially wealthy provinces, Alsace and Lorraine.

The loss of Alsace and Lorraine should be viewed against a broader demographic background. Under Louis XIV, one European in five was French; at the time of Napoleon I, the figure was one in seven; under Napoleon III, one in eight. In 1900, it fell to one in 10, and by 1945, to one in 13. The relative decline in population that occurred after 1789 was due partly to losses in wars and civil strife (perhaps 1.5 million deaths overall), but mainly to a considerable reduction in the size of families in France early in the 19th century, while other European nations maintained high birthrates. This trend may have been linked to laws of partible inheritance introduced in the Revolution, in that peasants realized that division of their holdings among too many offspring would mean economic ruin, and therefore limited their family size – normally, it would seem, through the practice of coitus interruptus (the condom became standard issue to troops only in World War I). Just as the earlier military and political strength of France had been founded on its demographic supremacy, so now, it seemed, its eclipse owed less to fighting on the field of Waterloo than to the bedroom habits of 20 million peasants.

The loss of Alsace and Lorraine to the new Germany was all the more significant in that the German population continued to grow. In 1870, it roughly equaled that of France; by 1914, Germany had over 50 percent more inhabitants than France. This imbalance aroused fears of national decadence in France, which was variously ascribed to alcoholism, syphilis and racial degeneration. Although the buildup of a colonial population (some 50 millions by 1914) offered some compensation for France's losses in Europe, getting the lost provinces back remained a priority. The *revanchiste* dream was at the heart of

French foreign policy through to 1918, when the dream was achieved. Indeed, the reintegration of Alsace and Lorraine in 1918–19 compensated to some extent for the appalling losses that the French sustained in World War I – over 1.4 millions dead and more than twice as many wounded or maimed. The population had stood at 39.6 millions on the eve of the war; in its aftermath, even with the addition of Alsace and Lorraine, it stood at only 39.2 millions.

The Third Republic
The downfall of Napoleon III after his defeat by Prussia led to the birth of the Third Republic, which was to last for 70 years. The veteran statesman Thiers (1797–1877), who headed the government until 1873, stated that a republic was essential as it was the regime that "divides us least". Bourgeois France recoiled in horror from the left in the aftermath of defeat by Prussia, as the protest of Parisian radicals against the provisional government gave way to an insurrection. The Paris Commune, as it was known, was put down by Thiers with massive bloodshed – 25,000 were summarily executed, nearly 10 times as many as died at the hands of the Revolutionary Tribunal in Paris in 1793–4. While a move to the left was clearly unthinkable, the right saw Thiers' moderate republic as a prelude to the restoration of the monarchy. Thiers was succeeded as President in 1873 by MacMahon (1808–93), an avowed royalist

The French colonial Empire
France's colonial experiences were especially strong in two periods. The "first colonial empire" was established as part of France's long political and economic struggle against Great Britain in the so-called "Second Hundred Years War" (1689–1815). These territorial gains, many of which passed from French to British hands and back again in rapid succession, were almost all nullified by British action during the French Revolutionary and Napoleonic Wars. Then, in the 19th century, following early successes such as the conquest of Algeria in 1830, France acquired a "second empire", mainly in Africa and southeast Asia. Since the 1950s, France has divested itself of many of its old, colonial possessions.

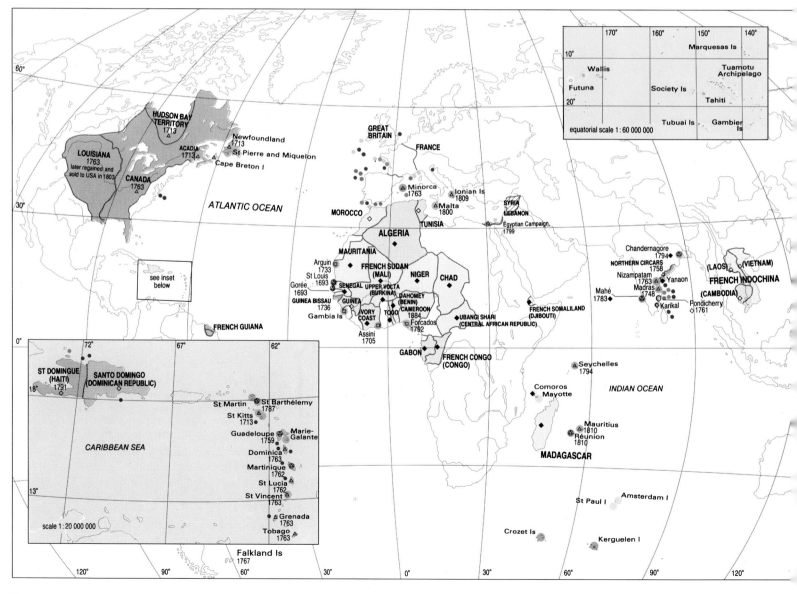

Industrial and population growth
The French Revolutionary and Napoleonic Wars shifted France's economic center of gravity eastward, away from the Atlantic seaboard ports and cities which had represented the most dynamic elements in the economy of the Ancien Régime. The north was better served than the south. It had a railroad network sooner; canal improvements were more significant there; and the geography of mineral endowment also favored the north. The railroad network (*bottom right*) which grew toward the end of the 19th century, was an important indicator of economic development. Railroads mobilized capital and labor, stimulated demand for coal and steel and opened up regional markets. The locomotive powered the French economy forward and severely disrupted traditional and archaic social patterns. Industrial production made a bigger social impact on the lives of northerners than southerners. The urban problems associated with rapid industrial growth were thus most apparent in the industrial cities of the north, although in the Midi too, new urban and industrial conurbations appeared. The south and west were still dominated by a peasant economy which showed, by 1914, serious signs of collapsing.

French colonial gains
- before 1748
- 1748–83
- 1784–1829
- 1830–81
- 1882–1919

1783 date colony lost
△ colony lost to Great Britain
○ colony later regained by France

independence gained
◇ before 1960
◆ 1960 and after

▨ area under French mandate 1920, became independent 1941–44

naval battle between France and Great Britain
- 1689–1748
- Seven Years War, 1756–63
- War of American Independence, 1775–83
- Revolutionary Wars, 1793–1802
- Napoleonic Wars, 1803–15

equatorial scale 1 : 115 000 000

PACIFIC OCEAN

New Hebrides (VANUATU)◆   Futuna

New Caledonia

see inset above for detail on Pacific Islands

180°

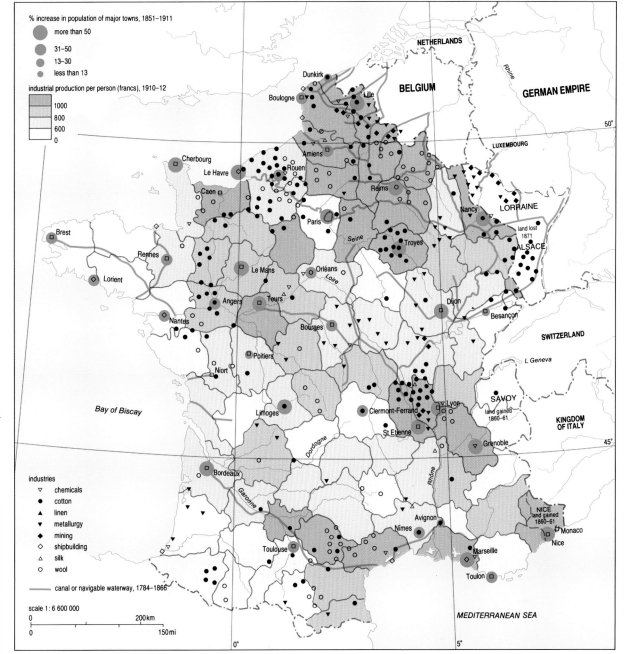

% increase in population of major towns, 1851–1911
- more than 50
- 31–50
- 13–30
- less than 13

industrial production per person (francs), 1910–12
- 1000
- 800
- 600
- 0

industries
▽ chemicals
● cotton
▲ linen
▼ metallurgy
◆ mining
◇ shipbuilding
△ silk
○ wool

—— canal or navigable waterway, 1784–1866

scale 1 : 6 600 000
0 ———— 200km
0 ———— 150mi

sympathizer. When, however, the Comte de Chambord (1820–83) emerged as the legitimist candidate and would-be Henri V, he alienated support by signaling his intention to be like Charles X rather than a conciliatory monarch like Henri IV. Sincere republicans, such as Léon Gambetta (1838–82), Jules Grévy (1807–91) and Jules Ferry (1832–93), gradually prevailed over the "monarchical republic", establishing a parliamentary rather than a presidential style of government in that the president was chosen by the legislature rather than voted in by the people. Occasionally, the system was challenged – notably in 1886–9, when the populist demagogue General Boulanger (1837–91) threatened an anti parliamentary coup d'état. Ultimately it prevailed, and ensured a political tradition of weak presidents and unstable governments which lasted until the Fifth Republic.

The social basis of the Third Republic was as bourgeois as its predecessors. However, manhood suffrage and the evolution of the economy reduced the importance of the upper middle classes, allowing lesser groups – merchants and traders, state functionaries and members of the liberal professions – to

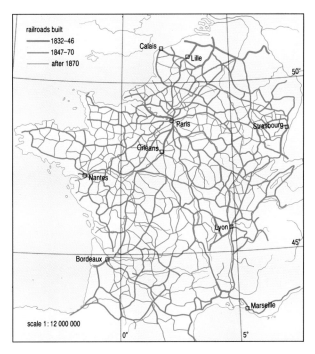

railroads built
—— 1832–46
—— 1847–70
—— after 1870

scale 1 : 12 000 000

play a more significant role. The regime's dependence on strong support from the peasantry proved something of a liability, when an economic depression occurred in the 1870s as a result of the mass importation of cheap grain from North America. Many peasants were unable to cope, and moved away en masse particularly from poorer regions such as the Alps, the Massif Central and Aquitaine. The depressed rural areas became more radical, so that the political center faced opposition not only on the right, from the traditional, proclerical "white" peasantry, but also from the new "red" peasants on the left.

The republic, whose origins and social base were fragile, found allies on the left and in the center by supporting the battle-cry of Gambetta: "Le clericalisme, voilà l'ennemi!" ("Clericalism is the real enemy"). The arena of struggle in the 1880s was education. Antirepublicanism was ascribed to ignorance and brutality: French was not spoken in about a quarter of French communes; one-third of the population was illiterate; religious congregations ran the schools in clericalist areas. A series of important measures piloted through parliament in the early 1880s by Jules Ferry ensured free and obligatory lay primary education for children between the ages of 6 and 13. Provision for secondary education for girls was also introduced. The post-Revolutionary missionary activity of the Catholic church had targeted

Above Primary education of both girls and boys was one of the most distinctive and important achievements of the Third Republic before World War I. Deliberately excluding religious indoctrination, state schools became an important agency for lay republicanism. The photograph shows an open-air lesson at Vénissieux, in the department of the Rhône.

Left The Eiffel Tower, on the Champ de Mars in Paris, was constructed by the Burgundian engineer Gustave Eiffel (1832–1923) for the Universal Exhibition of 1889, the centenary of the French Revolution. Seen here surrounded by other exhibits since dismantled, the tower, over 300m high, represented a considerable feat of engineering and symbolized the triumph of science and modernism. Its vulgarity and its sheer size, however, won it unqualified disapproval from a group of intellectuals including Dumas and Maupassant.

The Dreyfus Affair

The Dreyfus Affair (1894–1906), which established a new and acrimonious division between left and right in the Third Republic, began in a wastepaper basket in the German embassy in Paris. There, in September 1894, a cleaning woman working for the French secret services discovered a note suggesting that a French staff officer was passing classified information to the Germans. An internal inquiry led to suspicion falling on a Jewish captain, Alfred Dreyfus (1859–1935). He was court-martialed and convicted, and in 1894 condemned to life imprisonment on Devil's Island.

The trial was exploited by the anti-Semitic right-wing press, keen to prosecute an allegedly unpatriotic Jew. In fact, the evidence used to establish Dreyfus's guilt was unreliable, depending on handwriting identification and outright forgery. Dreyfus's brother refused to let the matter rest, and was aided by internal inquiries that pointed to another staff officer, Esterhazy, as the guilty man. However, when Esterhazy stood trial in 1898, the court found in his favor.

The spy story became a major political scandal and a *cause célèbre* when the novelist Emile Zola accused the war office outright of a cover-up. Public opinion was inflamed, as right and left stood diametrically opposed over the issue. On the left, the League of the Rights of Man provided a powerful lobby around which the Dreyfusards (Dreyfus's supporters) rallied. On the right, the growth of anti parliamentary views at one moment even threatened to give rise to a coup d'état. A retrial in 1899 found against Dreyfus but with extenuating circumstances, and later that year he was pardoned. He received a full pardon in 1906.

Bottom left Emile Zola's open letter to the President of the Republic on 13 January 1898 published in *L'Aurore*, the crusading newspaper of the radical politician Georges Clemenceau. The impact of Zola's celebrated "J'accuse" owed much to a massive growth in newspaper readership in the Third Republic aided by the growth in literacy. The affair changed Zola's life, making him a hero of the left but forcing him into exile.

Below center The anti-Dreyfusard *Le Petit Journal* was among the most widely read popular newspapers of the late 19th century, with a circulation of nearly a million, mostly outside Paris. The military degradation of Dreyfus shown here was widely known, as was the captain's quiet reply, "I am innocent".

Above A German caricature of how the Dreyfus Affair split some French families down the middle. Europeans found it difficult to understand how the incident could have such a significant impact inside France.

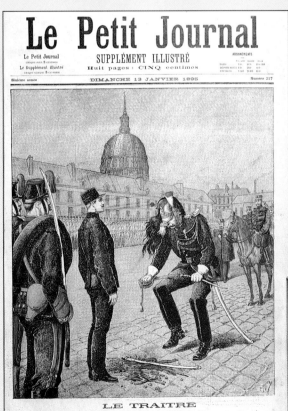

Above A French caricature of Dreyfus in which he is depicted as running for president. In fact, there was never much chance of this happening. After his pardon, Dreyfus served in the army during World War I.

Paris through the Ages

Founded on an unattractive site, Paris developed into a substantial urban stronghold under the Romans. It was not until the Dark Ages, however, that it was made the capital city, by the Frankish king Clovis, and not until the Middle Ages that it developed as a powerful urban center. Yet it was still small: the fortified wall erected by Philip Augustus (1180–1223) covered only a tiny fraction of the Paris of today.

The location of the court in Paris ensured that the city played a significant administrative and cultural role. It endured hard times in the later Middle Ages, passing into English hands during the Hundred Years War. The Renaissance and the economic boom of the 16th century revived its fortunes. The decision of Louis XIV to shift the court to Versailles might have spelled the eclipse of Paris. In practice, courtiers were only too anxious to slip away from the pretentiousness of court ritual for the more exciting carnal, cultural and intellectual pleasures of Paris. The city became synonymous with pleasure and has remained so ever since. The Revolution of 1789 seemed to open up a new vocation - that of Revolutionary city. Until 1871, and the crushing of the Paris Commune, it was said that whenever barricades went up in Paris, the monarchs of Europe trembled in their beds. In the 20th century, Paris has grown into an international metropolis.

The development of Paris
The dynamism of historical Paris is captured in this set of city plans, which highlight built-up areas (in pink), roads (in red) and major urban construction (black).
1 Paris in Roman times and in the Dark Ages. Based on a bed of gravel (Ile St-Martin), between what had been two branches of the river Seine, the site had first been seriously occupied by the Parisii tribe in the 3rd century BC. During the Roman occupation of Lutetia, name of the Roman city, urban functions developed, as well as a cultural dimension evident in the baths and arena. The earliest major area of settlement was on the south bank and on the highly defensible Ile de la Cité.
2 Medieval Paris grew onto the northern (right) bank. The fortified wall of Philip Augustus enclosed a thriving urban center. Church building and the development of the university (Sorbonne) recalled the city's cultural vocation, while administrative and court buildings, show the breadth and diversity of the city's roles.
3 Renaissance Paris developed less rapidly. The walls of Philip Augustus did not restrict urban sprawl, while bridge-building showed the growing internal dynamism of the city. Its fortifications (including the great Bastille fort) and the development of its palaces (notably the Tuileries) showed that Paris was still the residence of the king.
4 Ancien Régime Paris. Even though the Monarch moved to the Versailles palace constructed by Louis XIV, this did not inhibit the

city's exceptional dynamism in the two centuries following the Wars of Religion. New forms of urban development such as city squares (*places*) were a distinctive development of this period along with prestige building, such as the Invalides military pensioners' home, and the erection of sumptuous private dwelling-places (*hôtels, palais*). The Champs-Elysées was located in a still semi-rural area. There was considerable development beyond the Customs wall erected on the eve of the French Revolution.
5 Nineteenth-century Paris witnessed massive development. The city's vociferous urban working classes, were crammed into heavily built up central areas which only from the time of the Second Empire were redeveloped. Baron Haussman extensively remodelled the city by bulldozing into existence a network of boulevards. Associated projects included: the prestigious Eiffel tower, the Arc de Triomphe and the Sacré-Coeur; commercial developments such as the Galeries Lafayette; communications centers such as the big rail termini; and leisure facilities such as the Longchamp racetrack.
6 Twentieth-century Paris has grown within this shell, but perhaps most distinctive has been the development of the whole conurbation around Paris and dependent upon and often servicing it. The city enclosed within the Ile St-Martin of ancient times has become the super-conurbation of the late 20th century sprawling ever denser across the Paris basin.

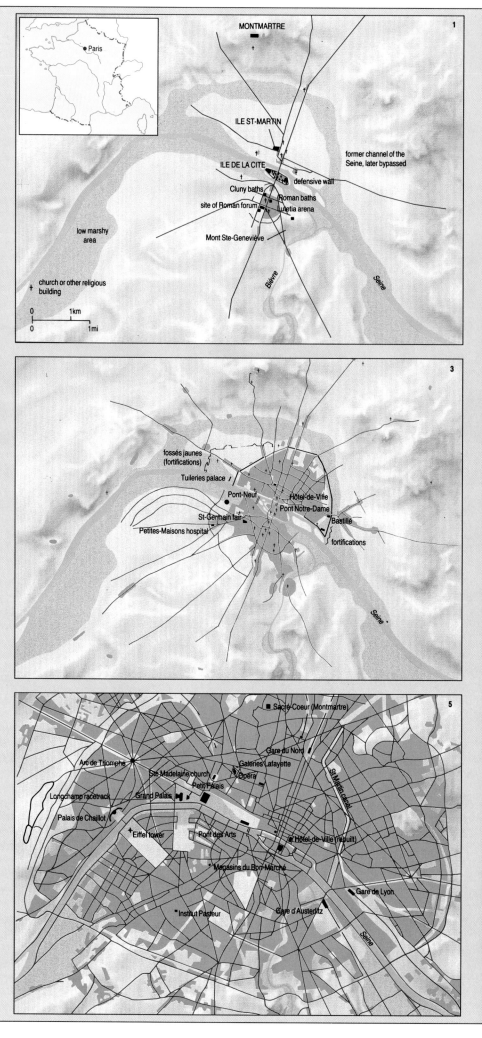

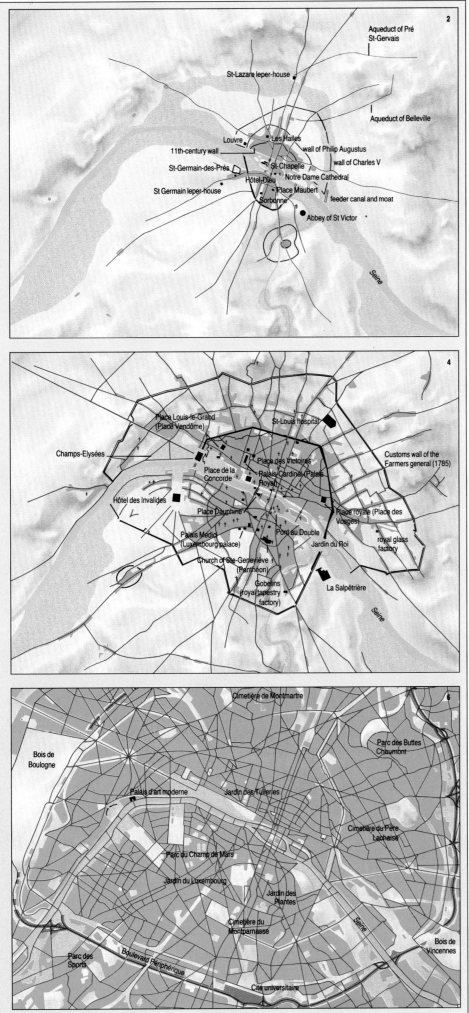

women, whom the anticlerical lobby now viewed as an obscurantist group poisoning the minds of their children against the Republic. These suspicions had long roots: Napoleon's Civil Code had effectively made women legal minors, and they were not to receive extensive civil rights until well into the 20th century, or the vote until 1945.

The astute politicians of the Third Republic thus used schools as a means of civilizing and republicanizing backward peasants and their families. The celebration of the centenary of the French Revolution in 1889, marked by an international exhibition and the erection of the Eiffel tower in Paris, was a climax of the new, confident republicanism. The heyday of militant anticlericalism came in the 1890s with the Dreyfus affair. This scandal – which split the social elite between a clericalist, traditionalist and nationalist right and an anticlerical, pro-republican left – made a profound mark on French politics. Although the affair was not fully concluded until 1906, by then the left had won the initiative. An important law passed in 1904 prohibited religious congregations from teaching, while a year later, church and state were separated, ending Napoleon's Concordat of 1801.

Material and scientific progress

For many on the right, the triumph of anticlericalism was the triumph of materialism over spiritual values. The left in contrast was more approving of the material progress of *la belle époque* – the carefree period up till 1914. The writer Charles Péguy (1873–1914) remarked shortly before his death that the world had changed more since the 1880s when he went to school than it had done from the time of the Romans up till the 1880s. Exaggeration apart, the changes referred to were extremely significant and generally for the better. For instance, the poorest peasants in 1900 could expect to live twice as long as their ancestors under Louis XIV. This owed something to the advances of medical science (especially smallpox vaccination since 1798 and the "bacteriological revolution" wrought by Louis Pasteur (1822–95) and others after 1870), but much also to improvements in public health. The economy, after a lull in the 1870s and 1880s, made further advances to bring about improved living standards. The proportion of bread in the national diet fell, as other foodstuffs were made available. The emergence of big department stores showed a growing market for consumer goods: the famous Galeries Lafayette dates from 1895, preceded by the Bon Marché (1852) and Samaritaine (1869) stores. Similarly, the wide distribution of gas and electric lighting and heating, and the emergence of mass leisure activities (soccer, rugby, cycling, rowing and others), demonstrated that this society was not on the breadline. The communications revolution, brought about by a national rail network and a massive program of road building, also contributed to the quality of life of this mass society. The appearance of the airplane and the motorcar was significant too, though their impact was probably less than the bicycle, which enjoyed a considerable vogue.

The benefits of material growth were, however, far from evenly shared. To some degree, France had a dual economy, one modernizing, one traditionalist. Pockets of industrial development and urban prosperity coexisted with pitiable workers' suburbs and impoverished rural areas suffering erosion of traditional lifestyles. The growth of the working-class

consciouness brought a new acuity to a politics long obsessed by clericalism and constitutionalism. The legalizing of trade unions and expansion of their powers (1864 and 1884) were important in this process. The nascent working-class movement proved as fraught with division, however, as the classical right. The Marxist Workers' Party, founded in 1879 by Jules Guesde (1845–1922), was widely viewed as providing "impossibilist" solutions to political problems while Guesde attacked his opponents as offering mere "possibilist", "gas and water socialism". The formation in 1895 of a trades congress, the CGT (Confédération Général du Travail), helped coordinate such energies, though its progress was still slow. Antiparliamentary anarcho-syndicalism in the workers' movement delayed the emergence of a unified and effective socialist party until the creation in 1905 of the SFIO (Section Française de l'Internationale Ouvrière) or French Section of the Workers' International. Its presence in parliament helped shift the center of gravity of French politics to the left.

A further, highly significant achievement of the Third Republic before 1914 was the building of a worldwide colonial empire in north and west Africa, Madagascar, Oceania (New Caledonia, Tahiti) and Indochina. Often the work of the same men – such as Jules Ferry – responsible for the influential educational reforms, this development led to rivalry with other European powers, notably Britain. In the Fashoda incident (1898), the two powers almost came to blows in the Sudan, and French withdrawal kindled popular Anglophobia. The growing threat of war against Germany, however, led Republican France first into alliance with autocratic Russia in 1894, and then toward closer cooperation with Britain (by the Entente Cordiale of 1904). A new belligerence evident in international relations in 1914 pitted the "Triple Entente" powers against the Triple Alliance (Germany, Austria-Hungary and Italy).

Le Petit Journal

Le Petit Journal
CHAQUE JOUR — SIX PAGES — 5 CENTIMES
Administration: 61, rue Lafayette

Le Supplément illustré
CHAQUE SEMAINE 5 CENTIMES

5 Centimes · SUPPLÉMENT ILLUSTRÉ · 5 Centimes

Le Petit Journal militaire, maritime, colonial..... 10 cent.
Le Petit Journal agricole, 5 cent. ⚜ La Mode du Petit Journal, 10 cent.
Le Petit Journal illustré de La Jeunesse..... 10 cent.
On s'abonne sans frais dans tous les bureaux de poste

ABONNEMENTS

Seizième année   DIMANCHE 19 MARS 1905   Numéro 748

M. SAVORGNAN DE BRAZZA
Le vaillant explorateur au milieu de son escorte pendant son dernier voyage au Congo

Above left The Galeries Lafayette in Paris. Created in 1895, it was a relative latecomer compared with other *grands magasins* such as Au Bon Marché (1852) and Au Louvre (1855). These big retailing outlets, which sold a wide range of products under the same roof, were like fairy-tale emporia for the growing numbers of consumers not only in Paris but also, through the mail-order businesses they built up, throughout France. In the 1860s chain stores also began to appear. These businesses continued to prosper in the 20th century, when they formed a distinctive feature of France's trading sector.

Above Pierre Savorgnan de Brazza (1852–1905), who explored along the river Congo and founded Brazzaville, was typical of French explorers of the second half of the 19th century. He was supported in his efforts by the prime minister Ferry, who won large tracts of central Africa for France at the international conference of Berlin in 1881. The popular press helped to promote the spread of the French empire to the public. Success in the colonies perhaps in some ways compensated for the loss of Alsace–Lorraine to Germany in 1871. Much of the pro-imperialist propaganda which justified the "civilizing mission" of the French exuded racism.

Right Bicycle manufacturer's advertising poster from the late 19th century. The poster industry developed with the rise of mass consumerism. Posters were viewed as more eye-catching, more durable and less expensive than newspaper advertising. Of all sports, cycling was among the first to adopt advertising and marketing techniques. Cycling was popular and it represented one of the few forms of mass leisure with a branch of manufacturing behind it. Often, as here, cycling posters celebrated the bicycle as a form of liberation for the working man that offered hope for a brighter tomorrow.

RUDGE

16, RUE HALÉVY

PARIS

PNEU "CLINCHER"

IMP. PAUL DUPONT, 4, RUE DU BOULOI, PARIS.

France's Scientific Tradition

France boasts a long history of scientific achievement. Lavoisier, Pasteur and the Curies are among a whole legion of outstanding French scientists.

Most important to French scientific achievement throughout has been the close connection between science and the state. From the time of Louis XIV onward the central government has always given high priority to the patronage of scientists. Following the establishment of the Académie française by Richelieu in 1634, Louis XIV's minister Colbert created the Académie des Sciences in 1666. The requirements of the state often determined the areas in which these scientists operated, engineering, such as road- or canal-building, for example, or military surgery. The two greatest scientists of the Enlightenment, the zoologist Georges Buffon (1707–88) and the chemist Antoine Lavoisier (1743–94), were both richly awarded by the government: Buffon was ennobled and received a huge pension, and Lavoisier became a multimillionaire as a high-ranking tax official.

The Committee of Public Safety mobilized science for the war effort in 1792–4. The mathematician Monge served as Navy Minister, while the chemist Chaptal organized the collection of saltpeter for gunpowder throughout France. The Revolutionary assemblies destroyed most of the educational institutions of the Ancien Régime, but set up new ones. Those were modified and added to by Napoleon, and have provided the framework for education and science until well into the 20th century. The world renown of Pasteur and the Curies, and contributions in photography and cinematography, took France into the 20th century with a high scientific reputation.

Above Marie Curie (née Sklodowska) (1867–1934) was the most brilliant Polish scientist since Copernicus. With her French husband Pierre (1859–1906) she discovered radium (1898), from which radiography and radium treatment derived. She was awarded the Nobel Prize in 1903 (with her husband) and then again in 1911.

Left Louis Pasteur (1822–95). His early studies on the souring of milk – from which the process of pasteurization resulted – led to the establishment of the science of microbiology. The "germ theory" developed by Pasteur – that diseases are spread by bacteria (germs) – was most clearly demonstrated in his isolation of a vaccine for rabies (1885). Gifts of money enabled Pasteur to open the Pasteur Institute in Paris as a center for microbiological

Right The hot-air balloon was invented in 1783 by the Montgolfier brothers Joseph (1740–1810) and Etienne (1745–1799). They proceeded to demonstrate it, to the amazement of all, throughout Europe. One ascent, at Versailles in September 1783, is said to have attracted a crowd of over 100,000.

Below France was a world pioneer in cinematography. The first public film show was put on by Lumière in Paris in 1895, and such was his acclaim that he was soon making a great deal of money. Traveling showpeople helped popularize film in the provinces, where public taste ran strongly in favor of comedy – as here, "the sprayer sprayed". French motion pictures increasingly lost out to American movies in the interwar period.

Below and bottom Photography was one of the great popular visual arts of the 19th century. The inventor was Jacques Daguerre (1787–1851). By 1849, it was said that 100,000 "daguerreotype" portraits were being produced in Paris alone. Besides portraits, a flourishing market also grew up in erotic and pornographic photography. The invention of photography had a considerable impact on the evolution of art: some artists strove to achieve quasi-photographic results, while others went the opposite way – toward impressionism, for example.

The Belle Epoque

The carnage of World War I reinforced the image of prewar France as a paradise of comfort, elegance and security. Certainly, it was easy to imbue the years at the turn of the century with false glamor, as a time of relative innocence; mass wars, economic collapse and political and technological revolutions were to come.

Yet there is more than myth to the idea of the *belle époque*. These years were remarkably rich artistically and culturally. This was the time of art nouveau, the wildly colored posters of Toulouse-Lautrec, the Moulin Rouge and the Folies-Bergère, Sarah Bernhardt and boulevard theater, Marcel Proust, early cinema, impressionism and its successors. Moreover, as the Universal Exhibition held in Paris in 1900 showed, technology could still be viewed as a benign instrument of social advancement rather than as a means of mass destruction or social alienation. The benefits of this society were shared by more people than ever before, as consumerism reached further down the social scale, while the well-off enjoyed material comforts of which their grandparents could hardly have dreamed.

However, the *belle époque* certainly had its darker side too. Much of the urban population faced the harsh reality of poverty; the continuing rural exodus caused feelings of resentment; the spread of working-class militancy signaled growing discontent at social injustices; and the Dreyfus Affair showed how politically divided the social elite remained. The *belle époque* contained the seeds of its own destruction.

Far left The Paris Opéra, founded in 1862, was opened to fanfares of publicity in 1875. Its architecture was characteristic of florid and grandiose Second Empire styles. One of its striking features was the great staircase, complete with marble columns and frescoed ceilings.

Left The play *Gismonda* by Victor Sardou (1831–1908) proved a triumph for its star, Sarah Bernhardt (1844–1923), and its publicist, the Czech A. Mucha (1860–1939). The Théâtre de la Renaissance where it was staged was situated on the Boulevard Saint-Martin and was one of the best-known showcases for boulevard theater. The poster by Mucha won enormous public acclaim and set the style for other posters. It also heightened the taste for art nouveau in Paris. The play itself was a great personal success for Bernhardt. Born Rosine Bernard, she sprang to fame in 1866 and became an institution of the Parisian theater until her death in 1923. Even after having a leg amputated she did not quit the stage.

Left The late 19th century saw a revolution in leisure for the middle and upper classes of Paris. A wide variety of public spectacles, including circuses, waxworks, music halls and theaters of every kind vied for their custom. The Théâtre de Vaudeville, shown here, was built in 1866–68 on the Boulevard des Capucines, and was one of the most successful institutions offering boulevard theater. It had a seating capacity of 1260. The painting is by Jean Béraud (1848–1935), who specialized in capturing the Parisian bourgeoisie, whether on the street, at the theater or at home. His works are a valuable record of the lives of the well-to-do in the capital of the *belle époque*.

Below left The French Riviera, a fashionable location where each year the rich spent the "winter" from October to April. Improved communications helped make summer holidays there popular too, and this considerably boosted the local economy. Nice, for example, was one of the fastest-growing cities in Europe between 1860 and 1914. The Riviera maintained its reputation for fashionable and leisured lifestyles down to 1914 and beyond.

Below, right One of the beneficiaries of the growth of consumerism in the late 19th century was the fashion industry. The fashion press was eagerly read by a mass middle-class, largely female, audience. The 24 April 1909 cover of the fashion magazine *Le Frou Frou* evokes the *joie de vivre* accessible to many in the *belle époque*.

Left Cartoon by the Alsatian writer and caricaturist Jean-Jacques Waltz (1872–1951) suggesting that, four decades after the annexation of Alsace, a German officer still required an armed escort for the purchase of a box of chocolates. French resentment at the conquest of Alsace and Lorraine in the Franco-Prussian War of 1870–1 lasted until World War I and beyond. Although in language and culture most Alsatians were closer to the Germans than to the French, the harsh manner in which the Germans administered the conquered territories angered the locals as well as the émigrés.

Right The city of Verdun, gutted by heavy artillery fire in World War I. Its population fell from 15,000 to 3,000. Very many French cities near to the main battle theaters suffered colossal damage.

The battleground of World War I Fighting in World War I was concentrated on France's northern frontier, where trench warfare exposed the futility of aggressive tactics in an age of automatic and mass firepower. Millions died in a conflict that, at least for France, had the merit of restoring the provinces of Alsace and Lorraine, previously lost to Germany.

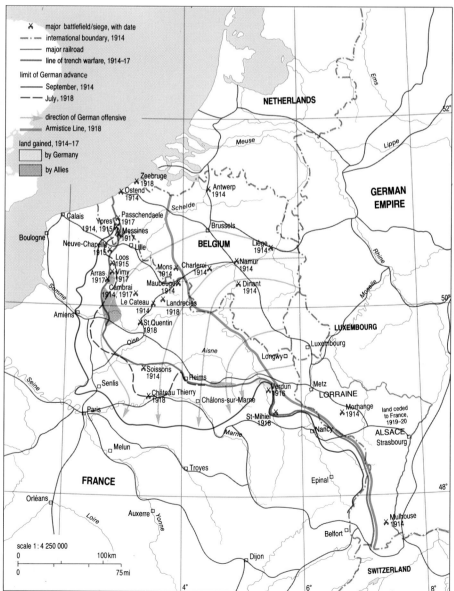

The Great War

Social divisions seemed temporarily blurred as French men and women supported a war of revenge against Germany in August 1914. Poincaré (1860–1934), President of the Republic, called for class harmony, invoking the "sacred union" which would, it was hoped, carry victory. The union scored an initial success when the French troops led by Joffre (1852–1931), and supplied with men and equipment carried by Parisian taxis, checked a German advance on the capital in the first battle of the Marne. Thereafter, it was sorely tested. From Christmas 1914, the war became one of attrition, with a long, barely shifting line of trenches from the Channel to Switzerland. The names on the war memorials found in every town and village of France testify to the extent of the bloodletting. Following massive casualties in the defense of Verdun in 1916, some regiments came close to mutiny, which was speedily put down by General Pétain (1856–1951). The war also tested the civilian population by bringing unemployment, inflation and enforced austerity, though government control over the economy helped stabilize the situation. The northeast – the battle zone – was the most damaged. The city of Reims was left with only 17,000 of its prewar population of 117,000, and many smaller towns and villages were even worse affected.

So great was the social, economic and demographic harm caused by World War I that, after 1918, the French prized security above all else. The severe demands that they made at the Versailles peace conference of 1919 reflected this view. Although Clemenceau (1841–1929), prime minister since 1917, did not achieve everything he wanted at the conference, he ensured that German reparations and the demilitarization of the Rhineland were written into the peace settlement. Concern with security led to full participation in the newly formed League of Nations as well as to the exploration of other means of ensuring defense, such as the building of the fortified

Maginot line on the German frontier, completed in 1929. France's economy, however, was still frail. Population levels continued to slip further behind those of economic and military rivals, and economic growth remained sluggish.

The interwar years

Social stagnation bred a politics of fear and resentment. More than ever, the Third Republic was the regime of the center, for both the far left and far right developed an antiparliamentarian stance. Quasi–fascist ideologies made a significant impact on the right, where *Action française* of Charles Maurras (1856–1952) became the standard-bearer of traditional antirepublicanism and developed an ultranationalistic hatred of so-called "aliens" (Jews and freemasons as well as foreigners). On the left, the Socialist Congress of Tours in 1920 saw the movement split by the formation of a pro-Moscow Communist Party on avowedly Bolshevik lines.

The victims of attack from both extremes, the politicians of the center continued in their time-honored tradition. Government rapidly followed government, with leading politicians regularly exchanging ministerial portfolios. The parliamentary left, denied the support of the Communists, could make little impact: the so-called "left cartel" of 1924–6, headed by Edouard Herriot (1872–1957), failed to win sufficient support for a radical program. A scandal of corruption in high places in 1934 – the Stavisky affair – also rebounded to the discredit of the radicals. Consequently, power was mostly held by a series of unimaginative conservative alliances, which found it difficult to cope with economic difficulties. The Slump came late to France – in 1931 – but it

Left Georges Clemenceau (1841–1929), the "Old Tiger", was the most consummate politician produced by the centrist Radical Party. A deputy from 1875, he became notorious for bringing down governments. He was a Dreyfusard stalwart and served as prime minister from 1906 to 1909 and then again from 1917. Enormously popular for leading France to victory in World War I, he was a major architect of the postwar world through the Treaty of Versailles (1919).

Bottom left The Colonial Exhibition held in Paris in 1931 offered "a tour of the world in one day", reflecting the French imperial presence in all the major continents.

Below left In the wake of the imperialist, there followed the tourist: The Touring Club de France was founded in 1890. By 1895, it had 20,000 members and by 1939, 300,000. The romantic lure of foreign locations was aimed initially at the leisured, wealthy and literate classes.

Below Cartoon satirizing crowded seaside holidays. It was only in 1936, under the Popular Front government, that the working classes won the right to free paid holidays. The tourist industry, though slow to develop compared with that of, say, the United Kingdom, had nevertheless been going for a long time. Seaside holidays became especially popular.

stayed longer too: its effects were still being felt in 1938, three years after world recovery had begun.

The failure of a right-wing coup d'état, on 6 February 1934, brought closer cooperation between left-wing political groups. The left finally had its chance in 1936, with the formation of the Popular Front. Hitler's smashing of the German Communist Party led French Communists to look more seriously at possible alliances with other left-wing groups. Elections in May gave Communists, Socialists and Radicals a parliamentary majority and, though the Communists abstained from government, they allowed a left-wing Popular Front government to be formed by Léon Blum (1872–1950). Expectations ran high, but times proved unfavorable for such a government to live up to them. The Popular Front succeeded in blocking the progress of the far right, but the tenseness of the international situation and the poor state of the domestic economy ruled out great reforms, if not grand gestures. The social program of the Blum government, notably the Matignon Agreements (7 June 1936), included wage rises, a 40-hour week and paid holidays for all workers. This last measure led to the mass migration to the seaside, pointing the way toward the pattern of tourism of the future.

759 — 19 Août 1933
39e ANNÉE

Ame d'Éditions Périodiques, Boulevard de Clichy, Paris-IXe
Téléphone : TRINITÉ 19-30 et 19-31
Compte chèques postaux Paris 436-38
out changement d'adresse doit être compagné de un franc et de la dernière nde. — Les abonnements partent du 1er de chaque mois.

Le Rire

JOURNAL HUMORISTIQUE PARAISSANT LE SAMEDI

Le Numéro : 1 fr. 50

	1 an	6 mois
France et Colonies	70	36
Étranger (Série A)	85	44
Étranger (Série B)	100	52

La série A comprend les pays ayant consenti la réduction de 50 % sur les tarifs postaux.
La série B, tous les autres pays.

Copyright 1933 by LE RIRE, Paris

APRÈS LE BAIN

— Et maintenant où se rince-t-on ?

Dessin de Pierre FALKÉ.

REGIMES 1789–1944

1789–92	**Constitutional monarchy:** Louis XVI Constituent Assembly 1789 Legislative Assembly 1791

10 August 1792: overthrow of Louis XVI

1792–9	**First Republic:** National Convention 1792–5

1792–4 **The Terror (directed by the Committee of Public Safety)**

First Republic: Directory 1795–9

9 November 1799: 18 Brumaire coup d'etat of Napoleon Bonaparte

1799–1804	**Consulate:** First Consul = Napoleon Bonaparte
1804–14	**First Empire:** Napoleon I
1814–15	**First Bourbon Restoration:** Louis XVIII
1815	**First Empire:** "the Hundred Days" (March–June): Napoleon I
1815–30	**Second Bourbon Restoration:** Louis XVIII 1815–24 Charles X 1824–30

1830 Revolution: overthrow of Bourbon monarchy

1830–48	**The "July Monarchy":** Louis-Philippe

1848 Revolution: overthrow of the July monarchy

1848–52	**The Second Republic** 1848: Election of Louis Bonaparte as President of the Republic 1851: Coup d'etat: Bonaparte head of state for 10 years 1852: Coup d'etat: Second Empire proclaimed
1852–70	**The Second Empire:** Napoleon III (Louis Bonaparte)

1870: defeat of Napoleon III in the Franco–Prussian War; overthrow of the Second Empire

1870–1940	**The Third Republic** Presidents: Adolphe Thiers 1871 Patrice de MacMahon 1873 Jules Grévy 1879 Sadi Carnot 1887 Jean-Casimir Périer 1894 Félix Faure 1895 Emile Loubet 1899 Armand Failleres 1906 Raymond Poincaré 1913 Paul Deschanel 1920 Alexandre Millerand 1920 Gaston Doumergue 1924 Paul Doumer 1931 Albert Lebrun 1932

1936–8: Popular Front

Etat Français (Vichy Government 1940–4)
President: Philippe Pétain 1940–4

1944 liberation of France and proclamation of the Fourth Republic

The fall of the Popular Front in 1938 was over-shadowed by the growing threat posed by Hitler's Germany. The rightist government of Edouard Daladier (1884–1970) participated in the Munich agreement of September 1938, but simultaneously put the emphasis on rearmament. When in 1939 France joined Britain in declaring war on Germany over the invasion of Poland, there was none of the popular enthusiasm that had characterized August 1914, only a quiet confidence in the strength of the armed forces. Opinion was, however, more divided than it looked. Some on the right were still shaken by the threat posed by the Popular Front – "rather Hitler than Blum," ran the table-talk – while the signing of the Nazi–Soviet

Europe during World War II
Allied landings from Italy and Normandy ultimately led to the overthrow of Nazi power, which had extended from Poland to the Atlantic seaboard of France. The French Resistance also played an important part in the German defeat despite the repression of the

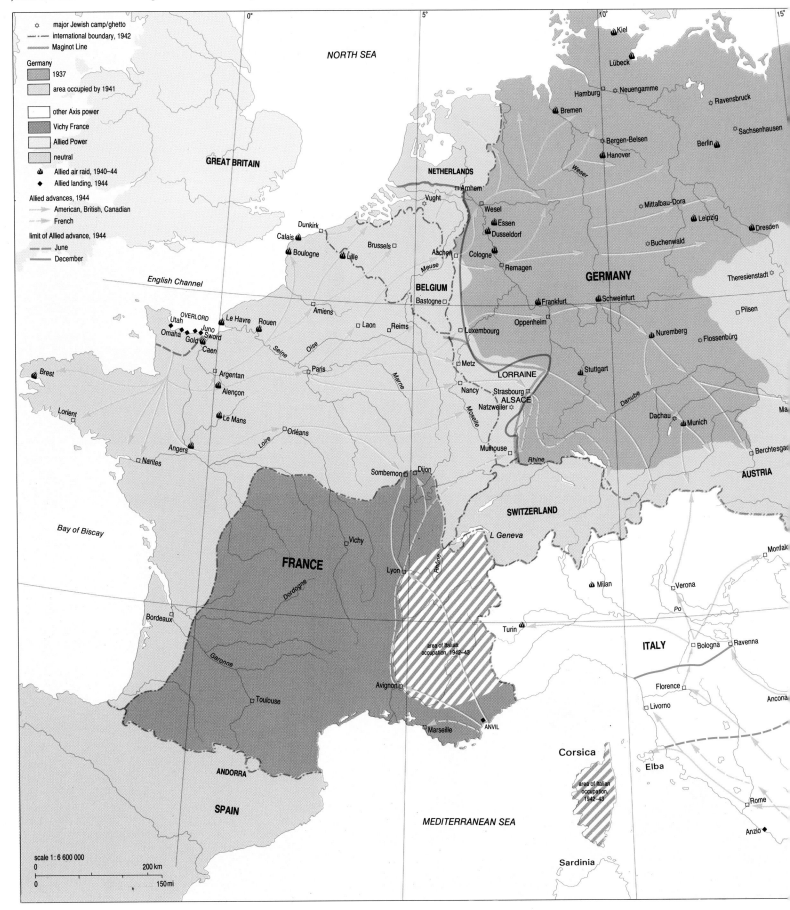

scale 1 : 6 600 000

French puppet regime of Vichy which bolstered German power in the early 1940s – and sent many Jews and other "aliens" to Nazi concentration camps and death camps.

pact in 1939 made many Communists less committed than before to oppose Hitlerism. Uncertainty was fueled by the "drôle de guerre" – the "phony war" period from September 1939 to May 1940 – when little happened. This only increased the awful shock of what historian Marc Bloch called France's "strange defeat" and "the most terrible collapse in all the long story of our national life".

The left, paralyzed by the internal situation and by France's international isolation, had failed to prevent the rise of Hitler and the growth of the Fascist movement in Europe, and Blum had had little alternative but to agree to France's nonintervention in the Spanish Civil War (1936–9).

Vichy France

Perhaps the generals had learned the lessons of World War I too well. Anticipating trench warfare, they were faced with blitzkrieg instead, as the Germans sidestepped the Maginot line and raced for Paris and the coast. Too old to contemplate new forms of warfare – "a mere boy" was one geriatric general's view of the 49-year-old General Charles de Gaulle (1890–1970) posted into the War Office in June 1940 – the high command proved inflexible. Belgium capitulated, the British expeditionary force had to be evacuated from Dunkirk and, on 14 June, the Germans entered Paris, which they found strangely empty. Panic had forced 2 million Parisians to join 6 million others from the north of France on the road southward, all their possessions hurriedly packed onto cars, motortrucks, pushcarts, bicycles and any available form of transportation. The 83-year-old World War I veteran, Pétain, was called into the government and ended hostilities. In a subdivision of France almost Merovingian in its brutality, the northern half of the country was occupied by German troops; Alsace and Lorraine were restored to the Reich; departments on the Belgian border were administered from Brussels; while in the south, Pétain established the so-called *Etat français*, with its capital at Vichy.

Vichy France self-consciously set itself above the political struggle and posed as a regime to which all French men and women of goodwill would rally. In practice, it proved one of the most viciously partisan governments of French history. The year 1940 was

viewed as a defeat for the republican values that had dominated the French polity since 1789, and the new regime attempted to turn back the clock to the days of clericalism, authoritarianism and paternalism of "traditionalist" France. The slogan "work, family and fatherland" replaced the 1789 triad of "liberty, equality and fraternity". There were several touches worthy of the Ancien Régime: election gave way to nomination – there was not even a Bonaparte-style plebiscite to approve the regime – and a mystique of leadership was cultivated, notably among Vichy's

Above The aged Marshal Pétain (1856–1951), former hero of World War I, signed an armistice with the advancing Germans and negotiated the creation of the Vichy state. He was the subject of a personality cult, aimed especially at the young.

Left The LVF – Legion of French Volunteers – was a collaborationist force organized in occupied France which soon won the backing of the Vichy government. It recruited in Paris and its members fought with the Nazis against the Soviet army on the eastern front. Collaboration was an easy option for a great many Frenchmen and women in the war years.

numerous youth organizations. Trade unions were banned; a witch-hunt against Communist and dissident civil servants was organized; religious congregations were again permitted to teach; and a strongly nationalistic ethos was encouraged, which justified attacks on Jews, freemasons and other "aliens".

At his trial after the war, Pétain pleaded that his intention had been to save France from a fate similar to Poland's and to form a "shield" against the worst excesses of Nazi occupation. If there was ever any truth in this plan, it looked especially unconvincing after the arch-collaborator, Pierre Laval (1883–1945) took charge (1940, then 1942–4), when the regime seemed to be striving to become part of Hitler's "New Order". The southern zone was occupied by the German army in 1942. Anti-Semitism became state policy and deportations of perhaps as many as 150,000 people were organized with an alacrity that haunts France half a century later. The establishment of the STO (Service du Travail Obligatoire) in 1942 involved enforced conscription of labor for German industry. Nearly a million workers were transported to Germany, where they joined the 1.6 million prisoners-of-war and other deportees. Within France too, factories worked to Nazi orders. The economic performance of the regime was unimpressive: output declined from lowish prewar levels; and, despite calls for population growth, Vichy failed to boost the birthrate. A police agency, the *Milice*, was established in 1943 with the specific aim of hunting down members of resistance organizations and, for the first time in France since the Ancien Régime, systematic torture was used. By the time of its overthrow, Vichy was a fully functioning collaborationist Nazi police state until 1944.

The French Resistance

If Vichy had been the sum total of France's experience of World War II, it would have been a terrible memory to live down after 1945. But there was, of course, another France, that of the Resistance and the Free French. When Paris fell in June 1940, Charles de Gaulle escaped to London where, on 18 June, he broadcast a radio message calling for the continuation of the armed struggle. This was a humble beginning for the Free French: the appeal was little heard in France, and de Gaulle's followers were initially few and unimpressive. He later sardonically recalled how, at first, "we had on our side only Jews, hunchbacks, cripples, failures and cuckolds." De Gaulle, however, proved a pivotal figure. Internationally, he was the focus for dissidence, particularly within French colonies – North Africa came over to the Free French by 1943 – as well as an accredited (if unpopular) go-between with the Anglo-American allies. Britain also helped to give greater cohesion to the internal French Resistance movement. Until his death under torture at the hands of Klaus Barbie, the "butcher of

Above right The photograph, by Henri Cartier-Bresson (1908–1990) shows forces of the Free French outside Lorient, then still held by the Germans. The Resistance movement attracted all types of individual, from the left and the right, men and women, old and young.

Right The liberation of Paris on 25 August 1944, photographed by the American Robert Capa (1913–54). Resistance forces had begun open warfare against the Germans in the city in June, but had been repelled. The Allied capture of the city signaled the overthrow of the Vichy regime.

LA LIBÉRATION DE LYON

Above Charles de Gaulle, who led the triumphant march down the Champs-Elysées to Notre-Dame cathedral the day after the liberation of Paris. De Gaulle, a junior general, fled to London in 1940 and founded the Free French. He became the most respected opponent of Vichy France and a military ally of Britain and the United States. Following the liberation of Paris, he toured the major cities of France, attracting support for the new Provisional Government. He was in liberated Lyon on 14 September.

Lyon", Jean Moulin (1899–1943) had played a crucial role in coordinating Resistance operations carried out by Gaullist units, Communists (notably after Hitler's invasion of the Soviet Union in 1941) and other forces.

The strength of the Resistance in France probably never exceeded 100,000 men and women, who engaged in armed struggle and sabotage, sheltered Allied airmen and agents, or collected intelligence. Listening in secret to BBC radio broadcasts – the number of radio sets had risen from 500,000 to 3 million in the 1930s – gave a larger number a feeling of participation. The efficacy of the military role of the Resistance is difficult to assess, even in the aftermath of the Allied landings of June 1944. The plans for postwar France that were debated within the Resistance – itself a highly fragmented grouping ranging from Communists to crypto-royalists – remained contradictory and unfocused, though it became increasingly clear that a new, Fourth, Republic would be established. Yet, the importance of the Resistance in giving France a myth on which to found its morale and its self-respect in the postwar era is incalculable. When de Gaulle organized the march up the Champs-Elysees in liberated Paris on 26 August 1944 he helped the French to erase the recent past and look hopefully toward the future.

FRANCE SINCE 1945

Recrimination and reform

The Liberation of France was accompanied by an ugly period of revenge and bloodletting, as local people took justice into their own hands and real or suspected collaborators were shot or otherwise punished; perhaps as many as 40,000 died in this way. Women who had befriended German soldiers were stripped and shaved. The anger was understandable, but often those accused did not receive a fair trial. In due course the new government set up proper courts to try suspected collaborators and sentence the guilty: among them, Laval was executed and Pétain sentenced to life imprisonment. During the postwar years, many former Vichyists claimed – like Pétain – that they had simply been doing their duty for France and should not be seen as traitors. The ensuing bitterness between them and the Gaullists and other former *Résistants* was to have a souring and divisive effect on French public life for years to come, until this older generation began to die out.

Like the Gaullists, the Communists emerged in a strong position at the Liberation and, for a period in 1944–5, some of their units in the southwest virtually controlled a few towns. However, backed by orders from Moscow, the Party decided not to try to take power by force, and instead it settled into uneasy collaboration with de Gaulle's new administration. De Gaulle came to power amid promises of major economic and social reform. Indeed, his initial provisional government of 1944, and the first postwar elected government of 1945, both carried out nationalization programs – a task made easier by capitalism's taint of Nazi collaboration. They took over the coal mines, Air France, the Renault motor-vehicle works, gas and electricity, and the larger clearing banks and insurance companies. In a France with so strong a tradition of state centralism, these changes seemed less drastic than they might have done in many other countries. More important to the French were the new social security system introduced under de Gaulle, the setting up of works councils in factories and the granting of votes to women – three major, if belated, steps toward modern welfare democracy.

Politically, however, the new deal of the postwar dawn did not fulfill its hopes. The first provisional government was based on a wide consensus of opinion, but after the 1945 elections the old party rivalries returned. De Gaulle, who never hid his contempt for political parties, found he could not govern as he wished and, in January 1946, he retired to private life – for the next 22 years. A new Constitution was finally drawn up and approved, and the Fourth Republic was born: but it rapidly came to look as unstable as the Third had done. A series of short-lived governments came and went, based on center–left coalitions of Socialists, Radicals and a new progressive Catholic party, known as the Mouvement Républicain Populaire (MRP). At first, the Communists were included too: with some 26 percent of the vote they were for a while the largest party,

followed by the MRP and Socialists (the traditional right was still weak and discredited). But, predictably perhaps, the Communists soon fell out with their partners and retreated to the sidelines, where they used their control of the largest trade union, the CGT (Confédération Général du Travail), to call disruptive strikes, which largely failed. In 1947, de Gaulle formed his own political movement, the Rassemblement du Peuple Français (RPF), but this took little part in the succession of weak, unstable governments that continued into the 1950s. Despite some able individual leaders, such as Robert Schuman (MRP), the parties, it seemed, were still prisoners of old structures and attitudes, and had not learned any of the lessons of the past.

Postwar recovery

In some ways France began to stir and change deeply after 1945, and this led to the major economic and social tranformations of the postwar decades. One important factor was the rise in the birthrate. In the 1930s the population was gently falling, but in 1945–6 the birthrate leapt from 93 to 126 percent and then stayed for many years at well above the European average. For this reason and because of immigration and longer life-expectancy France's population has risen from 40 to 56 million since 1945. The postwar *bébé-boom*, as it was called, was spurred by the generous new family allowances, though sociologists believe that its cause was also partly psychological – a survival instinct and reaction against prewar decadence. Certainly, the 1940 defeat and the Nazi occupation shocked a number of French people outside politics into reconsidering the future. In the civil service, the innovating technocrat emerged alongside the conservative bureaucrat, while, in the country, young farmers began to challenge the attitudes of the older peasants. At first, this new ethos of renewal and progress was confined to a few pioneers, but gradually it spread to infect public opinion more widely.

The Monnet Plan

A key figure in France's postwar reconstruction was Jean Monnet, a brandy-merchant from Cognac. A pro-European idealist and visionary, in 1945 he won de Gaulle's support for a central state Plan and then became its first Commissioner-General. Monnet cut through the usual barriers in France between different interest groups and succeeded in bringing civil servants, business representatives and trade-union leaders around the same table and persuading them to work together. The Plan was not the only force behind postwar renewal, but it made a major contribution and created its own mystique, which bred widespread optimism. Helped by Marshall Aid funds from the United States, the Plan became the prime motor of early French postwar recovery in austere times when much infrastructure still lay shattered and poverty was severe in many areas. Industry soon regained its prewar peak, and annual growth in the 1950s exceeded 5 percent. Meanwhile, mechanization of farming

Right In the form of de Gaulle's Cross of Lorraine, this memorial to victims of the Resistance stands on the Larzac plateau in the Massif Central. Today there are many such memorials dotted around France, especially in the southern uplands. Some are plaques marking the spot where hostages were shot by the Germans. But not all of these freedom-fighters were Gaullist. Both during the Occupation and at the Liberation, there were bitter rivalries between Gaullist, Communist and other factions within the Resistance.

Below At Chartres, directly after its liberation in August 1944, a woman with an illegitimate baby is marched through the streets in shame, her head shaven; she is accused of having had a German soldier as her lover. Throughout France, there were many incidents of this kind at that period. Many thousands of collaborators and Vichy militiamen were summarily executed by the Resistance, notably by the Communists; often there was little semblance of a fair trial. Later de Gaulle's new provisional government restored order and justice.

produced a rural exodus that provided labor for the booming new industries, as towns swelled in size and France finally shifted from an agriculture-based to an industrial economy.

This progress, however, was accompanied by high inflation, an endemic French ill that the Fourth Republic had inherited from the Third and one which it seemed unable to cure. The resulting devaluations, party feuding and shifting coalitions earned France the label "sick man of Europe". But behind the facade of political chaos, a strong civil service provided stability and a basis for dynamic planning. In foreign affairs, far-sighted leaders such as Robert Schuman and René Pleven helped France to play a major role in shaping a new destiny for Western Europe, and in laying the foundation for Franco-German reconciliation. The creation in 1951 of the European Coal and Steel Community, bringing together France, West Germany, Italy and the Benelux countries, paved the way for the signing in 1957 of the Treaty of Rome, which set up the so-called "Common Market", or European Community (EC), as it is known today. French industry was at first afraid to risk exposing itself to German competition in this way, but the venture was successful, and soon the EC was providing a further incentive for economic growth, as French businesses steadily revised their old protectionist attitudes and became more export-oriented. From 1958 to 1962, France trebled its trade with the other five EC partners. In matters of defence, France was a founder-member of the North Atlantic Treaty Organization

(NATO) in 1949. However, MRP-led proposals for a joint European army – the European Defence Community – were opposed by Gaullists, many Socialists and others and was abandoned in 1954.

The colonial legacy

In the early years of the Cold War, France thus made a significant and positive contribution to rebuilding the West. But this was also a time of worldwide decolonization, and the Fourth Republic was markedly less successful in dealing with its huge overseas empire, which finally brought about its downfall.

In 1947 a severe revolt in Madagascar, bloodily put down, pointed to a new restive spirit in the French colonies. Then, in Indochina, a lengthy war began with the Communists from the north, which led in 1954 to the fall of Dien Bien Phu, a French citadel of high strategic and symbolic importance. France was forced to make peace and withdraw. This was skillfully handled by the charismatic prime minister of the Fourth Republic at that time, Pierre Mendès-France, a progressive and energetic Radical. But his various attempts at much-needed reform, at home and abroad, won him so many enemies that in 1955 he was defeated after only eight months in office.

Trouble was also brewing in North Africa. Whereas freedom was granted relatively easily to Morocco and Tunisia, Algeria, with over a million French settlers, presented more of a problem. After an armed Muslim

Left Poster commemorating the French soldiers who died at Dien Bien Phu, the citadel in northern Indochina (today the Republic of Vietnam) that fell to the Communists in 1954. After this defeat, the French government of Pierre Mendès made peace with the Communists under their leader, Ho Chi Minh, and the French withdrew from Indochina. The Communists took control of north Vietnam, but the south remained pro-Western, until the United States, like the French, became involved in a hopeless war there and were defeated.

Left French troops and armored cars in the streets of Algiers, during the bitter Algerian war which lasted from 1954 to 1962. As in Indochina, the French faced a growing revolt against their colonial rule. But here the situation was complicated by the presence of more than a million French settlers, which made the granting of independence to the Algerian Muslim majority more difficult. It was only de Gaulle who managed to solve the problem, after his return to power. During the war, in which many thousands died, atrocities and torture were committed both by the French army and by the Muslim rebels.

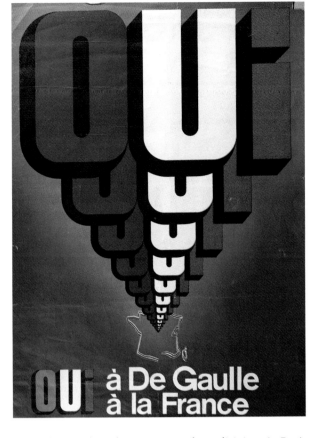

OUI à De Gaulle à la France

THE FOURTH REPUBLIC (1946–58)
Provisional Government (1944–6) headed by General de Gaulle 1944–6, Félix Gouin (1946) and Georges Bidault (1946)
Presidents: Georges Bidault 1946 Vincent Auriol 1946 Léon Blum 1946 Vincent Auriol 1947 René Coty 1954
1958 constitutional crisis and proclamation of the Fifth Republic
FIFTH REPUBLIC (1958–)
Presidents: Charles de Gaulle 1958 Georges Pompidou 1969 Valéry Giscard d'Estaing 1974 François Mitterand 1981

revolt began there late in 1954, the politicians in Paris were unsure whether to suppress it or negotiate. In 1956 a Socialist premier, Guy Mollet, opened talks with the Algerians, but the French settlers rioted and forced him to stop. He then switched to military repression (which resulted in France joining Britain in the fateful Suez adventure against the Algerian rebels' ally, Egypt). Although France sent a huge army to Algeria, the revolt spread and the conflict became more ugly, as both sides resorted to terror and sometimes torture. By 1958 the mood in Paris was moving toward peace talks, but when a new government favoring negotiation emerged under Pierre Pflimlin (MRP), the settlers staged a massive coup d'état in Algeria on 13 May, backed by army generals who still believed that their war was winnable. Demanding that Algeria remain French – *Algérie française* was their slogan – the generals threatened a military takeover of France itself. Whether they could have achieved this, given that the rank-and-file was made up of wary conscripts, is debatable. Even so, as the prospect of civil war loomed, the menace was sufficient for most politicians to believe that it was time to call on de Gaulle, the one man who might be capable of solving the crisis.

The Fifth Republic

General de Gaulle during all these years had been living at his home at Colombey-les-Deux-Eglises, eastern France, and had played no direct part in the army plot against Paris. However, he never believed that the Fourth Republic could last, or that its parties could solve France's many problems. He declared himself ready to serve the nation again, on condition that a new constitution be drawn up on his terms. On 1 June the National Assembly voted for him to return as prime minister. His first main action was to have executive presidential rule written into the new tailor-made constitution that was massively supported by

referendum. He was thus elected President of the Republic, and a new-style Gaullist party ready to do his bidding won a huge majority in the now weakened National Assembly. In this way, the unpopular Fourth Republic gave way to the Fifth.

De Gaulle next set about untying the Algerian knot. Believing that independence was inevitable, he began talks with the Algerian nationalist leaders, and thus effectively betrayed those of his supporters who had taken him for a champion of *Algérie française*. Several times the settlers, and even some army generals, organized revolts in an attempt to frustrate his efforts. But his authority carried the day, and in 1962 Algeria was granted its freedom. Some 800,000 North African settlers (known as *pied-noirs*, "black-feet") were repatriated to France, mostly to the south, where they were absorbed into the fast-expanding economy.

De Gaulle's new regime brought a stability that revived the self-confidence of the French at home and improved the nation's standing abroad. His measures to strengthen the French franc reduced inflation, and he completed the process of granting independence to France's West African colonies. But his foreign policy was tinged with an assertive nationalism which, while pleasing many of his own voters, often irritated his allies. His dislike of US dominance led him to pull France out of the military structure of NATO, and he publicly encouraged French Canadian separatism – "*Vive le Québec libre!*" ("Long live free Quebec"). He pursued an independent policy toward the Soviet Union and the Middle East (after the Algerian war, France became pro-Arab, much to Israel's annoyance, and was later to play a large part in selling arms to Iraq) but put brakes on further EC integration. He also recognized that friendship with West Germany was essential for France, and for peace, and so continued the policy of close cooperation with Germany's Chancellor Adenauer.

With a largely docile parliament and two loyal prime ministers, first Michel Debré, then Georges Pompidou, de Gaulle was able to govern much as he wished. Often he ruled by decree, or he applied his favorite tactic of appealing directly to the people by referendum. In another break with the practices of the Fourth Republic, he introduced a technocratic style, filling some key ministerial posts with non-politicians, such as prefects or bankers. Although these steps were controversial, they helped a dynamic government to

The Events of May 1968

The great national uprising of May 1968 began in March as a political revolt by a few extreme-left students near Paris; it then spread, and 9 million workers joined in, as well as the liberal professions. Many leading intellectuals, such as Jean-Paul Sartre, took the students' side. The actor-manager Jean-Louis Barrault, in charge of the state-owned Odéon Théatre, allowed militant students to take it over for public debate and said "I am fully on your side". For this he was dismissed by de Gaulle.

The revolt had many diverse strands. First, it had an element of national carnival and street theater, a reaction against boredom and routine. Second, it was a bid for political and social revolution, but only by a tiny minority of the rebels. Third, it had far wider materialistic aims – better pay for workers, better study conditions for students. Fourth, it was a demand for reform of many of France's outdated structures. In the short term, the revolt largely failed, at least politically. But as a catalyst it was to have a deep influence on French society. It helped to indure a more liberal and easygoing spirit – to create a dialogue, as the French say. It paved the way toward the more open society apparent today.

NOUS SOMMES TOUS INDÉSIRABLES

Above A student poster of solidarity with their best-known leader, Daniel Cohn-Bendit, a German born in France of Jewish parents. With his passionate, fiery oratory, he became a star of the barricades, but the government then deported him as "undesirable". "We are all undesirable" says this poster.

PAS DE RECTANGLE BLANC POUR UN PEUPLE ADULTE

INDÉPENDANCE et AUTONOMIE de l'O.R.T.F.

Above The staff of the state-run radio and TV networks (ORTF) were among those whose revolt was sharpest. This protest against state censorship of TV demands independence and autonomy for the ORTF. The rebels broadcast what they wished, but after their revolt ended, many were dismissed.

Below Intellectuals and leaders of the Communist-run CGT trade union, demonstrating together on a Paris boulevard.

Top Georges Pompidou (1911–74), de Gaulle's faithful lieutenant, was his Prime Minister in 1962–68, then in 1969 succeeded him as President, but died suddenly in 1974. Pompidou was not a career politician, but had been a teacher and then a banker before de Gaulle returned to power. A cautious pragmatist, who had an affinity with the more conservative elements in French society, he had peasant roots in the Massif Central, as well as many friends in the banking world. He was less in tune with the new post-1968 mood in France that demanded social reform.

Above François Mitterrand (b. 1916), seen here in front of a giant picture of himself at an election rally, has left a stronger mark on French politics than any other postwar figure except de Gaulle. First, in the early 1970s, he rebuilt the moribund Socialist Party into an effective and united force. Second, after becoming President in 1981, he moved the party away from Marxist ideology, toward modern social democracy. He survived a difficult period of *cohabitation* with the right in 1986–8, and was then reelected President for seven more years. His own brand of socialism is hard to define, and he did not join the Socialist Party till he was over 50. He has flexibility and realism, which his critics call opportunism. He is a wily, reserved, very private man, always something of an enigma, growing more aloof and regal with old age.

make full use of French centralized planning, and to carry through some difficult and much-needed reforms – in agriculture, the school system, housing, and other areas – which had eluded its weak predecessors. Symbolically, a new decree obliged Parisians to scour clean the fronts of their houses to restore brightness to a city that had grown gray.

During the world boom of the 1960s, France's domestic economy made huge advances. Much of the early postwar groundwork of Monnet's Plan, or of grass-roots movements, was completed, for which the Gaullist regime took more credit than it properly deserved. The country was rapidly modernized, as quiet old streets became filled with shiny new cars, suburbs were ringed with high-rise estates, and tractors replaced horse-carts. "Le drugstore" and other novelties imported from the United States made their appearance while local stores closed under the impact of giant new hypermarkets. The Caravelle jet conquered Europe's air-travel markets. These developments triggered more profound social changes. Peasants emerged from their traditional isolation in the countryside, while consumerism and the new mobility widened people's horizons and their expectations. Holidays abroad and in particular the Club Méditerranée became popular. Television also made an impact, reaching a wider audience than ever before. But suburban living induced new frustrations, as churchgoing declined and freer, more relaxed codes of morality (denounced as "permissiveness") emerged.

Clearly de Gaulle, in some ways a conservative, even archaic figure, was not responsible for all these changes but he did help to provide the framework of prosperity that made them possible. As the decade wore on, his star began to wane, and in the 1965 presidential election his share of the vote fell to 54 percent. Criticism of his autocratic style, and of his concern with costly prestige projects and grandeur, grew. More importantly, the new prosperity was very unevenly shared.

The May 1968 revolution

Despite the government's reformist zeal, many of the structures and institutions of the old France, bureaucratic and authoritarian, had remained intact, including the university system. The fast-growing student population had become dissatisfied with its bad study conditions, overbearing professors, ill-adapted curricula, and much besides. In May 1968 a largely political revolt by students of the far left on the Nanterre campus, near Paris, suddenly and unexpectedly escalated into a nationwide student uprising. Nine million workers struck in support, and to win better pay. They were joined by large sections of the intelligentsia and professional classes, such as doctors, architects, scientists and producers in state radio and television, who, for their own reasons, vented their frustrations at hierarchy, bureaucracy, over-centralization and entrenched privilege. Thus, arguably, May 1968 was above all the protest by a newly affluent middle class at the failure to match economic change with social and political change. For four weeks France was in a state of chaos. The waving flags, anarchic graffiti, and workers' picnics in occupied factories belonged to the kind of theatrical street-happening and explosive outburst that are part of the French tradition. But the implications were grave. For a while, de Gaulle wavered and it seemed he would fall: then he sternly called the nation to order, helped

by prime minister Pompidou, who bought off the workers with big pay rises. The President quickly called a general election, which his party won by a landslide, resulting from the "silent majority's" backlash against feared anarchy and leftism. Strangely, half the nation wanted reform, half wanted law and order – and yet many, it seemed, wanted both.

As the status quo ante returned, it was clear that those leftist student rebels who had hoped to instigate the overthrow of capitalism had failed. Moreover, de Gaulle did little to meet the demands for reform, apart from a reshuffle of the universities to give them a little more autonomy, and the granting of a better legal status to trade unions inside firms. Despite its failure to achieve its objectives, however, in many subtle ways May 1968 was widely influential and many French people today still regard it as a watershed. In relations between parents and children, teachers and pupils, officials and the public, and notably between employers and workers, it broke the old authoritarian mold in France.

Paradoxically, its prime casualty was de Gaulle himself. Although he restored order, the revolt had exposed his inability to understand the mood and needs of a fast-changing nation. Already showing signs of old-age, he began to retreat into isolation and in 1969 found a pretext to resign. He died the following year. Although de Gaulle did not finish on a note of triumph, most French people nowadays accept that they owe him an enormous debt, both for his wartime record and for his achievements after 1958. He was a father-figure of the kind to whom, in the past, the French rallied in time of need but who, by the later 1960s, had become an anachronism.

De Gaulle's successor was his close associate, Georges Pompidou. He modified the General's rigorous foreign policy to some extent – for example, by lifting his veto on British entry into the EC – but pursued much the same line in home affairs. Pompidou, a former banker, was a pragmatic conservative who, believing that France could cure its ills simply by getting richer, had little time for radical reform. He did however appoint a very liberal-minded prime minister, the Gaullist Jacques Chaban-Delmas, who pledged himself to reform in line with some of the ideals of May 1968. But the two men quarreled, and in 1972 Chaban-Delmas was dismissed. Under the Fifth Republic, a prime minister cannot easily defy his president and expect to remain in office.

Giscard d'Estaing's reforms

When Pompidou died suddenly in 1974, the Gaullist party's undisputed 16-year dominance of French politics came to an end. Neither of the finalists in the ensuing presidential election were Gaullists. The defeated candidate, François Mitterrand, was the strong leader of a revivified Socialist Party. He polled 49.2 percent, only slightly behind the leader of the non-Gaullist center-right, Valéry Giscard d'Estaing. This new president was an enigmatic figure, patrician and elitist, but was also a modernist and convinced "European", and an admirer of the American "open society". True to his electoral promises, he began his mandate with a flurry of liberal reforms. He made divorce easier, relaxed the abortion laws in face of hostility from his own coalition in Parliament, and introduced more equality of opportunity in school education. He also began to loosen state control of television. More ostentatiously, he breakfasted with his garbage collectors at the Elysée Palace, and invited himself to dinner in ordinary people's homes. Soon, however, he found that some of his key reform plans were obstructed by the right-wing Gaullists in his coalition, led by the young and energetic prime minister, Jacque Chirac. The world oil crisis of 1973 led to a mild recession, and further forced Giscard to switch his priorities and cut funding for reforms. The gifted economist Raymond Barre succeeded Chirac, who resigned in 1976. Barre launched an austerity program but this had only a limited success, as inflation soared and high unemployment became a problem in France for the first time since World War II. Giscard meanwhile had abandoned his earlier style, and was now perceived as aloof and secretive, which made him unpopular. By the late 1970s France, like other Western countries, was in a somber mood. Faith in economic growth had fallen victim to the recession, and the brave community ideals of May '68 gave way to a new egotism and an emphasis on private satisfactions, alike hedonistic, spiritual and material.

By the end of Giscard's seven-year mandate, in 1981, the left had been out of power for 23 years and the center-right regime, whether Gaullist or Giscardian, was appearing stale and cynical. Many French people, of all political persuasions, were well aware of the harm caused by this lack of a normal democratic alternation of power. However, the crucial middle-class voters were afraid to entrust power to a left regime that inevitably would include Communists. The Socialist Party, after a bleak period in the 1960s, had been strongly reconstituted around François Mitterrand in 1971, and was now much the larger of the two main parties of the left, but for electoral reasons it was forced into an alliance, uneasy and often fragile, with its hated Communist rivals. De Gaulle, for a few years, had created a superficial national consensus around himself, but in reality his system served to polarize France politically into two blocks – left and right – in accordance with the old French ideological tradition.

A Socialist government

Mitterrand had come close to winning the presidency in 1974, and the left the general election of 1978: its star was rising. Finally, in the 1981 presidential poll, the desire for change, coupled with growing disillusion, sufficed to override many floating voters' earlier fears, and Mitterrand defeated Giscard by 3.5 percent. The National Assembly was dissolved, after which the Socialists won an absolute majority, with 38 percent of the vote, against the Communists' 16 percent. It was a turning-point in French politics. The new government did not embark on the Marxist revolution that some on the right had predicted. Indeed, although Mitterrand had promised a decisive change in French society and his party's program still included some Marxist ideas, he appointed a very moderate government, led by the affable Pierre Mauroy. To win the Communists' acquiescence, Mitterrand allotted them four junior ministries, but they gave him little trouble. Some of the government's reforms, including major regional reform, were considered undoctrinaire and won wide popular approval. Others were Socialist in intent – notably the nationalization of nine key industrial groups and nearly all private banks – but, given the French tradition, this was not seen as such a drastic step. Moreover these state takeovers were prudently conducted so that some big firms became more efficient and profitable than before.

More controversial were the government's attempts to cure France's economic crisis by reflationary measures, such as massive public-spending increases, relaxation of credit controls and raising the wages of the lower-paid. These changes did help to stimulate production a little, but they also added to inflation and failed to reduce unemployment, which was nearing the two million mark. Moreover, France's internal economic policy ran counter to the prevailing monetarist trend in the West. By mid-1982 the effects of inflation were so dire that the French government faced an unpleasant choice: impose protectionist measures, which would break EC rules, or betray its own principles by switching to an austerity program. Mauroy and his Finance Minister, Jacques Delors, argued for the second option, and narrowly won the day. In 1982–3 the Socialist Party made a historic U-turn which had a profound effect on French politics. It introduced austerity of the kind that had earlier been advocated by Raymond Barre; it pursued Barre's relaxation of price controls and other "liberal" economic measures and succeeded better than he had done. In the process, the Party learned to live with the market economy, an effective repudiation of its old semi-Marxist ideals. The Communists were furious and quit the government; the Socialist left was unhappy too, but could do little to oppose a shift that had Mitterrand's own seal of approval.

The Socialist Party thus, in effect, moved to the center-left and became "social democrat" in all but name – a move that was generally welcomed by other center-left parties in Europe. To some, it was the French Socialist Party's greatest achievement of its years in power between 1981 and 1986, and represented a victory over itself. It had also carried through some valuable reforms, and left the economy in better shape than it had found it. But it had largely failed in its aim of redistributing wealth and privilege in France. Mitterrand's artful maneuvering also contributed to the French Communist Party's historic decline. From a postwar peak of 28 percent its support had fallen to an average of 20 percent in the 1960s and 1970s, then to a mere 9.7 percent in 1986. The main reason for its decline, however, was the intransigence of the Stalinist Georges Marchais and other leaders, and the Communists' failure to appeal to workers' aspirations or to permit dissent.

Political "cohabitation"

Despite the Socialists' shift toward the center, they lost the general election of 1988: but Mitterrand remained President, as constitutionally his seven-year mandate was two years longer than the National Assembly's. Consequently, for the first time under the Fifth Republic, a president faced a parliament of an opposite political color. Mitterrand had little choice but to appoint a prime minister acceptable to the Assembly, and he picked the most obvious candidate, Jacques Chirac. In practice, this novel period of "cohabitation" (as the French called it), between two leaders with strong personalities and contrasting temperaments, worked fairly well. They broadly agreed on defense and foreign affairs, so Chirac allowed the president to exercise his constitutional right to oversee these matters. In home affairs, however, Chirac made all the running and, as parliament was sovereign, Mitterrand could do little to stop him. Chirac then

Above Jacques Chirac (b. 1932) has been leader of the neo-Gaullist Party, the Rassemblement pour la République, since 1974, and a highly successful mayor of Paris since 1977. He was Prime Minister in 1974–6, when the non-Gaullist Valéry Giscard d'Estaing was President, but he soon fell out with Giscard, and resigned. He was then again Prime Minister in 1986–8, under the Socialist presidency of François Mitterrand, and this partnership went more smoothly, despite the political gulf between them. Thrusting and ambitious ("the bulldozer" was his youthful nickname), the demagogic Chirac has charisma and political flair, but has always been controversial. In the 1970s he rejuvenated the Gaullist party. His critics have said that he lacks any clear political philosophy beyond a crusading antileftism.

Above right The National Assembly, with its 577 directly elected deputies, is the lower house of the French parliament. It has more power and influence than the indirectly elected upper house, the Senate. Its debating chamber is in the Palais Bourbon, a handsome old building with a Greek-style portico, beside the Seine and opposite the Place de la Concorde. The deputies sit in a semicircle, with the left-wing parties to the left of the rostrum, the right-wing parties to the right (this arrangement is at the origin of the political labels "left" and "right"). The Assembly has a great tradition of oratory and fiery debate, but its powers have been somewhat clipped since de Gaulle introduced the presidential system of the Fifth Republic.

Right Young Muslim immigrants in the Marseille area, protesting against the killing of an Algerian youth in Avignon in 1985. During the 1980s, rising unemployment served to increase tensions between North African immigrants and the local French population, especially in southern France. This also helped to fuel the rise of the racist extreme-Right National Front party.

started on a sweeping program of privatization that went well beyond removing from public ownership the firms that had just been nationalized. This did not please Mitterrand, and indeed caused some friction, but both men knew that their alliance was popular with the public, and neither wished to be seen to be the cause of its rupture. Such a remarkable balancing act, which cut right across old traditions, would have been inconceivable only a decade earlier. It showed how far, since the Socialist U-turn, French politics had moved away from polarization and toward an Anglo-Saxon or German model of government.

This process continued to some degree, even after Mitterrand was reelected President in 1988 (defeating Chirac) and regained a Socialist majority in the Assembly. He appointed as Premier an able technocrat from the right of the Socialist Party, Michel Rocard, who chose a few ministers from the non-Socialist center parties. Rocard pursued a low-profile style of government, with the accent on sound management and, above all, on European integration. He was replaced in May 1991 by Edith Cresson, France's first woman prime minister. Mitterrand, Rocard and most other senior ministers were all dedicated "Europeans" who, in close liaison with their fellow French Socialist Jacques Delors (President of the Commission in Brussels from 1900), championed the 1992 "single-market" program and moves toward monetary and political union. Until the fall of the Berlin Wall and the subsequent unification of Germany, the French held the undisputed political leadership of the EC. The emergence of the new German giant was seen by some as a threat to France's position and aroused past anxieties. Official French policy was to take Chancellor Kohl at his word and to join him in pressing for rapid European union, as the best and safest way of containing an ultra-powerful Germany.

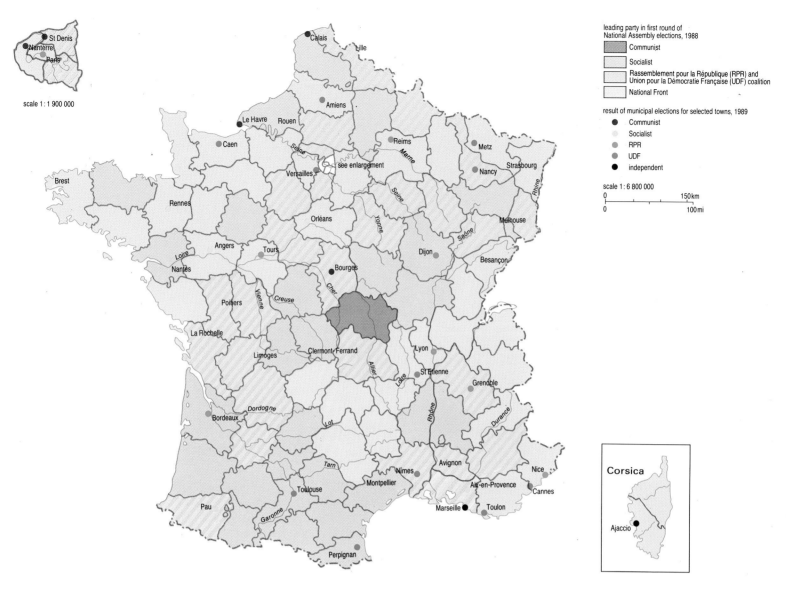

leading party in first round of
National Assembly elections, 1988

Communist

Socialist

Rassemblement pour la République (RPR) and
Union pour la Démocratie Française (UDF) coalition

National Front

result of municipal elections for selected towns, 1989

● Communist

○ Socialist

◔ RPR

◑ UDF

● independent

scale 1 : 6 800 000

0   150 km

0   100 mi

scale 1 : 1 900 000

Corsica

The presidential legacy

The consitution that de Gaulle devised for the Fifth Republic in 1958 has on the whole served France well, though it has its faults. For instance, the president's relations with parliament remain somewhat equivocal, as both are elected by direct suffrage and both are equally sovereign. The prime minister therefore has to serve two masters, which, as the "cohabitation" period showed, can lead to tensions. Many people have argued that the president's mandate should be cut to five years and synchronized with that of the Assembly, on the lines of the US model, to reduce the chance of the two being from opposing political parties. But, arguably, a strong presidential system, in which in a grave crisis the president can invoke emergency powers and rule by decree (as de Gaulle did once) does accord with the Franch tradition. Also, the double-round voting system that is used for all French elections, whereby the contest is decided in a runoff between finalists, has something of the same effect as proportional representation.

The old revolutionary left, till recently so vocal and potent in France, has gone into sharp decline, as elsewhere in Europe. The traditional French *manichéisme* – the tendency to see left and right in terms of black and white – has also waned, as a greater spirit of consensus has emerged. The antidemocratic extremes represent only about 20 percent of voters, half with the Communists, half with the new racist

National Front, an ugly but limited phenomenon. Between them are the big center-focused groups and parties, heated rivals but broadly in agreement on many matters, such as how to deal with unemployment, which remains a key issue.

Despite these developments however, since the 1970s there has been a growing public disillusion with politics, as opinion polls show that many people feel that the parties misunderstand their needs and are divorced from the real life of the nation. Certainly political parties sometimes seem to be too much concerned with their own feuding, which may be a matter more of personal rivalry than of policy or doctrine. At a Socialist congress in 1990, for example, far less time and energy was devoted to topical issues than to a slanging match between rival claimants for the future leadership of the party. The old contentious French spirit has not altered even in a period since 1945 that has seen wide and deep changes.

France today faces three challenges for the future: first, that of building on the new consensus and moderation in politics, in order to create a more equal society, less bound by privilege; second, discovering a new role for itself in the new Europe of political and monetary union, now taking shape; third, finding a way for the modern "high-tech" economy to transfer society without spoiling the traditional *douceur de vivre*, culture and lifestyles that are the cherished hallmark of French civilization.

Political trends and voting patterns
In the June 1988 elections to the National Assembly, the two main right-wing parties in coalition, RPR and UDF, won 40.4 percent of the votes and a roughly equal number of seats; the Socialist Party scored 37.5 percent, the Communists 11.3 percent and the extreme-right National Front 9.7 percent. With some exceptions, the spread of party votes around France is fairly even, and it is not always the case that industrial areas vote left and rural areas vote right. Some big industrial towns such as Lyon and Toulouse elect right-wing mayors and deputies; on the other hand, the Socialists have been making inroads into some traditional right-wing areas such as Brittany in the northwest and Alsace in the northeast. The Communists' vote has been steadily declining, and they have lost control of many town halls, but their vote still holds up remarkably in some rural areas. The Socialists also do well in the rural southwest, which has a radical tradition. However, their main bastions are the industrial north, and the Marseille area where the mayor is an independent Socialist. In some regions, there is bitter conflict between the mayor of the chief town and the right-wing regional assembly – for example in Languedoc-Roussillon (Montpellier) and Alsace (Strasbourg).

PART THREE
FRANCE TODAY

FRENCH SOCIETY TODAY

The conflicts between change and tradition in modern France have been sharper than in most European countries. The massive rural exodus and rapid urban and industrial growth that the country experienced in the decades following World War II helped to change the attitudes and life-styles of a nation. A formerly static and in some ways backward people, whose gaze was fixed on the past and on narrow local horizons, became more mobile and obsessed with novelty. In the area of high technology, the French love of modernization has produced impressive results, from the high-speed train (*Train à Grande Vitesse* or TGV) to the Ariane space rocket and the controversial nuclear power program, the world's most extensive. Recently, however, the French have become aware, in a land with so potent a civilized heritage, of a certain loss of old-world charm and have been turning back to their cherished traditions, to try to combine the best of the old and the new.

Problems of decentralization
Whereas the nation's much-needed economic and physical modernization has been managed rather

brilliantly, the success in adapting social and official structures to this new framework has been more uneven. Above all, the structures of the state have been slow to evolve, in this most centralized of Western countries. De Gaulle, who adored *la France* but thought less well of the French, said of them in 1966, "They can't cope without the state, yet they detest it; they don't behave like adults". In other words, the state's imperious paternalism has caused the people to grouse constantly, yet to complain equally loudly if the state fails to provide, though they are unable to provide for themselves. Dating in part from Napoleon, in part from Louis XIV or earlier, French centralism has put education, the police, justice, welfare and medical care, public utilities, many firms, and major aspects of local government and of public credit and finance, all in the hands of the state. Some dismantling has now begun, and in the past decade governments of both left and right have made moves to decentralize, under pressure from public opinion. But the debate rages as to how far this should go, and over the pros and cons of the whole system. Arguably, in the new age of open frontiers, not only does central

The transportation network in France
The French railroad network was built in the 19th century to radiate from Paris. Even in the 1930s it was still quicker to go from Toulouse to Lyon via Paris than to travel direct. But many fast direct intercity services have now been opened, for example Lyon–Bordeaux. The first TGV (*Train à Grande Vitesse*) line to open was Paris–Lyon, in 1983. Others are now being built toward Marseille and Bordeaux, and to Lille and beyond to link up with the Channel Tunnel and the German network. Cross-country air services have also developed, for example Nancy–Bordeaux, and more than 70 airports have regular scheduled flights. As for ports, the biggest ones (Marseille, Le Havre, Dunkirk) handle, above all, oil for refining and heavy industrial exports. The main passenger ports are those along the English Channel coast, led by Calais.

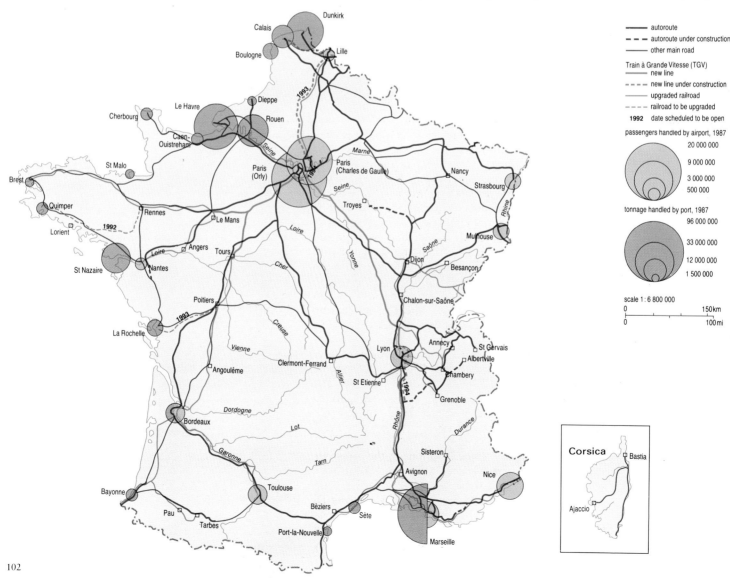

planning lose its value, but industries should become more self-reliant and market-oriented, ceasing to rely so much on supervision and subsidies from the state with its political considerations.

Another problem facing reformers has been how to lighten France's cumbersome bureaucracy. Life is governed by countless laws and regulations, often abstruse and involving heavy paperwork. The French, however, have little respect for them and find ways of circumventing the absurdities. This sport, known as *le système D*, is a cardinal feature of French life: that is, even the authorities tacitly accept that red tape can sometimes be ignored. The following story is by no means untypical. An Englishman with a villa in the Midi wanted electricity installed and was told by the village mayor that it would take years of delay and form-filling. "But", he added, "there's some wiring stacked in the vaults of the *mairie*, and René, our electrician, might fix you up, but keep it quiet."

Recent governments, aware of the problems, have made efforts to reduce the bureaucracy, simplify the rules and shorten the delays. It is a mammoth task, but some progress has been made, thanks in part to computerization. For example, in Bordeaux in 1989, the time needed to renew a vehicle licence was reduced from three weeks to three hours; and in the 1970s the list of categories of tax exemption, in the awesome French fiscal system, was cut by half. But the trouble with French bureaucracy is not just that the rules are complex: junior officials, not graced by *système D*, have tended to be unhelpful and officious in applying them. Aware of this too, governments have tried, with mixed results, to retrain staff to stop thinking of the

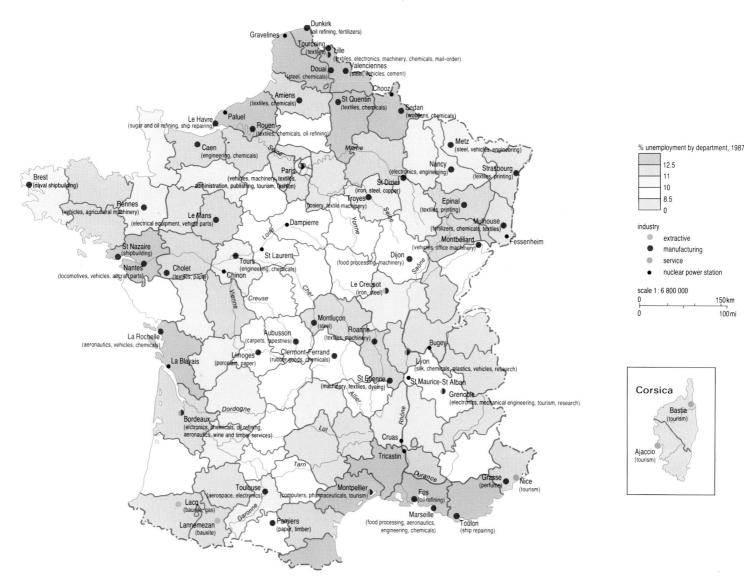

Dunkirk
(oil refining, fertilizers)
Gravelines
Tourcoing
(textiles)
Lille
(textiles, electronics, machinery, chemicals, mail-order)
Douai
(steel, chemicals)
Valenciennes
(steel, vehicles, cement)
Chooz
Amiens
(textiles, chemicals)
St Quentin
(textiles, chemicals)
Sedan
(woollens, chemicals)
Le Havre
(sugar and oil refining, ship repairing)
Paluel
Rouen
(textiles, chemicals, oil refining)
Metz
(steel, vehicles, engineering)
Caen
(engineering, chemicals)
Marne
Nancy
(electronics, engineering)
Strasbourg
(textiles, printing)
Brest
(naval shipbuilding)
Paris
(vehicles, machinery, textiles,
administration, publishing, tourism, fashion)
Seine
St Dizier
(iron, steel, copper)
Troyes
(hosiery, textile machinery)
Epinal
(textiles, printing)
Rennes
(vehicles, agricultural machinery)
Le Mans
(electrical equipment, vehicle parts)
Dampierre
Seine
Mulhouse
(fertilizers, chemicals, textiles)
Montbéliard
(vehicles, office machinery)
Fessenheim
St Nazaire
(shipbuilding)
Tours
(engineering, chemicals)
St Laurent
Loire
Dijon
(food processing, machinery)
Saône
Nantes
(locomotives, vehicles, aircraft parts)
Cholet
(textiles, paper)
Chinon
Vienne
Le Creusot
(iron, steel)
Creuse
Cher
La Rochelle
(aeronautics, vehicles, chemicals)
Montluçon
(steel)
Roanne
(textiles, machinery)
Bugey
La Blavais
Aubusson
(carpets, tapestries)
Limoges
(porcelain, paper)
Clermont-Ferrand
(rubber goods, chemicals)
Lyon
(silk, chemicals, plastics, vehicles, research)
St Etienne
(machinery, textiles, dyeing)
St Maurice-St Alban
Grenoble
(electronics, mechanical engineering, tourism, research)
Bordeaux
(electronics, chemicals, oil refining,
aeronautics, wine and timber services)
Dordogne
Allier
Rhône
Lot
Cruas
Tricastin
Durance
Garonne
Tarn
Toulouse
(aerospace, electronics)
Lacq
(bauxite, gas)
Montpellier
(computers, pharmaceuticals, tourism)
Fos
(oil refining)
Grasse
(perfume)
Nice
(tourism)
Lannemezan
(bauxite)
Pamiers
(paper, timber)
Marseille
(food processing, aeronautics,
engineering, chemicals)
Toulon
(ship repairing)

% unemployment by department, 1987
12.5
11
10
8.5
0

industry
○ extractive
● manufacturing
● service
• nuclear power station

scale 1 : 6 800 000
0   150km
0   100mi

Corsica
Bastia
(tourism)
Ajaccio
(tourism)

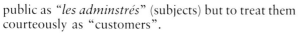

public as *"les adminstrés"* (subjects) but to treat them courteously as "customers".

Industrial relations

The French tradition of a somewhat authoritarian society has tended to color work relations inside firms or public offices, which are beset with rigid hierarchies and chains of command. Once again, however, recent years have seen changes, with the uprising of May 1968 acting as a catalyst. While the shopfloor then went on strike mainly for better wages, the junior technicians and management grades in many firms were rebelling against employers' secretiveness, aloofness and failure to delegate, or the lack of group discussion. Since then, many firms have taken personnel relations more seriously, or they have set up job-enrichment schemes or Japanese-style "quality circles" based on group discussion. The autocratic style, and the sense of formal hierarchy, have diminished a good deal in the private sector, but they remain strong in the public sector, where the systems of command are still formalized, and senior staff are afraid of delegating responsibility to subordinates.

The private employers' campaign to woo their staff with this new humane approach has largely bypassed the trade unions, which in France have less influence than in many Western countries. Only some 15 percent of the work force is unionized, and their numbers have been falling for years. Perhaps one reason for this is that the French are so individualistic. More

importantly, the workers have grown weary of the incessant feuding between the big unions, which in France are divided on political lines. The largest, the Confédération Générale du Travail (CGT), claiming 1.2 million members, is virtually controlled by the Communist Party, which has kept its hold despite its own decline. Its two main rivals, the Confédération Française Démocratique du Travail (CFDT) and Force Ouvrière (FO), each with some 900,000 members, are both pro-Socialist but in different ways. The former has "revolutionary" aims, like the CGT, while the latter is reformist. As the main unions have only limited funds, and can seldom agree on strategy, they cannot easily stage long strikes. Disruptive short-term stoppages in the public services are quite common in France, but in industry they are less frequent than in many countries.

Union weakness may also explain why French workers, and the unions themselves, were slower to gain representation inside firms than in many countries. De Gaulle, after the war, set up obligatory works councils (*comités d'entreprise*) in larger firms, but these "served little purpose save to arrange the Christmas parties", according to one common jibe. Only after May 1968 did the unions win a proper legal status within companies. Then, in 1981–2, the Socialists introduced a series of measures that finally gave workers and unions the same kind of rights – on wage-bargaining, representation, information about company policy, and so on – as had long been the

Industry, mineral resources and unemployment

Industry used to be concentrated in the east and northeast, but is now a little more evenly spread, thanks to the success of postwar regional policies. The former coal mines in Lorraine, the Lille area and the Massif Central are largely exhausted and many have closed. Instead, nuclear power has been developed, notably in the Rhône and Loire valleys. Older heavy industries around Nancy, Metz and Valenciennes in the north and St-Etienne in the mid-south have declined, but some new ones have arrived. Modern high-technology industry is especially strong in Lyon, Grenoble and Toulouse, and there is still much industry, both old and new, in the Paris region. The unemployment rate is highest in areas where older industries are in decline, for example in the north and northeast (coal mining, steel, textiles, shipbuilding), and in the St Nazaire and Toulon areas (shipbuilding and repairing). It is low in areas of successful modern industry, such as Lyon, Grenoble, Mulhouse, and the Paris basin. In some farming and vinegrowing regions of the Mediterranean coast, real unemployment is less high than the figures may suggest, because of seasonal part-time jobs in agriculture.

benefits for the disabled have since been raised to a decent level. State hospitals have greatly improved, too, and are now well funded; but the price is a heavy annual deficit in the social security budget.

Class and income

France is a country where class divisions have traditionally been strong. The peasantry has lived in a world apart; the working class has felt alienated from the powerful bourgeoisie; many subtle and snobbish gradations have divided the middle classes; and the aristocracy has kept aloof in its own exclusive circles. Since the war a new social mobility has developed, blurring some of the old distinctions between these classes (notably between the farmers and the rest), though major inequalities of wealth and of opportunity remain. Today, *Egalité*, one of the three great slogans of the Revolution, means to the French a civic equality among citizens all with the same rights. This produces a mutual respect between individuals, but also creates a kind of legal fiction that other very real

Above The old-style peasant, tilling the fields with an ox-drawn hand-plow, is today becoming a rarity in France, though a few still exist, as here in the uplands of the Massif Central. This kind of drudgery has largely given way to modern, efficient farming, as the old social gulf between *paysan* and *citadin* narrows and farmers become more like business people, as in Britain or the United States.

Right The inequalities of income and of privilege remain great in France; and in Paris and other cities the working class and the rich bourgeoisie still inhabit different worlds, even if in their leisure interests and their dress they have been drawing closer. Here an auction at the famous Drouot salesroom in Paris can attract high bids from wealthy Parisians as well as from foreign buyers.

norm in, for example, West Germany and Sweden. Workers even won the right to a few seats on management boards in the larger state-owned firms (though French unions have been skeptical about this kind of comanagement, which they see as irrelevant to their main aims).

In welfare and social security, French workers and their families are protected by a system that is one of Europe's most advanced, accounting for some 28 percent of GDP, about the same level as in Germany. Until the 1970s its main failing was that it was heavily employment-related: it tended to favor those in jobs, or otherwise useful to society, such as young mothers (the large family-allowances remain among its most generous features), while the elderly or handicapped fared much less well. However, old-age pensions and

inequalities do not exist. These in a way are accepted: although the left has long proclaimed the ideal of "revolution", in practice the narrowing of the gap of wealth and privilege has seldom been a major feature in electoral debates.

However, the relations between the classes, and the influence of each class, have been changing. The aristocracy, which in pre-1914 days set the tone in all Europe for taste and gallantry, has retreated onto the sidelines of national life. The great families still enjoy their own social world, with cocktail parties or an occasional ball, while the rest of France quietly ignores them. Although the French public may adore foreign royalty, or the idea of an English *milord*, it cares little for its own nobility. At one time aristocrats used to scorn the business world, but today, with their landed fortunes eroded by inflation or taxation, many of them have been obliged to take up salaried posts in firms. Often they use some of this income to maintain their cherished family châteaux, where they will spend part of the year. In professional life, many a count or baron discards his title and is called simply "Monsieur". Economically, the aristocrats have been merging into the upper bourgeoisie, even if socially they retain their own exclusive identity, and their intense family pride.

The upper bourgeoisie still holds much of the real power and influence in France. Its financial grip on the world of business and industry may have relaxed a little, as the big private firm gives way to the public corporation, but, even under Socialist governments, the upper bourgeoisie has retained control of many of the key salaried posts in the economy, through the system of educational privilege. This is the social milieu today that is popularly known as "BCBG" (*bon chic bon genre*), whose members dress impeccably, have perfect, rather formal manners, and work very hard. This upper-middle class is roughly divided into the *grande bourgeoisie*, of which de Gaulle was typical, and the *bonne bourgeoisie*, perhaps exemplified by Mitterrand, an ex-lawyer and the son of a businessman.

Lower down the social scale, modern economic expansion has produced a new, affluent middle-middle class whose numbers and influence have been growing fast. They include advertising and sales executives, skilled technicians, modern-minded tradespeople and small industrialists – such as the master-butcher whose former modest small-town store has multiplied into a chain of big ones, and who now lives in high *nouveau-riche* style in a country house with a swimming pool. This new, status-seeking upwardly mobile milieu resembles its American or German counterpart. But many others in the traditional *petite bourgeoisie* have slumped into decline, unable to cope with economic change. Meanwhile, as millions of peasants have become towndwellers, the farmers remaining on the land have been largely integrated into the commercial class, both in outlook and life-style – and so the old barrier between *paysan* and *citadin* has been fading away.

The other great barrier, between *bourgeois* and *ouvrier* (worker), has been slower to come down. French workers have long felt a sense of alienation from the middle class and its values, and many have given vent to this by voting Communist. The working class has tended to live in its own social world, especially in its ghetto-like strongholds of the older industrial areas, where it has had its own life-style, its own pastimes and its own mode of dress. The recent decline of the Communist Party is both cause and consequence of a decline in workers' old emotional solidarity, their sense of community bred of hard times. Moreover, with prosperity, many workers have been acquiring bourgeois habits. They now watch the same programs on television (a great leveler), and the young frequent the same discotheques. Whereas the old bourgeoisie was scornfully ignorant of the lives of workers, younger people are beginning to mix across the class barriers. The working class has itself become less homogeneous: its new elite of skilled workers and technicians now identifies more readily with junior management than with unskilled workers; a skilled worker may own the same kind of car as a bourgeois and, off duty, will dress in the same way. On the new urban estates, workers, tradespeople, *petits cadres*

(junior executives) and ex-peasants rub shoulders together, as do their children attending the same state primary schools. However, although the social classes are now mingling more, real barriers remain, especially at the upper levels, where snobbery and privilege are rife and family connections are invaluable.

These social barriers are a reflection of the inequalities in wealth and income. The net pay (after tax) of a managing director in France is 7.3 times that of an unskilled worker (the comparable figures are 4.5 for Germany and Italy, and 3.6 for the UK). In terms of disposable income, the differential for France may, in fact, be smaller, as the welfare allowances are larger than in many other countries. Even so, the French tax system still benefits the higher-paid. Income tax evasion by the liberal professions and others among the self-employed is a very rewarding old French pastime, which costs the state an estimated 60,000 million francs a year. A successful lawyer or private doctor, for instance, will declare for tax only a small

Above An old-style *clochard* (tramp) has found a bedroom for the night in a Paris bus stop. The true *clochard* used to be a Paris institution: usually he chose this way of life freely, hating to sleep in a bed and rejecting society's attempts to integrate him. Such people were usually drunk, but harmless. There are fewer of them today, and their place has been taken by a more sinister breed – the desperate jobless and homeless, often young, who resort to mugging and theft with violence to scrape a living. The sharp recent rise in the Paris crime rate is due in part to them.

part of his huge earnings – and the inspectors will turn a blind eye. As it is hard to get the French to pay direct taxes, the emphasis has long been on indirect taxation, such as value-added tax (VAT), which, as a consumer tax treats poor and rich alike. Recent Socialist governments have failed to redress these injustices. They did, in fact, raise the legal minimum wage faster than inflation, greatly increase death duties and capital gains taxes (hitherto well below the European average) and impose a new wealth tax. But although this went some way toward clipping the wings of the very rich, it failed to reduce the wage differentials. Many critics on the left argue that the Socialists never really fulfilled their electoral pledge to create a much more equal society.

Social mores

In many ways, in its day-to-day social intercourse, France has been spontaneously changing its style. Under the impact of new generations and of foreign influences, the old social formality of the French and their taste for ceremony have declined markedly in recent years. But even in the France of today, in office or public life, any ex-chairman will expect to be addressed all his life as "Monsieur le Président", while the ritual of handshaking continues and business letters are, by British standards, still overly formal and oddly stylized. Although outspoken in the voicing of opinions, the French are often still very conventional in their manners. However, for some years now, younger people have been showing impatience with this old formal approach, especially in social life, and ceremonial banquets with speeches are giving way to more informal home entertaining. The use of Christian names has increased steadily, and in some circles is now almost as common as in Britain or America. The use of "tu" (the familiar form of "you") remains restricted, but is gaining ground and is now almost universal among teenagers and students. Older people may still prefer to use "vous" (the more polite form of "you") and "Monsieur" or "Madame" unless they are on close terms. But this stylized courtesy can be meant quite cordially.

Freeing themselves from the strict standards of their elders, younger people are also now readier to invite friends casually to a meal at short notice – and the deeper you go into the provinces or rural areas, the warmer the welcome. In fact, the proverbial refusal of the French to entertain in their homes has long been a foreign myth, based perhaps on visits to Paris where often the upper bourgeoisie are genuinely too busy, or too snobbishly perfectionist, to be hospitable. (In this milieu, the notion persists that a party in your own home must be done with lavish excellence or not at all, and so it is done rarely.) In the smart social sets of Paris, the formality remains such that dinner-party habits can still be quite Edwardian, with printed cards, white-gloved waiters, probably evening dress, and rigid rules about the correct food and wines. Much social life also remains cliquey: people tend to invite their own kind, and will seldom risk mixing up, say, go-ahead bankers, bohemian artists and leftist intellectuals.

Compared with Anglo-Saxons, the French are more loquacious, but also much more *socially* reserved. They will readily start up an eager discussion with a stranger, but it will remain anonymous, without personal questions asked. By contrast, Anglo-Saxons are much more open about making new acquaintances and quickly developing them into friends; in a society still partly based on mistrust, the French are warier of making new friends. But, once made, their friendships are enduring, deep and loyal, while they find the easy Anglo-Saxon chumminess rather superficial, a facade to hide *emotional* reserve.

In France, as in other Catholic countries, the family plays a big role, and has long been a major focus of the individual's loyalty and sense of duty, ahead of community or state. "I can't pay my taxes: you see, I've a duty to support Aunt Hélène", has been a common attitude. Since the war, however, the focus has been narrowing from the extended to the nuclear family, from the big clan to the home cell of parents and children. In rural areas, as the young drift away, the big patriarchal peasant clan has been losing its influence; in the upper bourgeoisie, as salaried careers replace family managements, and property gives way to income, so the tight embrace of the big family gathering, the subject of so many anguished novels, has become less important for the members' security and future. Young people have become more mobile and independent, perhaps more self-interested, and less willing for an elderly widowed parent to live with them. As a result, officialdom has had to do more to help old people, through higher old-age pensions, new clubs and hostels. The senior citizens are also starting to build their own group social life, American style, with busloads of widows going on outings together – quite a new departure for France.

Even so, the family still has a stronger hold than in Anglo-Saxon countries, and within the nuclear cell of parents and children the links have recently become still closer, after a difficult period of transition. Around 1968, French teenagers rebelled sharply against traditional parental authority, and many young people refused to go on living at home until their marriage, as had been the custom. Now, having won their right to independence, teenagers have moved back to closer emotional ties with parents, on a more equal basis. Thus the family today is united less by convention and constraint, more by genuine affection and need.

The place of women

Women, too, in the past 30 years, have won a fuller emancipation – legal, professional and sexual. Although, socially, women have never been segregated as in some southern countries, they have been slow to push for full legal rights. They won the vote only in 1945, and until 1964 a wife even had to obtain her husband's permission to open a bank account or get a passport. Since then, however, all legal inequalities, relating to divorce, property and the right to employment, have been gradually eliminated. Moreover, women have been making headway in the professions, as ambassadors, prefects and even army generals. Some 34 percent of young doctors are women; and, in 1972, the first woman ever to enter the mighty Ecole Polytechnique, till then a male preserve, came first in the passing-out examination. However, in industry and big business there is still a strong male bias against giving senior posts to women. In politics too, they have been slow to make an impact: during the long period 1945–74, only three women even reached junior office, while the total of women deputies was sometimes as low as ten. Since then, both Giscard and Mitterrand made efforts to promote women in politics, with some success – for example, the Socialist

Edith Cresson (who became France's first woman prime minister in May 1991), and Simone Veil, a brilliant and popular Minister of Health under Giscard and later president of the European Parliament. Nevertheless, in all parties, there is still a bias against naming women as candidates or letting them climb up through party ranks.

In the past, French women preferred to exert power more subtly in the salon or boudoir, with de Pompadour as their prototype, not that most untypical of Frenchwomen, Joan of Arc. In fact, militant women's rights movements have never attracted much support in France, and even Simone de Beauvoir was little heeded for lecturing her compatriots, in *Le Deuxième Sexe* (The Second Sex), on how to escape from their "self-imposed inferiority". Today, most influential feminists still take care to remain very feminine, for what both French men and women enjoy is the subtle interplay of gallantry and romanticism between the sexes – a woman's use of charm to win her way. Domineering or aggressive women are treated with scorn. However, a younger generation does now insist on much more equality with a man in marriage or other relations, and an end to the egotism of a macho society. A woman will no longer allow her man to take all the decisions but do none of the household chores. If he does, she may well walk out. She expects the same degree of sexual freedom as a man, and from him the same degree of fidelity – and that in French life is new.

In the old days, the extramarital affair was more usual than the premarital one, and most women remained virgins till their wedding (or at least they were very secretive about any affair). Then, in the 1960s and 1970s, casual sex became common among teenagers, as in other countries, though since then, under the impact of AIDS and other factors, this tendency has waned. Today, nearly half of all couples live together before getting married, and many do not bother to marry until a child arrives. In the postwar years, marriage was the great ideal, but since 1972 the number of marriages performed annually has fallen from 417,000 to 266,000. The state even recognizes the status of *le concubinage* (cohabitation), and some 800,000 couples formally take advantage of it, for tax reasons. Of course, attitudes to such behavior vary by class: in the provincial bourgeoisie, older people will still frown on an unwed couple in their midst. But in all strata of society, divorce is now so prevalent that it no longer carries a stigma, and it has become easier, too: dissolution by mutual consent, introduced in 1975, now accounts for one-third of all divorces.

Repeal of the laws against birth control and abortion have also played a part in women's emancipation. A law passed in 1920 – not for religious but demographic reasons, to help repair the losses of World War I – forbade the sale of contraceptives and all publicity for birth control. By the 1960s, the law was being widely sidestepped, while the government turned a blind eye. Contraceptives were still hard to obtain, however, and most couples resorted to *coitus interruptus* or other equally unreliable methods. Clandestine abortions were then running at over 700,000 a year. A few richer women went off to clinics in London, Geneva or Morocco; poorer ones resorted to backstreet doctors or to clumsy self-abortion, which led to thousands of deaths annually. Finally, in 1967, the Gaullists repealed the 1920 law, despite opposition from Madame de Gaulle and others. Today, contraceptive pills are provided free by the

health service, on a doctor's prescription, to women of any age whether married or not. Also, sex education in schools has become compulsory. In 1974 abortion was legalized, despite a powerful Catholic-led opposition lobby, *Laissez-les-Vivre* (Let them live). Abortions within the first 10 weeks of pregnancy are now available under the health service, and though many Catholic doctors refuse to cooperate, there are enough of those who do so for the new law to be working fairly well. Some 180,000 legal abortions are carried out every year, while the number of illegal ones has fallen to an estimated 80,000.

The school system

In education, both in schools and universities, the French have been trying to adapt their highly academic and competitive system to the mass needs of a modern age, without letting standards fall too low. Any reform must come through the Ministry of Education, which tightly controls 83 percent of schools (most others are run by the Catholic Church). Although these state schools are free and open to all, by tradition many of the best *lycées* (high schools) in the big cities have tended to be middle-class preserves, and French social barriers and prejudices have often deterred workers from pushing their children very far up the educational ladder. Only 13 percent of the million or so students in higher education are from working-class homes. In efforts to make the system more equal in practice, postwar reforms have obliged all pupils to attend the same schools till the age of 15,

Above Edith Cresson, seen here attending a Socialist Party congress in 1981, was in 1991 the first woman to be appointed Prime Minister of France. She is a lifelong militant Socialist, but Mme Cresson comes from a well-to-do upper bourgeois family. Although an ardent feminist, she always dresses with true Parisian chic: when she was Minister of Agriculture in 1981–3, the rough French farmers nicknamed her *la parfumée* (the scented lady). She has often complained that there is an unfair male prejudice against women in politics in France; her own success has now helped a little to disprove this.

and have introduced modern-style mixed-ability classes where – in a sharp break with tradition – the academic grind is leavened with the learning of manual skills such as sewing and metalwork. Also, examinations have been made easier. Many teachers have now voiced their fears that the changes have gone too far, and that children are no longer being properly taught the basics of spelling, history and so on.

The French concept of education, traditionally, is not to develop the whole personality but to train the intellect rigorously, with the accent on rhetoric, style, deductive reasoning, and much encyclopedic knowledge. This system, with its stress on *culture générale* rather than early specialization, has molded an elite of technocrats who can later tackle any problem with the same clarity that they were taught to apply to a Racine text. The system is still largely in force in the senior classes of *lycées*, where life is lived in a shadow of that hallowed French institution, the *baccalauréat* leaving exam, the passport to a university. As people's social expectations have risen, the numbers attempting and passing the "*bac*" have grown steadily, from 7 percent of the age group in 1953 to 30 percent today. Under this populist pressure, the exam has gradually been made easier, though by most non-French standards it is still very tough and demanding. The Ministry has been trying to divert the less academically inclined away from the posh *lycées* into technical education: but this, unlike in Germany, has low prestige and the bourgeoisie tends to spurn it. The problem is, how to combine the old ideals of scholarship with new, broader social and economic needs.

The debate also centers on how a school should be run. Most schools used to have rigid discipline and a bureaucratic ambience (teachers in state schools are civil servants). Then followed the May '68 explosion, and for a year or two there was cheerful chaos. Now, a certain order has returned, but less strict than before. Teachers are more friendly and informal toward their pupils, putting more emphasis on group work and dialogue, and the pupils are more relaxed. But there is still little attempt to make a school into a living community, in an Anglo-Saxon way. Teachers tend to treat their job like an office job, and will seldom stay behind after class to organize clubs or cultural activities. To them, the children's out-of-school life and character development are the parents' responsibilities. Sport in schools has increased, it is true, but solely within school hours. Many *lycées* do not even have an orchestra, drama club or school magazine. Furthermore, there is no training in leadership or civic responsibility, as parents look on school as an academic utility that should not compete with them as a focus of loyalty. Indeed, much of the French mistrust of authority may well stem from attitudes inherited at school, where competitive academic individualism is still the touchstone. However, some younger teachers are beginning to adopt different modes, and in 1988 the Socialist government introduced new teacher-training programs to induce a more modern and community-minded ethos.

Higher education

Some of these school problems are echoed in higher education, whose most distinctive feature is the gulf between the privileged elite of the Grandes Ecoles – smallish colleges with a highly selective entry system – and the "student proletariat" of the overcrowded, amorphous universities, which tend to have low prestige. By tradition, anyone with the *bac* has the right to a university place. But, already by the 1960s, the numbers passing the *bac* far outstripped the funds and facilities allowed to the universities. This has led to a running crisis that was one of the main factors

Below Students sitting an examination in Bordeaux. As university entry is fairly easy, student numbers have swelled to over one million and there are not adequate funds for dealing with them. Lecture rooms and laboratories are overcrowded and most students have little personal contact with their professor, except at postgraduate level. A first degree is of little value, and many students face unemployment, or are forced to take jobs far below their abilities. There is little romance or fun about student life in France. Outside the teeming universities, however, there exists a group of elitist colleges, the Grandes Ecoles, which rigidly control their numbers and afford golden career prospects to those clever enough or lucky enough to pass their fiercely competitive entrance examinations.

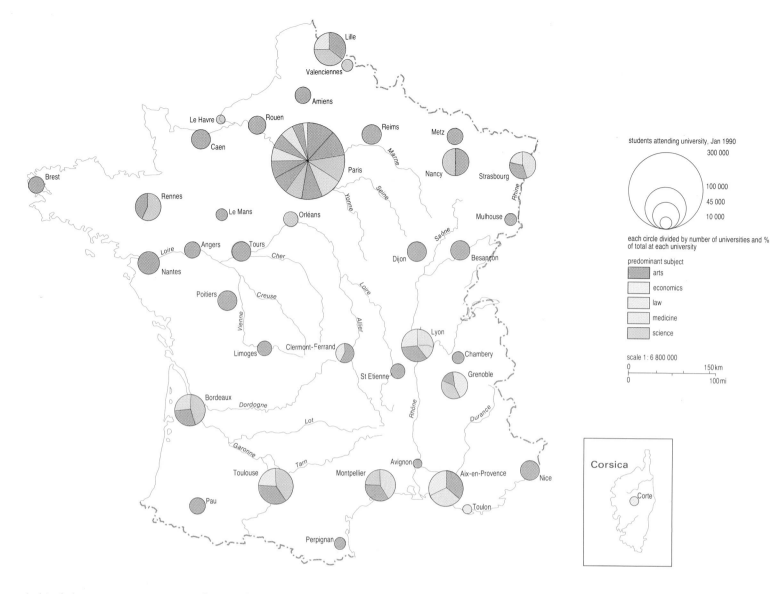

students attending university, Jan 1990

300 000

100 000
45 000
10 000

each circle divided by number of universities and %
of total at each university

predominant subject

arts
economics
law
medicine
science

scale 1 : 6 800 000

0   150 km
0   100 mi

Corsica

Corte

behind the May '68 uprising. Afterward, the government did make a few reforms to the structure, and the 77 or so French universities, almost all of them state-owned and previously under tight central control, now have some limited internal autonomy. There is also now more emphasis on group work and seminars, and teachers have become less remote and highhanded – another lesson of '68. But many faculties are still racked by political feuding.

The most serious problem is that overall student numbers have continued to rise. From 122,000 in 1939, they moved to 612,000 by 1968 and are today over a million, some 90 percent of the students being in the universities and the rest in technical colleges and Grandes Ecoles. In some disciplines, such as medicine, a *numerus clausus* has now been imposed, so that the *bac* no longer guarantees a place in the faculty of a student's choice, but he or she is still assured of a place somewhere. So strong is this tradition that politically it has not been possible to introduce an overall selective entry. Many students deselect themselves by dropping out after the first year; others survive the junior two-year degree course, but find that its diploma has little value on the job market. Indeed, graduate unemployment is a serious problem. Only the higher degrees, such as the prized *agrégation* or *maitrise*, really ensure a promising career. On the outskirts of towns, where the big modern campuses have been built, the students tend to lead lonely lives.

Their numbers are such that in the junior years they still have only minimal personal contact with their professors, and feel little inclination to create their own clubs or cultural activities, in the Anglo-Saxon manner (nor are they provided with the amenities for doing so). Very few students are today politically active. They work hard, they cling to their family life, they try to find part-time jobs to eke out their meager stipends, but they enjoy little of university life as an enriching experience. The government is thus caught between trying to preserve the old ideals of scholarship, answering the new populist demands for more higher education, and providing the economy with the trained specialists it needs.

Quite separate from the universities are the 150 or so Grandes Ecoles. These are also nearly all state-run, but each has much freedom and controls its numbers with its own highly competitive entrance examination, which requires two years' special study after the *bac*. Their privileged students have close contacts with their teachers, and are virtually assured of a good career — especially if they graduate from one of the more prestigious of these colleges, such as the mighty Ecole Polytechnique. This is one of the many Grandes Ecoles devoted to engineering or applied science; others are business and management schools, such as the Ecole des Hautes Etudes Commerciales, while the famous Ecole Normale Supérieure educates future professors in the humanities as much as in science. Not

French universities
Many of the universities have been created since the war in towns that had none before, such as Nice and Amiens. Almost all are state-owned. Under the 1969 reforms, universities were split into smaller units, so that many towns have two or three – and Paris, with its 300,000 students, has 13. Its famous Sorbonne, founded in 1253, is now simply the building housing the administration offices of a few of them. Many universities have split on political lines, and there is much feuding between professors in rival camps. Most universities teach a variety of subjects, but some have noted specialities. Montpellier's renowned medical faculty dates from the 13th century; Toulouse and Grenoble are noted for science; and Aix-en-Provence and Poitiers are famous for literature studies.

The Ecole Polytechnique
Known for short as "X" because of
its badge of two crossed cannon,
the Ecole Polytechnique is the most
prestigious of the handful of elite
colleges, the Grande Ecoles, that
soar above the mere universities
and provide France with much of
its top talent, in industry, finance
and the public service. Among its
many famous alumni is Valéry
Giscard d'Estaing, the former
French President, seen here as a
pupil (*above*). Founded in 1794,
Polytechnique was made a military
college by Napoleon, to train
engineers for the armed forces.
Today it is still run by the Ministry
of Defence, with a serving general
at its head. And "*les X*" go on
parade four times a year (*right*) in
full dress uniform, with swords and
strange curly hats. But apart from
this, little military spirit remains,
especially since the school's
transfer in 1976 from its monastic
home in central Paris to a breezy
modern one in the suburbs. Few
students opt today for a military
career: they are more likely to be
found running a bank or factory,
or near the top of some state
service. Since 1972 the college has
admitted women students. The
power of the graduates'
freemasonry remains as strong as
ever. An *X* in a senior position will
usually try to fill a vacancy on his
staff with another from the school,
or give that person preference in
business dealings. The closed-shop
camaraderie causes bitterness
among outsiders.

strictly speaking a Grande Ecole, but today as influential as any of them, the postgraduate Ecole Nationale d'Administration (ENA) was founded in 1946
to train senior civil servants.

These colleges account for only about 5 percent of
students in higher education, but they attract much of
the brightest young talent and produce a high proportion of France's top engineers and administrators. In
theory, they are open to all on merit, but in practice
their intake tends to be heavily middle class, especially
at ENA. Some of the more powerful colleges, such as
ENA, have exclusive old-boy networks that monopo-
lize the best jobs in some state services so that, if you
lack the right diploma, your way to promotion may be
permanently blocked. Whatever advantages this elitist
system may have in providing the state and the
economy with a pool of devoted talent, it is clearly
divisive, and its critics have long argued that the
Grandes Ecoles should be closer to the university
structure. Others disagree, and their view has prevailed, as the Grandes Ecoles retain their privileges.

ENA, "Polytechnique" and one or two other
grander colleges supply the recruits for that potent and
unique French phenomenon, *les Grands Corps de
l'Etat*. These are a dozen or so exclusive state club-like
bodies that operate parallel to the ministries; each has
a specific technical job, but, more crucially, their
informal function is to keep state and industry supplied with top talent. The *corps* are in two rival
groups, one administrative and economic, staffed
largely from ENA (the Inspection des Finances, Conseil d'Etat and Cour des Comptes are the leading
bodies), the other more technological and composed

largely of *polytechniciens* (one of its main bodies is the
Corps des Mines). Some members work within their
corps, but the more ambitious ones take key jobs
outside, at the head of bodies such as French Railways
or other state agencies and firms, or they enter politics.
Increasingly, today, some of the best are attracted by
the higher salaries in the private sector, where they can
be found running banks or industries. This archi-
complex system lies at the heart of France's technocratic prowess and the strength of its upper civil service.
But, as with the Grandes Ecoles, the barriers between
these elites and the less privileged public servants lead
inevitably to resentments, even to apathy, and this can
be counterproductive. Today, as the central power of
the state wanes, so the influence of the Grands Corps
and Grandes Ecoles is waning a little, too. In the new
consumer and service sectors, modern firms are
becoming readier to promote people on their merits
rather than for the elite diplomas they hold. However,
within the state apparatus itself, little has changed.
Governments, even Socialist ones, prefer to hold to a
trusted system that has served them well, rather than
risk reform. Indeed, many of their leaders are products
of the system: the Socialist Michel Rocard is himself
an Inspecteur des Finances.

Religion

Another French institution, the Catholic Church, has
seen huge transformations since the war. The old
central authority of the Church has waned, but a
new-style Christian spirit is taking lively and diverse
forms – perhaps a sign of the changed moral climate in
France, which is seen by some as a sad decline of old

firm and moral values, but by others as the rise of a new tolerance and openness.

Although since 1905 the state has been secular and the Church disestablished, its leaders, at least until the 1940s, identified closely with the upper bourgeoisie and defended the social status quo: in rural areas, priest and gentry were natural allies. Under the Occupation many bishops were pro-Vichy: yet, at the grassroots, profound change was under way. In the cities, some priests vowed to "devote their lives to the rechristianization of the working class", and from this came the radical worker–priest movement. Militant Catholic laymen took a lead in the Resistance, and after the war some of them founded influential social reform movements in the farming world and in industry. As a result, the Church shifted from its old rightist, antitemporal stance, and became more involved in social action. But at the same time, as in other countries, churchgoing declined. Today, most people still are married, baptized and buried by the Church, but weekly attendance at Mass is down to 14 percent (10 percent in Paris); the parish *curé* has lost much influence even in villages, and the priesthood is gravely short of new recruits. The Church, from being a central pillar of society, has become more like a dynamic minority pressure-group – or rather, a series of such groups, for there are rival tendencies. Some Catholics, rejecting formal churchgoing, have formed private "charismatic" groups or other fellowships that meet for prayer and discussion in private homes; others have moved into leftist social action on the worker–priest model; and, partly in reaction against this, other Catholics have turned to right-wing "integrism", in a bid to guard the old liturgical purities. Amid this turmoil, the Church hierarchy has become much less assertive, disciplined and unified: priests openly express different views on such matters as abortion and contraception.

As well as having lost much of its power, the Church has also lost its old enemies. The ancient Catholic–Huguenot conflict has now faded into history, in this ecumenical age of cordial relations with France's 3 percent Protestant minority. More important by, the old bitter feuding between clericals and anticlericals, which for over a century divided many villages, has now died out. Parliaments of the Third and Fourth Republics used to fight and bleed over the vexed issue of state aid given to Church-run schools, but today the two school systems coexist easily in most areas. Many of the teachers and pupils in the Church schools are non-Christian; many of those in the state system are Christian. If there is one last bastion of anticlericalism, it is the large teacher lobby in the Socialist Party, who in 1984 pressured the government to remove the Church schools' privileges and integrate them into the state system. This met with such a nationwide outcry, even from millions of non-Christians, that the parliamentary Bill was dropped. The issue was perceived as one not of religion, but of freedom of choice.

Young people and patriotism

While the role of the Church has declined, so too has the impact of other ideologies, even the youthful community ideals of the post-1968 period. This was followed, in the later 1970s, by the much-analyzed trend of *le repli sur soi* – the return to private satisfactions both hedonistic and spiritual, for instance the warmth of family and friends, nature and arts, good food and foreign travel. It was accompanied

by a greater dependence on personal resources and a cynicism about politics and other forms of public action. The booming 1980s, in France as in other countries, was the "yuppie" era when careerism, the cult of success, the spirit of personal enterprise, all came back into vogue among the serious-minded young. A leading media star and idol of the young in the late 1980s was Bernard Tapie, a showman entrepreneur, prophet of dynamic achievement. Twenty years earlier, the idols had been leftist philosophers like Jean-Paul Sartre, or stormers of barricades. In the *lycées*, bright pupils formed ambitions to start their own businesses, a trend that was welcomed in economic circles as the token of a new vitality and realism among French youth, though it seemed a long way from the old ideals of public or community service.

A few public causes, however, do still interest young people. They are noticeably readier than their elders to show solidarity with disfavored minorities and, after a slower start than in Germany or Britain, are now showing greater concern for ecology. The Green movement, bedevilled by its own internal conflicts, has been rather weak in France, and even the sit-ins against nuclear projects have made little impact on a public opinion that generally supports France's ambitious nuclear program and, for good or ill, is less anxious and hazard-conscious than are, for instance, the Germans. However, threats to the environment, such as ugly new buildings at beauty spots, are now being taken more seriously and the Green vote at elections has been increasing.

One of the most striking changes of the past 20 or so years is that the French have become much more international-minded, and for some of them a united

Above In the 1950s and 1960s, huge blocks of high-rise workers' flats, known as HLMs, were built on the outskirts of many towns, as here in Marseille. This was done in order to meet a severe housing shortage caused by prewar neglect and the mass exodus from the countryside. Few of the blocks were attractive; and their inhabitants, many of them ex-peasants, found it hard to adapt to living there. Today, new building of this kind is more modest and human in scale, and the flats are of better quality. Most French people would rather have a small house with a garden.

Right Teenagers outside a *lycée* (high school) in Tours. In the senior classes, life is lived under the shadow of the crucial *baccalauréat* leaving examination, but pupils still have time for fun. They go to discos, and the boys parade their *vélos* with *macho* pride. Promiscuity, among young people, common in the 1970s, has since declined, partly because of AIDS, but drugs are a problem in many urban areas.

Europe is now a kind of ideal. The old flag-waving patriotism, epitomized by de Gaulle, has waned very sharply. Younger people, though still attached to the French way of life, do not share this vision, and the opinion polls bear this out. When Americans in a national survey were asked "Do you feel very proud to be American?", 80 percent of them said "yes". The corresponding figures were 55 percent for Britons, 41 percent for Italians but only 33 percent for the French, who scored little higher than the Japanese (30 percent) and West Germans (21 percent), two peoples still obviously subdued in their national pride.

French foreign policy can still be assertive in defence of national interests, especially outside Europe, and the French remain highly competitive toward other peoples, while within Europe France has been keen to retain a dominant role in the European Community. This competitiveness, however, is closely allied to a real spirit of cooperation – a more healthy attitude than the insularity and protectionism that were so common before. In the new Europe, young people travel abroad with little sense of frontiers, and businesspeople are forced to think in European terms.

This change is especially noticeable in attitudes to speaking other languages. As theirs was once the leading world language of culture and diplomacy, many French are, of course, resentful at its having been eclipsed by English; and in de Gaulle's time public servants were forbidden to speak anything but French at international meetings. But now the French have decided that, in the interests of their foreign trade and their position in the world, they have no choice but to use the world's leading language, as others are doing. Thousands of firms have promoted in-service

language courses for their staffs, and foreign language classes are now compulsory in universities and at most school levels, with 83 percent of students making English their first choice. As a result, especially in business circles, the majority of young educated French people now speak English, which was not the case 20 years ago.

France and its neighbors

The European Community (EC) has long been accepted as part of the landscape. According to recent surveys, 61 percent of the French think membership has been good for their country, and only 5 percent think it bad – much the same proportions as in Italy, Germany and Benelux. "Europe" today is in vogue, and even though few people have a clear idea of what the complex "1992" single-market operation really involves, most of them back the official policy of close EC integration; among political parties, only the National Front and the Communists, and a fraction of the Gaullists, are opposed. A survey in 1989 showed that 78 percent of the people favored European monetary and political union, while among the under-25s the figure rose to 89 percent, and among executives it was 92 percent. More than half wanted a European Government, with only 27 percent hostile to the idea. Why should a people historically so proud of their nationhood today seem ready to accept so much loss of sovereignty? By and large, they have come to believe that France can best retain its influence by joining a bigger European unit and by trying, through positive cooperation, to retain a major role in its leadership. This new-style patriotism extends even to official cultural policy, for the government recently invited hundreds of European intellectuals and writers to an ambitious conference in Paris on "European cultural identity".

France's change of attitude toward its neighbors is most marked in its relations with the Germans. Ever since the war, official policy in both Paris and Bonn has encouraged reconciliation, through well-funded youth exchanges, town-twinnings and other activities; and today it seems that the old hatreds have largely died away, except among some French Jews and older people who suffered directly at Nazi hands. In the main, the qualities of the Germans are admired, and the school exchanges work well. The unification of Germany has led to some misgivings among some leftist intellectuals and older people, as well as to fears that the balance of power in the EC will be tilted away from France. But generally the French accept the official view, that unity is the Germans' right, and that within a tightly integrated Europe assertive neo-nationalism need not be a danger.

French attitudes to Britain are more ambivalent. On the one hand, many things British carry a snob-appeal – from the Savile Row suits, malt whiskies and nursemaids imported by the upper classes, to the popular music, casual clothes and slang in vogue with teenagers, not forgetting the fascination with British royalty. On the other hand, there is not much interest in what Britain is really like as a modern society; it is considered too "different", too much a special case, to be worthy of serious study as are, say, the Germans, Americans or even Russians. Yet, as the success of town-twinnings shows, when the British and French take the trouble to get to know each other, and stay in one anothers' homes, the mutual prejudices melt away. Since 1972, the number of such twinnings has

Religion Today

Christianity in France is predominantly Catholic, and the Protestants account for only about 3 percent (there are also important Jewish and Muslim minorities). However, the role of the Church has been changing since World War II. As fewer people attend Mass and society becomes more secular, so the Church has been losing its wider conventional influence, but gaining a new one as a militant pressure group of true, dedicated Catholic believers.

In the years after the war, new Catholic lay movements played a large part in social reform, and in forging a new idealistic spirit of progress. These new-style leaders were influenced by Teilhard de Chardin and his optimistic philosophy, and by Emmanuel Mounier who urged all Christians to engage in improving the world. Active alike in farming, industry and commerce, the neo-Catholics were the spiritual leaven in the material modernization of France.

At the same time, churchgoing has declined. The proportion of children baptized has fallen from 90 percent to less than 50 percent since the 1950s; attendance at Mass can still reach 80 percent in some rural areas, but in industrial centers it can drop to 4 or 5 percent. Despite the efforts of worker-priests, the Church has largely lost touch with the working class. It also faces a severe lack of new recruits to the clergy: only about 100 are being ordained each year, against about 1000 in the 1960s. Significantly, perhaps, over 85 percent of today's priests are said to oppose compulsory celibacy for the clergy.

Nevertheless, among practicing lay Christians there has been a sharpening of the faith; and the old local pageants, festivals and pilgrimages are maintained with varying motives. The patriotic Bretons at the *pardons*, the old-style pious Catholics who go to Lourdes, and the young, eager ecumenicists at the Taizé rallies, are three different kinds of Christian.

Some new religious communities are blossoming. L'Arche, founded by a disciple of Mahatma Gandhi, is based in a remote Languedoc mansion: here young people from many nations live the simple life, pooling their money and possessions. They campaign not just against war and violence, but against profit, machines and other perceived evils of modern society.

Above right Sick people hoping for a miracle cure are among the crowds of pilgrims outside the church in Lourdes, near the Pyrenees. In 1858 Bernadette Soubirous, aged 14, daughter of a local miller, claimed that the Virgin had appeared to her near a grotto; these visions were followed by miraculous gushing of water. Bernadette was canonized in 1933, and today more than 3 million pilgrims a year flock to Lourdes. Many miraculous cures have been claimed. The main pilgrimage, on 15 August includes spectacular torchlight processions.

Left One of the largest of Breton *pardons* is held in August at the little chapel of Ste Anne-la-Palud, on the Finistère coast. The *pardon* is a Christian festival unique to Brittany, when people pay tribute to their local saint, or make a special vow. Clergy and costumed pilgrims parade with candles, banners and statues of saints. *Pardons* are a typical expression of the piety of Bretons, who have created hundreds of their own saints.

Below The late Monseigneur Marcel Lefèbvre, kneeling at the altar, is here seen ordaining "integrist" priests at his "traditionalist" seminary in Switzerland. The integrist movement, a return to ideological purity, developed in France as a reaction against modern forms of liturgy and Catholic social action. It was condemned by the Pope, who forbade Lefèbvre to say Mass or ordain his own priests: but he went ahead. Lefèbvre died in 1990, but his deeply conservative movement goes on, with the support of maybe some 10 percent of French Catholics.

Left Young pilgrims outside the modern church at Taizé, in Burgundy, Europe's leading ecumenical center. Founded in 1940 by a Swiss pastor, it provides a forum where Protestants, Catholics and others, priests and laity alike, live, pray and work together. Taizé has fired the imagination of new generations of Christians, and up to 40,000 young pilgrims of all nations camp on its hillside at rallies and Christian festivals. The Pope and Archbishop of Canterbury have been among its visitors. Taizé has played a leading part in postwar reconciliation between France's Catholics and its 3 percent Protestant minority.

Above The seaside town of les Saintes Maries, in the Camargue, lies at the heart of old legends about Christianity's arrival in Provence. A boat without sails or oars is said to have come ashore here from the Holy Land, bearing the Virgin's sister St Mary Jacobe, St Mary Salome, St Mary Magdalene, other saints, and their African servant Sara who became the patroness of the gypsies. At the great gypsy festival here in May, the statues of Mary Jacobe and Mary Salome, in a little boat, are taken from the high fortified church and carried down to the sea and back again. Two days of Provencal merriment then follow.

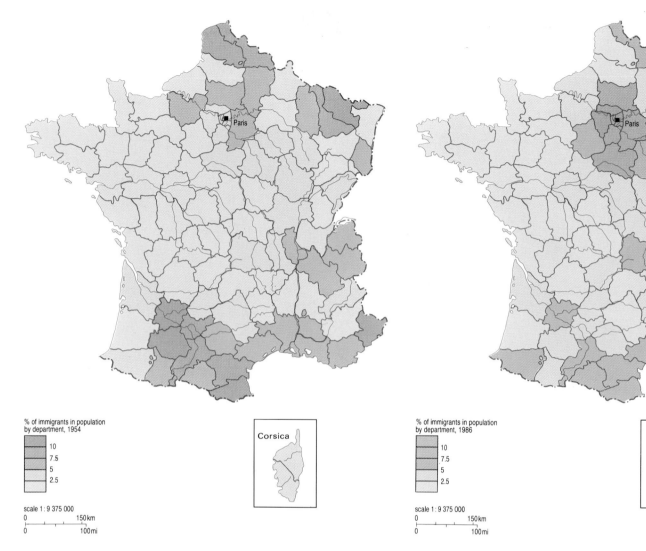

% of immigrants in population
by department, 1954

10
7.5
5
2.5

scale 1 : 9 375 000
0   150 km
0   100 mi

Corsica

% of immigrants in population
by department, 1986

10
7.5
5
2.5

scale 1 : 9 375 000
0   150 km
0   100 mi

Corsica

risen from 150 to over 300, but is still well behind that of the Franco-German total, which is some 600.

Racial tensions

Although now good Europeans, the French have in some ways grown more racist, and this today is a major problem and talking-point. Before the war, most foreigners in France, whites and others, were eyed with some hostility: but today the long-established European minorities are much more warmly accepted, and anti-Semitism has declined too. Moreover, France has a good record of aid to the Third World (thousands of teachers, doctors, technicians and others work abroad on aid schemes) and a fine tradition of granting asylum to political refugees, from Latin America and Indochina as well as Eastern Europe. But the public has become much less generous toward the large nonwhite groups within France, mostly North African Muslims. Some 4.5 million foreigners live in France, many of them migrants who came to find jobs during the boom years and have since put down roots. The main white minorities – the Portuguese (860,000), Italians (425,000) and Spanish (380,000) – are all easily accepted, but frictions have been growing with the Algerians (780,000), Moroccans (520,000) and Tunisians (215,000).

Until recently, the North African minorities, though never encouraged to integrate socially, coexisted quietly with the French and tensions were few, even during the Algerian war. However, since the early 1980s, rising unemployment has led to accusations that the Muslims are taking jobs from the French – and this has fueled the rise of the extreme-right racist National Front under Jean-Marie Le Pen. The Muslims are also feared for their very high birthrate, as many primary schools become filled with brown faces, and for their alien customs, as scare stories have spread of sheep being slaughtered in bathrooms. Pro-Iranian fundamentalists who have fomented strikes of Arab workers, or tried to prevent the immigrants, especially young women, from adopting French customs, have only made matters worse. Tensions have been greatest in southeast France, where the large repatriate *pied noir* community has continued the old colonial feud, venting its anger on the Muslims who "robbed" them of Algeria. But there has been trouble too in the Paris area, where the immigrants, living in high-rise working-class ghettos, are shunned and despised by the French. One immigrant worker said that in 26 years he had never once been invited into a French home.

The Socialist government has taken some steps to try to ease daily life for Muslims. It improved their welfare rights, and ordered the police to be less brutal in questioning suspected illegal immigrants, who are very numerous. All governments have also tried to bribe foreign workers to return to their country of origin, but this has not had much success. Many of the younger ones were born in France and have little desire to go to live in a very poor Algeria where they might feel equally out of place. The one hopeful development is that many young French people have

been shocked by their elders' racism and have launched a national campaign of support and solidarity for young North Africans in France.

Compared with the North Africans, the 650,000 or so Blacks in France have an easier time. Most of them come from the Caribbean *départements* of Guadeloupe and Martinique, so they are full French citizens; many are educated and middle-class, whereas the Arabs are mostly proletarian; and the French tend to find them more easygoing and friendly than the Muslims, and with a more emancipated attitude to women.

France's 700,000-strong Jewish community is the largest in Europe outside the Soviet Union. Anti-Semitism has a grim history in France – witness Dreyfus – and few citizens did much to prevent 117,000 French Jews being sent to the Nazi gas chambers. This has left a sense of remorse, and in the main anti-Semitism has now died down. When Arab terrorists have attacked synagogues or kosher restaurants in Paris, big public rallies have expressed their solidarity with French Jews. Even so, among Le Pen supporters some latent anti-Semitism lingers, and occasionally fringe neofascist groups have committed outrages, such as the desecration of Jewish cemeteries.

Life-styles

French life-styles have centered traditionally on the long leisurely meal with good food and good conversation in a big family gathering, whose concern for wit, style and originality is greater than for efficiency and tidiness. Visitors often remark on such outward symbols of Frenchness as the long, crispy *baguette* loaf, the rough, strong *Gauloise* cigarette, the game of *boules* and the bathroom *bidet*. Modern economic and social change has had little effect on the old picturesque way of life in some ways; in others, such as

the use of gadgetry, the impact has been very great.

As France modernized, a superficial Americanization spread fast in the 1960s and 1970s, and today some of its results appear odd in a French context – the fast-food and hamburger bars found on some main streets (including the Champs-Elysées), the rock stars with American-sounding names and, above all, the invasion of the French language by the hybrid "newspeak" known as *franglais*. Many English words for which there was thought to be no real French equivalent, such as *le weekend*, *le marketing*, *le cash-flow* and *le check-up*, are now in daily use, while some verbs have been Frenchified, for example, *elle est interviewée* (she is interviewed). But the *franglais* craze, which infuriated the purists, is now past its peak, except in business circles. Although, in some respects, the tendency was certainly ludicrous and overdone, French, like any language, needed to remain receptive to foreign imports if it was not to become sterile. (In English, for example, there are *cafés* and *maisonnettes*, just as the French have *le snack* and *le parking*; the purists must accept this.)

To many modern activities the French have managed to bring their own flair, taste and creativity. The small personal local store has often been ousted by the new massive hypermarket, but this is invariably crammed with French cheeses, charcuterie and fresh vegetables, rather than with American-style packaged goods. Similarly, *le drugstore* may have borrowed an American formula of late-closing multipurpose shopping, but its style owes more to Paris than to any New York pharmacy. Perhaps most inventive of all, to replace their quaint old men-only outdoor urinals (*pissotières*) the French have devised the ultra-hygienic unisex *sanisette* – an example of true Gallic creativity which is now found in other countries.

However, it is in the countryside that life-styles and

attitudes have changed most dramatically. The mechanization of the farms, and the great increase in their
average size caused by the massive rural exodus and
the sale of land, have transformed local life. The
old-style peasant, poor and backward, suspicious and
hyperindividualistic, is everywhere disappearing; and
a new, modern-minded generation has emerged, more
dynamic and prosperous, much readier to use up-to-
date marketing methods and to share facilities – in
short, more businessperson than peasant. Such farmers did exist before, on the big wheat-plains of the
north, but they were few; now they are the majority.

Of course, this bright picture is not universal. On
the arid Breton uplands, and in parts of the Massif
Central, peasants can still be found eking a living from
useless polyculture, with a cow or two, some mangy
chickens and antiquated barn-like housing. But these
are mostly elderly people, the young having long since
left. Yet, though most farmers today have far wider
horizons and more mobility, perhaps some of the old
local human warmth, bred of poverty, has at the same
time been lost. In the old days, in Breton farmsteads
young people would draw round the stove on winter
evenings to hear grannies reciting Celtic legends; in the
Auvergne, villagers would gather in one farm to weave
baskets or shred maize, and make it the excuse for a
party. At harvest time, scores of seasonal laborers
would hold noisy parties every night: today, a
combine-harvester does their job and the workers are
in the local factories. Now that all farmers have cars,

Left A customer in a Paris shoe shop. Small, smart boutiques of this kind still do well, but a dominant trend of recent years has been the rise of the hypermarkets. These American-style emporia can be found on the outskirts of most towns, and they are the largest stores of their kind in Europe, with up to 70 checkouts. They sell furniture, toys, kitchen and electrical goods, as well as food and drink in amazing profusion. Their range of traditional French produce, such as charcuterie, cheeses, fresh fruit and vegetables, is usually excellent. And they have wooed the French housewife away from the old local corner shops, thousands of which have been forced to close.

Below Traditional outdoor food markets, like this one in Paris, continue to flourish in most towns, despite the hypermarkets. Their little stalls sell fresh produce direct from the farms, and they provide a picturesque ambience and personal touch valued by their customers.

and their children have *vélos* (mopeds), social activity in the country towns or big villages has regrouped around the discotheques, dance halls and modern sports centers. And country people now wear modern clothes, not their traditional costumes, except on occasions such as weddings or special festivals.

However, in the past 10 or 20 years, with the battle for modernization now largely won, some people, particularly from the newer generation, have been seeking to revive some of the old rural traditions. This interest is, in part, the legacy of May 1968, and is linked also to the revival of regional awareness. A few of those who of necessity migrated to the cities after the war have been trying to come back to their *pays* – not to work on the farms, for economically that is seldom possible (indeed, the rural exodus is still going on, if more slowly), but to find other jobs – in tourism, or crafts or local industry. Modern technology has made it far more feasible than in the old days to run a small factory in a rural location. In addition, some long-time city-dwellers, smitten by a yen for country life, have been migrating to the villages, to try to make a living as potters, weavers or other craftworkers, or to try their hand (less successfully) at goat-breeding or other upland farming. Besides these, there are the hundreds of thousands of middle-class Parisians and others who have bought up old cottages or farmsteads and use them as weekend, holiday or retirement homes. Some stay aloof from local life, but others make real efforts to get to know the country people and their customs, and so, to some extent they become countrified. Often, farmers convert barns or outhouses into *gîtes* (lodgings which they rent to townspeople for rural holidays), and as a result many lasting friendships are made, further narrowing the old gulf between peasant and towndweller.

Many of the migrants to the country, and the local people too, are concerned to help preserve its heritage. They restart old folk festivals, or sometimes try to revive dying handicrafts, and regularly spend time and money on restoring the old rural homes they have bought, or other fine buildings falling into ruin. This trend to preserve and improve France's *patrimoine* (heritage) became very marked in the 1980s and won much official support, embracing towns as well as country areas. While the downtown parts of cities have their share of modern glass-and-steel constructions, much work has been done to embellish and restore the lovely older buildings, and to make these areas into attractive, neatly paved pedestrian zones. In the Marais district of Paris, and elsewhere, it is now fashionable among well-to-do people to live in such places, rather than in the smart suburbs.

The French, at heart, are either country people or city-center dwellers, and since the war they have not found it easy to adapt to living in modern suburbs. In the 1950s and 1960s a large number of graceless high-rise estates were erected hurriedly on the edge of Paris and other towns, to house the rural emigrants, slum evacuees and others. The most notorious of these was Sarcelles, just north of Paris, an austere gridiron of gray box-like blocks. At first, these dormitories were poorly provided with shops and other amenities, or with local employment outlets, that could make life easier for their inhabitants, many of whom had to commute long distances to work. But since about the early 1970s, as standards have risen, the new suburbs have been better designed, and more thought has been given to supplying them from the outset with shops

and schools, cafés and sports centers, bus services to the city and, if possible, local light industries. The value of such improvements is seen when the ugly Sarcelles is compared with a more recent "new town" in the Paris area such as Cergy-Pontoise.

Community relations

The much-discussed *ennui* of the suburbs was the fault not only of the planners and designers, but also of the inhabitants, who were cautious about making friends and sharing resources and found adaptation very difficult, psychologically. The rural emigrants missed the warmth of their old tight-knit village communities, where rival families might feud and bicker, but at least had known each other for centuries. Similarly, the huge numbers evacuated from insanitary slum tenements, under rehousing programs in Paris and elsewhere, liked their new little modern flats, but missed the old neighborliness of the slums. In particular, housewives would grow bored and lonely, and some would even nostalgically trek long distances to their old home areas, to do their weekly shopping and see familiar faces. It hardly occurred to them to make friends with their new neighbors down the stairway, as British or Americans would have done.

In each suburb, a few dedicated do-gooders, mostly left-wing or Catholic activists with some education, or social workers, would try to forge a new sense of community that might coax people out of their solitude. They founded all kinds of clubs, crèches and get-togethers, but the response was not great, and most people preferred to hug their privacy. The new craze for television discouraged the old habit of café-going, and the few cafés that dared to spring up in the new spiritual wasteland were mostly drab, uninviting places. To complicate matters, many of the do-gooders were politically motivated and quarreled among themselves, so that those whom they were trying to help suspected them of ulterior motives.

Because French social life has always tended to center on the family, or the café, or professional contacts, the people are not used to an Anglo-American style of club or community activity or voluntary self-help movements. In recent years, especially in the new suburbs, they have been trying to develop what they call *la vie associative* (clubs, private welfare, pressure groups and so on), but it has not been easy. In this legalistic land, any private initiative is regarded with mistrust unless it secures official approval by adhering to the complex statutes of 1901 that govern all non-profit-making bodies, from arts centers to old people's clubs. But, with the role of the Church now in decline, and officialdom often short of funds or initiative, citizens are coming to realize that they ought to do more to organize things themselves rather than expect all the money and the work to come from the *mairie* (mayor's office) or some state body. The more disinterested do-gooders are, in fact, making progress with genuine community ventures, and the migrants to the new suburbs have finally put down roots and made local friends. Some of these new towns are now quite lively with good human relations. But the process has been slow and traumatic.

The home

It has also taken time to solve the French housing shortage, which in the 1950s was catastrophic. A long legacy of neglect meant that most people were living in archaic conditions, and not much new housing was yet being built, for the postwar priority was industrial recovery. The 1954 census showed that only 10 percent of French homes had a bath or shower, and only 27 percent had flushing toilets. A crash building program followed, and by 1984 the proportion of homes with a bath or shower had risen to 88 percent, and those with an indoor flushing toilet to 89 percent. People have become more concerned for comfort, and readier to spend money on it. The average share of family income devoted to rent or mortgage, and other basic charges, has risen since the war from the incredibly low figure of 3.4 percent (the result largely of low-pegged rents) to over 25 percent, bringing France into line with Britain or Germany. In the towns, most people live in flats, but new villas have been spreading in the suburbs as more of the French realize their dream of a house with a garden.

The middle and upper classes tend to furnish their homes either in striking modern style or else in the classic tradition, with heavy period-style furniture or with antiques and spindly Louis XV chairs. None of these styles is exactly cosy, but the French care less about furniture than about modern consumer durables. Their love of gadgetry, and in particular of electrical goods, has put them in the lead in Europe, ahead of the Germans. Since 1954 the proportion of homes with refrigerators has risen from 7 to 97 percent, with washing machines from 8 to 83 percent, with color televisions from 0 to 69 percent, and with cars from 21 to 73 percent.

The most striking technical change has been in the public telephone service. Until the mid-1970s, France had only one-fifth as many lines per capita as Sweden, and fewer than Greece, and a private applicant had to wait, on average, 16 months for an installation. The state was then ambitiously experimenting with highly advanced electronic schemes, such as videophones, but could not be bothered to meet the public's simple daily needs. Finally, a crash program brought the number of lines up to British and German levels, and today the system works well and is fully automatic. The government has even gone further, providing millions of homes, free of charge, with the famous Minitel, a French-made videotex service that links into the big central computer banks and serves as an electronic telephone directory. As a consequence, many people, bored and lonely or just perverted, use the Minitel to dial other subscribers anonymously and conduct pornographic conversations on the screens: this has become a major nationwide game.

Another remarkable change has been in the patterns of domestic spending. Expenditure on food and drink accounted for 50 percent of the average family budget before the war, but today only 21 percent, even though, in real terms, it is still rising. But this has been eclipsed by the vast new sums spent on holidays, homes, clothes, "health and hygiene", and *le bricolage* (do-it-yourself). Indeed, improved home comforts plus television have meant that people visit cafés much less than they used to. The big terrace-cafés still do well at apéritif-time, or from tourists, but there have been thousands of closures of the kind of little local *bistrot* where, once, groups of men would sit in the evening, debating and gossiping.

Eating and drinking
Lunch is traditionally the main meal of the day, but its role has been waning, except for Sundays. Until about the late 1950s, Paris and other cities went dead for two

Left In a land with more than 300 different cheeses, some bearing famous names like Camembert, Brie and Roquefort, cheese is considered an important part of a serious meal; and it is always eaten *before* the dessert, accompanied by red wine. This cheese store in Reims is typical of the thousands of small speciality food shops that cater for the revival of interest in serious cuisine, at least for special occasions. The French still prefer fresh foods, and remain wary of canned or frozen goods.

hours, as all offices and even the big stores closed, and everyone went home for a leisurely family lunch. However, migration to the far suburbs, coupled with other modern pressures, began to make this impractical, so firms staggered lunches, opened canteens, or gave vouchers, and gradually a shorter lunch-break has been adopted. Nevertheless, many shops and banks still close completely for an hour. In smaller towns in the drowsy south, near to Spain and its siestas, everything still shuts up from twelve till two, including post offices and hypermarkets. But generally, it is realized that however delightful a long lunch may be for those taking part, it can be maddening for a visitor, and also harmful to the economy. Although many now leave work a little earlier, as a result of the changed routine, the French remain conservative about their dinner time, which in all classes of household rarely begins before 8 p.m. After this, not much of the evening is left, which may help to explain why there is not more weekday social and club activity in the new suburbs.

The French, however, have become less conservative about what and how they eat – though not always with the best results. Good cooking has long been central to the French way of life, in a land whose cuisine has rightly been judged to be the world's best, based on regional dishes of exceptional variety and subtlety. Today, on the one hand, young people line up for *le fast-food*, frozen and canned goods make inroads, and ordinary restaurants' standards become more erratic. On the other, there is much talk of a renaissance of French cuisine: the quality restaurants are fuller than ever, and the top chefs of so-called *nouvelle cuisine* are idolized like film stars.

French eating habits are becoming strangely polarized. The middle classes, at least, used to eat really well every day as a matter of routine, especially at home. But, to a modern nation in a hurry, daily meals both in and out of the home have become more

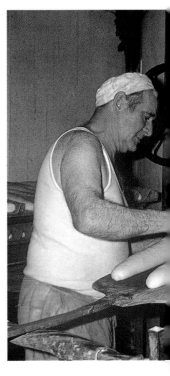

Above Those long thin *baguettes* of French bread have a special quality, with their crispy crusts and chewy insides. Modern industrial baking, with over-bleached flour and too-swift fermentation, has been lowering their quality. But some small local bakers have now launched a crusade to keep up standards, and many rural areas still have their own delicious varieties of country bread.

Wine and brandy production
Wines are carefully graded and controlled by the government. The better grades, which must come from a precise area and indicate that on their label, are known as *Vins d'Appellation d'Origine Contrôlée*. Some 40 percent of French wine, mostly table wine, comes from the southeast in Languedoc; the main areas producing quality wines are Burgundy and around Bordeaux. The best brandies come from the Armagnac and Cognac districts, but many other areas have their local *eau-de-vie*. Apple spirit (*calvados*) comes from Normandy in the north, which is outside the wine producing area; good fruit liqueurs are produced in Alsace in the northeast.

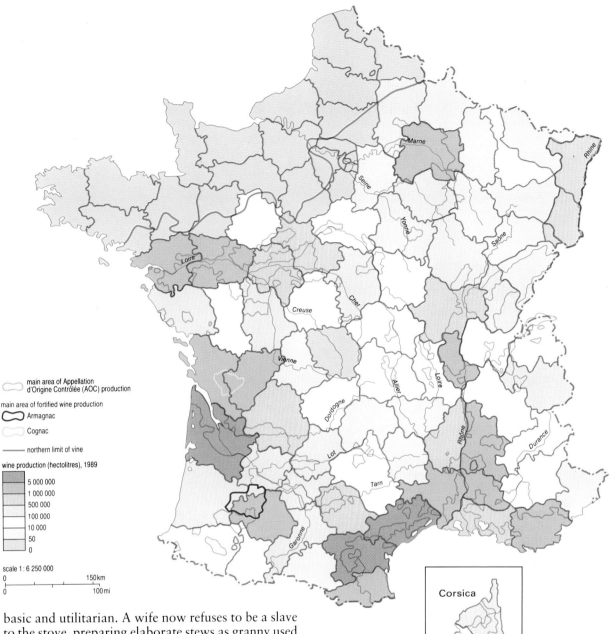

main area of Appellation d'Origine Contrôlée (AOC) production

main area of fortified wine production
Armagnac
Cognac

northern limit of vine

wine production (hectolitres), 1989
5 000 000
1 000 000
500 000
100 000
10 000
50
0

scale 1 : 6 250 000
0 — 150km
0 — 100mi

Corsica

basic and utilitarian. A wife now refuses to be a slave to the stove, preparing elaborate stews as granny used to do. Instead, she will grill a steak or open a can, and watch television. Ordinary restaurants, too, faced with rising costs, cut corners with mass-cooking techniques, and their customers accept it. Yet the French love of gastronomy has not vanished; it has merely taken a new turn, or is reserved for the once- or twice-a-week special occasion, the dinner party at home for friends, the ritual Sunday family lunch, or the really good restaurant meal with a loved one. The luxury foodshops, the serious cookbooks, the little bistros that take real trouble to keep up the old standards, all do a roaring trade. When they wish to, the French still eat better than any other nation, and they talk about food with great expertise, in a way that an Anglo-Saxon might find boring, or even distasteful.

The prime motor for the new gastronomic trends, though not the only one, has been nouvelle cuisine, which emerged in the mid-1960s and has so much influenced sophisticated cooking both in France and abroad. Led by a few youngish regional owner-chefs, such as Paul Bocuse near Lyon, Michel Guérard near Pau, Roger Vergé near Cannes, the movement was a reaction against the classic repertoire that allowed no scope for inventiveness, and against the heavy sauces and high calories of grand-hotel haute cuisine. It

marked a return to a lighter, purer manner, using very fresh, high-quality ingredients cooked in their own juices, to bring out their flavors. This attuned with a new diet-conscious mood of the French public, who wanted smaller meals, less likely to produce the *crise de foie* – that occupational liver disease of the middle-aged Frenchman.

The nouvelle cuisine chef is expected to deviate from classic recipes and try out daring new combinations, such as oysters cooked with leeks, or foie gras with apple. In the hands of a great chef, using seasonal local produce, nouvelle cuisine can be sublime, but in lesser hands (of which these are many) it can amount to no more than bland-tasting minuscule portions arranged over-decoratively around the plate. Yet, as this style is still in vogue with a moneyed clientele, many owner-chefs can get away with charging high prices. Indeed, nouvelle cuisine is never cheap, and its excesses have been much criticized. It has, however,

The Taste of France

Haute cuisine evolved from French regional cookery, "invented" in country kitchens through the ages. With rudimentary roads and no system of transportation, food in bygone days had to be grown easily and reared (or caught) locally. Geography dictated the ingredients – not least the cooking fats.

From Poitou-Charentes, across the north and down into Burgundy and Franche-Comté, lush pasture ensured fat cattle – so butter became a prime ingredient. Dairy produce was plentiful in the east, too, with the Vosges mountains and the Alps providing good grassland in high summer. A temperate climate encouraged fruit and vegetables.

The stony *garrigues* of Provence and the hot harsh landscapes stretching west across the Rhône into Languedoc-Roussillon did not favor cattle-rearing, and the prime source of meat and cheese were goats. But the olive thrives in this unpromising soil, and its oil became the mainstay of the southern kitchens. Heat-loving herbs, tomatoes, peppers, garlic and citrus fruits vividly flavored the region's cooking.

Much of central and southwest France was impenetrable forest or wild windy upland, and therefore impossible for conventional crops. Chestnut or maize flour often stood in for wheat. Peasant women raised quick-growing pigs and geese, whose abundant fat flavored every dish, even sweet ones. By chance, the lentils and beans (fresh or dried) that also grow here are perfect for offsetting the richness of these meats. In the far southwest, the Basques have also had the widest choice of cuisine styles. Fertile land, in an ideal climate, seems to grow anything.

Game, in the country's extensive woodlands, provided extra protein everywhere, and so did water. The English Channel and Atlantic teemed with seafood of all kinds: there were tunny, sardines and anchovies in the Mediterranean and even its bony rockfish were good for soup and *bouillabaisse*. Further bounty, from great salmon through eels to freshwater crayfish, came from France's magnificent rivers.

Right Dawn landing: silvery sardines, fresh or preserved, have been an important protein source in the south.

Center right Partridge served with butter-fried apple slices and a cream sauce. Butter is used for cooking everything in Normandy and other cattle-rich regions. Fruit with meat has been popular all over France. When fresh fruit was not available, dried fruit was used instead, for example, prunes in the plum-growing southwest, raisins in grape regions, or pears and apricots from one's own garden.

Below Garlic is probably France's most famous flavor, and nowadays grows nearly all over the country. Said to have almost magical medicinal powers, it is used cooked or raw, with or without the skin, not only as flavoring but for sauces, stuffings for birds, or even baked whole as a vegetable.

Left Small mussels stuffed with garlic-and-herb butter and served with cider. Shellfish are plentiful around the English Channel and Atlantic shores. They are especially famous in Brittany, eaten straight from the sea or lightly grilled.

Far right Bean and lentil dishes are warming, and complementary to the rich flesh of the pig or goose. They originated in central and southwestern areas, where there are many varieties of *cassoulet*. The flavor and richness of the fat, pork sausage and *confit* of goose is absorbed by the white beans during long, slow cooking. Foie gras and truffles – expensive luxuries today – were readily available to humble peasants: extra maize for the goose provided one, the others were free for the finding.

Below right "Waste not" has always been the French cook's motto. As with the household pig ("everything used but the squeak"), nothing pulled from sea, lake or river is discarded. If fish is too small or bony to be cooked in the usual way, it can be fried whole such as whitebait as *petite friture*, or used in fragrant soups and stews. *Cotriade, matelote* and *bouillade* are some important versions from the north and inland regions. Most famous of all is *bouillabaisse*, made from spiny rockfish, tiny crabs, and crayfish and other shellfish from the Mediterranean. Ingredients are the subject of much controversy, but olive oil and saffron feature in most recipes.

rejuvenated a tired classic haute cuisine, and revived interest in gastronomy. In fact, the better nouvelle chefs are using old regional recipes as a basis for their innovations, resulting in a subtle blend of old and new.

The new style seldom finds its way into daily home cooking, however, and has had little effect on cheaper restaurants, or on the traditional regional ones in a land where cuisine has strong peasant roots. There are still clear distinctions between *cuisine paysanne* (country cooking, using simple ingredients, but often spicy and subtle), *cuisine bourgeoise* (the solid home fare of the middle classes) and expensive haute cuisine, a mainly 19th-century elaboration by chefs such as Auguste Escoffier, of which nouvelle cuisine is a variant. Serious good eating in France is not a bourgeois importation, as it tends to be in Anglo-Saxon countries: the working class cares greatly about its food, and now has more money to spend on it. In many factories, unions and works committees are more exacting about the quality of the canteen's food than about most other aspects of working conditions: subtle, classic dishes, carefully cooked, regularly appear on their menus.

The French have also been discovering foreign cuisines, which previously they despised, and this has modified their old rooted belief in other nations' culinary inferiority. During their holidays abroad they have found that Spanish, Turkish or Hungarian food is not as coarse and unsubtle as they once thought, and they may even try out a goulash or paella at their dinner parties. Also, foreign restaurants, and not only the ubiquitous Italian and Chinese, have been spreading in many towns. So too have the snack-bar and the burger-bar and, more generally, the American-style normalization of foodstuffs, to the detriment of quality. French consumers may have proved relatively resistant to frozen foods and canned vegetables, but the broiler has begun to oust the farm-reared chicken, tomatoes and carrots are grown on fertilizers, making them larger and prettier but not tastier, and chewy French bread is losing some of its quality. However, the better shops and restaurants find ways round these problems.

Drinking habits have been changing, too. The old French convention that no meal is complete without wine has been losing ground. Many people now take mineral water instead, which is considered healthier: its sales have trebled since 1960, while those of fruit juices have quadrupled. Fruit juice costs twice as much as cheap wine, which limits its sales to the poorer classes but lends it a prestige appeal in well-to-do circles, where consumption of champagne and Scotch whisky have also increased hugely – *le Scotch* is now the favorite apéritif of the bourgeoisie, ahead of any French one. However, alcoholism remains a serious problem in France, though this is due less to the excessive intake of strong spirits by the middle classes, than to massive drinking of very cheap red wine by poorer people. Alcoholic consumption per head has declined by over 20 percent since 1951, yet the French remain the world's heaviest drinkers, after Luxembourgers. Curiously, it is not in the vinegrowing areas of the south that wine is drunk most heavily, but in Brittany and the Nord, where many men consume more than 4 liters a day. Deaths from cirrhosis of the liver or alcoholic excess currently run at some 16,000 a year, but the figure is declining, and the strenuous official anti-alcohol campaigners seem to be making quite considerable progress.

Sport and holidays

The new concern for health among the French shows itself also in the postwar craze for sport. The main traditional spectator sports are still the annual Tour de France cycle race, motor racing, football (soccer and rugby) and (in some parts of the southwest), bullfighting. The major growth has been in the energetic practice of sport for fitness or pleasure. Amateur soccer clubs' membership exceeds 1.7 million, while rugby is played eagerly in the Midi. However, the individualistic French tend to put less stress on team games than on solo activities. They excel at sailing (Eric Tabarly, the single-handed transatlantic yachting champion, was a national hero) and the number of private yachts in France has risen since 1960 from 20,000 to over 650,000. Each year some four million people, many of them working class, go on skiing holidays, mostly to the French Alps. Tennis and riding, once minority sports of the rich, have also become widely popular. Membership of riding-clubs has risen tenfold since 1972, to reach 300,000, and scores of new golf courses have been built recently to meet growing demand. Of the more traditional French outdoor pursuits, *la chasse* (hunting) is mostly conducted with a rifle, not horse and hounds; it was once the preserve of peasants and gentry. Now, so many clumsy urban amateurs have taken to the woods at weekends, with accidents ensuing, that the gun-licensing laws have been tightened. The traditional game of *boules* or *pétanque*, a rough kind of bowls, is much played by groups of older men, and some younger ones too, mostly in the Midi. But this rather

Right Paris's one surviving vineyard, in Montmartre, is kept going for reasons of tradition, and its thin white wine is drunk at a harvest festival each autumn. This is typical of the French desire to retain and renew their folklore and traditions in a modern age. Also in Paris, the old 17th-century fair on the Pont-Neuf has been revived.

Below The French have become devoted to sport, physical fitness and outdoor exercise. Almost every town has its municipal *piscine*, but not all of them are as overcrowded as this private club in Paris. Skiing, yachting, tennis, golf and riding have all increased hugely in popularity, and many holidays are of a sporty kind. All beaches are "topless" and naturism is widely practiced, too, in special club centers.

Below right The traditional game of *boules* (or *pétanque*) remains hugely popular. It originated in Provence, still its heartland, and spread all over France. It can be played on a proper pitch, or any piece of ground, by two teams. As in bowls, the winner is the team that gets closest to the jack without hitting it. In Provence, a game usually ends with a glass or a few glasses of *pastis* in a café and a good gossip.

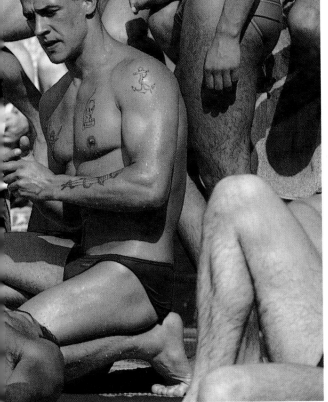

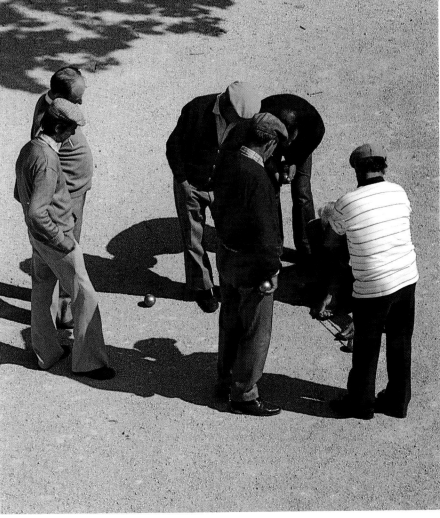

The Tour de France

"An army from Mars could land", it has been said, "governments could fall and the recipe for *sauce béarnaise* could be lost; but if it happened during the Tour de France no one would notice." Certainly the three weeks in July in which this greatest of cycle races unwinds through the French countryside is something of an institution.

The first Tour was in 1903 and the first races were ridden over dirt roads on single-gear machines with balloon tires. In 1913 when the cycle frame of the race leader snapped, he had to run 16 kilometers down the road with the bicycle slung over his shoulder to find a blacksmith to weld it together – a far cry from the massive backup of mechanics provided these days. A huge entourage of offical, technical and press vehicles follows the riders; publicity and endorsements are key to covering the costs of the Tour.

While the overall aim of the Tour is to complete the course in the fastest time, a host of other competitions are included within this framework: stage races, races against the stopwatch, the team competition, prizes for the best mountain rider, for the best young rider and so on. For many years, the Tour was dominated by the French and the Belgians. The Belgians Jacques Anquetil and Eddy Mercx and the Frenchman Bernard Hinault are the only riders to have won the Tour on five occasions. The growth of international interest in the 1980s, however, led to a fresh influx of riders, including the American Greg Lemond (Tour victor in 1986, 1989 and 1990) and Colombians, who have made a big impact in the mountain stages.

Above The route of the first Tour de France, from the newspaper *Le Vélo*. Each year, the route and starting place vary. Starts have included foreign cities such as Amsterdam (1954), Brussels (1958), Cologne (1965), The Hague (1973), Leiden (1978) and Berlin (1987).

Above The Tour de France is fast, exciting, colorful, competitive and dangerous. Mass crashes in bunched sprints have caused numerous injuries over the years. From the late 1980s riders showed greater concern for safety by wearing helmets.

Left The first Tour was started as a publicity venture by Henri Desgranges, owner of the sports newspaper *Le Vélo*. Shown here is the winner of that event, Garin. His bicycle contrasts with the hyperefficient, wind-dynamic and scientifically-tested machines ridden nowadays. The first Tour covered 2248 km – nowadays the average distance is well over 3000 km.

static sport contrasts with the new French craze for physical fitness, which has led to the spread of health clubs, with gymnasium, massage, sauna and swimming facilities. *Le jogging* is also very popular.

Even more than sport and fitness, holidays now rival cuisine as the primary national indulgence. Before the war, only the well-to-do took long holidays, but today French wage-earners have won the longest annual paid leave in Europe, a legal minimum of five weeks, plus the various one-day public holidays, such as 14 July (Bastille Day) and 1 May (Labor Day). When one of these falls on a Tuesday or Thursday, they will *faire le pont* (literally, make the bridge) to take the Monday or Friday off too, to have a long weekend. In the urban middle classes, hordes of people make a getaway each weekend to their second home in the country, either a new villa or converted farm or cottage, and the French have more of these per capita than any other nation. But they have to crawl through the traffic jams of similar migrants, so the weekend escape can be a tiring business.

The strongest element in the new holiday cult is a "back-to-nature" urge, allied to the sport-and-fitness urge. Besides the popularity of sailing, cycling and skiing holidays, the numbers who practice *le camping* have risen dramatically, from one million in 1950 to five million today. While many make for the crowded, organized campsites of the coast, others like to lose themselves in lonely mountain valleys. Among the millions who sunbathe on the beaches, many of the women now go topless. Even in the staidest resorts this is now accepted and in some seaside towns toplessness extends to the shops and cafés too. Total nakedness, however, is formally illegal outside the nudist camps, but these have soared in popularity. The French are also now venturing outside their own frontiers almost as much as the sun-starved British, with one holiday in six spent abroad. Italy, Spain and Greece are the favorite destinations, but many people travel much farther, to India or Mexico, for example. All these new holiday trends — back-to-nature, sport, and exotic foreign venues, plus a fourth, gastronomy — are epitomized by that spectacular French postwar invention that has colonized many parts of the globe — the Club Méditerranée.

Going away in late July or August remains a rooted French habit that is hard to break. As a result, the hotels, campsites and other amenities in France are packed out in that period and fairly empty at other times (except for the ski resorts). This annoys the tourist industry, which would go bankrupt were it not for foreign visitors who are prepared to stagger their holidays. The traffic jams in the crowded resorts are maddening, while the congested superhighways add to the accident rate. Moreover, the nation's economic activity, compared with that of most countries, slows right down in high summer. The government has tried to induce people to spread their holidays into June and September, and has set a lead by staggering school vacations a little, but the main effect has been merely to shift some of the burden from August to July. If Paris shuts down in August a little less than it used to, this is not so as to be able to serve local customers, but rather because theaters, shops and restaurants want to take advantage of the tourist trade. The true Parisian is probably to be found somewhere on a beach, along with all the other Parisians. Paradoxically, the French remain individualistic about their right to share the same herdlike conventions.

Left In few sporting events is the backdrop as impressive as in the Tour de France. Here cruising through the sunflowers, the pack, or *peloton*, awaits attempts by the ambitious to make an attack, or breakaway, and establish a lead. Each competing team has a flexible team strategy which aims to cosset their star riders and bring them through to the best positions from which to make a bid for the lead.

Above The Mont Ventoux (1912m) in the Vaucluse is the site of the Tour's only fatality. In 1967 the English rider Tommy Simpson collapsed here from fatigue and drug-use and died on the mountainside. A memorial on the side of the road marks the spot.

Below The final stage of the Tour sees the riders circling the Place de la Concorde in Paris before converging on the Champs-Elysées, the traditional finishing-point for the Tour.

Club Méditerranée

The Club Méditerranée, founded in 1950, has grown to become the world's largest holiday organization and a living legend – a marvellous expression of French stylishness, sensuality and fantasy. It was invented by Gérard Blitz, a Belgian athlete and diamond cutter, and its first "villages" (never called holiday camps) were little groups of straw huts by beaches, for simple, back-to-nature holidays. The idea caught on, and has spread: there are now over 100 of these villages around the globe, most of them solid bungalow-type buildings, though the few straw-hut ones are still popular. Some 60 percent of Club members are not French, and the North American market has been expanding very fast.

The concept was seductively original, and has since been much imitated. First, the camaraderie. The young staff, called *gentils organisateurs* (nice organizers), mix freely with their guests, the *gentils membres* (nice members), as if on holiday with them, and do not "serve" like normal hotel staff. Everyone is supposed to be on informal "*tu*" terms – rare in France – and the gargantuan buffet meals, with free wine (food is a strong point at Le Club), are taken communally. Second, the outside world is banished: no money, only beads; no radios or newspapers; no locks on doors. Third, sport, cabaret and other fun-and-games are laid on lavishly (but the Club is not the sex-den that is sometimes alleged). This joyous escapism appeals to the French, and has even helped to break down some of the barriers and tensions in their society. "Sophistication amid back-to-nature, and the liberated right to be ridiculous, that's the secret of our formula", says Gilbert Trigano, who now runs it.

Below Windsurfer at Sveti Marco,
Yugoslavia. The straw huts here are
scattered amid the trees by the
beach: most villages are well
landscaped in this way. The Club
puts a strong emphasis on sport,
especially watersports –
windsurfing, waterskiing, sailing –
and there are trained instructors
on hand.

Above The new village at Opio,
on the Côte d'Azur, is aimed at
upmarket holidaymakers and the
convention trade. It has modern
conference rooms with fax and
video, while the bedrooms have
TVs, hair-dryers and even locks on
the doors! It is all part of Le
Club's relentless move up market,
to the regret of many of its earlier
idealistic supporters. The
primitivism now comes
prepackaged and the earlier
mystique is diluted.

Below This girl is wearing a
necklace of popart plastic beads,
which are used for buying bar
drinks, cigarettes, and so on.
Simpler than carrying money
around, it is all part of the Club's
mystique. Some villages have now
introduced magnetic "house"
credit cards in place of the beads.
But no cash changes hands within
a village: it is all banked on
arrival.

Paris Fashion

Above Drawing of a turban designed by Paul Poiret, 1911. Paul Poiret, the most influential designer of the first decade of the 20th century, liberated women from the corset and the formal ornate costumes of the previous century. His fascination with the Orient, reflected in the rich colors and flowing styles of his designs, stemmed from an inspiring visit to the Indian department at the Victoria and Albert Museum in London, and coincided with a frenzy of "orientalia" sweeping Paris with the advent of the Ballet Russe.

Right top Yves Saint Laurent at work in his fashion house. He began his career as assistant to Christian Dior. On the death of the master, he succeeded to the position of designer of the house, but his career was interrupted by conscription to the French army in the 1950s, an event which led to a breakdown. He was soon discharged, only to find that his position at Dior had been taken by Marc Bohan. Saint Laurent recovered to found a fashion house of his own, which would soon eclipse that of his master. With his marvelous cut and brilliant use of color, he is today the leading designer of Paris.

Right Mademoiselle Gabrielle "Coco" Chanel was a milliner who became a close friend of the Duke of Westminster and his circle. Her own daring dress-sense made her a trendsetter of society women and led to her beginning a career in design when she was in her 40s. She introduced the sporty look, the fashion for suntanning, the simple elegant use of jersey fabrics and tweeds, and the lavish use of imitation jewelry.

Far right Country tweeds by Madeleine Vionnet, 1938. To Madame Vionnet is owed the bias cut, which causes fabrics – whether tweed, satin or silk – to follow the body's lines in a great subtlety of movement. She herself was elegant to the end: at her last interview, given when she was 94, she appeared dressed in a pink satin trouser suit by her own favorite designer, Balenciaga.

The origins of France, and especially Paris, as the center of world fashion lie in the royal courts of the 14th century. Given such a long tradition, it is little wonder that fashion has made such an important contribution to the arts in French society, and has become absorbed into the blood of the French. French women are said to have an intuitive trait for beautiful clothes: they have always loved them and known how to wear them. Possessors of a heritage of centuries of elegance and chic, society and working women alike have fostered the renown of "*la couture*".

Until the 19th century, wooden dolls known as "Pandoras", were dressed in the current fashions of the ladies of the court and sent to foreign courts, whose ladies would copy them. Royal marriages, alliances, the exchanges of ambassadors and merchants of fine materials, contributed to the spread of French modes. Later, as printing processes developed, dolls were replaced by fashion drawings or plates and, as ladies' magazines emerged, an awareness of fashion was extended to a greater public.

By 1775 some 1700 dressmaking houses existed in Paris, despite the enormous cost of each garment. With the advent of the sewing machine in 1850, more cloths become available to more people. However, it remains as true today as it did in the past that changes in fashion tend to be a difference in detail rather than in the silhouette. After the two world wars, Paris soon re-established itself as the fashion center of the world with names as famous as Dior, Balenciaga, Givenchy, Balmain, Courrèges, Cardin and Yves Saint Laurent.

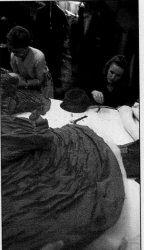

Above No designer can work on their own but, as here, in the workshop of Christian Lacroix, he relies on brilliantly trained staff. The cutter and the fitter are the heads of the workroom, able to interpret the master's designs into working "toiles" – models in calico – to see how they work in three dimensions. Workroom hands and assistants are the lifeblood of the house. It is demanding work, and one of the few crafts left that is not dependent on machinery (although this changes when the wholesale range is designed). The system has changed little from the early days, and the workroom staff are extremely loyal and proud of their own "house".

Left Another new line from Dior in 1954 with the long slim body line. Christian Dior sold his first fashion sketches of hat designs when he was 30. He went on to work with the prestigious houses of Robert Piguet and Lucien Lelong. He was introduced to Marcel Boussac, financier and textile magnate, who backed him to open his own fashion house. In February 1947, he opened with the historic collection named the "New Look" with its huge swirling skirts and nipped in waistlines, which caught the attention of the world. His brief but brilliant career lasted until his sudden death, 10 years later.

Transportation

The French have put great efforts into developing their transportation network, which is now one of the most modern and effective in the world. Most of the equipment is French-built, including the locomotives and rolling stock, aircraft such as Airbus, and the Métro systems in Paris, Lyon, Lille and Marseille, now being developed in other cities too.

French railroads, the Société Nationale des Chemins de Fer Français (SNCF), were nationalized in 1937. After World War II, some 10,000 kilometers of uneconomic branch lines were closed down, and replaced by buses run by the SNCF. French trains are known for their punctuality and comfort, and generally low accident rate. Only some 30 percent of all track is electric, but this carries over 75 percent of all traffic. One main problem is that freight services, although subsidized, have been losing custom to trucking, which users find more convenient.

Super highways were at first developed slowly, being perhaps less urgently needed than in more densely populated countries. But now France has a fairly good network of 7000 kilometers of *autoroutes*, some built by the state, some by private firms. Controversially, they nearly all carry high toll charges, which is unusual in Europe, and is why many drivers therefore prefer to stick to the old busy main roads. The *autoroutes* are well landscaped.

Below Concorde, the Anglo-French supersonic jetliner built so slowly and expensively in the 1970s, was a graceful bird and a technical triumph, but a commercial disaster. The only two airlines that bought Concorde were the "captive" ones of the nations that had built it – Air France and British Airways. Air France still uses Concorde on some transatlantic flights, but relies mainly on Boeings and Airbuses. Air France, state owned, has the most extensive network of any world airline; its domestic subsidiary, Air Inter, plus a few smaller private airlines, provide France with the most elaborate domestic network in Europe.

Left Motor traffic in Paris moves very unevenly – fast along the new expressways by the Seine and some broad boulevards, but very slowly in the honeycomb of old, narrow Right Bank commercial streets where jams can be horrendous. Despite excellent public transportation facilities, Parisians still regard the use of their own cars as a sacred right.

Below The Paris Métro has been given a face-lift, with, at some stations, decor that mirrors the *quartier*, as here. The trains are swift and frequent, but so alas are thieves and muggers.

Above The Train à Grande Vitesse (TGV), pioneered during the 1980s is claimed to be the world's fastest express, with a top speed of over 270km/h. It has cut the 460km Paris–Lyon journey from four hours to two, and has thus stolen half of Air Inter's custom on that busy route. It is now also being used on other lines.

Right Modern French trains are known for their comfort. Some coaches resemble the first-class sections of an airliner.

FRENCH CULTURE AND INTELLECTUAL LIFE

Above The writer Marguerite Yourcenar (1903–87) was the first woman ever to have been elected to that male bastion, the Académie Française. Born in Brussels, she spent much of her early life in her family's country home near Lille. There she became imbued with that deep love of nature that marked her writing and led her in later years to champion ecological causes from her home in Maine, United States (this photograph was taken there). She is known for her historical novels, such as *Mémoires d'Hadrien.* She also wrote movingly about "the slow-burning Flemish ardor" of her own background.

France is a land where culture and ideas, and those who create or disseminate them, have long been held in unusually high respect; and it has always managed to show off its culture to the best advantage, partly with an eye to national prestige. Generous state patronage of the arts has played a part in this process, not only providing funds, but also helping to give culture a higher official status than in many countries. Today culture's share of the overall French budget is just under 1 percent, about three times the figure in Britain. France also has a Ministry of Culture, with considerable power. The state's influence has, of course, tended to be conservative and pro-establishment, but the avant-garde has found ways of exploiting the patronage.

It was Colbert, Louis XIV's finance minister, who initiated the systematic policy of promoting the arts as a vehicle for French power and prestige: he founded academies of architecture and science, he developed the Louvre as a museum, and it was in his time that the Comédie Française, the world's oldest national theater, was set up. Even earlier, in the 1630s, Richelieu had created the Académie Française, a typically French institution that sanctified the formal status of the writer in France. Even today, its 40 members, *"les Immortels"*, wear embroidered uniforms and carry swords on ceremonial occasions: yet most of them are literary men, along with a few clerics,

diplomats and scientists. In protocol ranking, an *académicien* comes before a minister or ambassador, and just after a prince or cardinal. The Académie's task is to uphold standards of literary taste, and unsurprisingly its influence has always been conservative and opposed to innovation: social critics such as Balzac in the 19th century, and later Sartre, did not enter its ranks. It is also a bastion of male chauvinism, and did not admit any women until Marguerite Yourcenar, in 1980. Since her death, there have been two other *Immortelles.* To be elected remains a great honor, but the Académie no longer wields great influence and most younger people think of it as an anachronism.

Malraux and Lang

In a country where, at least until 1950, Paris had tended to drain the lifeblood from the rest of France – in the arts as in other fields – almost any creative performer or artist with ambition would make for the limelight of the capital. Writers such as Balzac (1799–1850), Mauriac (1885–1970) or Maupassant (1850–93), though deeply influenced by their native *pays*, went to Paris to live and to make their name. Paris may still account for most of the best creative work, but, increasingly, artistic talents are now ready to make a career away from the capital. Moreover, since the war the main official emphasis has been on helping culture in the provinces.

In the early 1960s, the enigmatic André Malraux, former left-winger turned visionary mandarin of art and prophet of Gaullism, embarked on the grandiose policy of building a provincial network of huge multipurpose arts centers – the famous Maisons de la Culture. These, he claimed, would enable France "to become again the world's foremost cultural nation" (a telling admission that it was no longer). Each Maison, he said, should present only works of quality, thus spreading Paris standards across France; there would be no place for mere entertainment or local amateur productions, as many might have wished. Malraux also wanted the Maisons to woo the working classes into the theaters and art shows, thus destroying the idea of culture as a bourgeois preserve. But workers, frightened off alike by the highbrow programming and by the cathedral-like nature of these vast temples of culture, never accounted for more than 2 or 3 percent of audiences. Malraux also ran into conflict with local mayors, more philistine than he, for the Maisons were planned to be run on a 50–50 partnership between state and town councils. After he left his post in 1969, the building of new Maisons was halted and the ethos was relaxed a little (pop concerts are now sometimes allowed, but not amateur work). Today, about a dozen Maisons operate: the biggest are at Grenoble, Rennes and Amiens. However, as they struggle with vast overheads and inadequate funds, the Maisons cannot afford full programming and so are half-deserted much of the time.

More realistically, today the accent is on building much smaller local centers, and the burden of arts

patronage has shifted a little, away from the state and toward the city councils and new regional councils. Most big towns now have their own active cultural policies, funded with up to 10 percent of the civic budget. Unlike in Britain, this is seen as a vote-catching matter of municipal prestige, amid intense inter-city rivalry. Culture is a matter of local pride, a status symbol, like having a good football team.

Very different in attitude from Malraux, Jack Lang, the young Socialist who became Culture Minister in 1981, and again in 1988, believed that "all the arts matter, even minor ones". He extended patronage to new fields, setting up a strip-cartoon museum at Angoulême, a costume museum in the Louvre, a school for photography at Arles, and even a school for circus performers. He also put money into jazz and rock music. Some 5500 little local bodies and theater groups benefited from his largess. Today, the animateurs – those who go out to remote areas to start up festivals, organize poetry-readings, pottery classes or other small-scale local activities – are a key French profession, even filling the gap left by the declining roles of the *curé* and *instituteur*. The trend in French culture in recent years has thus been away from the solemn and cerebral, toward the colorful and amusing.

For a long time the French attitude to *la culture* has tended to be reverential. In schools, it is a *valeur*

(value) that children imbibe passively from the teacher, rather than learn to perform and enjoy for themselves. Outside school, culture tends to be spoon-fed to audiences by professionals, in theaters or opera houses. It is the getting of wisdom. But the newer approach, typified by Lang, is that culture is also entertainment, a means of personal expression and participation. Lang was more concerned with grass-roots action than with helping venerable institutions such as the Comédie Française, and he inspired what has been called "a nonstop atmosphere of carnival".

An allied but much older conflict is that between the classical and the avant-garde. The French venerate their classics, perhaps too much, but at least in Parisian circles they also have a passion for novelty, for its own sake. In such a milieu, to follow the avant-garde is chic, and to hold views on the latest in the arts is a must at the best dinner parties. As a result, much that is phony or pretentious is admired, then forgotten; but at the same time, the French openness to the new has produced a climate where creative originality has found it easier to flourish and be accepted than in most societies. The novels of Flaubert and Zola, for instance, or the paintings of the Impressionists and Cubists, may have been shockingly revolutionary in their day, but are now part of the French cultural heritage.

France has a very fine tradition in literature and

Above A 1791 painting of a performance at the Comédie Française, in its theater near the Louvre which is still its home today. Founded by Molière's regular troupe of actors just after his death in 1673, this old French institution is the longest-established national theater in the world. It is also a kind of cooperative, run by its team of 40 permanent actors: past members have included Sarah Bernhardt and Jean-Louis Barrault. "Le Français", as it is known, had long been a sanctuary of the stylized rhetorical tradition of French acting. By 1970 it has become rather fusty and archaic, but was then revitalized by the great actor-manager, Pierre Dux. He shocked its regular bourgeois audiences with the première of Ionesco's *La Soif et la faim*, where one scene lampoons Christianity. He also introduced foreign and contemporary plays, from Aeschylus to Brecht and Sartre. But Molière remains the central pillar of its repertoire.

Above Pierre Mignard's portrait of Jean-Baptiste Molière (1622–73), much the greatest of French comic dramatists. He had a sharp eye for human foibles, for the vanities, vices, hypocrisies and affectations that he observed in the society around him, and he exposed these wittily, but not cruelly, in a number of masterly plays. *Tartuffe, Le Misanthrope, L'Avare* and *Georges Dandin* are perhaps the best. He began life as an actor, and founded his own company which toured the provinces. In Paris, he won the patronage of the king, but some of his satires so shocked the court that they were banned.

passed on elsewhere – possibly even to New York.

The reasons for the decline are not easy to assess. Perhaps a period of rapid industrial and social change has diverted the nation's energies elsewhere, and that the technocratic ethos, so strong under de Gaulle and Giscard, has damaged creativity. Perhaps the rise of a consumer-oriented society, and the waning of the old ideologies of the left, has caused many thinkers and artists to feel empty and bewildered. France is not alone in this problem, for the creative malaise is much the same in Germany and Italy. When Mitterrand and Lang raised the state's budget for culture, and spread new subsidies around, one of their aims was that a better cultural climate might stimulate new creative work, but alas it has not happened.

Presidents Pompidou and Mitterrand (Giscard less so) both made efforts to revive the cultural prestige of Paris, through ambitious new building projects such as Beaubourg and the Bastille Opera, and through majestic festivals and pageants. In fact, they succeeded in refocusing some international attention on the city, as was evident at the time of the Revolution's bicentenary celebrations in 1989. They hoped also to draw more foreign artists and writers to live and work in Paris, as in former days. Those who came have in recent years included political exiles from Latin America and Eastern Europe, such as the Argentine stage director Jorge Lavelli and the Czech writer Milan Kundera, and fashion designers such as Karl Lagerfeld (German), and Kenzo (Japanese). Indeed, the Paris cultural scene today is remarkably international, utilizing the best foreign talents, while most of the state culture-palace projects have been entrusted to foreign architects. Yet, although culturally Paris may be very lively, some people detect a certain staleness, even decadence, in its desperate search for novelty and cultural chic.

Theater
The French tradition of great drama dates essentially from the 17th century, with the tragedies of Corneille and Racine, and the social comedies of Molière, who had his own theater company. Racine's ornate, rhetorical style today seems somewhat dated, but Molière's acute satires on human weakness remain as fresh and relevant as ever, and he is still much the most performed of the French playwrights. Later came Marivaux (1688–1763) with his light and frothy comedies of love, and Beaumarchais (1732–99) whose *Le Barbier de Séville* and *Le Mariage de Figaro* were turned into operas. The 19th century was a dull time for French theater, despite the efforts of Victor Hugo in the 1830s to wage war on its rigid dramatic conventions, with his vigorous romantic dramas, *Cromwell* and *Hernani*. Later, some lesser figures such as Alexandre Dumas the younger (*La Dame aux Camélias*, 1852) and Edmond Rostand (*Cyrano de Bergerac*, 1897) enjoyed great popular success. In more recent times, the period roughly 1920 to 1960 was quite a golden era: philosophical thought is combined with poetic lyricism in the works of Giraudoux and Claudel, and with stylish comedy in the plays of Anouilh, while among the many noted playwrights of the early years after World War II were Sartre and Genet, de Montherlant and Audiberti. The genre known as the "theater of the absurd" was pioneered mainly by immigrant writers who settled in Paris – Adamov from the Soviet Union, Ionesco from Romania and Beckett from Ireland. Since then,

philosophy, in the visual arts and cinema, perhaps a shade less so in theater and music. Among the very greatest names, Descartes, Pascal and Voltaire, Balzac and Proust, Berlioz and the Renoirs father and son, and – more recently – Gide, Sartre and Camus, to name but some, are giants of Western culture. The unique intellectual climate of Paris has also attracted and assimilated many immigrant geniuses – Rousseau the Swiss, Picasso the Spaniard, Beckett the Irishman, and so on. France has been a powerhouse of new ideas, new books and paintings, and all kinds of creative endeavors.

Culture and art today
In many Western countries, and in France more than most, the stress is no longer on the solitary painter or poet of genius, at work in a studio or study, but on innovation by little groups of actors or musicians, or by workshops of decorators, sculptors or video directors, all in close touch with their public. This kind of culture is less spiritual and philosophical, probably more ephemeral, and more social, than the classic pattern. The revival of the performing arts, and the popular eagerness for them, have brought a new vitality to French life. At the same time, however, there is a lack of new novelists, playwrights, painters, composers or filmmakers of distinction. French undisputed leadership in the creative arts seems to have

however, in the past 30 years, no substantial new playwrights have emerged.

In other respects, the French theater today is flourishing, in both Paris and the provinces. It is true that there has been a decline in the old Parisian commercial playhouses, the *théâtres du boulevard* that used to provide the bourgeoisie with its staple entertainment of easy comedies: these suffer from the rival lure of television. But the state-subsidized repertory companies, which attract younger, more serious audiences and can afford to experiment, are doing well. Their doyenne, the Comédie Française, has been brought up to date; great producers such as Jean-Louis Barrault have been given state funds to do interesting work; and the Théâtre de l'Odéon has an enterprising policy of inviting foreign visiting companies, such as Britain's Royal Shakespeare, to perform plays in their own languages. The Paris theater today is cosmopolitan and open to new ideas: significantly, the great British experimental director, Peter Brook, has chosen to base himself not in London but Paris, where his multiracial company finds better funding and a better working atmosphere.

Even more remarkable has been the change in the provinces, where, before the war, theater was almost dead. Soon after 1945 a number of talented young actor-producers decided to forgo the Parisian rat race and set up repertory theaters in other cities, and these soon won state support. One of them was Roger Planchon, in the Lyon suburb of Villeurbanne: here his pioneering work won such renown that, in 1972, the government honored him by letting his company take over the mantle and title of the Théâtre National Populaire (TNP), which had been founded in Paris in 1951 by the great Jean Vilar but had later gone into decline. Some of the most brilliant new directors, notably Patrice Chéreau, have worked with Planchon in Lyon, where his TNP is still regarded as France's foremost theater company after the Comédie Française.

At Avignon, the summer drama festival created in 1956 by Vilar and the actor Gérard Philippe, remains the foremost of its kind in Europe, featuring some 400 productions of all kinds, most of them on the "fringe" and some wildly avant-garde. Other cities such as Marseille, Strasbourg, Toulouse and Rennes also have notable repertory companies, while hundreds of little *ad hoc* troupes have emerged too, often transient, seldom brilliant, but always lively. Performances range from improvised or experimental playlets to staple classics (Shakespeare is popular).

In the Paris theaters, too, the diet is largely one of classical revivals or modern plays from abroad plus insipid new comedies on the "boulevard". English playwrights such as Harold Pinter and Tom Stoppard are in vogue, as are some Austro-German ones including Thomas Bernhard and Botho Strauss. The serious new French writers of the past 30 years, such as Marguerite Duras, Michel Vinaver, Jean-Claude Grumberg and Bernard-Marie Koltès, are probably not in the first rank. Producers tend to feel that foreign playwrights provide them with "meatier" subjects that relate to the modern world; and even the state-subsidized theaters make little effort to seek out new French talent.

Perhaps the major reason for this dearth of new writing is that the clever and fashionable directors who have come to dominate the scene in the past 20 years have an entirely different concept of theater.

They are not interested in receiving a text from an author and then staging it faithfully; to them a living author is a potential nuisance, an obstruction to their own creative fantasies. They prefer either to devise their own texts, or else to reinterpret radically the plays of dead authors, who cannot interfere. This is a new visual theater of lighting, movement and gesture, more than of the spoken word – and French critics are divided on whether it marks a brilliant new advance or an artistic dead end.

Sometimes a director and cast take a theme – often historical – and collectively improvise a play around it during rehearsal. The talented Ariane Mnouchkine and her Théâtre du Soleil company did this with the Revolutionary years 1789 and 1793 and even with the subject of genocide in Cambodia. Alternatively, a director will work a literary or political text into a dramatic piece, as the late Antoine Vitez did. But the favorite method is to take a classic, maybe by Racine, Molière or Marivaux, and, by adding various visual fireworks, and possibly even rearranging the text, to turn it into something almost unrecognizable. Planchon, Chéreau and Vitez have been the high priests of this cult, which is not confined to France: Peter Zadek has done much the same in Germany. Some critics are delighted by the virtuosity of the mise-en-scène, or will

Above Ariane Mnouchkine, seen here directing a film, is one of the most talented of a new wave of French theater directors who prefer to take a theme and improvise a play around it, rather than use a playwright's text. After 1968 she formed the Théâtre du Soleil as a kind of workers' cooperative, in a disused factory in the Paris suburbs. This company created a dramatic collage around the French Revolution, to brilliant effect. Mnouchkine has applied similar techniques to Klaus Mann's novel *Mephisto*, and even to the subject of genocide in Cambodia. She has also made films, notably a rollicking biopic about Molière.

Right Pierre Boulez (left in picture), looking at the model of his research center for modern music, IRCAM, before it was built in Paris in 1977. Boulez (b. 1925) is France's leading modern composer, an innovative pioneer of what is called "serialist" music, and a noted conductor too. For years he was spurned in France, so he worked abroad, in Germany, Britain and the United States, where he conducted some leading orchestras. Since 1972 he has been back in Paris, where he has evangelized a small but devoted public with his own passionately held theories on modern music. This is still a minority taste among music lovers, but his chamber concerts can draw over 1000 people.

claim that the directors have found new depths and meanings in the text. Some also argue that the method helps to liberate great plays from the cumbersome strictures that for centuries had been imposed on them by the Comédie Française. But other critics are horrified by the distortions, and acuse producers of willfully misrepresenting the authors, especially those who are dead, possibly out of envy for their talents. It is a trend very much in the French tradition, where some fashionable coterie – whether in theater, literature or cuisine – for a while imposes a "tyranny of taste" on the rest. But at least the French theater shows vitality, and, when the current vogue has passed, new playwrights may again emerge.

Music

Over the past 20 years France has experienced a revival of musical activity, and of public enthusiasm for music, after a lean period when the nation seemed to have been neglecting a noble tradition. In the 18th and mid 19th centuries France was a leading musical nation. Paris, around the 1830s, in the time of Hector Berlioz (1803–69), a native composer of world rank, attracted great names to live and work there, including Chopin, Liszt and Rossini. The city also enjoyed preeminence in ballet, dating from the time of Noverre (1727–1810), and this continued into the early 20th century, with the creation of Stravinsky's principal ballets. As in literature and the visual arts, the later 19th and early 20th centuries were a fertile period when a number of excellent composers – among them, Debussy, Saint-Saëns, Ravel and Bizet – produced music that was sensuous, elegant and poetic, some of the best of it written for ballet, or for opera, such as Bizet's *Carmen* (1875).

However, the social reformers of the later 19th century not only starved music of funds, but they gave it a very minor place in the new school curriculum:

generations of French children grew up with virtually no musical education. By the 1950s some 30 provincial conservatoires were still surviving, but they were run on stuffy, academic lines, closed to any sense of enjoyment. André Malraux as Culture Minister in the 1960s did nothing to improve things: he even declared that music was a "secondary art" and the French were "not a musical nation". The official prejudice against modern music at the time of Malraux was such that France's leading composer-conductor, Pierre Boulez, was spurned in his own land, and to study the serialism that he had pioneered meant going abroad. After Malraux, a remorseful President Pompidou persuaded Boulez, who had boycotted France in protest, to return and run an ambitious new center for modern music, the Institut de Recherche et de Coordination Acoustique (IRCAM). This was opened in 1977 and has been a great success, with teams of musicians and scientists working on new approaches to music. Boulez has also created a new chamber orchestra for modern music, and with evangelistic fervor has done much to build Paris into a major world forum for the kind of music that he cherishes. Another Parisian modernist, Olivier Messaien, has also played a significant part. An English expert who has worked in Paris remarked: "In London, the music is of high quality but very conservative; Paris has other intellectual traditions, but has now turned to music as a novelty."

Pompidou, who cared for music, also managed to revive the fortunes of the Paris Opéra, once so renowned but by then in sorry decline. At huge expense he renovated its home, the elegant neobaroque Palais Garnier, and hired as artistic manager the great Swiss, Rolf Liebermann, who with help of a giant budget brought it back into the European front rank. Liebermann was responsible for some magnificent productions, such as Alban Berg's *Lulu*, directed

Left Dancers of the National Ballet of Marseille, which Roland Petit has directed for many years. Petit (b. 1924) has been one of the major postwar creative influences in French ballet – a dancer and choreographer whose ballets combine modern realism with imaginative fantasy. Despite France's great tradition of classical ballet, it has more recently been most successful with modern dance. The classical ballet of the Paris Opéra, France's premier company, has had a checkered postwar career. It greatly improved under Nureyev, who was its artistic director in 1893–90, but declined when he left. Meanwhile, contemporary dance has flowered, notably in the provinces: inspired by Merse Cunningham and other Americans, a new generation of talented young French choreographers have developed their own styles and ideas.

Below Children at an outdoor summer music festival in Paris. The playing of music, as well as listening to it, has increased hugely in popularity especially among young people. But as music is still taught very little in schools, children can only learn by attending part-time classes in local *conservatoires*. These charge fees, and thus tend to be middle-class preserves. In a nation that prides itself on its free education, this is widely regarded as socially unfair. Pressure has increased for more musical activity in state schools, but this is still opposed by a powerful lobby of conservative teachers.

by Chéreau, with Boulez conducting. But after he left in 1980, standards again fell. Moreover, the Palais Garnier was unsuited to the large modern productions now in fashion. This prompted Mitterrand, with the eager backing of Lang and Boulez, to devise a scheme for a new, lavish opera house at the Bastille, which opened in 1989. Its career so far, however, has been beset with troubles, including some much-publicized squabbles between politicians, administrators and musicians that led to the spectacular dismissal of Daniel Barenboim as musical director. The Bastille Opéra has not been properly funded, and remains encumbered with the Palais Garnier's legacy of archaic bureacracy, overstaffing and labor-relations problems. The Garnier is still used for ballet, and Rudolf Nureyev, who took over the Opéra's ballet company in 1983, raised it to a high standard. But then he too quarreled with his masters and was sacked in 1990. Apparently, Paris has not yet found the political unity of purpose to run a high-level opera company as well as Hamburg, Milan, London or New York can and consequently the music suffers.

The main thrust of the French postwar music revival has been not so much qualitative, at the top level, as quantitative, in public enthusiam at the grassroots. With the great classics taught so little in school, a new generation seems to have suddenly discovered the delights of Beethoven and other composers. The French have also rediscovered Berlioz, long ignored in his own land. Not only are concert halls and opera houses far fuller than before, but the French are also increasingly turning to amateur music-making – to choral singing and learning to play instruments, both hitherto much neglected. The number of part-time pupils in the municipal or state-run *conservatoires* has multiplied fourfold since 1960; and some two million attend dance or ballet classes, a new craze with the French. The new passion for music is evident on all sides – a Chopin sonata floating through the thin walls of a suburban council flat, medieval ballads performed in the floodlit courtyards of old castles, and in some families a revival of the old custom of making music together after dinner.

How is this new phenomenon to be explained? One music critic summed it up thus: "In the postwar decades, and until after 1968, the French were preoccupied with ideologies and social issues, and this climate favored the art forms that best deal with these – literature and theater. But today people shun political idealism; they would rather seek an inner world. So they turn to an art form that appeals joyously to the heart and senses, more than to the intellect or conscience." The revival has also been boosted by a belated increase in state funding. Even Malraux, toward the end of his term of office, accepted that the miserable infrastructure must be improved, and between 1966 and 1979 the Ministry's budget for music was increased from 11.5 to nearly 400 million francs. In that time, 12 new orchestras were created, and scores of new conservatoires, while the 12 provincial opera companies were revivified.

The two state radio networks mainly devoted to serious music, France Culture and France-Musique, have also done much over many years to stimulate public taste. When Jack Lang took office, he raised the state music budget a further threefold. Yet while he poured more money into symphony orchestras and classical opera, his main accent was on helping more popular kinds of music. He gave money and recognition to hundreds of local folklore troupes, he helped amateur choirs and brass bands, he created a major jazz orchestra and built a huge stadium for jazz and rock in Paris, and – to the horror of some Ministry mandarins – he funded rock and pop. This was a break with tradition, and it set off a debate as to which kinds of music are part of "culture" and which are not. Lang also instituted an annual one-day nationwide Fête de la Musique (Music Festival), held every 21 June since 1982: some 10 million people, more than for the Bastille Day festivities of 14 July, take part in this mammoth popular jamboree – a mix of sambas and sonatas, reggae and requiems, Bach and Beatles.

Lang has also given support to modern dance, a field where even 15 years ago France was nowhere, but now has quite a reputation. Jean-Claude Gallotta, Dominique Bagoué and Maguy Marin are among the talented young choreographers in charge of 16 companies devoted to modern-style ballet, nearly all of them in the provinces. With opera, however, in the provinces as in Paris, matters have gone less well, for high costs have forced some towns to forgo the prestigious luxury of having their own full-time opera company. Today there are only six of these, but several cities mount their own productions from time to time. Lyon, Strasbourg and Toulouse, in particular, have restored their fine old musical traditions. In Toulouse, where the gifted conductor Michel Plasson has led the revival, a big disused cornmarket has been converted into a concert hall seating 3,300. Leading musicians such as Isaac Stern and Igor Oistrakh have performed there, with Beethoven drawing larger audiences – mainly of young people – than the Rolling Stones and other pop and rock groups.

Standards of performance in France, professional and amateur alike, are still variable, for, after the long neglect the French still have a way to go to catch up with the British and the Germans. There is a lack of first-rate instrumentalists, and in opera most lead singers have to be imported. There is a shortage of good teachers, too – and music teaching in schools remains much the weakest point of the system. However generous the Ministry of Culture may be, it

has no control over its sister Ministry of Education, which is still hesitant to allow music a real place in the curriculum. In *lycées*, music is an "extra" subject that few pupils take, except in the few schools that prepare for the new music option in the *bac*. Thus, nearly all music learning takes place out of class, in local conservatoires which charge fees – socially most unfair, in a land priding itself on its free education. In recent years, music has been made a compulsory item in the training of primary teachers, and the number of schools with a choir or orchestra has doubled (in the 1960s, only 8 percent of French secondary schools had an orchestra, compared with 46 percent in Britain), but most of the teaching corps are adverse to change and to anything nonacademic, and remain hostile to music in schools. The great French music revival has happened in spite of French school education, not because of it.

Painting

As in some other fields, the visual arts in France today are marked by a great deal of activity and public interest, but a dearth of new creativity. The museums are crowded, with many splendid special exhibitions, but they almost always relate to dead or foreign artists. Throughout the 19th century, and until the middle of this one, France appeared as the most fertile land of art, producing many great painters and attracting others from abroad to settle. Paris was then considered the world capital of art, but today is no longer so, despite its glorious art history.

Early 19th-century painting after the Revolution featured the conflict between Neoclassicism and Romanticism. The first major exponent of the former in France was Jacques-Louis David (1748–1825), who became Napoleon's official painter. J.A.D. Ingres (1780–1867) was a pupil of David who became his successor and the leader of Neoclassicism; he was noted for his nudes and for his portraits. The leaders of Romanticism were Théodore Géricault (1791–1824), who loved to paint horses and whose best-known work is *The Raft of the Medusa*; and then, after Géricault's early death, Eugene Delacroix (1798–1863), who for decades dominated French painting with his bold fresh colors and strong emotive subjects. Naturalistic landscape painting blossomed in the mid 19th century, influenced by the Barbizon school, which was founded in the village of that name near Fontainebleau; the wistful landscape scenes of Camille Corot (1796–1875), and the realistic peasant studies of François Millet (1814–75), are among the best examples.

A bolder kind of realism emerged with the work of Gustave Courbet (1819–77), whose left-wing views informed many of his social scenes, though he is noted also for his landscapes and still-life painting. Another realist, Edouard Manet (1832–83), was even bolder, and some of his now-famous works such as *Le Déjeuner sur l'herbe* and the nude *Olympia* at first shocked the public. Manet was a precursor of the Impressionist group, founded in the early 1870s by Claude Monet (1840–1926) and Auguste Renoir (1841–1919). The Impressionists, whose main concern was the effects of light and shadow, had a revolutionary impact on art. In his search for the very essence of light and color, Monet painted, time and again, the facade of Rouen cathedral, the Normandy cliffs at Etretat, and the water lilies in his own garden at Giverny. Renoir is distinguished for his warmly

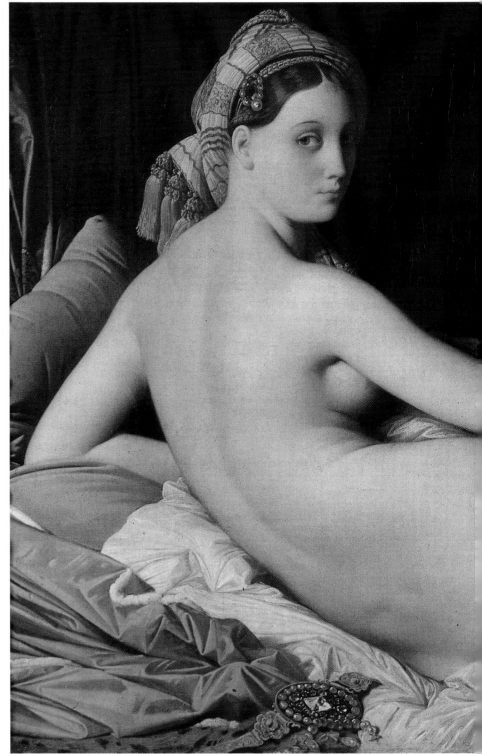

colored, richly sensuous studies of women, often in rural settings. Paul Cézanne (1839–1906) was influenced by Impressionism but later diverged from it, though he never lost his fascination for the effect of light on landscape – notably in his native Provence. Edgar Degas (1834–1917), also on the margin of the movement, was less concerned with light than with rapid motion, which he caught in the gestures of dancers and horses. Following on from the Impressionists came three highly individual artists: Paul Gauguin (1848–1903), whose passion for bold areas of color and exotic subjects took him finally to Tahiti; Henri de Toulouse-Lautrec (1864–1901), who vividly depicted the bohemian life of Montmartre; and the wild, Dutch genius, Vincent Van Gogh (1853–90), inspired like no one else by the brilliant light and

Above La Grande Odalisque is one of the best-known and most typical works of J.A.D. Ingres (1780–1867), leader of the Neo-classical school of French painting after the death of David. As in this painting, he was greatly concerned with contour and balance, and his cool, detached style with its clear colors was the antithesis of the Romantic school that flourished alongside Neoclassicism. His feud with the Romantics' leader, Delacroix, was famous. Ingres greatly influenced some artists who were otherwise very different, including the later Renoir and Picasso.

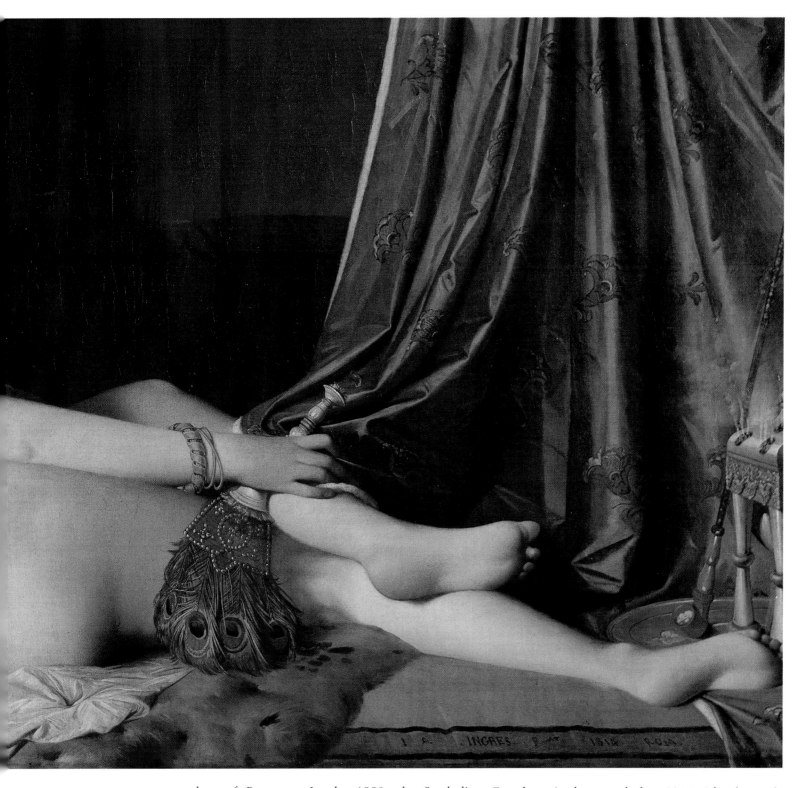

colors of Provence. In the 1890s the Symbolist painters came to the fore: most notable among them was Odilon Rédon (1840–1916).

The early 20th century saw two major developments in French art: fauvism and cubism. To the fauvists, subject matter and realism were unimportant, and the whole emphasis was on vitality of color and design. The movement's leader, and one of the notable giants of modern art, was Henri Matisse (1869–1954): the still-lifes and odalisques of his later period, at the end of a long career, were among his finest work. Others associated with the *fauve* group included Georges Rouault, Maurice de Vlaminck and Georges Braque. Braque was also the cofounder, along with the Spanish-born Pablo Picasso (1881–1973), of the cubist school, which dominated

French art in the years before 1914. After his early "blue" and "pink" periods, Picasso broke into the revolutionary new style of cubism with his famous *Demoiselles d'Avignon* (1906), and then carried it further. Later, his prolific genius led him toward surrealism and symbolism, culminating in one of his greatest works, *Guernica* (1937). Fernand Léger (1881–1955), another leader of cubism, was much preoccupied with machinery and the impact of factory life. Between World Wars I and II, surrealism was the most influential new movement, but its main exponents, such as Ernst, Magritte and Miro, were not French. At about the same time, the French artistic scene was enriched by the arrival of a number of immigrants from eastern Europe – most notably Marc Chagall (1887–1985) from the Soviet Union, who

The Impressionists

The Impressionist movement, which was revolutionary at the time and greatly influenced subsequent painting, developed in Paris in the 1870s. Edouard Manet had led the way in the 1860s. But the true creators of the group were Claude Monet and Auguste Renoir, joined later by Camille Pissarro, Alfred Sisley and others. After their work had been rejected by the Salon of the French Academy, they held their own first show in 1874, and were derisively dubbed "mere impressionists" by the critics.

They rejected the academic teaching which had long dominated French art, favoring grandiose, historical or emotive subjects. They wanted to get close to a new kind of visual reality, by depicting precisely the transient effects of light and shadow. The "subject" in any literary sense thus became less important than color and form: but they were not abstract artists, and painted directly what they saw. They were guided by new scientific discoveries that color did not belong inherently to an object but depended on the light it reflected. Monet was insistent that outdoor scenes should be painted on the spot, not in the studio. So he, Renoir and others, went to the Seine near to capture the fleeting effects of light on water and trees.

Right La Loge, one of the greatest works of Pierre-Auguste Renoir (1841–1919), dates from his earlier period, soon after his pioneering of Impressionism in the 1870s. Using short, multicolored strokes, he could capture the effects of shimmering light, of vibrating foliage or the luminosity of a woman's skin. In the 1880s he moved away from Impressionism, turned to a more severe discipline, and settled in Provence. But his work blossomed into new styles of color and sensuality, a festival of naked women, flowers and sunlight. Toward the end, crippled with rheumatism, he painted with the brush strapped to his arm.

In the late 1880s the Impressionists broke up, but greatly influenced a number of contemporaries. Edgar Degas tried to capture the rapidly changing poses of dancers and horses in movement. Paul Cézanne began as an Impressionist before diverging. A little later came Seurat, Gauguin, Toulouse-Lautrec and the Dutch-man Vincent van Gogh: they were loosely labeled Post-Impressionists.

Left Paysage à Eragny, by Camille Pissarro (1830–1903). Born in the West Indies, son of a Jewish merchant, Pissarro moved to Paris where he met Monet and Renoir. He was more concerned with social problems than they, and many of his subjects were the peasants and workers of the Paris region, against a background of fields, trees, houses, and city streets in varying lights.

Right Manet's painting of Monet in his boat. Edouard Manet (1832–83) was a precursor of the Impressionists and one of art's great innovators. Like Gustave Courbet before him, he was a Realist, and he broke new ground by choosing real-life subjects from the world around him. Influenced by Japanese prints, he also used bright colors on a white ground. Born in Paris, he first caused a stir with his painting *Le Déjeuner sur l'herbe*, which showed a naked woman sitting with clothed men, and with his realistic nude *Olympia*.

Above A typical Provençal landscape by Paul Cézanne (1839–1906), who was much influenced by Impressionism. After years in Paris he settled back in his native Aix-en-Provence, where his searching analysis of color and tone led him to paint again and again, in varying lights, the limestone pyramid of Mont Ste-Victoire. He also did still-life paintings and portraits. Misunderstood in his time, he was to have a huge influence on modern painting.

Above right This painting by Claude Monet (1840–1926) of a girl with a sunshade typifies the Impressionist use of light and color. Monet, the chief apostle of the movement, derived his feeling for nature and its shifting moods from his boyhood by the sea in Normandy. Later, he specialized in series of paintings of the same subject seen in different lights – Rouen cathedral, the Norman cliffs, haystacks, and above all the water-lily garden which in the 1890s he created beside his country home at Giverny, west of Paris. Today it is a museum.

persevered to a very ripe old age with his particular peculiar style of luminous, sensuous fantasy.

During the 1939–45 war, many artists left Paris to escape the Nazis. Many of them never returned, but, together with refugees from other parts of Europe, settled in the United States. This is partly why Paris has ceased to be the world's capital of art; great painters no longer flock to live there. New York and even Cologne and London have all become more important as markets for dealers. The mecca of young artists is now New York, much more than Paris, and France has contributed little to recent developments in modern art. With the possible exceptions of Jean Dubuffet, the abstract artist Nicolas de Stael, and the sculptor Daniel Buren, very few postwar French artists have had any wide international impact.

The Ministry of Culture has made some effort to assist modern art, though less than for theater or music. Jack Lang provided new funds for museums to buy contemporary works, and he set up new modern art centers in the regions. His major emphasis, however, was on revitalizing the state museums in the provinces, which had tended to be fusty and badly organized. Here he was building on the growing new public interest in museums, in France as in many other countries. Museum-going is now in vogue as a leisure activity, and the tally of visitors has increased hugely. The French today excel at mounting large imaginative art exhibitions, generally retrospectives of a single artist or period, and these draw big crowds – for example, the Pompidou Center's surveys of the historic cultural links between Paris and cities such as Berlin and Moscow. Paris certainly knows how to display its illustrious cultural heritage to great effect, and despite the comparative lack of native talent, it is still a city where art is eagerly discussed.

Cinema

Not only did the French pioneer cinematography in the 1890s, but arguably they have produced more great directors and great films than any other nation, even the United States. The cinema in France may be in part a mass-entertainment industry, as elsewhere, but it is also regarded as a major art form, and has long enjoyed high intellectual respectability. In the 1920s Cocteau was turning to film as a medium for his poetry, and writers such as Malraux, Sartre and Robbe-Grillet have taken part in filmmaking or even directed films. Today France's star classic theater director, Patrice Chéreau, is moving to cinema. However, as in the other arts, creativity is flagging, and few good directors have emerged recently to take over the torch from the now aging veterans of the *nouvelle vague* (new wave).

Often literary in flavor, or full of poetic fantasy, or warmly humanistic, the French cinema appears as the natural inheritor of the best traditions of French painting or novels. Significantly, one of its greatest directors, Jean Renoir, was the son of one of the leading Impressionists. As distinct from Hollywood, where traditionally a director is simply an employee of a big studio, working to a rigid system, the French have long held to the concept of the "*film d'auteur*", that is, the film as the director's unique personal creation. The independent cinema in France has been conducive to such freedom of expression, far more so than television, which has done little to promote good fictional filmmaking or new drama (almost the opposite of the situation in Britain). Especially in the "new wave" period, much of the best creative talent was being drawn to cinema, rather than to other art forms, which may partly explain the recent poor state of painting, the novel and play-writing.

Above left The gifted and versatile Louis Malle (b. 1932) is seen here directing a film in the 1960s. Though often classed with the *nouvelle vague*, he is not really part of it but a lone figure. Most of his best films have been set in the past or abroad. He has excelled at focusing intimately on embarrassing or taboo subjects, such as suicide (*Le Feu follet*), incest (*Le Souffle au coeur*), wartime collaboration (*Lacombe Lucien*) or child prostitution (*Pretty Baby*). His warmth and humanism show in these films, and in others such as *Au revoir les enfants*, a moving study of wartime France.

Above Alain Resnais (b. 1922), seen here directing *La Vie est un roman*, has been a great innovator in the cinema. The Cannes Festival in 1959 was stunned by his first feature, *Hiroshima mon amour*, with its incantatory style and strange interweaving of themes of public and private tragedy. *L'Année dernière à Marienbad* was equally provocative. *Muriel* and *Providence* were the best of his later films. Resnais is an elusive, enigmatic person, and elusiveness has been one of his major themes.

Jean Renoir

The golden age of French cinema, in the 1930s, was dominated by some great directors who combined strong lyrical gifts with a radiant humanism. Undeniably the greatest of them was Jean Renoir, whose career as a filmmaker spanned 45 years, from 1924 to 1969. Renoir was a realist: but his work had its own poetry, as well as a sensuous, painterly quality, much influenced by his father, Pierre-Auguste Renoir. A feeling for landscape and sunshine, for human form, for the physical joy of living, informed the work of both of them.

Renoir also had left-wing sympathies and a warm feeling for working people, expressed in his film of Zola's *La Bête humaine*, as well as in *La Grande Illusion* and *Le Règle du jeu*. He worked abroad for a while, then crowned his later years with some mellow films such as *French Cancan*, a study of Montmartre in the *belle époque*. A gentle humanist and fervent lover of life, he reflected these qualities in his films. He was also a craftsman and an innovator. Renoir was adored by the young.

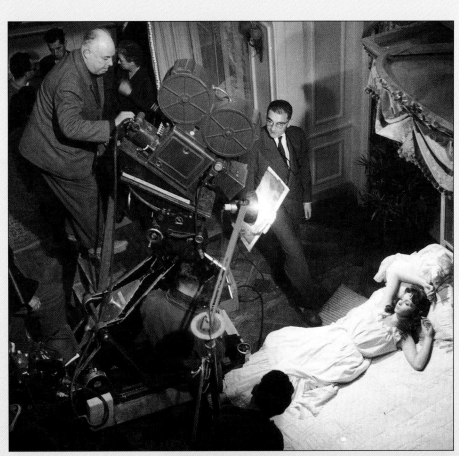

LA GRANDE ILLUSION

JEAN GABIN • PIERRE FRESNAY • ERIC VON STROHEIM
IN
A STORY OF THE 1914-18 WAR

Above right Renoir in the studio, directing a scene from *French Cancan* in 1955. Although he accepted studio constraints, his fluid, improvising style was often at its best when he was filming on location or outdoors.

Above left Renoir himself acted in several of his prewar films, as here (left, in picture) in *La Règle du jeu* (1939). This film, often considered his masterpiece, was a study of the moral decadence of the bourgeoisie in the 1930s. On the outbreak of war it was banned by the French censor as being "demoralizing".

Left La Grande Illusion (1937), another of his very great films, was a pacifist story of the futility of war and the primacy of comradeship. Eric von Stroheim (seen here) played the German commander of a 1914–18 prisoner-of-war camp, whose friendship with one of his French officer captives, a fellow-aristocrat, transcended the national barriers between enemies.

Right Renoir at work with Paulette Goddard on *Diary of a Chambermaid* (1946), one of several mediocre films that he made in Hollywood in the 1940s, after fleeing German-occupied Paris. The best films that he made outside France were *The River*, set in India, and *La Carrosse d'or* (Italy), both visually ravishing.

The French cinema is funded quite generously by the government, and films of artistic merit are eligible for special grants, on the basis of a promising script or the director's previous work. This helps the so-called "art movie", though of course the film industry also produces plenty of commercial tosh, from low comedies to gangster movies and pornography. Indeed, the mass public taste is no loftier than in other countries, but the serious intellectual audience, notably of young people, is much larger. In Paris, with its scores of little art-houses, the choice of good films to see, old or new, is far wider than in any other city, even New York. Hundreds of ciné-clubs flourish all over France.

The French are proud of having been the cinema's foremost inventors. Louis Lumière, a photographer, devised an early motion-picture camera, and in 1895

Above left Quatorze juillet (1932) was typical of René Clair's lighthearted satiric comedies set in Paris. This director (1898–1981) was born in the working-class central Paris that inspired much of his best work. He began in silent films, then in the early 1930s made *Sous les toits de Paris*, *Le Million*, *A nous la liberté* and other movies that mixed joyous humor and burlesque with touches of surrealism. His work was always gentle and optimistic, rarely concerned with any social message, save that of individual freedom.

Left Jean Renoir's film *La Bête Humaine* (1938) was based on Zola's 1890 novel of that name, a steamy melodrama about an engine driver's affair with a stationmaster's wife. It gave a powerful part to Jean Gabin in the main role. With its moody camerawork and its feeling for human passion, the film was typical of the "poetic realism" of that golden age of French cinema in the 1930s.

Above This farcical poster gives a somewhat false impression of *Orphée* (1950), Jean Cocteau's mysterious poetic fantasy, based loosely on the Orpheus and Eurydice myth. Poet, novelist, actor and painter as well as film director, Cocteau (1889–1963) was a fashionable figure in the prewar Paris artistic world. "Etonne-moi" ("astonish-me"), Diaghilev told him, so he did. This being France, he turned to making films as a natural outlet for his poetic talents, as displayed in the startling *Sang d'un poète*.

Right Jeanne Moreau was the star of François Truffaut's dazzling *Jules et Jim* (1961), a celebration of happiness and freedom of spirit. Much influenced by Renoir, Truffaut (1932–84) was a lyrical humanist whose films were about love or childhood, or even about the joy of making films (for instance, *La Nuit américaine*) and rarely touched on social or political themes.

made what is considered the first film; then Georges Méliès, a professional magician, produced over 400 short films between 1899 and 1913. Apart from the work of Abel Gance, whose *Napoléon* (1927) is a great classic, the French did not contribute so much to the golden age of silent films, but with the coming of the "talkies" some marvellous directors emerged. Jean Vigo (1905–34) made two great poetic films, *Zéro de conduite* and *L'Atalante*, before his early death. René Clair (1898–1981), who had started in silent films, is remembered for his exuberant satires (such as *Le Million* and *A nous la liberté*), while possibly his best postwar film was *Belle de nuit*. Marcel Carné (b. 1909) directed some powerfully moody romantic dramas, notably *Quai des brumes* and *Les Enfants du paradis*, while Jean Renoir (1894–1979), whose successes included the *Partie de campagne*, *La Grande Illusion*, *La Régle du jeu* and *The River*, was one of the cinema's greatest lyrical humanists.

If the 1930s were the golden age of French cinema, then the early postwar years were at least silver, with such films as Jacques Becker's *Casque d'or*, René Clément's *Les Jeux interdits*, and the earlier work of that austere master, Robert Bresson. But, by the later 1950s, the French cinema had lost its sparkle and was in a dull, stereotyped phase. It was then that the *nouvelle vague* burst upon the world – an explosion of new talent with few parallels in world cinema. Although these young directors were all labeled "new wave" by the press, they were really very diverse. The rebel coterie of critics from the magazine *Cahiers du Cinéma* (Chabrol, Godard, Rohmer, Truffaut and others) were very different from the more reserved group around Alain Rensais, or from the lone rider Louis Malle. Moreover, while some of the directors (Resnais, Godard) were true cinema revolutionaries with a new film language, others such as Truffaut were simply applying a new personal style to older themes. What they all had in common was the *film d'auteur* approach – a freshness of vision, and a desire to get away from the star system, and to do location work rather than rely on studio sets. Most of the early "new wave" films were made on tiny budgets, and critics and public responded to them. The first features of Resnais and Truffaut won the two top prizes at the Cannes Festival in 1959.

Perhaps the most typical of the new directors was François Truffaut (1932–84), whose first feature *Les 400 coups* was in part autobiographical. Quite unconcerned with social or public themes, he was a humanist in the Renoir tradition whose lyrical gifts and gentle wit were seen at their best in *Jules et Jim* and *La Nuit américaine*. Claude Chabrol (b. 1930),an erratic but striking talent, also began with films based on his own experience, and then made a series of elegant thrillers (*Le Boucher*, for example) that were also acute satires on bourgeois hypocrisy. The idiosyncratic Eric Rohmer (b. 1920) is known for his wordy but subtle conversation-pieces on themes of love and private morality, in such slight but charmingly original films as *Le Genou de Claire* and *Un Conte de printemps*. Even more *sui generis* is the work of Jean-Luc Godard (b. 1930), the most provocative, influential and talked-about of the "new wave" directors, and a true child of the 1960s. His first feature, *A bout de souffle*, was filmed in streets and flats with a hand-held camera. Though quirkily whimsical, almost surreal, his earliest and best films (among them, *Pierrot le fou*, and *Alphaville*) were also a subtle critique of French society, but his later work has been untypically solemn and abstruse.

Alain Resnais (b. 1922) is just as controversial and unusual as Godard, but in a very different way. His films, withdrawn and enigmatic, have recurrent themes of time and memory, the erosion of love and loyalties, and the elusiveness of reality. But as he has generally relied on a script by a star writer, the impact has varied – hauntingly powerful in *Hiroshima mon amour* (script by Duras), teasingly trite in *L'Année dernière à Marienbad* (Robbe-Grillet). Agnès Varda (b. 1928), France's best woman director and, like Resnais, a leftist intellectual, has explored themes of women in modern society, with irony in *Le Bonheur*, with warmth in *L'Une chante, l'autre pas*, and disturbingly in *Sans toit ni loi*. The gifted and versatile Louis Malle (b. 1932) has made films around the world, with an eclectic variety of moods and themes – very private in *Les Amants*, *Le Feu follet* and *My Dinner with André*, exuberantly escapist in *Viva Maria*, serious in his treatment of wartime or social subjects, as in *Lacombe Lucien*, *Au revoir les enfants* and his Indian documentaries.

There were scores of other "new wave" directors. After the success of the first films, producers eagerly joined the new-style low-budget vogue, and almost any young hopeful with a new idea found a camera thrust into his hands. Between 1959 and 1963 more than 170 French directors made a first film. The boom did not last. Few of the newcomers had real talent, and most of their films were frivolous and self-indulgent. In sum, the *nouvelle vague* worked wonders to restore the lyric, personal style of French cinema, and it yielded many great films. But today, 30 years later, most of its directors except for Malle and Rohmer, who are both still in high form, seem to have run out of inspiration. Since 1970, the one truly outstanding French filmmaker to have followed them is Bertrand Tavernier, a gentle humanist in the Renoir tradition. He has made films on serious social themes, but his best ones have been his sympathetic studies of family life and personal relationships (*Une Semaine de vacances*, *Dimanche à la campagne*, *Around Midnight*). Another modern director, Maurice Pialat, who has a far more misanthropic view of the human condition, has made some memorably powerful if gloomy films (*Loulou*, *A nos amours* and a version of Bernanos' novel *Sous le soleil de Satan*). Other directors of note include Claude Miller and André Téchiné, responsible for sensitive, realistic studies of local life, and Claude Berri, with his popular two-part remake of Marcel Pagnol's *Manon des Sources*. Some interesting women directors have also emerged – Diane Kurys, Claire Denis, Nelly Kaplan – while the most trendy newcomers have been the "video-clip" school of young filmmakers whose flashy thrillers have a teenage appeal – Luc Besson (*Subway, Nikita*) and Jean-Jacques Beineix (*Diva*, and notably his more serious and passionate *Betty Blue*).

Certainly, the French still make a few good films each year, but they tend to be slight, nearly always dealing with very private themes, or are set in the past. Seldom do they tackle the more sensitive political or social subjects of the day. Producers argue that the public may want "slice of life" films, but not ones dealing with controversial topics like racism or trade unions. After the glorious liberty of the "new wave" era, producers have again become wary of taking risks, for French cinema, like many others, is in

Balzac

Below An early edition of a volume of vignettes, part of Balzac's main work, *La Comédie humaine*. Balzac would write a first draft very fast, then make elaborate proof corrections which would drive his printers mad. His printers' bills often exceeded the sums he was paid for his writing, and were one cause of his constant debts.

Honoré de Balzac (1977 – 1850) was one of the most prolific of novelists, as well as perhaps France's greatest. Most of his vast output is contained in the 17-volume *Comédie humaine* with gives a sweeping panoramic survey of the French society that he knew. He had an intuitive understanding of the depths of human nature, and a sharp gift for evoking mood and personality. Many of his characters and scenes remain so alive that it has been said of him, "he not so much observed society as helped to create one".

Balzac was of provincial origin, in Touraine, but spent most of his life in Paris where, vain and ambitious, he struggled to be accepted by fashionable society. Many of his books are concerned with the mutual scorn and jealousy between Paris and the provinces. But his overriding theme was the power of money, and the self-interested search for money, prestige and success. Balzac sought to apply scientific principles to his rigorous analysis of human motives and social nuances. Many of the 2000 or so characters in *La Comédie humaine* keep reappearing in different books. But his approach was anything but detached. He passionately dissected the bourgeoisie, the Paris artistic milieu, the greedy tradesmen. But he ignored the working classes, despised the peasantry, and was too rough in nature to have a true empathy with the aristocracy.

Above A contemporary sketch of Balzac. He was a heavy man with a big round face, not handsome. But he was a dandy who liked dressing extravagantly, and a man-about-town with snobbish tastes for high society. He was a passionate man who had many loves – notably Eveline Hanska, a wealthy Polish countess, who married him just before he died.

Below A contemporary illustration for *Le Lys dans la vallée*, a story of doomed love set in a country château in the Indre valley, south of Tours. Several of Balzac's novels had provincial settings, for which he would do special field research: among them, *Les Chouans* (Brittany), *Illusions perdues* (Angoulême) and *Eugénie Grandet* (Saumur).

Right A drawing for *L'Illustre Gaudissart* whose eponymous hero, a shrewd and vulgar commercial traveler, was one of the archetypal characters in *La Comédie humaine*. Others included Vautrin the clever criminal, Cousine Bette the greedy ex-peasant, and Rastignac the provincial *arriviste* seeking fame and fortune in Paris.

financial crisis. It has, in fact, held up better than most to the impact of television, and audiences, after declining steeply in the 1960s, have now leveled off at some 50 to 60 percent higher than in Britain or Germany: the French are still a filmgoing nation. But the export trade has fallen badly, reflecting a decline in the quality of serious French movies. It is also arguable that, in economic terms, France still produces far too many films (about 130 features a year). After much haggling, the industry has at last reached an entente with the main television channels, which now help to finance some feature films, and are restricted in their screening of new films that can still earn money in cinemas. Other money-saving measures are less satisfactory, in particular the temptation, in the new age of Europe, for film and television companies to spread their costs through hybrid multinational coproductions – for example, a film set in Germany with a French, English and Italian cast, all talking English. Artistically, this is nearly always disastrous – and the French are just as bad offenders as others. Without doubt, the best French films, from *L'Atalante* to *Jean de Florette*, have radiated a genuine Frenchness, and this has been a secret of their success abroad.

Literature

The universality of French literature, its supreme appeal around the world, has resided perhaps in two main factors: one, a passion for ideas; two, a strong sense of place and of detailed social observation. Some of the greatest French writers have been philosophical – Montaigne and Pascal, Rousseau and Voltaire, and, in this century, Sartre and Camus. Others have been rooted in some native corner of France and have evoked the human condition in a precise local context – the novels of Flaubert set in Normandy, or of Mauriac in the Bordelais, or of Giono in Provence.

The conflict between reason and emotion, between feeling and observation, has recurred constantly in French literature. In the 18th century, Montesquieu, Voltaire and other writers in the classical tradition placed the accent on reason, clarity and objectivity. But then, gradually, a sense of poetry and passion emerged, and a feeling for nature that was fairly new in France. The precursor of this trend was the Swiss-born philosopher Jean-Jacques Rousseau (1712–78), who believed that only by living in close harmony with nature could human beings, corrupted by society, recover their innocent and happy state. Next, came the early Romantics: Madame de Staël, a great traveler who wrote an influential book on German Romanticism, *De l'Allemagne*; and François-René de Chateaubriand, a Byronic figure who truly lived the part and has left some fine memoirs. The Romantic movement at its height was led by four great poets, Lamartine, de Vigny, de Musset, and notably Victor Hugo (1802–85). Alphonse de Lamartine, who also played a part in politics, was a Burgundian aristocrat whose moody poetry is imbued with a characteristically romantic love of nature. Hugo, the Romantics' self-styled spokesman and perhaps the greatest of all French poets, championed the cause of total liberty for the artist, which led him to clash with the classicists in the "quarrel of the ancients and moderns". As well as being the author of much fine verse, he wrote plays and some famous popular novels, notably *Les Misérables* and *Notre Dame de Paris (The Hunchback of Notre Dame)*.

Stendhal and Balzac, two contemporaries of Hugo,

were much greater novelists than he. Stendhal (1783–1842) whose real name was Henri Beyle, believed that people were ruled by their passions and that literature should show this. His best novels are *Le Rouge et le noir*, a tale of fatal ambition, and *La Chartreuse de Parme* which reflects his lifelong love affair with Italy. Honoré de Balzac (1799–1850) gave a detailed panorama of French society, in Paris and the provinces, through his titanic series of novels that make up *La Comédie humaine*; his creative vigor, his portrayal of passion, his acute and ironic observations of character and of social mores, single him out as a writer whom many consider the equal of Tolstoy. A very colorful figure is the woman novelist who used the pen name of Georges Sand (1804–76): she alternated a boldly bohemian existence in Paris (including love affairs with de Musset and Chopin among others), with a quiet country life among the peasants of her beloved native Berry, whom she idealized in her novels such as *La Mare au diable*.

Two other major novelists dominated the latter half

Above Illustration for Victor Hugo's *Les Misérables*. This particular *misérable* is the sad, maltreated child Cosette, and this famous 19th-century sketch of her has been posted on billboards all around the globe in recent years, to advertise the rock musical version of Hugo's sprawling, big-hearted epic novel. It is a fresco of life in France in the 1820–30 period. Hugo was the leader of the French Romantic movement in literature. Besides *Les Misérables* and *Nôtre Dame de Paris*, a novel of medieval Paris, he wrote plays, and much powerful poetry where he laid bare his soul, in the Romantic manner.

Right The lowly born but ambitious Julien Sorel meets the well-to-do Madame de Rênal, whom he later seduces, at the start of Stendhal's great novel *Le Rouge et le noir*. This drawing is from the 1854 edition. *La Chartreuse de Parme*, set in the Italy that he adored, was Stendhal's other masterpiece.

Below Albert Auguste Fourie's artistic evocation of the suicide of Emma Bovary. Gustave Flaubert's *Madame Bovary* (1857), the study of a bored provincial wife destroyed by her misplaced romanticism, was partly based on a real-life drama in the village of Ry, east of Rouen. Flaubert detested bourgeois pettiness, yet was understanding of human frailty and thus could empathize with his heroine. "Madame Bovary, c'est moi", he said.

of the 19th century. Gustave Flaubert (1821–80) was a supreme stylist and a realist who painted a sharp picture of the bourgeoisie of his native Normandy, notably in *Madame Bovary*, an ironic tale of romantic frustration that at the time was found so shocking that he was prosecuted for it (but was acquitted). Then Emile Zola (1840–1902) pioneered the "naturalistic" novel. In his many powerful books, such as *L'Assommoir*, *Thérèse Raquin*, *Germinal* and *La Terre*, Zola gave a vivid account of the social conditions of his day. Another "naturalist" writer, but in a quieter vein, was Guy de Maupassant, a disciple of Flaubert and, like him, a Norman; he is best known for his ironical short stories. A third Norman novelist of that time, Barbey d'Aurevilly, was very different: a flamboyant Romantic and keen Royalist, his tales of rural passion are hauntingly macabre.

Charles Baudelaire (1821–67), the leading poet of the period, was a highly original writer, often regarded as the precursor of modern poetry. In *Les Fleurs du mal* and other work, his sonorous rhythms and sense of melancholy introduced a new sensibility into French verse, closer to the ennui of urban life than the joys of nature. His work influenced the equally evocative poetry of Paul Verlaine, and that of the turbulent and precocious Arthur Rimbaud, who had ceased to write by the age of 20. They, in turn, paved the way for the symbolist movement, which centered on the poet Stéphane Mallarmé, an aesthete concerned with the search for ideal beauty. A little later, the poet

Above Charles Baudelaire is one of France's very greatest poets. But his brooding evocation of evil and squalor so shocked the public at the time that he was prosecuted, like Flaubert, for "offence to morals". Unlike Flaubert, he lost and was fined; some poems were banned, and the ban was not lifted until 1949!

Above right Renoir's portrait of Stéphane Mallarmé (1842–98), a teacher of English whose often abstruse verse, aiming at an idealized beauty, had a great influence on modern poets.

Left Emile Zola (here as portrayed by Manet) was a left-winger and political activist, whose powerful "naturalistic" novels were aimed at portraying the life of the poor, and the injustices of society, in the later 19th century. He used journalistic techniques, doing research down the coal mines for *Germinal*, and among peasants for *La Terre*. His books are lurid and melodramatic, but very powerful.

Right The powerful novelist Alexandre Dumas *père* (1802–70) is best known for his historical adventure stories, *Les Trois Mousquetaires* and *Le Comte de Monte-Cristo*. He wrote with gusto and imagination.

Charles Péguy was one of a number of writers, around the turn of the century, who combined a fervent Catholicism with a patriotic worship of France; another was the right-wing novelist Maurice Barrès, from Lorraine.

Four very disparate figures stand out as giants in the literature of the early 20th century – Proust, Valéry, Claudel and Gide. The multivolume, semi-autobiographical masterwork of Marcel Proust (1871–1922), *A la recherche du temps perdu*, was both a precise portrait of the smart Paris high society that he knew, and the private exploration of an inner imaginative world, built on the themes of time and memory. The originality of Proust's poetic vision of life, and of his hypnotic prose style with its lengthy, complex sentences, are quite truly remarkable. Paul Valéry (1871–1945), also a great stylist, and much influenced by Mallarmé, wrote poetry that is difficult and sometimes obscure, combining sensuous beauty with deep philosophical thought – for example, in *La Cimitière marin*, a soliloquy on the theme of death. Paul Claudel (1868–1955), a career diplomat who was emotionally bound up with Catholicism, wrote poetry and drama with lyric fervor on religious themes notably *Le Soulier de satin*. André Gide (1869–1951) was a freethinker torn between accepting and rejecting his severe Calvinist background, who espoused a creed of personal liberty. His questing moralism, seen in some of his fine short novels, such as *La Porte étroite*, had much influence at a time when such an outlook seemed bold and modern.

While Matisse, Picasso and others were pioneering the avant-garde in art, it began to appear in literature too. Around 1910, the poet Guillaume Apollinaire and others dispensed with punctuation and explored surrealist imagery. Then in the 1920s, the surrealist movement made its appearance, aiming to capture in art or in words the chaotic images of dreams and the

Above Sidonie-Gabrielle Colette (1873–1954), the leading French woman writer of her time, wrote short novels about love and other personal themes, notable for their vivid sensual evocation of sounds, colors, tastes and smells. With a touch of autobiography, she dwelt on the poignancy of adolescence. She also adored cats, and they feature in several of her books.

unconscious. In French literature, its leaders were the poets André Breton, Louis Aragon and Paul Eluard. Other, more accessible writers of great quality, mainly novelists, were also at work in the interwar years – among them, Jules Romains (*Les Hommes de bonne volonté*), Sidonie-Gabrielle Colette (*Chéri, La Chatte*), the best woman writer of the time, and Raymond Radiguet (*Le Diable au corps*) who died aged only 20. François Mauriac, who touched on the conflicts between religion and passionate sensuality, and Georges Bernanos, who described the spiritual struggles of young priests, were two more writers in a strong Catholic tradition. At the same time, in Provence, Jean Giono, prophet of a radiant pantheism, extolled the mysterious cosmic links between human beings and nature.

Just before and during World War II, some important writers emerged who were as much thinkers and critics as novelists or dramatists, and who expressed the anxieties of the time. André Malraux (1901–76) wrote political and philosophical novels based on his experiences in China in the 1920s and in the Spanish Civil War, before turning mainly to art criticism and to a political career. Jean-Paul Sartre became known more as a philosopher and political activist than as a writer of fiction. His first novel, *La Nausée* (1938), caused quite a stir, and his plays such as *Huit-clos* have worn well. Albert Camus, who shared with Jean-Paul Sartre a sense of the absurdity of human existence, truly was a very great writer, who expressed his courageous humanism in novels such as *L'Etranger* and *La Peste*, and in several philosophical works.

In the earlier postwar years the world reputation of French letters was still high, with no less than five French writers receiving the Nobel Prize for Literature – Gide, Mauriac, Camus, the epic poet Saint-John Perse, and Sartre (who refused it on political grounds). Then, with the rise of the "*nouveau roman* (new

Left center On a profound and metaphysical level, Marcel Proust drew on childhood and youthful memories, weaving them into the complex poetic fabric of his seven-volume *A la recherche du temps perdu*, one of the greatest novels in world literature. Some of the best scenes evoke his boyhood visits to Illiers, the "Combray" of the book: here his ritual walk beside a hawthorn hedge becomes, in the novel, a central metaphor for the mystery of Time itself. Other scenes evoke holidays on the Normandy coast at Cabourg ("Balbec" in the book) where his passionate image of Albertine was inspired by one of his homosexual loves. In real life Proust was a neurotic and an invalid, who lined his room with cork to exclude noise, and wore a heavy coat even in summer. He died of asthma.

Left Albert Camus (1913–60) was born in Algeria, which was the setting for his best-known novel, *La Peste*. This study of life in a plague-ridden city can be read as an allegory of the human condition. *L'Etranger*, *La Chute* and *L'Exil et le royaume* are among his other well-known works. Camus was an agnostic whose writing reflects his agonizing search for a meaning to existence, and he was much admired for his courageous humanism. He played a part in the Resistance, and in 1957 won the Nobel Prize for literature. He died in a car accident in 1960.

Right Alain Robbe-Grillet (b. 1922) has been the standard-bearer and leading theoretician of the *nouveau roman* school of French fiction that was dominant in the 1950s and 1960s. A statistician and agronomist by background, he has written novels – *le Voyeur* and *La Jalousie* are the best-known – that studiously exclude emotions and narrative, and deal just with objects, minutely described. And he has passionately promoted this kind of writing, denouncing anyone who still dares to write in a traditional way. His influence has now waned.

novel) and of structuralism in the 1960s, the humanism that had informed writers gave way to an arid technical experimentation with form and language. For a while, these trends were so dominant that they seemed to crush other kinds of writing. The "new novelists" – Alain Robbe-Grillet, Michel Butor, Nathalie Sarraute and others – were a mixed bunch, no more a "school" than was the "new wave" in the cinema. What they had in common was a rejection of narrative, social comment and character portrayal, and an obsession with minute physical description, of objects or sensations. Their semiscientific approach linked them to structuralism. By far the most extreme of them was Robbe-Grillet, their self-appointed leader, who vehemently attacked the Balzacian, even the Proustian, tradition, or any kind of novel that included emotion. His own books, such as *Le Voyeur* and *La Jalousie*, are written in a sonorous, dreamlike prose, given over to detailed descriptions of, for

instance, the shape of a window or the physiognomy of centipedes. Michel Butor's novels are concerned mainly with the relativity of time and space, while Nathalie Sarraute, in her manner a psychological realist, uses a stream-of-consciousness technique to explore a living tissue of tiny, subtle sensations. Claude Simon, who won the Nobel prize in 1985 for such books as *Le Palace* and *La Route de Flandres*, has perhaps wrongly been dubbed a "new novelist". The same may be said of Marguerite Duras, a warm-hearted writer with a feeling for real people, despite her elliptical techniques of dialogue and narrative.

Needless to say, the rarefied and esoteric "new novel" found little success with the public, and its sales were usually small. Today its vogue has largely passed. For some years, however, its ideas and those of the structuralist Roland Barthes, exerted a mental tyranny over younger novelists, making them feel unable to write any more in a traditional manner. No coherent group or trend has emerged since then. A few good solitary writers have for many years continued quietly along their own lines, unaffected by fashion – notably, Michel Tournier, whose reworking of historic myths has some affinities with Tolkien; J.M.G. Le Clézio, whose cosmic allegories are an attack on the materialism of modern society; the late Marguerite Yourcenar, a gifted historical novelist; and Patrick Modiano, who has written evocatively about the Occupation period. The baleful satirist Georges Perec and Jean Carrière, whose *L'Epervier de Maheu* was a potent parable about rural poverty in the Cévennes, also deserve attention. But it is noticeable that nearly all the good recent French novels – and there are not so many – are set either in the past, or abroad, or in private worlds of childhood. France is still far from producing, even on a modest level, a new Balzac or Zola who will chronicle today's society.

Indeed, publishers and critics alike still tend to disdain works of modern social realism, and they exert much influence over public taste, especially through the great annual literary prizes – the Goncourt, Fémina and others. A new novel that might otherwise be expected to sell, say, 10,000 copies, will jump to the top of the bestsellers' lists, with sales of up to 300,000 if it wins the coveted Goncourt. Any status-conscious dinner-party hostess will then be sure to display the latest Goncourt-winner on her coffee-table within days of publication. Sometimes the best new books win these prizes, but there have been allegations that the awards are rigged by three top publishers who control the juries.

Intellectual life

The term "intellectual" is seldom used pejoratively in France, as it is in many countries. Intellectuals are a respected and recognizable species, very conscious of their own status and duties; they may not have a great influence on public events, but they are expected to pronounce on them and debate them publicly, as Jean-Paul Sartre did with such vigor in the postwar decades, and they often make headlines. They can be found all over France in academic circles, but those who seek the limelight cluster, above all, on the Paris Left Bank, where they hold teaching posts, or make a living from part-time jobs in publishing or journalism, writing novels or pamphlets, or giving radio talks and appearing in highbrow television chat shows. Most intellectuals have tended to be on the left, but a vocal right has reemerged in recent years, while the influence of left-wing ideas has waned.

The debate between left and right, notably the nationalist, Catholic right, dominated French intellectual life from the late 19th century until the 1930s – and its origins lie partly in the "Dreyfus affair" of the 1890s. It was then that intellectuals first discovered their power, and the term *intellectuel* first became widely used. Alfred Dreyfus was an army captain, and a Jew, who was falsely convicted on a charge of giving military secrets to the Germans. Some writers and others sprang to his defence, notably Emile Zola whose famous open letter *J'accuse* (I accuse) claimed that Dreyfus was the victim of a right-wing anti-Semitic plot. The scandal split France into two camps, roughly left and right, and it lasted until 1906, when Dreyfus's finally received a full pardon and he was reinstated. The Dreyfus case was unique: never before or since in France has the intelligentsia intervened so decisively on a public issue.

Although defeated over Dreyfus, in the next decades the nationalist Catholic right was extremely active, both before and after the 1914–18 war. Its leaders were the novelist Maurice Barrès and the militant nationalist Charles Maurras, with his *Action Française* movement. Then, in the 1920s, Communist intellectuals began to come to the fore, such as the novelist Henri Barbusse; and, in the 1930s, even writers such as Gide and Malraux were flirting with Communism (Malraux fought as a pilot on the Republican side in the Spanish Civil War), while the pacifist ideas of Jean Giono, the Provençal novelist, had an influence too. Intellectuals both of left and right made some impact on public opinion during that time, as the threat of war grew closer. During the Occupation some liberal thinkers, such as Albert Camus, played a key role in the Resistance, while part of the right collaborated. For this, the pro-Nazi writer Robert Brasillach was executed at the Liberation, while the gifted novelist Drieu La Rochelle, who had edited the *Nouvelle Revue Française* under the Germans, committed suicide.

For some years after the war, Jean-Paul Sartre dominated the intellectual scene, mixing existentialist ideas with an open sympathy for Communism. Some others went further and joined the Communist party, but many left it after the Soviet interventions in Budapest (1956) and Prague (1968). The Algerian war was for a while a rallying-point of opposition by leftist intellectuals, and 121 of them, in 1960, signed a manifesto urging conscripts not to fight. They were hostile also to the technocratic ethos and the growing consumerism of the 1970s and 1980s. When Mitterrand took power, although nearly all of them had gladly voted for him, their attitude became equivocal, for many felt that a self-respecting intellectual should not side with *le pouvoir* (the government) and that integrity was best preserved in opposition. Yet, while for the past hundred years French intellectuals have seldom been slow to take sides on big public issues, they have equally seldom been able to change the course of events (Dreyfus was an exception).

Jean-Paul Sartre has been the best French example in this century, of an active politically committed intellectual, very influential within his own circles. He is best known for the existentialist ideas of responsibility and freedom of choice that he developed from the German thinkers, Husserl and Heidegger. He and his lifelong companion Simone de Beauvoir used to sit in the St-Germain-des-Prés cafés, where disciples and hangers-on would often mistake rigorous Sartrian liberty for easy licence. Sartre himself was really more interested in Marxism, asserting that existentialism was merely its handmaiden. But gradually, he broke with Communism, though until his death in 1980 he continued publicly to support various leftist and humanitarian causes, going to the Elysée palace to plead the cause of the Vietnamese "boat people" with Giscard. Sartre commanded wide respect, but the apparent shifts and ambiguities in his thought steadily alienated many of his disciples. As was often said, his was the tragedy of a man with a deeply religious nature who had killed God. Even so, his intellectual influence was to force a reappraisal of old ideas and introduce a freer, more skeptical climate.

The existential movement had largely faded away by the later 1960s, when a new, intellectually high-powered trend emerged: structuralism. This was not a philosophy so much as a method, nor was it a

Above The literary critic Roland Barthes (1915–80) was one of the best-known of the very diverse group of intellectuals loosely referred to as "structuralists". They had a huge influence in some academic and avant-garde circles during the 1970s. Barthes, a Marxist, applied structuralist ideas in the fields of semantics or "semiology" – the study of the signs or symbols which he believed shaped thoughts and actions. He wrote in a precious style full of neologisms, which was often parodied. But academically he was distinguished, holding the chair of literary semiology at the august Collège de France.

Right Simone de Beauvoir (1908–86) and Jean-Paul Sartre (1905–1980), seen here at a rally in Paris in 1970, were lifelong companions and lovers, though they never married. Both of them were on the left, and they constantly urged their fellow intellectuals to leave their "ivory towers" and indulge, as they did, in political activism. This was the theme of de Beauvoir's novel *Les mandarins*. She was also an active feminist, and in *Le Deuxième Sexe*, she urged French women to rebel against the inferior status imposed on them by a male-dominated world. Sartre wrote his first novel *La Nausée* while he was a *lycée* teacher in Le Havre, and it is set in that seaport. He and de Beauvoir espoused an existentialist philosophy which was largely misunderstood by many of their followers. Sartre was a Marxist who gradually became disillusioned with orthodox Communism. Although not a great literary stylist, he was an original thinker of the first rank, and was awarded the Nobel Prize in 1964. He refused it, for political reasons.

Following pages A typical café-restaurant with sidewalk terrace, in the Paris Latin Quarter. While many have been modernized, this one has been kept deliberately in its pre-war style. Although much invaded by tourists, this part of Paris remains a public meeting point for intellectuals, artists and others, as in the immediate post-war years when Jean-Paul Sartre held court at St-Germain-de-Prés. The literary café is in decline, but certain restaurants remain haunts of the intelligentsia; Parisians like them to be crowded and noisy, with swift, brusque service.

"school", for its leading exponents were most diverse – the literary critic Roland Barthes, the philosophers Michel Foucault and Jacques Derrida, the psychoanalyst Jacques Lacan, and the great anthropologist Claude Lévi-Strauss. In a sense, structuralism grew out of existentialism, with which it shared an atheistic rejection of the classic view of history and morality. But whereas the humanist Sartre saw the individual as the free captain of his or her own destiny, the structuralists saw the individual as the prisoner of a predetermined system. Foucault, in his seminal work *Les Mots et les choses* (1966), argued, "Man with a capital M is an invention" – and an educated public reacted with fascinated horror. Sartre had killed God: this new lot were killing Man too! Many critics saw the trend as a symptom of the belated French discovery of anthropology and other social sciences, which the structuralists seized on imaginatively but

with typical French extremism. They had much influence in academic circles outside France, especially in the United States. But they were also criticized for a willful aridity, arrogance and obscurity; and by the later 1980s, with many of its leading exponents dead or very aged, the fashion seemed to be petering out.

In a Paris always hungry for intellectual novelty, other trends have emerged since the mid-1970s. First the so-called *nouveaux philosophes* (new philosophers), led by André Glucksmann and Bernard-Henri Lévy, erupted noisily. These were young men from the left who wrote books and articles proclaiming their disenchantment with Marxism or their other leftist ideals. The left hit back, denouncing these attacks as "a media racket mounted by the right". Then, in 1979, it was the turn of *la Nouvelle Droite* (the New Right). The intellectual hard right had been fairly quiet since the war. Now, encouraged by the decline of the left, it

reemerged and began to be taken seriously. The New Right's propagandist-in-chief, Alain de Benoist, announced a somewhat confused Nietzschean doctrine of mystical elitism and paganism, not at all nationalist in the Maurras vein, but harking back to the spiritual fount of early European tradition – Hellenic, Celtic and Germanic. This eccentric vogue soon passed, and though the right is still intellectually vocal, no real trend has emerged since. By 1990, "ideological vacuum" was the phrase most often used to describe the Left Bank scene, where all the "isms", Marxism included, seemed to have lost their power to excite.

Left Bank intellectuals tend to cling together, meeting in their modest flats or in well-known haunts such as the cafés Lipp and Le Balzar. It is an intense, narcissistic world of rival cliques, constant intrigue and instant fashion, whose members often review one another's books. London and New York of course, have similar circles, but in Paris the closed surroundings and the French love of polemic raises the temperature of the argument. Visiting foreigners are often captivated by the climate of eager debate, the curiosity about new ideas – a world where, for instance, Boulez and Barthes once held public talk-ins to explore the links between structuralism and serial music, and drew full houses. It is also a world infatuated by novelty, where new ideas become seasonal fashions like the *haute couture* collections. As one witty pundit wrote, "Paris, obsessed by its own navel, gobbles up an ideology a week, an ontology every month." This milieu also sometimes appears as one of the last bastions of French insularity, and while intellectuals may feel involved in world events, their debate is often Paris-focused. This mattered less in the old days, when French thought and culture were universally acclaimed, but today the Paris debate makes much less impact on the world, and intellectuals are loth to admit this.

In his analysis of the origins of French intellectual power, Régis Debray has suggested that the main center of persuasion has shifted three times in the past 100 years: first, in about 1880, from the Church to the universities, then, in the 1930s, to the big publishing houses with their monthly or quarterly reviews, and, since about the 1960s, to television and the other media. Certainly, the reviews, such as *Les Temps Modernes* which Sartre used to edit, or Gallimard's *Nouvelle Revue Française*, are still more numerous and influential than in most countries, but in recent years they have lost ground to the quicker mass outlets provided by the new media. Debray has alleged that true intellectual debate has been trivialized by the new media, which are dominated by a new class of "mediacrats" who lure serious thinkers into prostituting their talents, with high fees and easy fame. Of course, this problem is not confined to France. But in Paris, where American media techniques arrived late, the impact of television on a milieu already so intense, polemical and exhibitionist, has been explosive. The media exploit the polemics as show biz, and a mass public enjoys the jousting. So professors and writers compete with each other to become stars on the chat shows – and they did so especially for the famous Friday night *Apostrophe* literary program which, with up to 6 million viewers, was the highpoint of the intellectual week. Its presenter, Bernard Pivot, was denounced by Debray as a "literary dictator", though when he brought his show to an end in 1990, France's television was certainly the poorer.

French Popular Culture

French popular culture has always produced its own idols. Some, such as the singer Alain Souchon, were little known abroad, but others have become stars as renowned across the globe as in France itself. They have even become symbols of a certain image of Frenchness – the saucy suavity of Chevalier, the chic sexiness of Bardot, the Latin charisma of Montand. Juliette Greco and Charles Aznavour too won international acclaim.

In the world of song, there is possibly less of a gap in France than in many countries between "popular" and "serious" tastes. This may be due to the tradition of the *chanson* (the word just means "song"), a truly French *genre* that carries intellectual respectability. With its roots in the Middle Ages, the *chanson* is a poetic ballad, highly personal, and the singers often write the words themselves. Some, such as Greco, began in the little Left Bank *boîtes* of Paris, then with stardom moved to the huge music halls. Some of the greatest of these singers have been true, serious poets with a vision of the world, and not just entertainers – among them, Georges Brassens, Charles Trenet and Jacques Brel, a Belgian.

Right Josephine Baker (1906–75) was a black American entertainer who conquered France and settled there. In the 1920s she moved from New York to Paris as a dancer, introduced *le hot jazz* there, and was adored for it. Her flamboyant style made a diverting contrast to the classic French *chansons* that she often sang. In World War II she played a part in the Resistance.

Below Edith Gassion (1915–63) was given the stage name of Piaf (Parisian slang for "sparrow") because of her petite, frail appearance and her plaintive voice. Piaf was perhaps the greatest French popular singer of her time and became a living legend. Abandoned at birth by her mother, she sang on the streets of Paris as a child, to earn *sous*. Discovered and trained, she quickly became a major star. Her dramatic style, her ringing voice with its hint of tragedy, won audiences' hearts wherever she played.

Below Yves Montand (b. 1921: this poster dates from the 1950s) has regularly headed French opinion polls as the most popular living Frenchman. Of Italian peasant origin, he grew up in poverty in Marseille. Besides making over 60 films, he has starred as a music-hall singer, with a deep-timbered, rasping voice.

Below Brigitte Bardot was only 17, not yet a star, when she went on the cover of *Paris-Match*. She made 50 films, few of much value, but was ruthlessly exploited by the media as a sex-kitten. In a way the image was true, and she never concealed her stormy love-life. Today she is a dedicated campaigner against cruelty to animals.

Below Maurice Chevalier (1888–1972) was a debonair star of the Paris music hall and musical comedy who made many films both in France and Hollywood. With his gilt-topped cane, tilted straw hat and suave manner, he came to epitomize Frenchness for many foreigners. In later years his suspected pro-Vichy role caused his popularity in France to slump.

Television

Although television is not in itself an art form, it is a key medium for the spreading of culture and information, and in France it does not do that job very well. For decades it was under state control, timid and self-censoring, with low prestige, and so it never attracted the talent or built up the standards essential for good programs. Today, the state monopoly is ended and some networks are in private hands, so *la télé* is now freer, and more outspoken. But its output has become even more mediocre, for competition has produced a downward spiral of pandering to the lowest common denominators of public taste, in the battle for ratings that attract advertisers.

Television after the war depended directly on either the Ministry of Information or the prime minister's office. Under the Fourth Republic, antigovernment views in broadcasts were frequently suppressed. De Gaulle's regime then made matters worse, by placing its loyalists in key positions to run the networks. In that period, programs on economic or social issues were vetted in advance by the appropriate ministry and news bulletins were edited to show the government in a good light. On the other hand, the proportion of cultural programming, under Malraux's influence, was high, with long hours devoted to the arts and history. Television, though uninspired, was didactic in the French pedagogic manner; as there was no competing with commercial channels for audiences, few concessions were made to popular taste, and very little American "pulp" was imported.

However, many directors, technicians and journalists had liberal or leftist sympathies, and were profoundly frustrated. During the May 1968 uprising their resentment boiled over; they staged a virtual putsch and for a few glorious days said what they liked on the screen. The government retaliated by sacking more than 60 radio and television journalists. But some lessons had been learned, and during the Pompidou and Giscard eras a few efforts were made to liberalize television, though without ending the state monopoly. Opposition leaders, including Communists, were now allowed to take part in live debates; the practice of direct interference by ministries was ended; and Giscard split up the television monolith into three separate network companies, still state-owned but in competition with one another, and partly financed by advertising. Mitterrand then went further: he set up a new independent High Authority, somewhat on British lines, that was to ensure balance and objectivity. As a result, news programs became more lively and investigative, and more open to minority views, and senior television executives were no longer all government loyalists. This was a move toward the German *Proporz* system, where top posts are shared out between the parties. However, for political reasons, Mitterrand also sanctioned two new private commercial channels on the dubious Italian model, breaking earlier Socialist promises that an ending of the monopoly would not involve a debasement of program quality or a sellout to big business. Chirac, as prime minister, went still further, privatizing outright the main state network, TF1, which was purchased by, among others, the British media magnate, Robert Maxwell.

Today there are seven networks of one kind or another, four private, three in state hands. They include a pay channel with some 3 million subscribers, used mainly for films and sport, and a state regional network. TF1 has by far the largest audiences, well ahead of its main rival, Antenne 2, which is still state-run and whose output tends to be more serious. But on almost all networks the shortage of funds for program-making is so grave that they have to rely heavily on cheap foreign imports, many of them American soap operas. This is because the revenue available to the networks from advertising, and from their shares of the licence fees, is not adequate. Moreover, the programs that they do make are seldom of quality. French television excels at big live debates, political or literary, where the national gift for passionate argument is given full scope, but probing documentaries on current issues are rare, and little effort is made to stimulate new fictional drama. Television has become much less prudish than in the old days, and will now screen nudity as the cinema does, and also occasionally show features on sensitive topics such as AIDS or homosexuality. It has thus grown more in touch with French society, but the proportion of cultural programming, as opposed to light entertainment, is much lower than in the severe Gaullist days. French television, though now unmuzzled, has not yet acquired the tradition and the professional values needed for work of high quality; as compared with, for example, the BBC, its recruiting and training are haphazard, and its executives and producers seem to lack the commitment that the French display in the arts or in industry. One positive development is that in 1990 the French and German governments launched a multilingual European satellite network, *la Sept*, to be used solely for cultural programs, and to be publicly funded, free from the constraints of the ratings. It is ironic that the much-derided state should have to step back in, to save at least a corner of French television from the ravages of commercialism.

In radio, the situation is a little different. Parallel to the main state-run networks, a number of popular commercial stations – notably Europe 1, Radio Monte Carlo and Radio Luxembourg – have for a long time broadcast from just outside France, beyond the reach of the monopoly. The government did find subtle ways of controlling them, mainly by acquiring majority shares in them through holding companies, but these have now been privatized, while the state networks have been liberalized as in television. At the same time, local radio has been sanctioned, and some 800 small stations now operate around France, often run by town councils or other local self-financing bodies (they are not allowed to be commercial). The quality of radio broadcasting is often little higher than in television, though the big stations such as Europe 1 are excellent for news and comment, while two of the state networks are strong on classical music.

The press

The French are not great newspaper readers, and their dailies tend to have modest circulations. Interestingly, despite the French centralizing tradition, provincial papers account for over two-thirds of the dailies' total sales. There is no real national press, and *Le Monde* is the only daily paper that is read at all widely outside Paris. The French daily with the highest circulation is not, in fact, a Parisian one, but *Ouest-France*, which is published in Rennes and serves the northwest. It sells some 750,000 copies, whereas no Paris daily paper has a circulation of more than about 500,000.

Politically, rather more of the capital's dailies

support the right than the left. *Le Figaro*, though middlebrow and a little dull, is owned by the controversial tycoon Robert Hersant, who holds strident right-wing views. The business paper *Les Echos* belongs to the British *Financial Times*; *La Croix* is a very good Catholic daily, and *France-Soir* a mediocre evening paper. On the left, while the Communist Party's *L'Humanité* staggers on with falling sales, *Libération* has come up strongly in recent years as a good independent radical daily, lively but serious, with more influence than its modest sales might suggest. The flagship of the French press, and one of the world's great newspapers, is *Le Monde*, which has retained an austere format, with virtually no photographs and with long serious articles whose elaborate sentences do not make for easy reading. Its political stance is left-of-center, generally but not always pro-Socialist, and it is independent of big-business ownership.

The weakness of the Paris dailies is to an extent offset by the rise of the weekly news magazines (there are virtually no Sunday papers of the British or American kind). Two of these, *L'Express* and *Le Point*, both right-of-center, have borrowed the *Time* and *Der Spiegel* formula: they have a high cover-price and look glossy, with lots of color advertisements, but their content is newsy. Their chief rival, *Le Nouvel Observateur*, pro-Socialist, is a little more wordy and intellectual. Other leading weeklies are *Paris-Match*, known for its photo-stories, *L'Evènement du Jeudi* and *Le Canard Enchaîné*, a famous French institution. This satirical paper with a lampooning style nevertheless conducts serious investigative political

journalism and its scoops can often embarrass the government. It thus fulfils a useful role, in a country where fearless reporting of this kind is none too common. Even *Le Monde*, despite its wide and thorough coverage, seldom makes effective probes into scandals behind the scenes, and other papers do so even less. Perhaps this is partly due to the traditional French deference toward power establishments, not only governmental but business too. Journalists depend on their contacts with official sources and are hesitant to prejudice them by making revelations.

The strength of the regional daily press can be traced back to the Occupation period, when France was split in two and the transportation difficulties prevented the sale of Paris papers in the provinces. Consequently, local papers were able to build up a position of strength that they have since held and even extended. Today, there are 72 provincial dailies, and they have managed to resist all attempts by Paris ones, notably *Le Figaro*, to invade their territories. After *Ouest-France*, the leaders are *La Voix du Nord* in Lille, *Le Dauphiné Libéré* in Grenoble, and *Sud-Ouest* in Bordeaux. These and other daily newspapers are prosperous empires with fine modern offices, making some Paris papers look like poor relations. However, their editorial content is generally bland. *La Voix du Nord* and *Les Dernières Nouvelles d'Alsace* (Strasbourg) will sometimes be controversial, but as each paper tends to have a monopoly on its area, most of the others avoid the risk of offending readers and aim for the widest possible appeal. They carry little foreign news, treat national news stories uncritically, and fill out their pages with reports of local activities.

Above A typical newspaper kiosk on a Paris boulevard. Kiosks of this kind display scores of daily papers French and foreign, as well as hundreds of magazines. "What Saddam is preparing next", says this poster (upside-down) for *L'Express*, one of the most successful of the weekly news magazines. Modeled on *Time* and *Der Spiegel*, these weeklies do well, whereas the daily Paris press is remarkably weak: in fact, provincial dailies sell more widely and are more prosperous, though not necessarily of better quality. No Paris daily sells more than about 500,000. The ultra-serious *Le Monde* has as high a circulation as any.

PART FOUR

A REGIONAL PORTRAIT OF FRANCE

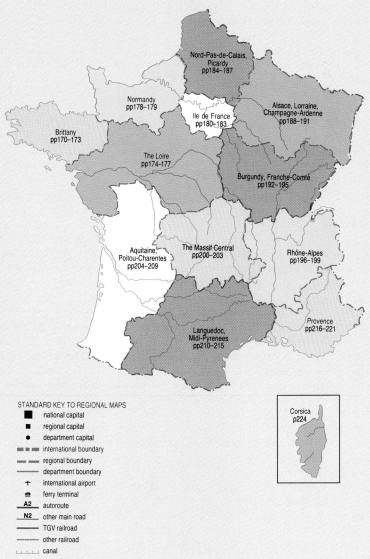

STANDARD KEY TO REGIONAL MAPS
- ■ national capital
- ■ regional capital
- ● department capital
- ▦ ▦ ▦ international boundary
- ▬ ▬ regional boundary
- ‒‒‒‒‒ department boundary
- ✛ international airport
- ⛴ ferry terminal
- **A2** autoroute
- **N2** other main road
- ▬▬▬▬ TGV railroad
- ———— other railroad
- ⊔⊔⊔⊔ canal
- ▲ mountain summit
  (height in meters)

Corsica
p224

RENEWAL IN THE REGIONS

Under the Ancien Régime, the old provinces of France enjoyed a certain autonomy, but after the Revolution they were divided up and replaced by artificial *départements* (departments), mostly named after rivers, and each was ruled over by a Paris-appointed prefect. Political and economic centralization increasingly went hand in hand. The railway network became centered on Paris, with few good cross-country lines. When heavy industry grew up, some settled near the coal mines of the northeast, but much went to Paris, to be close to the key ministries, as did the major banks. From 1851 to 1931 the Paris area's population went up by 4.4 million, that of the Nord and the Lyon-St-Etienne area by 1.8 million. The growth of industry in the east gave rise to the notion of "two Frances", divided roughly by a line from Caen to Marseille, with the poorer farms and towns without modern industry all to its west. The preeminence of the Sorbonne, and the pull of the Paris literary salons, also deprived the provinces of many of their cultural resources, as graceful, historic old towns such as Rouen or Dijon sank into dullness and lethargy.

Economic renewal and regional development

Curiously, the tide began to turn during the Nazi Occupation of World War II. Many provinces, cut off from Paris, were forced to act on their own initiative; at the same time many dynamic leaders left the troubled capital to settle elsewhere. After the war, a massive rural exodus coupled with the growth of industry brought a new vitality to stagnating towns. Many cities doubled or even trebled in size, led by Grenoble and Toulouse. The need for regional development became a high priority of Monnet's Plan and of state policy. The government also encouraged provincial universities to expand much faster than those of Paris, and it promoted major new arts centers in provincial towns to increase their appeal. Grants and other incentives were offered to encourage firms to transfer from Paris or set up new factories in the underindustrialized west and southwest: Brittany, Languedoc and the Massif Central were targeted, among others, in a bid to stem the rural exodus to the capital. For a time, there was a virtual ban on new factories in the Paris area. With the economy expanding rapidly in the later 1950s and the 1960s, this development policy was very successful. Although many firms still preferred to settle new plant in towns such as Reims or Orléans within easy reach of the capital, others did move out to, for instance, Rennes or Toulouse. Often they were enticed by some dynamic local figure, such as Jacques Chaban-Delmas, the Gaullist leader and mayor of Bordeaux, who used his influence in Paris to bring massive new industrial investment to a city that had too long rested on its laurels as a wine producer.

Altogether between 1955 and 1975 the regional incentives generated about 500,000 new jobs. Paris, on the other hand, lost some 77,000 industrial jobs between 1962 and 1973. It was still growing and modernizing fast, but in so doing it was becoming too congested and frenetic, and an inverted snobbery against Paris began to emerge among many younger professional people, countering the traditional anti-provincial snobbery of the Parisians. This new mood was linked with the ecological "quality-of-life" trend of the 1970s. Executives, engineers and college professors began to realize that life in some smaller city, such as Avignon or Annecy, in the warm south or near the sea or ski-slopes, could be more relaxed and pleasant than in Paris. Moreover, these places were no longer regarded as cultural deserts, having plenty of their own new theaters, concert halls and art galleries. Between 1975 and 1982, there was, for the first time, a net migration away from Paris of 291,000. That movement has continued and now includes not only the middle classes but also workers.

After its successes in the south and west, the government, in the later 1970s, switched its priorities to older industrial regions such as Lorraine and Nord Pas-de-Calais, which had been badly affected by recession and pit closures. Fortunately, the development of the European Community was at the same time turning investors' attention back east, so that these struggling regions turned out to be strategically well placed. Those areas of France that are today the worst-off economically are in the hilly, thinly-populated center. The old east–west divide is being replaced by a more complex pattern. For some years, population and new investment have tended toward the periphery, above all to the Mediterranean coast and Rhône valley, where there are good transportation links with the rest of Europe as well as fine scenery and plentiful sunshine. This applies also to Aquitaine and much of the west. The broad stretch of land from the Ardennes to the central Pyrenees, embracing most of the huge Massif Central, has an aging population in decline and finds it hard to attract new investment. This still worries the planners, even though their main regional objectives have been fulfilled, and Europe has entered a new age of open frontiers.

Local government and political devolution

Until the 1980s, the French government's economic policy of regional renewal was not backed up by any real political devolution. Yet the economic and cultural regeneration gave rise, in the 1960s and 1970s, to a growing new regional awareness, as in many other parts of Europe, from Scotland to Sicily. This took the form, in part, of a revival of folk culture, such as local music and dances, and crafts and costumes, as well as attempts to preserve the old local languages. The movement was led mostly by intellectuals, and often it seemed to provide compensation for the lack of political autonomy or even a means of fighting for it. Such movements were particularly strong in Brittany, Languedoc, Provence and the French Basque country. In most regions, and in Corsica, separatist movements arose which sometimes used violence to further their aims. But they generally lacked the support of the public and of local leaders, who did not want outright independence, but more internal autonomy.

French local government
The local administration of France is complicated. The country is divided into 96 *départements*, which today are grouped into 22 regions. The departments, created artificially in Napoleon's day, are all roughly the same size (except in the Paris area, where they are smaller), and nearly all are called after a local river, for example, Somme and Loire, or in some cases a mountain range. The regions were created in the 1960s. Many of them are based on old provinces or dukedoms, for instance Brittany and Provence, but some, such as Midi-Pyrénées and Centre, are more artificial. Reforms during the 1980s have modified the highly centralized structure of local government. Each department used to be ruled directly from Paris by a state-appointed prefect. Today the locally elected bodies in the regions and departments, as well as the town councils, have rather more power, and the prefect rather less. But France still remains quite centralized.

scale 1 : 1 070 000

■ regional capital
● department capital
— · — · — international boundary
— — — regional boundary
———— department boundary

scale 1 : 6 250 000

0 ————— 150km
0 ————— 100mi

CORSICA

The right-of-center governments of the time, however, refused even this much. Although they had moved some of the state service departments, and some Grandes Ecoles and other such bodies, out of the capital, they retained control over them. Local government of each of the 96 departments was administered by a prefect, a senior civil servant who with his own large staff was responsible only to Paris. Each department also had its own locally-elected *conseil général* (general council) but, with only a modest budget, this had little real power. Below department level were the 36,000 or so *communes* ranging in size from big cities to tiny hamlets. They also had their own elected councils but had to submit their budgets to the prefect for approval. Moreover, their local revenue was so limited by law that, for almost any project, they needed to obtain state financial partnership, which, in effect, placed them at the mercy of endless ministerial delays or vetoes, and of a slow and impersonal bureaucracy in the far-off capital.

The mayors of larger towns, however, had much personal, if little formal, authority, and in practice could often oppose the prefect. A key figure in French life, usually highly respected, a mayor could often stay in office over many decades, being reelected every six years. Many national politicians have sought a local

power base by becoming mayors of big towns, for example, Jacques Chaban-Delmas in Bordeaux, Gaston Defferre in Marseille, Pierre Mauroy in Lille, and Jacques Chirac in the *mairie* of Paris. There was often a degree of complicity and uneasy alliance between prefects and city mayors, as they necessarily shared common aims of economic expansion, the maintenance of peace and order, and dealing with the state bureaucracy of which they both, in a sense, were victims. Prefects had problems with rival ministries.

In many instances, dynamic central state planning did much for the regions economically, such as the imposition on sluggish, backward Languedoc of a big irrigation scheme and modern tourist resorts. Often, however, these projects were imposed by Paris technocrats who did not bother with local consultation. Cool relations between prefects and local politicians

frequently led to conservatism and inertia, while the state bureaucracy sapped the spirit of local initiative.

Under growing pressure, governments in the 1960s and 1970s did make a few reforms. The prefect's tutelage over communes' budgets was modified; ministries' local services were reorganized under his control, in the interests of efficiency; and in 1964, for the purposes of economic planning, the 96 *départements* were grouped into the 22 *régions* that exist today. Then, in 1972, these regions were granted assemblies of a kind, but they were not directly elected and had no real powers. In fact, it was little more than window dressing by a government fearful that "the state would fly apart" (in the words of one Gaullist leader) if more autonomy were granted. In 1981, the Socialists came to power, pledged to a thorough overhaul of local government. Prime Minister Mauroy and Gaston Defferre, who as Minister of the Interior was put in charge, were both keen "regionalists" and they won over a more cautious Mitterrand.

The reform was applied in stages in 1982-6. The prefect's tutelage over the communes was abolished, and he was formally renamed Commissioner of the Republic (though informally he kept his old title). His role was now largely confined to coordinating the local state services and advising the smaller communes. His executive powers passed to the elected chairman of the department's *conseil général*, the

major beneficiary of the reforms. The state also transferred some of its own responsibilities to each of the three main tiers of local government. To the region it handed over responsibility for professional training, the building of *lycées* (high schools) and many aspects of culture, tourism, road-building and aid for new industry; to the department it gave the enormous task of running the welfare and social services; to the communes it at last gave control of their own town-planning and environmental schemes and authority to grant building permits. All local bodies gained new powers to raise extra finance, from loans or higher taxes, and – most important – each region acquired a directly elected assembly.

The prefect's political role as watchdog of the Ministry of the Interior was ended, but he remained in charge of the police and of law and order. The state also kept control of many crucial areas that in Britain or Germany are largely in local hands, notably the health service (as opposed to welfare), education (as opposed to school buildings) and the judiciary. France's regional reforms were less radical than those of post-Franco Spain, and they stopped well short of a true federal system as in Germany or the United States. They were also applied unevenly, with considerable local variations. In some cases, prefects retained much influence, while in others they were pushed aside by powerful leaders of the *conseil général*.

Above The village of Kargenthal in eastern France. In France, a country with strong rural traditions, the village has long played a key role. Many villages have their roots in medieval times, and the inhabitants tend to live close together. But modern life has brought changes. Some villages have become enveloped in the surburban sprawl of towns; or the farm exodus has brought a decline in their population. All France is divided into some 36,500 *communes*, ranging in size from hamlets to big towns, all with some autonomy. So strong are local loyalties that even small villages have opposed attempts to merge them into larger, more rational units.

Right Nearly every village has its war memorial, where wreathes are laid on 8 May and 11 November by the mayor, in his tricolor sash, and other dignitaries. Even under the centralized system, the locally elected mayor has always been a potent figure in France, wielding power in uneasy rivalry with the prefect.

Overleaf Vaux-le-Vicomte, a château south of Paris, is one of many potent reminders of former royal power in France.

Weakness of the reforms

Although many observers felt that the Defferre reforms were a big step in the right direction, others pointed to their basic weaknesses. For instance, the reforms failed to address one of the worst problems: that the 36,500 separate communes are too many and are often too small. Yet, because they are each jealous of their identity, government efforts since the 1960s to encourage them to merge have met with little success. Many tiny villages have proved incapable of handling their new planning powers, and are still looked after by the prefect. In towns, the reforms have tended to strengthen the authority of mayors, who have been keeping their extra powers to themselves, rather than sharing them in accordance with Defferre's aim of "bringing democracy closer to the people".

The reforms, have, in some cases, also led to petty feuding and local corruption – for instance, mayors, anxious to please their own electors over such matters as building permits, are sometimes susceptible to bribery. In addition, the complex new structure is top-heavy and expensive, with some of the new responsibilities overlapping or ill-defined. Underlying these difficulties, the critics of the reform claim, is that the government failed to choose between region and department but instead promoted both, and their rivalry is destructive. Mauroy and Defferre wanted to downgrade the department and give the region huge powers: but they were overruled by Mitterrand who, with the backing of civil-service mandarins, forced an unsatisfactory compromise. As a result, the department has acquired more power, whereas the region lacks the resources to adequately discharge its responsibilities for economic development. Few major politicians are opting for the regional assemblies. Most prefer to be a mayor, or the chairman of the *conseil général*, or a deputy in Paris, and a new law limits the number of elected offices that they can hold at one time.

The reforms have thus failed to create a strong regional system; yet the French *départment* is too small to play a proper economic role and too artificial to command strong loyalties. Whereas some of the regions – Provence, Burgundy, Aquitaine and others – have deep roots in French history, the departments were all made by strokes on a map based on logistical criteria in the 1790s. The Jacobins and their heirs, who have always feared the region as a challenge to Paris, have argued that, if the government is of one color and a majority of regions are of another, this will undermine the stability of the state. Yet after 1988, the government was Socialist and all but two of the new regional assemblies were in center–right hands, but there was no crisis. For all their faults, the Defferre reforms have at least reduced resentment against Paris and given local areas a greater sense of being in control of their own destinies. For instance, in the context of a new Europe, Languedoc is forging economic links with Catalonia, Rhône-Alpes with Lombardy, and Lorraine with Saarland. To be truly effective in the new Europe, however, the 22 French regions are too numerous. Although some are historic realities, others such as Midi-Pyrénées are hybrids with badly drawn boundaries, while Normandy is split in two. Reducing the number of regions to about a dozen, by combining those that have affinities with one another, would be reasonable on political, economic and cultural grounds. The treatment of the regions in the pages that follow employs such a grouping.

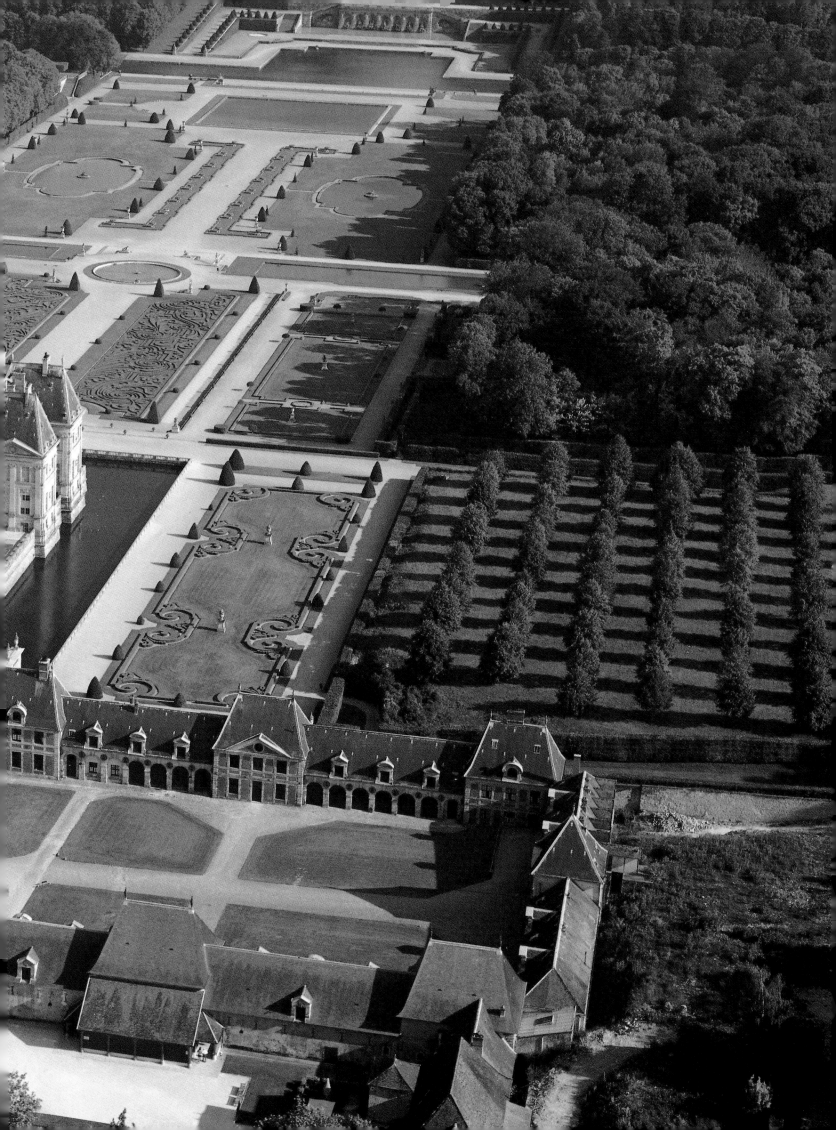

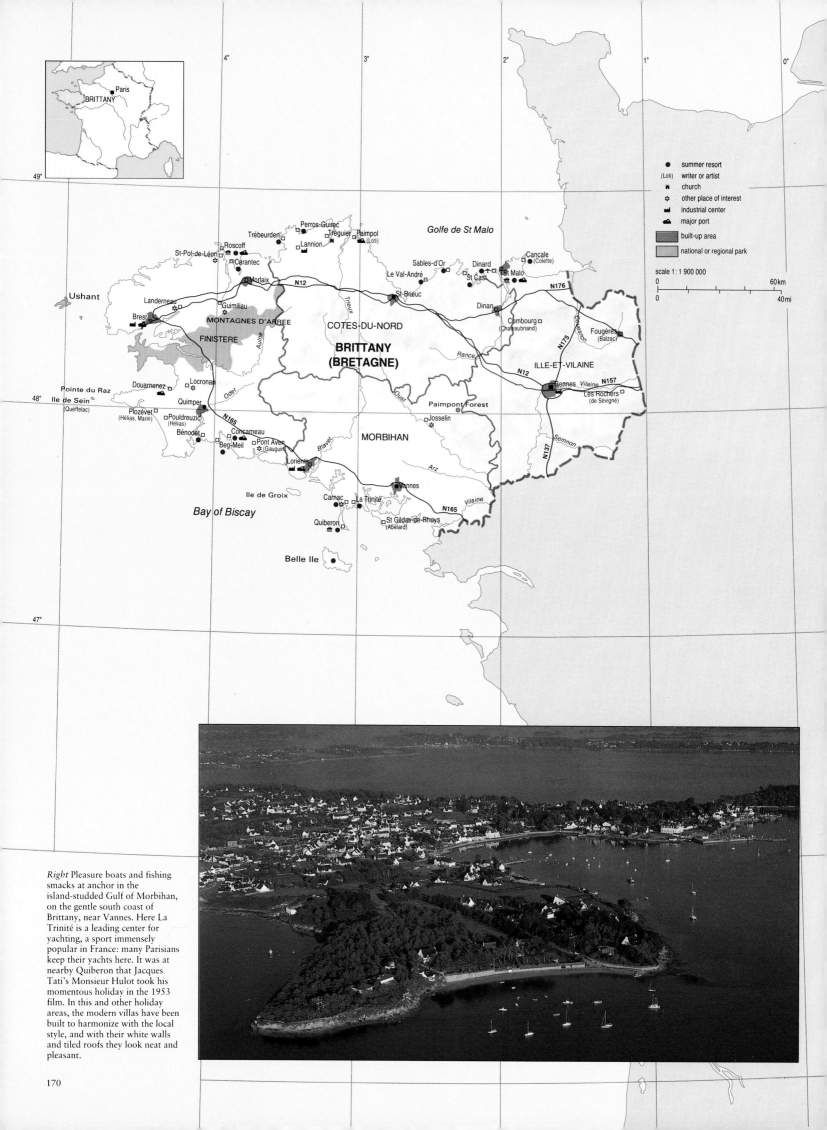

Map Labels

49°

4°   3°   2°   1°   0°

BRITTANY   Paris

Golfe de St Malo

● summer resort
(Loti) writer or artist
⛪ church
✤ other place of interest
🏭 industrial center
⚓ major port

built-up area

national or regional park

scale 1:1 900 000

0   60km
0   40mi

Perros-Guirec
Trébeurden   Tréguier   Paimpol
Lannion   (Loti)
Roscoff
St-Pol-de-Léon
Carantec   Cancale
Morlaix   Sables-d'Or   Dinard   (Colette)
N12   Le Val-André   St Cast   St Malo
Landerneau   St-Brieuc   N176

Ushant

Brest   Guimiliau   Dinan
MONTAGNES D'ARRÉE   Combourg   Fougères
FINISTÉRE   COTES-DU-NORD   (Chateaubriand)   (Balzac)
Aulne   N175
                                         ILLE-ET-VILAINE
                    BRITTANY
                    (BRETAGNE)   Rance
Odet   N12
Douarnenez   Locronan   Rennes Vilaine N157
48°   Les Rochers
Pointe du Raz   (de Sévigné)
Ile de Sein   Quimper
(Quéffelac)   Paimpont Forest
Plozévet Pouldreuzic   N165
(Hélias, Marin) (Hélias)   Josselin
Bénodet   Trieux
Concarneau   MORBIHAN
Beg-Meil Pont Aven
         (Gauguin)   Blavet
         Lorient   Arz
Ile de Groix   Vilaine
                                  N137
         Carnac   La Trinité Vannes   N165
Bay of Biscay   Semnon
         Quiberon St Gildas-de-Rhuys
                   (Abélard)

Belle Ile

47°

Right Pleasure boats and fishing
smacks at anchor in the
island-studded Gulf of Morbihan,
on the gentle south coast of
Brittany, near Vannes. Here La
Trinité is a leading center for
yachting, a sport immensely
popular in France: many Parisians
keep their yachts here. It was at
nearby Quiberon that Jacques
Tati's Monsieur Hulot took his
momentous holiday in the 1953
film. In this and other holiday
areas, the modern villas have been
built to harmonize with the local
style, and with their white walls
and tiled roofs they look neat and
pleasant.

BRITTANY

Brittany
Brittany is the most westerly and the most maritime of French regions, and one of the most individual, with a strong sense of its own identity, culture and history. Brittany's main industries are agriculture, fishing, tourism and electronics.

Population 2.8 million; area: 27,000sq km; capital, Rennes pop. 200,000, 347km from Paris. Other main towns: Brest, large port, pop. 160,000; Lorient, port, pop. 64,000; Quimper, pop. 60,000; St-Brieuc, pop. 51,000; St Malo, port, pop. 47,000; Vannes, pop. 45,000.

Below Traditional fishing vessels in a south Breton port. The fishing industry has been in decline for some years, badly affected by rising costs, falling prices, Atlantic over-fishing, foreign competition and poaching by Spanish vessels. There are only 10,000 Breton fishermen left. But deep-sea fishing, for cod and tunny, still takes place from Lorient, Douarnenez, St Malo and other ports. Also, coastal fishing still brings in a wealth of sole, turbot, sardines, langoustines, lobsters, scallops and other delicacies served fresh in local restaurants. Brittany is known, too, for its cultivation of oysters and mussels.

Once poor and isolated, now mainly prosperous, Brittany (population 2.8 million) is France's only Celtic province, and in some ways it has more in common with Ireland or Wales than with the rest of France. The people who inhabit this storm-tossed region are tough and industrious, yet dreamy and poetic. They have a strong sense of identity and cling closely to their own traditions and culture, yet are still touched by ancient Celtic legend.

Brittany is a huge granite peninsula jutting into the Atlantic. Of its highly indented, 3000 kilometer coastline, the northern and western parts are mostly rocky, with some dramatic headlands, but close inland are fertile plains. The south coast is gentler, with low wooded estuaries and a milder climate. Except for Rennes, the capital, almost all the main towns and population centers are on or near the coast: seafaring and ocean fishing have for many centuries been key Breton activities. The big town of Brest with its wide natural harbor is still the main Atlantic base of the French navy, though its importance has declined. The port of Lorient combines naval and fishery roles, while other fishing centers include Douarnenez, Paimpol, and the handsome old fortified ports of Concarneau and St-Malo. (It was sailors from St-Malo who first colonized the Falkland Islands, calling them Les Malouines, from which comes the Spanish name for them, Las Malvinas.)

The Brittany coast has many fine sandy beaches, which are attractive to holidaymakers, though the summer season is short. Dinard, Perros-Guirec and Benodet are major bathing resorts, while yachting is popular at La Trinité. In contrast to the sleek coastal areas, the hinterland is poor and empty – an upland massif where the soil is thin and the gales howl over the moors. It reaches its highest point (400 meters) in the arid Montagnes d'Arrée. Older Breton housing is

of plain gray local granite, austere but dignified. Everywhere there are modern villas, too, especially in holiday areas.

The climate, typically Atlantic, is mild and moist, with frequent alternations of sun and storm. It is said, as in other Celtic lands, that this may help to explain the temperament of the people – eloquent and passionate like the Irish, whimsical like the Welsh, yet also practical and hardworking like the Scots. Bretons tend to be stockily built, with fair complexions and blue or gray eyes, and, like most seafarers, are considered hardy. Their long struggle with the elements, which cost them so many lives, has left them with a keen sense of life's tragedy and an almost fatalistic attitude to death (as described in Pierre Loti's novel *Pêcheur d'Islande* about deep-sea fishermen in the Paimpol area). The strange stone calavaries and ossuaries found outside many churches, the huge array of local saints, and the Catholic festivals known as *pardons* are evidence of a special religious past. Bretons are less religious than they used to be, but still the attendance at Mass, over 25 percent in the villages, is twice the French average.

The religious spirit has pagan origins. The earliest inhabitants built long rows of menhirs and dolmens (still visible near Carnac), which the first Celtic settlers took over for their own druidic rites. The main Celtic invasion came from England and Ireland in the 5th century AD. As well as bringing Christianity, these Celts elaborated the tales of Merlin and King Arthur, which Bretons associate with "Brocéliande", a forest that is probably that of Paimpont, near Rennes. Even if Arthur's Camelot was more probably sited in England, these legends, and those of Tristan and his Irish love, Isolde, remain a basis of Breton mythology.

For 700 years an independent duchy, Brittany was annexed to the French crown in 1532. Even after this, it retained its parliament and commercial importance with Breton fleets sailing to the Americas and the Far East in the 17th and 18th centuries. Following the Revolution of 1789, it was divided into *départements*; then, when it became a modern region in 1964, it was shorn of its old capital, Nantes, which was hived off into the Pays de la Loire – to the anger of many Bretons. These proud people have kept a strong sense of their own nationhood, like the Scots, and since World War II many of them have indignantly felt neglected by Paris or – even worse – colonized. A tiny minority of separatists even resorted to violence but they never won much support. The mass of Bretons regard outright secession as unrealistic. Moreover, since the reforms of the 1980s, Bretons now have had more control over their own affairs and so feel less of a grudge against their "colonizers".

Already, in the 1960s and 1970s, the government did much to give economic help to a region that lacked any industrial tradition and suffered from its peripheral position at the far edge of the European Community. It encouraged French electronics and automobile firms to set up plant in Rennes and other towns, it created nuclear and spatial centers and

research institutes, and it made Brittany the leading pilot zone of its ambitious telecommunications program. In fact, the government poured more money into this region than into any other.

Although this did not satisfy the many who wanted political devolution, some of the more resourceful Bretons, in the meantime, took matters into their own hands, to modernize their farming, and to restore the old overseas trading role that had been theirs before the stranglehold of Napoleonic centralism. In this regard, they were delighted by British and Irish entry into the European Community. A major figure in local affairs is Alexis Gourvennec, of north Finistère. In the 1960s he organized the vegetable farmers of the fertile plain around Morlaix into a powerful cooperative able to dictate its law to the Paris wholesalers who, for a long time, had exploited them. Then, in the 1970s, he and other local farmers created Brittany Ferries, the highly successful shipping line that now carries Breton produce to Britain, and British tourists to France (said to be the only example in Europe of farmers starting their own shipping company). Gourvennec enthuses over the idea of creating a major new westerly trade route, from Spain via Brittany to Glasgow. "We Celtic lands have ignored each other too long," he says. "We must return to the historic links of our ancestors."

Gourvennec has also helped to revolutionize Breton agriculture. For a long time, the region long had possessed great potential, but it was underutilized since most farms were too small, ill-equipped and backward. Yet, although since the 1950s three-quarters of the farm population has left for Paris and local towns, agricultural production has soared. Brittany today accounts for 22 percent of France's milk output, 64 percent of its artichokes and cauliflowers, and 45 percent of its pigs, eggs and poultry. In some sectors, it has been too successful and dairy farmers are now angry at being obliged by the EC to cut back on surpluses. By contrast, the big Breton fishing industry is in decline, as in many parts of Europe.

Local cuisine relies heavily on this produce: fresh oysters and prawns, mussels *marinière*, clams baked with garlic, *cotriade* (a rich fish stew), lobster or monkfish *à l'armoricaine* (in a rich brown sauce with garlic and brandy), and so on. Special meat dishes are few, but *gigot* of salt-pasture lamb is tasty, as are Plougastel strawberries, when in season. *Crêperies* selling thin filled pancakes are everywhere. There is no local wine, but local cider is popular.

The modern era has brought great changes in traditional rural life, and though some upland farms are still poor, most have now emerged from their old stark poverty. But with it has gone much of the old picturesque folk culture. Except on special occasions, few women now wear the famous Breton *coiffes* (white lace headdresses); and modern clothes and cars, furniture and music, have made inroads into the old life-styles. However, the past 20 years have seen some attempts to revive this culture, led mainly by younger people, out of a desire by Bretons to retain their national identity. Costumed folk-dance and musical groups have been reborn, which perform the stately slow-swaying dances to the sound of a local *bombarde*, a kind of oboe, and *biniou*, a kind of bagpipes. Also, the lovely old carved rustic furniture, once characteristic of the region but until recently stored away in barns, is now back in vogue.

There have also been some attempts to revive the old Breton language, which is similar to Welsh.

Originally, the French tried to eradicate it, and any child heard speaking it in school would be punished. Then, in the 1960s, this policy was relaxed, and Breton is now even an option in the *baccalauréat* (though most students prefer to learn English as their second language). In daily use it is dying out even among older people, and only one Breton in four can now speak the language. The impulse for revival has come mainly from a few intellectuals. Pierre-Jakez Hélias, the best-known modern Breton writer, whose book *The Horse of Pride* gives a marvelous picture of Breton rural life, wrote in Breton, then himself translated the text into French. Altogether, the book has sold 2.2 million copies, but only 750 of them in Breton. Other Breton writers have used just French — including Chateaubriand, the great Romantic, who superbly described his boyhood at Combourg castle in *Mémoires d'outre-tombe* (Memoirs from beyond the grave; 1849). Other writers about Brittany have come from outside, such as Genet and Colette.

Below The wheat harvest in the Crozon peninsula, Finistère. Brittany is one of France's main agricultural regions, and many farms are grouped into strong cooperatives. Near the coast, its fertile plains yield cereals of all kinds, as well as onions, cauliflowers and artichokes; pigs, poultry and milk are also produced massively. But while coastal farms tend to be modern and prosperous, many on the uplands are still small and poor.

Left Selling locally made baskets and halters in Finistère. Traditional crafts, including pottery, still survive in some areas. But the lovely old rustic furniture is no longer made, though surviving items, such as heavy cupboards, chests and dressers made of dark oak with ornately carved surfaces, fetch high prices. Even a few of the curious old box-beds, virtual sleeping-cupboards, can still be found, often converted for other purposes.

Right The old Breton *coiffes* vary in style. This one is from Pont-Aven, while those from Pont-l'Abbé are tall and thin. *Coiffes* are seldom worn now except at special festivals. They take 30 minutes to iron before fixing to the elaborate hairstyles.

Above The old fortified port of St Malo has a majestic setting on a rocky promontory of the north coast. Much bombarded in 1944, it has been carefully rebuilt in the old style. Its people are known as Malouins. Some have been deep-sea fishermen, and they were the first to discover the far-off Falklands which they called Les Malouines. The Argentinians changed this name to Las Malvinas.

Left The most famous of all Breton calvaries is this 16th-century one at Guimiliau, Finistère, with its 200 stone figures depicting the Crucifixion. Typifying the Bretons' deep religious spirit, stone calvaries and ossuaries, mostly 16th-century, stand outside churches or alone by the sea, as memorials to drowned sailors. Some are venues for *pardons*, Christian festivals special to Brittany where people gather to pay homage to their local saint: they parade through the streets in costume, carrying banners, candles and statues of saints, and chanting hymns.

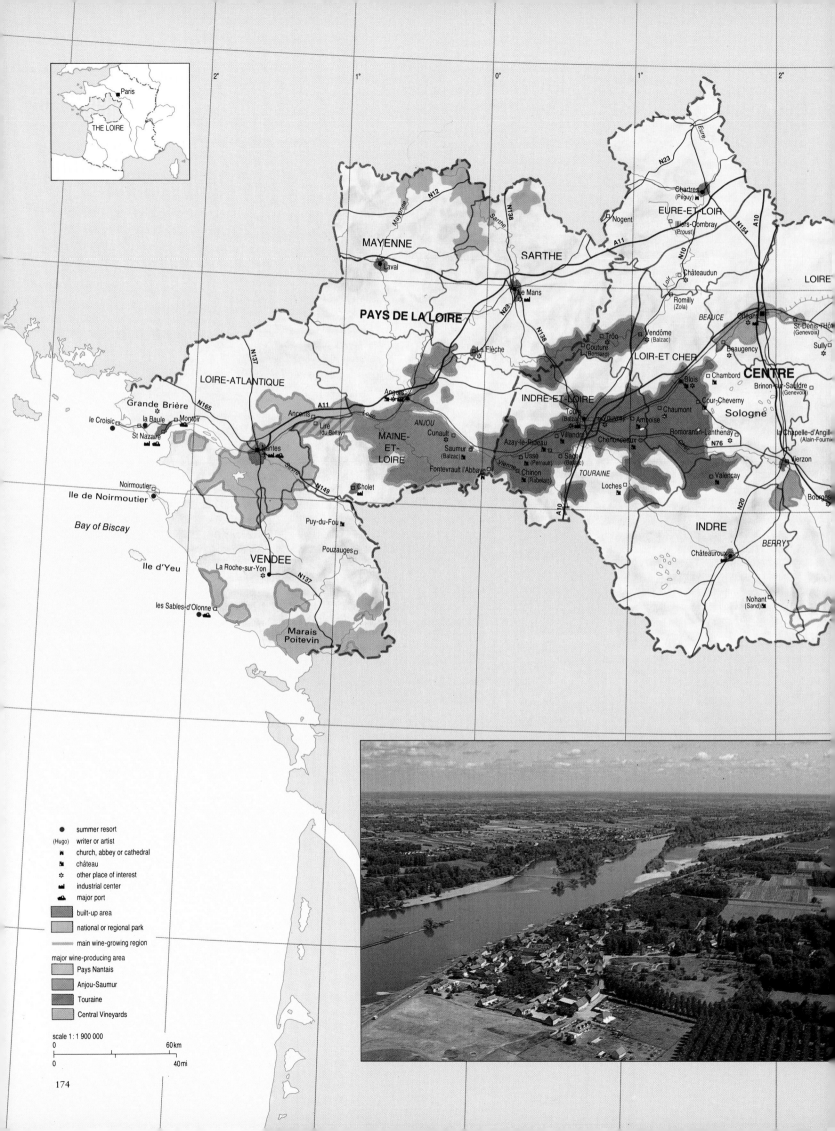

Inset (top left)

2° 1° 0° 1° 2°

Paris

THE LOIRE

Main map labels

Eure

N23

Chartres
(Péguy)

EURE-ET-LOIR

Nogent

N12

Mayenne

Sarthe

N138

Illiers-Combray
(Proust)

N154

A10

MAYENNE

SARTHE

A11

Laval

N10

Châteaudun

LOIRE

Le Mans

Romilly
(Zola)

BEAUCE

Orléans

St-Denis-l'Hô
(Genevoix)

PAYS DE LA LOIRE

N23

Vendôme
(Balzac)

Sully

N138

La Flèche

Trôo

Couture
(Ronsard)

Beaugency

LOIRE-ATLANTIQUE

LOIR-ET-CHER

CENTRE

Blois

Chambord

Brinon-sur-Sauldre
(Genevoix)

Grande Brière

N165

Angers

A11

INDRE-ET-LOIRE

Cour-Cheverny

Sologne

le Croisic

la Baule

Montoir

Ancenis

Loire

ANJOU

Tours
(Balzac)

Vouvray

Chaumont

Amboise

Romorantin-Lanthenay

la Chapelle-d'Angille
(Alain-Fournier)

St Nazaire

Liré
(du Bellay)

Cunault

Azay-le-Rideau

Villandry

Chenonceaux

N76

Nantes

MAINE-
ET-
LOIRE

Saumur

Ussé
(Perrault)

Saché
(Balzac)

Cher

Vierzon

Noirmoutier

Sèvre

Fontevrault l'Abbaye

Vienne

Chinon
(Rabelais)

TOURAINE

Valençay

Bourges

Ile de Noirmoutier

N149

Cholet

Loches

A10

Bay of Biscay

Puy-du-Fou

INDRE

BERRY

Pouzauges

Ile d'Yeu

VENDEE

La Roche-sur-Yon

Châteauroux

N137

les Sables-d'Olonne

Marais
Poitevin

Nohant
(Sand)

Legend

● summer resort

(Hugo) writer or artist

church, abbey or cathedral

château

other place of interest

industrial center

major port

built-up area

national or regional park

main wine-growing region

major wine-producing area

Pays Nantais

Anjou-Saumur

Touraine

Central Vineyards

scale 1 : 1 900 000

0   60 km

0   40 mi

174

THE LOIRE

The Loire
The two far-flung regions of Centre and Pays de la Loire contain many famous royal castles, lying on or near the banks of the broad river. These gentle regions have nurtured many great writers, including Rabelais, Balzac and Proust. Major industries include shipbuilding and food-processing.

Centre: population: 2.3 million; area 39,000sq km; capital, Orléans pop. 105,000, 131km from Paris. Other main towns, Tours, pop. 136,000, and Bourges, pop. 79,000. *Pays de la Loire*: population 3 million; area 32,000sq km; capital, Nantes pop. 247,000, 384km from Paris. Other main towns, Le Mans, pop. 150,000, and Angers, pop. 141,000.

Bottom left The river Loire flows through a fertile plain which produces fruit such as melons and apricots, and fine wines. Touraine, the sector around Tours, is called "the garden of France".

Below A chic cave-dwelling in the tufa cliffs at Montsoreau on the Loire, near Saumur. The many caves of the Loire and Loir valleys, inhabited since medieval times and then abandoned, are now being lived in again by ecological enthusiasts. Some are also used for cultivating mushrooms on a massive commercial scale.

Bottom A medieval bed in the museum at Rabelais's family manor house of La Devinière, near Chinon. This rebellious life-loving humanist, son of a wealthy local lawyer, was born here in 1494, in a lush valley which he used as the setting for the comic Picrocholean war in his satirical masterpiece *Gargantua*. Boisterous Rabelaisian banquets are still held today by the local wine fraternity, in the "painted caverns" below Chinon's royal fortress.

France's longest river, the Loire, broad and serene-looking, yet given to sudden flooding and treacherous currents, flows through a wide and fertile plain to the sea at the big port of Nantes. The two sprawling, low-lying regions of Centre (population 2.3 million) and Pays de la Loire (population 3 million) that make up the Loire region are mainly rural, and their farms and orchards yield some of France's richest produce. The important towns of the region are mostly along the Loire – Nantes and Angers, Tours and Orléans.

This river has witnessed many episodes in French history. Great fortresses and châteaux were built on or near its banks, first for defence in war, then as pleasure-haunts for the French kings in Paris. Anjou (capital Angers) produced a powerful medieval dynasty whose Plantagenet rulers were closely linked to the English crown, while Orléans was the site of Joan of Arc's triumph in 1429 that led the way to French victory in the Hundred Years War. On the fringes of the Loire valley are the monotonous wheat plain of the Beauce, the brooding forests of the Sologne and, seaward, the Vendée plain where the Royalist passions of 1793 still smolder.

At the very center of the region, around Tours, the province of Touraine with its gentle climate has long been seen as a heartland of true French tradition. Here the spoken French is the purest and most accent-free in France. The rich soil yields melons and asparagus, strawberries and fine wines, such as sparkling white Vouvray and robust red Bourgeuil.

Touraine's confident serenity has also been propitious to literature; indeed, the whole Centre region has nurtured more great writers than any other. The 19th-century novelist Honoré de Balzac was born in Tours and, though he later moved to Paris, he never lost his passion for Touraine and its way of life, which he "loved as an artist loves art". He used to stay with titled friends at the château of Saché (now a Balzac museum), in the Indre valley, the setting of his novel *Le Lys dans la vallée*. Before Balzac, the Renaissance lyric poet Pierre de Ronsard lived in the lush valley of the little river Loir (no "e"), north of Tours, where, through his verses, he dedicated a fountain to "la Belle Hélène". This is an area of strange caves in the tufa cliffs, some still inhabited. Today Tours has become a booming industrial city, and so has Orléans, the fast-expanding regional capital. Big modern firms such as St-Gobain and Thomson have moved in, and Chinon even has nuclear power stations. It was in Chinon castle that England's Henry II died and Joan of Arc met the Dauphin.

To the northeast, around Chartres, the even limestone plain of the Beauce has a rich clayey topsoil whose yields of wheat and barley per hectare are among the world's highest. Yet, despite the prosperity, the suicide rate here is France's highest, perhaps because of the awesome monotony of this plain, where Zola set his searing portrait of peasant life in the 1880s, *La Terre*. To the south, the Sologne has its own particular beauty – a distinctive flat district of heathland and forest, with reedy lagoons and low white cob-walled thatched cottages. It is great hunting country, with big estates of wild boar, deer and pheasant, which once used to teem with local poachers – as described in Maurice Genevoix's novel *Raboliot* (1925), in which an illegal poacher is identified with the animals he hunts.

A wistful picture of the Sologne is also presented in Alain Fournier's *Le Grand Meaulnes*, which mixes romantic fantasy with precise souvenirs of his childhood spent in the area and farther south at Epineuil-le-Fleuriel, a village in the Berry. The rolling Berry country (its main town, Bourges, has a fine Gothic cathedral) was also the *pays* of the novelist Georges Sand. Although perhaps best known as a Parisian bohemian, she was deeply affected by the wild Rousseauesque adolescence she spent among country-folk, around her family château at Nohant, where she retired in later life and set her novels of idealized rural innocence. Even today, her corner of the Berry remains one of the least spoilt, and least modernized, parts of rural France.

Back on the Loire, Anjou's historic capital, Angers, has a stately feudal castle with superb tapestries. During its heyday in the 12th to 15th centuries, the county and duchy of Anjou produced King Henry II of England, and "Good King René", who went off to rule as far afield as Provence and Sicily. Anjou was annexed to France in 1259. Today, as serene and fertile as Touraine, it is a center of market gardening, while mushrooms are massively cultivated in caves in the rocks near Saumur.

The lower Loire area centers on Nantes, which was part of Brittany until the 1789 Revolution. Many Nantais still consider themselves Breton, even though their big city is now the capital of another region. It is a busy Atlantic port, and this area has important new electronics and aerospace factories, which make up for the decline of the huge shipyards at St Nazaire. Other modern industry is over at Le Mans, best known for its fine cathedral and the annual 24-hour motor race. The lower Loire produces dry white wines, notably Muscadet; and its farmlands supply a thriving local food-processing industry, strong on biscuits and canned and frozen goods. Near the sea is the nature park of Grande Brière, a strange marshy area of peat bogs and fossilized tree trunks, up to 5000 years old. Here, too, is la Baule, one of France's largest and most fashionable seaside resorts.

There are more good beaches, and biggish resorts such as Les Sables d'Olonne, over on the Vendée coast south of the Loire estuary. But the Vendée plain is known, above all, as the scene of the bitter Royalist and Catholic uprising against the Revolution, after the execution of Louis XVI in 1793. Today this is still a heartland of old-style traditional Catholicism, where old hatreds die hard: during France's Bicentenary festivities in 1989, some right-wing mayors judged it "indecent" to celebrate the Revolution, and refused to do so. At the half-ruined château of Puy-du-Fou, a spectacular nocturnal pageant each summer portrays – albeit one-sidedly – the saga of the Vendée wars.

Characteristic of the cuisine of the Loire regions is the *beurre blanc* sauce that goes with many fish dishes, Nantes ducklings served with peas, bass or eels cooked in white wine, the *rillettes* (minced pork) of Le Mans, the *coq au vin* of Touraine, and the game dishes of the Sologne (pheasant casserole, venison with black cherry sauce). Quality Loire wines include white and red Sancerres as well as Touraine and Anjou.

Châteaux of the Loire

The banks of the Loire and its tributaries are embellished with scores of stately châteaux. Most of them were built by the kings of France, who loved this region for its mild climate, good food and wine, and forests well stocked with game. It was also within easy reach of Paris. The châteaux were used as grandiose hunting lodges, or as summer residences – or even for amorous purposes, when some favorite mistress was installed discreetly in one of them. Sometimes the king would move his whole court to a Loire château for several months, with vast retinues of courtiers, luggage and furniture.

The earliest medieval châteaux had been built for war, not peace, for example, the severe hilltop fortress of Chinon, where England's king Henry II died in 1189. In the 15th century Charles VII moved his court here, and in 1429 the 18-year-old Joan of Arc came to kneel before him and ask him for an army. He agreed. Then, in 1465, Louis XI built the château of Langeais, where Charles VIII married Anne of Brittany.

The finest châteaux were built in the Renaissance period, but some are later, and classical in style. One of the most romantic, Ussé on the Loire, festooned with pepperpot towers, is said to have inspired Perrault as his model for "The Sleeping Beauty".

Below Built in the 14th century by Louis, duke of Anjou, Saumur's massive square castle dominates the Loire. The poet René le Bon called it "the castle of love". It now houses a museum of decorative arts, and a museum of horses. An old house in a narrow street just below it was the setting for Balzac's novel *Eugénie Grandet*, a study of miserliness and provincial ennui.

Left Chambord, much the largest of the Loire châteaux, has 440 rooms, 365 sculptured chimneys, and 85 staircases. It was built as a hunting lodge by the flamboyant François I, and stands in a huge deer park. In summer it swarms with visitors, and stages a spectacular son et lumière show.

Above The double-spiralled staircase at Chambord where two people going up and down cannot meet except at top and bottom, yet never lose sight of each other.

Top right Described as "a lovely houseboat made of stone" the elegant Renaissance château of Azay-le-Rideau stands on the river Indre, whose waters reflect it magically in some lights. Inside are fine Renaissance tapestries and furniture.

Right Sturdy Chaumont château on the Loire, a 15th-century fortress, is associated mainly with famous women who disliked it. Cathérine de Médici, Henri II's widow, bought it to avenge herself on her late husband's mistress, Diane de Poitiers. She forced her rival to give up lovely Chenonceaux and live at grim Chaumont, which she came to hate. It was also disliked by the writer Madame de Staël, who lived here when exiled from Paris by Napoleon.

2°   1°   0°   1°   2°

50°

English Channel

Baie de la Seine

le Tréport

Dieppe

Cap de la Hague

Yport
(Maupassant)   Fécamp
(Maupassant)

SEINE-MARITIME

Falaise d'Aval
Etretat
(Maupassant, Monet)

Cherbourg

St-Vaast-la-Hougue

Cuverville
(Gide)

N128

Villequier
(Hugo)

Ry
(Flaubert)

N15

Cotentin

Le Havre
(Sartre, Maupassant, Queneau)

Harfleur
Honfleur
(Boudin)

Pont de Tancarville

Jumièges

Rouen
(Flaubert, Maupassant)

Utah Beach

Omaha Beach

St-Sauveur-
le-Vicomte
(Barbey d'Aurévilly)

Arromanches

Deauville   Trouville

Cabourg
(Proust)
Houlgate

UPPER NORMANDY
(HAUTE-NORMANDIE)

Louviers

les Andelys

Carteret
(Barbey d'Aurévilly)

Bayeux

Ouistreham

Pont-l'Évêque
(Flaubert)

Le Bec-Hellouin

N13

Giverny
(Monet)

A13

Seine

N14

Lessay
(Barbey d'Aurévilly)

N13

Caen

Pays d'Auge

Lisieux

N13

EURE

Evreux

St Lô

N138

A13

Coutances

CALVADOS

Livarot

Suisse Normande area

N175

N154

LOWER NORMANDY
(BASSE-NORMANDIE)

Camembert

MANCHE

Granville

Vire

See

Argentan

Risle

Baie du
Mont St
Michel

Avranches

SUISSE NORMANDE

Orne

ORNE

N12

Mont-St-Michel

Selune

Domfront

Bagnoles-de-l'Orne

Mayenne

Alençon

49°

48°

resorts

● summer
● spa

place associated with

(Gide) writer or artist
● cheese

⌂ church, abbey or cathedral
✿ other place of interest
⌂ industrial center
⚓ major port

█ built-up area
▓ national or regional park
▒ major area of calvados production

scale 1 : 1 900 000

0 .... 60km
0 .... 40mi

Right The entrance to the port of
Le Havre, France's largest after
Marseille. Some transatlantic liners
still dock here, but 80 percent of
the port's traffic is now oil-related,
and there are huge refineries in the
Seine estuary.

Center right Horses and jockeys
prepare for a race meeting at
Deauville, where the summer
racing season is highly fashionable.
Lower Normandy is the main
breeding ground of French
racehorses, and Norman
thoroughbreds are renowned for
their grace and toughness.

NORMANDY

Normandy
Old half-timbered houses, apple orchards, meadows where racehorses and dairy cows quietly graze, tall Gothic cathedrals and a coastline of chalky cliffs – all these make Normandy a picturesque province that exudes well-being. It also has much modern industry, including car factories and nuclear power stations.

Upper Normandy: population 1.7 million; area 12,300sq km; capital, Rouen pop. 105,000, 137km from Paris. Other main town, Le Havre pop. 200,000. *Lower Normandy*: pop. 1.4 million; area 17,600sq km; capital, Caen pop. 117,000, 240km from Paris.

Right The most-visited tourist sight in France after Versailles, the abbey of Mont-St-Michel stands just offshore on a granite peak rising 80m above the sea, and is reached by a causeway. In its Romanesque 12th-century church, Benedictine monks still say Mass daily.

Bottom right Normandy's countless orchards yield small bitter apples used for cider, from which the famous spirit *calvados*, named after the department, is distilled. It is drunk as a *digestif*, but also finds it way into the sublime, calorie-rich Norman cuisine.

Although today divided administratively into the regions of Upper Normandy (population 1.7 million) and Lower Normandy (population 1.4 million), this ancient province preserves a strong sense of identity, which, for historical reasons, is in some ways less Latin than Nordic. The people are more often fair-haired and blue-eyed than in other parts of France and more cautious in temperament. Indeed, this is the part of France most similar to southern England – in its people, its seafaring traditions, its climate, its coastline of chalky cliffs, and its pastoral scenery.

Rouen, Upper Normandy's proud capital, is a big river-port full of sprawling modern industry. Yet its medieval core, though badly bombed during World War II, still has many fine old half-timbered houses around the soaring cathedral and the market square where Joan of Arc was burned. From Rouen the broad Seine loops its way past the half-ruined 11th-century Benedictine abbey of Jumièges, one of many great Romanesque churches built by the early Normans (they imported the style into England, where it is just called Norman). The nearby ruined abbey and re-stored monastery of Le Bec-Hellouin, which produced

three archbishops of Canterbury, is another example.

At the Seine estuary is Le Havre, one of Europe's major ports. Destroyed in the war, it was then hurriedly rebuilt in an austere style and is the only big French town to have been uninterruptedly Communist-run since 1945. Submerged in its new industrial suburbs is Harfleur, where in 1415 Shakespeare's Henry V summoned his dear friends once more unto the breach. The coast northeast of the city, toward the major fishing ports of Fécamp and Dieppe, has high chalky cliffs which, around Etretat, stand out to sea in bizarre shapes.

To the west, Lower Normandy focuses on Caen, its capital, now a booming center of modern industry, but also home to two magnificent, well restored, Romanesque abbeys. Badly damaged in the epic 1944 battles, Caen has since been tastefully rebuilt, unlike many of the other towns destroyed in this area, which are now mainly concrete. Down on the coast are the 1944 invasion beaches, Omaha, Utah and others, and at Arromanches there is a vivid museum of the whole operation. The coast east of Caen has fine sheltered sandy beaches and a string of busy bathing resorts, of which Deauville is by far the most fashionable. Inland is the luscious Pays d'Auge, quintessence of rural Normandy, and Lisieux with its Gothic cathedral and modern basilica, where pilgrims throng to honor Thérèse, the local saint.

The western side of Normandy – the Manche department, where the Cotentin peninsula holds the busy port of Cherbourg – is different from the rest. It is formed of granite, not chalk, and its rugged coasts and severe stone houses have a Breton look. Also its peasant people are much poorer than those of Calvados, around Caen. But it has some stunning buildings – the soaring Gothic cathedral of Coutances, and the renowned Gothic abbey of Mont-St-Michel, towering up on its rocky offshore islet, always besieged by tourists.

Normandy has produced a large number of major authors and some have written critically. Guy de Maupassant, born in Fécamp, found the local peasantry wily and stubborn. His friend and mentor, Gustave Flaubert, who spent his life in Rouen, painted a harsh picture of the narrow-minded Norman middle classes, notably in *Madame Bovary*, which may have been based on a true drama in the village of Ry. Very different was flamboyant and eccentric Barbey d'Aurévilly. Normandy has nurtured great painters too. Poussin and Millet were both Norman, while Boudin was born and lived in Honfleur. Many of the leading Impressionists also worked in Normandy – notably Claude Monet whose water-garden by his home at Giverny, has been beautifully recreated.

Normandy is one of the richest of French farming regions, producing pungent cheeses (for example Camembert, pont l'Evêque, livarot), apple-liqueurs and racehorses. At Domfront, the world's largest cheese factory daily produces 350,000 camembert cheeses. Over one quarter of French beef and dairy products originate from the very rich clayey pastures.

ILE DE FRANCE

The heartland of royal France in early times was the small area between the rivers Seine, Oise and Marne, which came to be known as the Isle of France. Today the Ile de France region (population 10.2 million) spreads more widely, embracing the Greater Paris conurbation and some rural areas beyond. Only 2.1 million live in the City of Paris itself, with its own mayor and council – the trim oval-shaped area within the old city gates and the new Boulevard Périphérique (motorway). The rest live in the hundreds of surburban communes, some of them elegant ancient towns such as Versailles, others featureless concrete postwar dormitories.

This whole area is a great jumble, built haphazardly in phases. The interwar years saw a rash of unplanned *pavillons* – ugly bungalows with little gardens – in what are now the inner suburbs. Then, in the 1950s and 1960s, to meet an urgent housing crisis, new high-rise "social" housing estates were put up here and there, where space was available, on the edge of older suburbs: Sarcelles was the most notorious of these. At the same time, for the well-to-do, smarter estates of California-style villas and flats, with private tennis courts and swimming pools, began to spread mainly to the west of Paris, toward Versailles. Serious coordinated planning then began, and since the 1970s five well-designed "new towns", of 100,000 to 150,000 people each, have been built on the edge of the conurbation, whose size has swelled since the war from 5 to 9 million (due more to the French rural exodus, and to the magnetic appeal of Paris, than to demographic or economic growth). The whole area is interlaced with new motorways, and well served in places by the new high-speed rail-cum-Métro network, the RER. But the tangle of hospitals and hypermarkets, factories and filling stations, colleges and crèches, apartment blocks and asphalt, is still bewildering.

Here and there, a few interesting older places survive – Enghien-les-Bains, the only spa in the Paris region, the majestic early-Gothic basilica at St-Denis, the modest château of Malmaison, where Napoleon lived with Josephine, and the fort of Mont Valérien where the Nazis executed some 4,500 Résistants (it is now a memorial). The 30 metal-and-glass skyscrapers of the new La Défense business quarter, harmoniously grouped, are now as much part of the Paris scene as the Eiffel Tower.

Beyond Greater Paris stretches the limestone basin of the Ile de France, ringed with forests of beech and oak: "the lungs of Paris" they are called, for they help to purify the air of its industrial conurbation. The forests used to be royal hunting-grounds, full of deer. Now they are state-owned and open to all. Beyond the Paris sprawl, the Ile de France still has much rural charm: half-ruined abbeys beside streams, great châteaux with ornate parks, and wooded valleys such as the Chevreuse, where Parisians go for Sunday picnics (by car, in large numbers). Farming is still important, with wheat plains around Provins, and market gardens selling mushrooms and cut flowers.

Southeast of Paris, the Brie country is known for its large, soft, circular cheeses.

The kings of France built royal palaces in the Ile de France, the most important being Versailles. At St-Germain-en-Laye, nearby, is the great Renaissance château built by François I on the site of a much older one, where Mary Queen of Scots spent her childhood and James II died. St-Germain is on the edge of a handsome forest; so is Rambouillet, whose château dating from the 14th century (but since then much modernized) is now the official summer residence of the President of the Republic.

Second only to Versailles in the Paris region, the great Renaissance palace at Fontainebleau was built by François I. Napoleon much preferred it to Versailles, and used it as his royal home. Fontainebleau's big forest, mainly of oak and beech, contains outcrops of oddly shaped sandstone rocks, much used by trainee climbers. Another château in the area, Vaux-le-Vicomte, built for Louis XIV's finance minister, has superb terraced formal gardens by Le Nôtre. Of the major abbeys in the Ile de France, the 13th-century Cistercian monastery of Port-Royal-des-Champs became the headquarters of the Jansenist movement in the 17th century; only its ruins remain today. To the north of Paris, Royaumont Abbey was also 13th-century Cistercian and is also now partly ruined, but its lovely monastery survives, and today serves as a cultural and conference center, in an idyllic setting.

The clear shimmering light of the Ile de France has attracted numerous artists to the region. The village of Barbizon, near Fontainebleau, became the home of a 19th-century school of landscape painters led by Théodore Rousseau and J.F. Millet; Corot worked there too. In the 1870s the Impressionists and post-Impressionists moved out from Paris: Pissarro and Cézanne to Cergy-Pontoise, Renoir and Monet to Bougival and Argenteuil, then villages on the Seine where very often they painted boating-party scenes; today they are Parisian suburbs. Sisley, the English Impressionist, lived and painted at Moret, on the river Loing, and at Auvers-sur-Oise the disturbed Van Gogh spent his final months, and killed himself.

Some Parisian writers, too, have found inspiration or peace of mind in this quiet countryside. Jean-Jacques Rousseau, weary of the literary salon snobberies of the capital, spent six years in the village and forest of Montmorency, where he elaborated his philosophy of nature. His cottage still stands, now swamped by the suburban sprawl. The Vicomte de Chateaubriand, that great Romantic, lovingly planted trees around his country home of La Vallée-aux-Loups ("I know them all by their names...they are my family"): here Madame Recamier consoled him, and her bedroom can today be visited. Near the Seine, at Medan, Emile Zola bought a big gabled Victorian villa, where he wrote some of his novels. On the lawn outside, is a bust of him, scowling and bushy-bearded. The trains that ran between Paris and Rouen passed his garden and provided him with research material for his novel *La Bête humaine*.

Ile de France

The Paris conurbation of some 9 million people covers quite a large part of the compact little Ile de France region. Today less than a quarter of Parisians live in the city of Paris itself, within the old gates; the rest are out in sprawling suburbs, all separately governed. The region's limestone basin contains forests that were once hunting grounds used by the kings who built the great palaces and châteaux of Versailles, Fontainebleau, Rambouillet, and others.

Population: 10.2 million; area: 12,000sq km; capital, Paris pop 2.1 million.

Below Café-going may be in decline in France, but Paris's hundreds of terrace-cafés still do a lively trade – with Parisians at the apéritif hour, with tourists at all times.

ILE DE FRANCE

VAL D'OISE

Royaumont Abbey

l'Isle Adam

Auvers-sur-Oise
(Van Gogh)

Cergy-Pontoise
(Cézanne, Pissarro)

Montmorency
(Rousseau)

Sarcelles

Enghien-les-Bains

Charles-de-Gaulle

Meaux

Maison Laffitte

Medan
(Zola)

Argenteuil
(Monet)

Poissy

St Denis

Aulnay-sous-Bois

Marne

St Germain-en-Laye

Nanterre

Mont-Valérien

Bobigny

Thoiry

YVELINES

Bougival
(Renoir)

Malmaison

PARIS
Paris

SEINE-ST-
DENIS

Chelles

Petit Morin

Boulogne-Billancourt

Marne-la-Vallée

Coulommiers

Grand Morin

Montfort-l'Amaury

Versailles

HAUTS-DE-SEINE

Sceaux

SEINE-ET-MARNE

Port-Royal-des-Champs
(Racine)

Dampierre

Chevreuse

Rungis

VAL-DE-MARNE

Créteil

Orly

BRIE

Rambouillet

A10

Yères

Provins

ILE DE FRANCE

Evry

Vaux-le-Vicomte

ESSONNE

Seine

Melun

Etampes

Essonne

Barbizon
(Rousseau, Millet, Corot)

Fontainebleau

Seine

Moret
(Sisley)

A6

Loing

Nemours

Seine

Mantes

A13

Vallée de Chevreuse

ILE DE FRANCE

Paris

● spa resort

(Hugo) writer or artist

church, abbey or cathedral

château or palace

other place of interest

industrial center

built-up area

state forest

scale 1 : 1 000 000

0   30km
0   20mi

Below The entrance to Christian Dior's fashion house lends a touch of glamor to the Champs-Elysées district, which has been moving down-market. The broad majestic avenue has been filling up with fast-food shops, car showrooms and multi-screen cinemas. In the side-streets, a few grand old luxury hotels survive, most of them now British-owned.

Modern Paris Buildings

Paris is a city of great monumental buildings, often daring in design. It was the French kings, with an eye to their own glory, who initiated this tradition: Louis XIV, for example, built Les Invalides in grandiose style. Then in 1887–9 the Eiffel Tower was erected in a very different spirit: to mark the centenary of a Revolution that overthrew the monarchy.

The presidents of France have now revived the old royal tradition – in a prosperous age when Paris is keen to hold its place as both the most majestic and innovative of Europe's capitals. De Gaulle, despite his love of *grandeur*, did little for architecture. But his successor, Georges Pompidou, set the new trend by initiating the modernistic arts center that bears his name. This, like most of the new projects, was the work not of French but of foreign architects.

A project of this kind may take from five to ten years to complete. Launched by one president, it will often be finished by his successor, and both will try to claim the credit (rivalries for prestige are intense). Thus Giscard d'Estaing completed Beaubourg, and then launched two of his own projects – the Orsay and la Villette museums – which were left to his successor, François Mitterrand, to carry through.

Mitterrand, a lover of modern architecture, has poured billions of francs into ambitious ventures, as part of his plan to promote a French cultural renaissance. But his critics have accused him of self-glorification, of "suffering from a Louis XIV complex". Besides the Louvre pyramid, the Bastille Opéra and the Great Arch at la Défense, he had initiated a new home for the Bibliothèque Nationale, and put some much-contested modernistic sculptures into the 17th-century courtyard of the Palais Royal.

Above left The Cité de la Musique, completed at la Villette in 1991. It is the new home of the Conservatoire de Paris, and contains a concert hall for Pierre Boulez's modern orchestra.

Above The new Opera House at the Bastille, designed by the Canadian architect Carlos Ott. It was planned to provide Paris with a venue for large-scale modern productions, since the Palais Garnier, built in the 1860s, was no longer suitable. After many difficulties, the Bastille Opéra was opened at the 1989 Bicentenary.

Left Conceived by President Georges Pompidou, the Pompidou Center was opened in 1977 at the Plateau Beaubourg, and is the best-known postwar building in Paris. It is a multipurpose cultural center, designed by the Anglo-Italian team of Richard Rogers and Renzo Piano. Its service equipment – water mains, electric cables and so on – is all displayed on the outside, in bright colors. Nicknamed the "arty oil-refinery", it caused a furore at first but is now accepted.

Bottom La Grande Arche, formally opened at the 1989 Bicentenary, is a vast cube-shaped office block in white marble, 100m square, with a hollow interior. Designed by Otto von Spreckelsen, a Dane, it is set in the new skyscraper quarter of la Défense, west of central Paris.

Below The towering pyramid in the main courtyard of the Louvre, 21m high, is perhaps the most controversial of the new Paris buildings. Commissioned by President Mitterrand and designed by the Chinese–American architect I.M. Pei, the structure is modeled on the ancient pyramids of Giza in Egypt. It is designed to reflect the light, and is best seen from inside, where the Louvre's main entrance foyer has been greatly improved. But many Parisians feel that it is out of keeping with its classical surroundings.

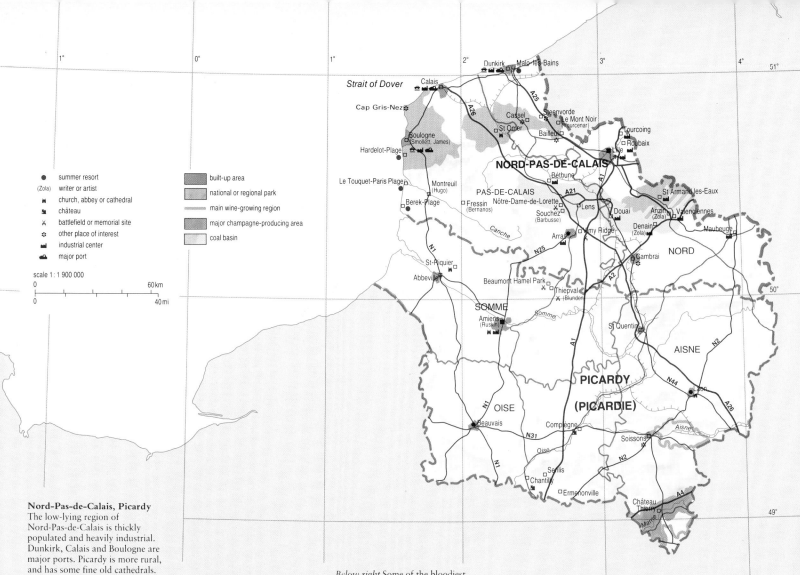

Nord-Pas-de-Calais, Picardy

The low-lying region of Nord-Pas-de-Calais is thickly populated and heavily industrial. Dunkirk, Calais and Boulogne are major ports. Picardy is more rural, and has some fine old cathedrals.

Nord-Pas-de-Calais: population 3.9 million; area 12,000sq km; capital, Lille; pop. 157,000. Other towns, Roubaix pop. 102,000, Tourcoing pop.97,000 and Calais pop. 77,000. *Picardy*: population 1.7 million; area 19,400sq km; capital, Amiens pop. 136,000.

Below Calais's town hall with its tall and ornate brick belfry. In front of it is Rodin's famous sculpture *The Burghers of Calais* (1895), honoring the six who in 1347 offered their lives if the besieging English armies would spare the town.

Below right Some of the bloodiest trench battles of the 1914–18 war took place in the Artois and Somme districts. Their reminders today are several graceful hilltop war memorials, and many thousands of neatly tended cemeteries, such as this one in Picardy.

Map legend:

- summer resort
- (Zola) writer or artist
- church, abbey or cathedral
- château
- battlefield or memorial site
- other place of interest
- industrial center
- major port

- built-up area
- national or regional park
- main wine-growing region
- major champagne-producing area
- coal basin

scale 1 : 1 900 000

NORD-PAS-DE-CALAIS, PICARDY

Below Lenten and spring carnivals are a popular tradition in these regions. Here young men in Amiens parade on stilts (in the nearby marshes, these were once used as a means of moving about).

The cemeteries of two World Wars, and the slag heaps of coal mines now closed or dying, lie dotted across the wide windy plain of the Nord-Pas-de-Calais (population 3.9 million), as symbols of its past travails. This densely populated region (and likewise Picardy next door) has for centuries been a major European crossroads both for traders and armed invaders. It was also, for a long time, the prime center of French heavy industry, until its mining, steelworks, shipbuilding and textiles fell into decline. But today, with the opening of the Channel Tunnel from Calais to Dover, and new high-speed rail links, it faces a bright future in the new single-market Europe of 1992.

The northern strip, from the big industrial port of Dunkirk to Lille, the capital, is Flemish in origin, closely similar to adjacent Belgian Flanders. The flat landscape has its own somber beauty, its horizons marked by high red-brick Flemish belfry towers. The people, tenacious, warm-hearted and open-minded, have long offset their harsh, industrial existence with a varied social and club life that might seem more Anglo-Saxon than French, and their sense of local folk tradition is unusually strong. They cherish their special sports and hobbies (puppetry, pigeon-fancying, archery, brass bands), and enjoy their Lenten and spring carnivals, when each town joyfully parades its own Giant, a costumed grotesque symbolizing its medieval founder or protector: Bailleul and Cambrai have the best ones. The Flemish have been invaded 22 times in 800 years, and they claim that is why they are so keen to preserve their identity by affirming their culture.

Often ravaged by the English, the area in the 17th century was under Spanish occupation, before Lille was ceded to France in 1713. Then, in 1914–18, the English came back as allies, many dying in the trench battles of Flanders, and of the Somme in Picardy. Today, the massive British hilltop memorial at Thiepval, the smaller Canadian one on Vimy Ridge, the 2500 neatly tended Commonwealth cemeteries, and the millions of French and German graves remain as grim reminders of a four-year nightmare, poignantly evoked by the soldier-poets such as Britain's Wilfred Owen. But the most powerful portrayal of those battles is in Henri Barbusse's novel *Le Feu*, set in the Vimy area below the high French memorial of Nôtre-Dame-de-Lorette. In World War II, the towns again suffered heavily, and Dunkirk found its place in history with the epic evacuation of the British army between May 25 and June 5, 1940, when some 350,000 soldiers were rescued by a fleet of ships.

Industry has been the Nord-Pas-de-Calais' greatest asset, but also its Achilles' heel. Lille was a major textiles center from the Middle Ages, and its traders toured the globe. Then, in the 19th century, heavy industry came in, based on the local steelworks and the coal mines south of Lille, whose world of bitter toil and poverty was captured in Zola's *Germinal*. Today workers are better paid, but work has grown scarce. Steel is in recession, the Dunkirk shipyards have closed, and jobs in the near-exhausted coal mines have dropped from 220,000 to 7000 since 1947. The textile firms have successfully modernized, but at the cost of shedding many jobs too. Local unemployment and emigration levels are well above the French average, and attracting investment in new industries has not been easy because of the area's image. "We're portrayed in the Paris media", one coal-belt official was quoted as saying, "as a place of gray skies, Zolaesque slums, alcoholism and badly paved roads. It's not really like that – but what can we do?"

However, prospects for the region are now brighter in the context of a new Europe. Whereas, in the past, this northern tip of France had always seemed somewhat peripheral to the country, now, with the abolition of trade frontiers, it has become central. Lille has been chosen as the hub of the new high-speed Euronetwork, where the TGV (Train à Grande Vitesse) from London to Paris via the Tunnel will link with the other TGV line from the Ruhr, Amsterdam and Brussels. The region hopes to become the pivot of the world's leading wealthy urbanized area, the so-called Golden Triangle of the EC. This will bring massive new investment in services and manufacturing.

Lille, the dignified old pink-brick Flemish city where de Gaulle was born, is a lively place with all-night restaurants and a good art museum; it has eagerly

Overleaf Mers-les-Bains, in the Somme, is one of several somewhat old-fashioned family bathing-resorts that line the sandy beaches of this coast. The best-known is Le Touquet-Paris-Plage, very elegant in Edwardian days and now popular again.

responded to the challenge by creating new business centers – under its assertive Socialist mayor, Pierre Mauroy, Prime Minister in 1981–4. This industrial region has long been the Socialists' main bastion in France, where in uneasy alliance with the Communists they have controlled the regional council and most town councils. Their politics, however, have always been very flexible, and even some Communist leaders have welcomed capitalist development. Calais, France's premier passenger port, feared the nearby Tunnel as a dangerous rival, but its Communist mayor came to terms with the project, and began to woo British and American financiers – with some success. Whereas the coal basin inland still does poorly, new investment has been flooding into the ports. Coca-Cola has set up a factory at Dunkirk.

The British especially, who owned Calais from 1346 to 1558, have returned as commercial invaders. They have bought up real estate, building or taking over hypermarkets, casinos and big hotels around Calais and the major fishing port of Boulogne, and down the Opal Coast to Le Touquet-Paris-Plage, which the British helped to create as an elegant resort in Edwardian days, but later forsook. The Tunnel has further prompted thousands of Britons to purchase cottages and farmhouses as holiday or weekend homes, in the pleasant rural hinterland of Boulogne and at Le Touquet, where house prices are a mere third of those across the Channel in rural Kent.

This coastal region, with its chalky cliffs and good beaches, is more hilly and scenic than the Flanders plain – and is rich in literary associations. Georges Bernanos (1888–1948) lived at Fressin, where he set his austere novels about young priests' spiritual struggles; and it was at walled hilltop Montreuil that Hugo's Valjean turned from petty thief into noble champion of *Les Misérables*.

Several old towns in the region have fine examples of that distinctive curly gabled Flemish architecture, so similar to Dutch and the Hanseatic style of North Germany. In Arras, in particular, two noble squares are framed by tall and elegant 17th-century houses with ornamented gables and covered arcades. St-Omer and St-Riquier have splendid old churches. But the best cathedrals are in Picardy – at Laon, where the Gothic seven-towered Nôtre-Dame stands imposingly on a hilltop, and at Amiens, Picardy's capital. Its cathedral, perhaps the finest Gothic one in France, so inspired John Ruskin that he wrote a book about it; he especially liked the "Madonna in decadence" at the south porch, with "her gay soubrette's smile".

At the southern edge of Picardy, not far from the Paris conurbation, are two famous towns. Chantilly is known for its fashionable racecourse, and for its lakeside Renaissance palace whose museum includes superb illuminated manuscripts. Compiègne's palace, even grander, was used by Napoleon as an imperial residence. In a clearing in the nearby forest, a memorial marks the spot where the Armistice was signed on 11 November 1918, ending World War I, and where Hitler then took the French surrender in June 1940.

Rolling Picardy (population 1.6 million) is a fertile agricultural region whose big farms grow cereals and sugar beet. Neither this region nor the Nord-Pas-de-Calais is renowned for its cooking, but the Flemish way of stewing beef in beer is tasty. So is *ficelle picarde*, a crêpe with ham and sauce, and *hochepot*, a heavy meat stew.

ALSACE, LORRAINE, CHAMPAGNE-ARDENNE

Alsace (population 1.6 million) and Lorraine (population 2.3 million), are very different in character, but they share the fate of being the only French provinces adjacent to Germany, and this has deeply marked their history. Although effectively united with France since 1648, they have frequently suffered German pressures and invasions, and were annexed by Germany from 1871 until 1918 and again from 1940 until 1945. Souvenirs of past wars are on every side, including the Maginot Line fortifications, built so confidently in the 1930s to keep out *les Boches*, but in 1940 so swiftly outflanked by the panzers (its forts are now tourist sights). Today, however, Alsace's great capital, Strasbourg, is the seat of the European Parliament and the Council of Europe, and is the very symbol of postwar Franco-German reconciliation and European unity.

The two provinces are separated by the long line of the Vosges, high hills more than mountains, nowhere rising above 1425 meters; their rounded summits can be reached on foot, while a good road runs along their central spine. Pine forests cover much of the range, but there are upland pastures too, and slopes for skiing. The hills descend gently on the western side, more steeply to the east. Here the Alsatian vineyards lie just above the broad Rhine plain, below some boldly perched castles such as feudal Haut-Barr and mock-feudal Haut-Koenigsbourg, and the strange 11th-century pilgrimage chapel of Sainte Odile.

The Alsatians are of Allemanic origin, close cousins to the nearby Badeners and Swiss-Germans; their dialect is very similar, as are their German-sounding place and family names. In fact, of all regions of mainland France, this is the least French in looks and feel. In the neat villages, the older half-timbered houses, many with flowery balconies, look much like those across the Rhine; the local costumes, the style of festival celebration, even the wine itself (white and fruity, from Riesling grapes), all recall southwest Germany. Yet the Alsatians suffered so much from German occupations that they have willingly implemented Paris' postwar policy of Frenchification. Alsatian is not taught in schools, though it is still widely spoken in rural areas.

Strasbourg is an exceedingly graceful city, with gabled 16th-century houses by the river Ill, and a splendid red sandstone Gothic cathedral noted for its "astronomical clock" and soaring tower. In the 15th century Gutenburg, in exile from Mainz, pioneered the printing press in Strasbourg. Goethe, too, lived and studied here, and had a love-affair with a pastor's daughter, Friedericke, in nearby Sessenheim. The Alsatian "wine road" winds south from Strasbourg, past picturesque villages such as Ribeauvillé and Riquewihr, at their best in high-spirited festival time when some fountains literally flow with free wine. Kayserberg, near Colmar, was the birthplace of the missionary surgeon Albert Schweitzer (1875–1965). Bigger and much more industrial than Colmar, Mulhouse has a Peugeot factory and a museum with over 400 vintage cars (the Schlumpf collection). Alsace, centrally placed in the new Europe, booms with modern industry and attracts more per capita investment from abroad – notably Japan, the United States and Germany – than any other part of France. It also contains many of France's biggest breweries, and is a region where much beer is drunk as well as wine. The people are outgoing and artistic, and their traditional talent as woodcarvers and sculptors can be seen in the ornate Renaissance or baroque decor of their fine churches and of secular buildings such as the curious Metzig in Molsheim.

Lorraine, by contrast, is generally poorer and more austere. The initial impression is one of gray, unkempt farms and villages. The differences may be due in part to the older tradition of heavy industry, and to the harsher climate on these wide austere plateaux. Yet southern Lorraine is a pleasant rolling region of woods and lakes, orchards and cornfields, with some famous spas such as Vittel. Lorraine has a notable history. In the Middle Ages it was the central focus of the kingdom of Lotharingia, then a powerful duchy: in the 18th century it saw a golden age under Duke Stanislas who built Nancy, his capital, into one of the loveliest of French cities.

Partly because of its frontier position, Lorraine has long enshrined French patriotism: it is the land of Joan of Arc (born at Domrémy-la-Pucelle), of Verdun, and of the double-barred Cross of Lorraine that de Gaulle adopted as his symbol of the Free French. Maurice Barrès, the right-wing nationalist, came from the Nancy area and used it as the setting for his patriotic novels, which won a big following around the turn of the century. His book *La Colline inspirée* is set on the "inspired" hill of Sion, which has long been a pilgrimage point for French patriots.

Alsace, Lorraine, Champagne-Ardenne
Alsace, beside the Rhine, is Germanic in character. Its famous vineyards lie below the wooded Vosges hills that stretch into Lorraine, a more industrial region. Champagne-Ardenne has rich farmlands on a rolling chalky plain.

Alsace: population 1.6 million; area 8,200sq km; capital, Strasbourg; pop. 252,000. *Lorraine*: pop. 2.3 million; area 23,500sq km; capital, Metz pop. 118,000. Other main town, Nancy, pop. 99,000. *Champagne-Ardenne*: pop. 1.3 million; area 25,600sq km; capital, Châlons-sur-Marne pop. 54,000. Other main town, Reims pop. 182,000.

Above "Little Venice", one of the prettiest corners of Colmar, a delightful medieval town, full of the gabled, half-timbered buildings that are typical of Alsace. Colmar holds two very great artworks, Grünewald's *Issenheim Altarpiece* (1510) and Schongauer's *Virgin and the Rosebush* (1473).

Left Harvesting time at Riquewihr, a picturesque old village on the Alsatian "wine road". Sheltered from the west winds by the Vosges hills, the grapes of these vineyards ripen late, and are not picked till mid-October. The "noble" grapes, such as Gerwürztraminer and Riesling, produce wines that are fairly dry but fruity and aromatic. They are much used in the cooking of the region.

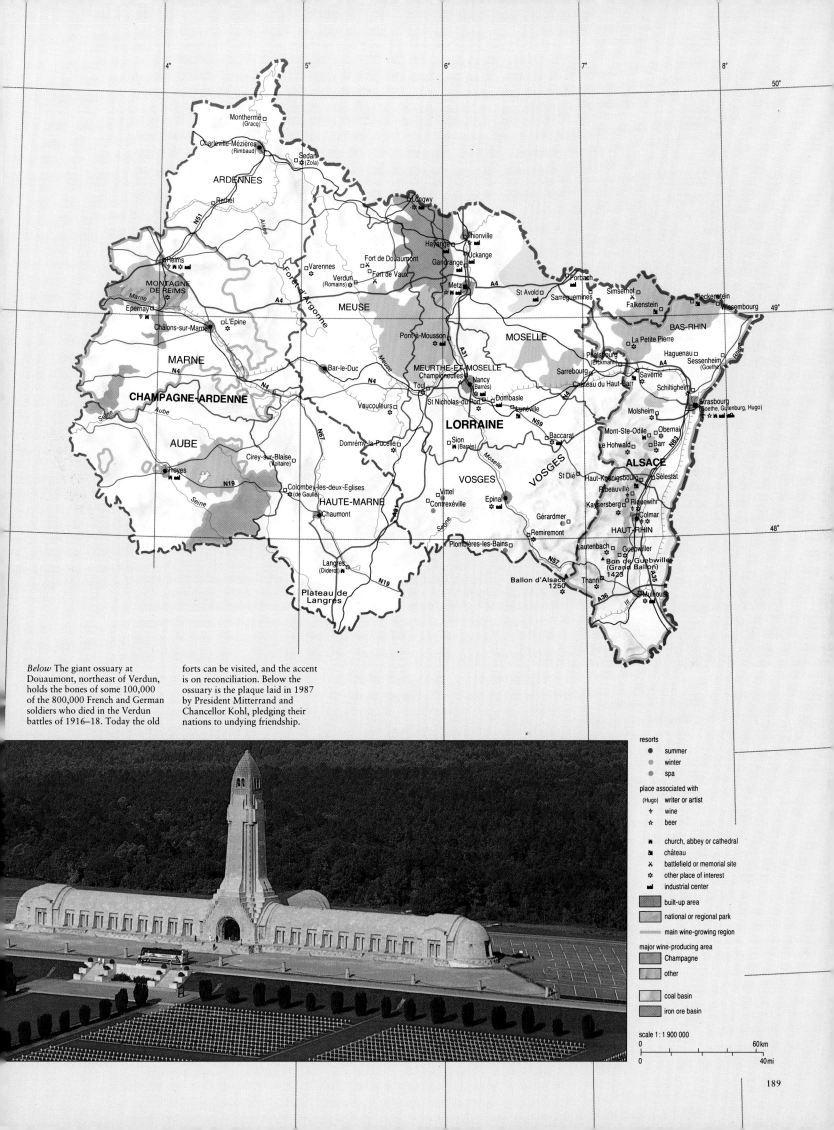

Monthermé
(Gracq)

Charleville-Mézières
(Rimbaud)

Sedan
(Zola)

ARDENNES

Rethel

N51

Aisne

Longwy

Thionville

Hayange

Uckange

Fort de Douaumont

Gandrange

Varennes

Verdun
(Romains)

Fort de Vaux

Metz

Porbach

St Avold

Sarreguemines

Simserhof

Falkenstein

Fleckenstein

Wissembourg

Reims

BAS-RHIN

MONTAGNE
DE REIMS

Marne

MEUSE

MOSELLE

La Petite Pierre

Haguenau

Sessenheim
(Goethe)

Épernay

Pont-à-Mousson

Phalsbourg
(Erckmann)

A4

Châlons-sur-Marne

L'Épine

MARNE

N4

Bar-le-Duc

Meuse

MEURTHE-ET-MOSELLE

Sarrebourg

Château du Haut-Barr

Savérne

Schiltigheim

Molsheim

Strasbourg
(Goethe, Gutenburg, Hugo)

CHAMPAGNE-ARDENNE

N4

Seine

Aube

N4

Championeulles

Nancy
(Barrès)

Toul

Dombasle

Lunéville

Mont-Ste-Odile

Obernai

St Nicholas-du-Port

N59

Barr

ALSACE

AUBE

Vaucouleurs

LORRAINE

Baccarat

Le Hohwald

N67

Domrémy-la-Pucelle

Sion
(Barrès)

Moselle

St Dié

Haut-Koenigsbourg

Sélestat

Troyes

Cirey-sur-Blaise
(Voltaire)

Seine

N19

Vittel

VOSGES

VOSGES

Ribeauvillé

Kaysersberg

Riquewihr

Colombey-les-deux-Églises
(de Gaulle)

Contrexéville

Épinal

Colmar

HAUTE-MARNE

Chaumont

Gérardmer

HAUT-RHIN

Remiremont

Lautenbach

Guebwiller

Plombières-les-Bains

Bon de Guebwiller
(Grand Ballon)
1423

Langres
(Diderot)

N19

Ballon d'Alsace
1250

Thann

A35

Plateau de
Langres

N57

A36

Mulhouse

Ill

Below The giant ossuary at
Douaumont, northeast of Verdun,
holds the bones of some 100,000
of the 800,000 French and German
soldiers who died in the Verdun
battles of 1916–18. Today the old
forts can be visited, and the accent
is on reconciliation. Below the
ossuary is the plaque laid in 1987
by President Mitterrand and
Chancellor Kohl, pledging their
nations to undying friendship.

resorts
● summer
● winter
● spa

place associated with
(Hugo) writer or artist
⚜ wine
✱ beer

⛪ church, abbey or cathedral
🏰 château
✕ battlefield or memorial site
✿ other place of interest
🏭 industrial center

built-up area
national or regional park
main wine-growing region

major wine-producing area
Champagne
other

coal basin
iron ore basin

scale 1:1 900 000
0   60km
0   40mi

Metz, with its lofty Gothic cathedral and other fine buildings, is now Lorraine's official capital, upstaging its jealous rival, Nancy. Metz is lively and progressive, while Nancy is quieter and more conservative. An important legacy of the dukes of Lorraine is the big château at Lunéville, modeled on the palace of Versailles. To the south, in the Vosges foothills, are numerous little textile towns that have seen better days. One of them, Epinal, also has a traditional industry of popular prints and engravings of stereotyped figures: "image d'Epinal" has come to mean "cliché" in French.

Old industry of a much heavier kind is located in thickly populated northern Lorraine, in the iron-ore belt around Longwy and Thionville and the coal-belt around Forbach. Here France's major iron and steel works were built up. But the mines became exhausted, the steel firms failed to modernize, and in the 1970s recession became severe. Since then, the steel firms have been restructured and their workforce pared down from 90,000 to 20,000, but they do now make a profit. There has been massive new investment in high technology, mainly from Germany, while as many as 25,000 Lorrains now find work across the border in Luxembourg and Saarland.

The cuisine of Lorraine is not particularly special, apart from the ubiquitous *quiche*. However, specialities of Alsace include *coq au Riesling*, spicy sausages, game in rich sauces, platters of *choucroute* (sauerkraut with pork) and *foie gras*.

The southwestern part of the Champagne-Ardenne region (population 1.3 million) is a wide rolling chalky plain whose name comes from the Latin *campania* (flat country). Its big farms have thrived and grown prosperous on cereals and sugar beet, but the great timber forests of oak, beech and poplar have been subject to soil erosion because of a lack of proper reafforestation. The grapes for the world's best-known sparkling wine, champagne, are grown exclusively in a small hilly district south of Reims. This, the region's biggest city (but not its capital), has a superlative ancient cathedral – as does Troyes, now a leading center of hosiery manufacture.

In southern Champagne, a 44 meter granite Cross of Lorraine towers on a hilltop above Colombey-les-Deux-Eglises, the village where Charles de Gaulle lies buried; it is now a tourist attraction. His manor house tactfully preserves his home just as it was, including the alcove study where he wrote his memoirs.

Up in the Ardennes to the north, the landscape changes into the forested plateau that sweeps on across south Belgium. Here the German army twice broke through at Sedan, in 1870 and 1940; and here, where the Meuse loops between high rocky cliffs, Julien Gracq set his superb novel *Un Balcon en forêt*, about a soldier's mystic communion with nature. Another writer, the tumultuous poet Arthur Rimbaud, was brought up in Charleville-Mézières, where he satirized the "wheezy bourgeoisie" and, at age 17, wrote *Le Bateau ivre*.

Above The old fortified townlet of Neuf-Brisach, near the German border east of Colmar, was built in the 17th century by Vauban, the great military engineer. With its rectangular streets, it still keeps its old character. Many other fortresses were built along this war-torn Franco-German frontier. Close by, at Markosheim, is one of the 1930s forts of the Maginot Line, now a memorial museum.

Champagne

Champagne is a region of France, around Reims, that produces a noble sparkling wine of that name, made in a special way. Only the wine from that area may properly be called champagne. If some other countries label their sparkling wines "champagne", they are cheating, and the French makers have sometimes taken them to court for it and won.

A mystique surrounds champagne more powerful than for any other drink. Light, heady and bubbly, it is *the* drink for celebration, much used at weddings and other special parties, not only in France but the world over. Its fizzy quality was invented by Dom Pérignon, a local Benedictine cellarer, in the 17th century. Its secret lies partly in the special method of fermentation, but also in the unique blend of soil and climate in the district south of Reims and around Epernay. The south-facing slopes, cold in winter, hot in summer, are backed by a sun-trap of forests, and the subsoil is chalky. So subtle and varied is this magical combination that each vineyard will produce its own quite distinctive taste.

Nearly all the wine of the area is white. Pink champagne, which the French think is rather a vulgar drink, is made by adding a dosage of the still red wine from the local village of Bouzy.

Grape picking has to be done carefully, nearly always by hand (*far left, center*). Some pickers are local people, but others come seasonally from abroad, or from the industrial areas of the Nord. The grapes are then quickly pressed in large long wooden presses, to extract their juice (*bottom left*). After this, the first fermentation takes place, usually today in vats of stainless steel. Next, in order to produce the sparkle, a slow secondary fermentation takes place in the bottle. Although this process is used elsewhere, too, for sparkling wine, in Champagne it is done in a very special way – the *méthôde champenoise*. For several months each bottle stands on its head and is gently twisted by hand daily (*bottom right*) by an expert who will twist up to 30,000 bottles every day. The sediment works down the neck of the bottle and this is periodically checked, here (*below*), over a candle flame, before being removed. The bottle is then topped up with sugar to strengthen the alcohol, and recorked. The growers sell to the producers and dealers in Reims and Epernay. They store and mature the wine in a rabbit-warren of great underground cellars in the chalk soil, before selling it. When it eventually appears on the dinner table, it will carry one of the famous labels of the producer (*left*). The Germans, British and Americans are major importers. But the French themselves each drink, on average, two bottles of champagne a year, and it is popular in all classes. In Reims, workers can be seen drinking it for breakfast in cafés.

BURGUNDY, FRANCHE-COMTÉ

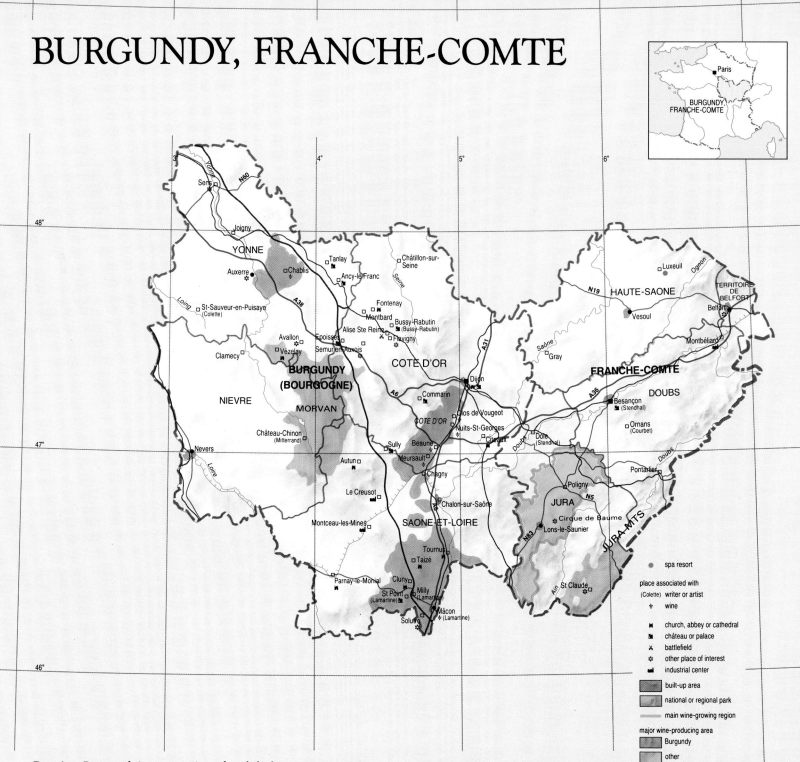

Despite Burgundy's reputation for bibulous conviviality, only two or three small stretches of this former dukedom are given over to wine producing. The rest is more notable for its splendid abbeys and châteaux, and for a distinguished history dating back to the Stone Age settlement (c. 15,000 BC) on the rock of Solutré, near Mâcon.

Set where the north French plain begins to break into hills, Burgundy (population 1.4 million) is a serene and rolling land, forested in places, agriculturally rich (the white Charolais cattle yield France's best beef). Most of the region is gentle, save for the wild Morvan, a beautiful, rocky granite massif with waterfalls, lakes and woods of beech and oak. Nearby, at the hilltop fortress of Alésia, the Gauls' leader Vercingétorix made his last stand against Julius Caesar in 52 BC. Later, Burgundy became a vital focus of medieval Christianity. In 1098 the Cistercians built the *maison müre* of their Order at Cîteaux; and in the

12th century the great abbey at Cluny was the most potent intellectual center in Europe. Only fragments of these buildings survive today. But the wonderful flowering of Romanesque architecture at that time can be seen in the basilica at Vézelay, and at Autun, Tournus and elsewhere. Today Burgundy is again a foyer of religious innovation: the church at Taizé, founded in 1940 by a Protestant pastor, has become Europe's leading ecumenical center.

Burgundy in the Middle Ages was a powerful independent duchy. Yet, being centrally located, it has also been closely associated with the French traditions of elegance and robust good living. Its stately Renaissance châteaux, such as Sully, Tanlay and Ancy-le-Franc, bear witness to the taste and prestige of its former noble families. Its small towns are picturesque, while some great classic buildings, such as the ducal palace in Dijon and the Hospice de Beaune are notable for the fine colored patterns of their tiled roofs.

Burgundy and Franche-Comté
Once a powerful duchy, Burgundy
is one of the most historic of
France's regions and holds some of
its finest abbeys, churches and
châteaux. It is also a land of good
living, famous for its wines. The
Franche-Comté region, thinly
populated, comprises part of the
beautiful Jura mountains along the
Swiss border. Both regions are
strongly agricultural but have little
industry.

Burgundy: population. 1.6 million;
area 31,600sq km; capital, Dijon
pop. 145,000. *Franche- Comté*:
pop. 1.1 million; area 16,200sq
km; capital, Besançon pop.
119,000.

The vineyards of the Côte d'Or
produce expensive, high-quality
wines which require much care. In
winter the vines are expertly
pruned and sprayed, sometimes
still by traditional methods, as here
in a field beside the Clos de
Vougeot (*right*). Most of the
harvesting is still done by hand
(*below*), for the grapes would be
damaged by the grape-picking
machines used today in areas
producing more ordinary wines.
After the harvesting come the wine
tastings and wine auctions. These
are pretexts for three majestic
banquets, known as the Trois
Glorieuses, which overflow with
Burgundian jollity and song
(*above right*).

Some châteaux were the homes of writers. The
Romantic poet Alphonse de Lamartine, though rather
solemn and hardly characteristic of the jolly, down-to-
earth Burgundian, still reveals in his poems a warm
feeling for his homeland in the Mâcon hills, where his
château at St-Point still stands. Perhaps more true to
type was the flamboyantly eccentric Count Roger de
Rabutin. Exiled by Louis XIV to his château at
Bussy-Rabutin for lampooning court life, he took a
lonely revenge by decorating his walls with cartoons
and epigrams about his ex-mistresses and others at the
Sun King's lascivious court. A third writer, Colette,
was born and brought up in a modest house full of
dogs, cats and children, at St-Sauveur-en-Puisaye. She
has beautifully described her magical childhood there,
and her equally magical mother.

Good red wines are produced in the Mâcon area,
and excellent dry whites around Chablis, in the north.
But the "great" Burgundy wine area is the Côte d'Or, a
sunny east-facing slope that runs from Dijon to south
of Chagny. Its wines, mostly reds, are sturdily full-
bodied – and expensive. Most have double-barreled
names, from the local village and its main vineyard,
for example, Gevrey-Chambertin or Vosne-Romanée.
These remain small-scale farming communities, not
great château estates as in the Bordelais. A traditional
vinegrower's home has the cellar as its centerpiece
(this is where the banquets and parties are held) with
the living rooms added on later.

These social functions are a key feature of local life.
In the 1930s, during a slump in the wine trade, the
growers invented the Confrérie des Chevaliers du
Tastevin, based on medieval orders of chivalry, as a
way of promoting their wines. They acquired the
lovely old Clos de Vougeot mansion, set amid
vineyards, and here, ever since, they have held regular
banquets, with fancy costumes, trumpeters,
boisterous drinking songs, and other trappings of
folklore. Distinguished guests are invited; in fact,
many leading politicians and Hollywood celebrities
have considered it an honor to be made a member of
the Confrérie. These banquets are therefore gastronomic elitist events, through which much valuable
publicity is gained for the wine producers.

The fun comes to a climax in November, with the
"Trois Glorieuses", three successive banquets to
celebrate the new vintage. The first is held at the Clos
de Vougeot, the second in the Hospice de Beaune,
combined with a major wine auction that draws the
world's top buyers, and the third in the wine village of
Meursault, at lunchtime. On these occasions and at
lesser local feasts throughout the year, there is genuine
merriment, accompanied by famous local songs – such
as *Joyeux Enfants de la Bourgogne* and *Chevaliers de
la Table Ronde* – belted out enthusiastically by the
participants. Burgundians of the Côte d'Or may have
a canny sense of business and public relations, but they
are also a naturally gregarious, fun-loving people who
know how to enjoy themselves.

Good wine habitually induces good cooking, and
Burgundy is one of the most richly gastronomic of

French regions. Ham with parsley baked in white wine, snails fed on herbs, and frogs' legs in garlic are all popular; so are the ubiquitous dark wine stews such as *coq au vin* and *boeuf bourguignon*. Many annual gastronomic fairs are held, notably in Dijon, the region's somewhat sleepy capital, known for its aromatic mustards. Also, a former mayor, Canon Kir, gave his name to his favorite local apéritif – cassis, a blackcurrant liqueur, with dry white wine.

As an industrial region, Burgundy is much less important. There used to be some heavy manufacture, mostly around the Le Creusot mining area where the Schneider family built up a big steel concern, Creusot-Loire. However, when the mines became exhausted, Creusot-Loire and other older firms collapsed, while new modern industry, such as Kodak at Chalon, has come in only slowly. Even President Mitterrand, for many years mayor of Château-Chinon in the Morvan, was unable to do much to improve things.

The smaller region of Franche-Comté (population 1.1 million) is less renowned than Burgundy. This former "free county", long disputed, was finally wrested from the Habsburgs by Louis XIV in 1678. Its stately capital, Besançon, is crowned by a fine Vauban citadel above the looping river Doubs. Stendhal set part of his novel *Le Rouge et le noir* in the town, and part in nearby Dole which he calls Verrières; Gustave Courbet came from the charming old town of Ornans which he so often painted.

The region also comprises the French half of the Jura mountains astride the Swiss border – a lovely rolling plateau cut by deep valleys, popular for holidays. Here the pipemaking town of St-Claude has a splendid setting. There is another imposing Vauban citadel at Belfort, whose heroic defeat of a Prussian siege in 1870 is commemorated by the huge statue of a lion above the town. At nearby Montbéliard, the Peugeot family opened a steel mill in 1810, and much later added a car factory that is still the main Peugeot production center.

Left Of the mighty Romanesque abbey of Cluny, little remains today except one octagonal belfry and a few other ruins. Built by Benedictines in 1088–1130, the abbey church was for over six centuries the world's largest, containing five naves and five belfries. It was also one of the most powerful centers of Christendom in the Middle Ages, in art and learning as well as in religion. It acquired huge wealth, but this finally led to decadence and downfall. Ransacked in the Wars of Religion, it was suppressed and dismantled after the Revolution.

Right A secular building of great beauty is the Hôtel-Dieu in Beaune, with its roof of patterned colored tiles. Also known as the Hospices de Beaune, it was built in 1443 in Flemish Gothic style, as a hospital for the poor, and was still used as such until 1948. Now it is the venue of the famous wine auctions in November, and of the principal banquet.

Below The majestic basilica of La Madeleine towers up from the fortified hilltop village of Vézelay. Its life has been tragic. Founded by Benedictine monks in 864, the church was gutted in 1120 by a fire that killed 1000 pilgrims. It was rapidly rebuilt, but was wrecked again at the Revolution, then restored in the 1840s by Viollet-le-Duc. It is noted for its Romanesque tympanum and beautiful barrel-vaulted ceiling.

RHONE-ALPES

With 5.2 million inhabitants, Rhône-Alpes is the most populous French region after the Ile de France. It is also one of the most prosperous and influential, thanks above all to two big, dynamic industrial cities: Lyon, its capital, and Grenoble. The region exudes self-confidence, and its central position astride the Rhône valley makes it well placed to benefit commercially from the new frontier-free Europe. It is also a modern amalgam of three very diverse areas: the great river valley, the eastern part of the Massif Central, and the Savoy and Dauphiné Alps.

The Rhône flows in from Lake Geneva. The city of Geneva is so close across the Swiss border that some of its suburbs are inside France, and its wealthy economy contributes to that of Rhône-Alpes. Many workers commute across the border and this kind of traffic is not new. In 1760, to escape harassment by the city's strict Calvinists, the freethinking philosopher Voltaire moved to a château at Ferney-Voltaire just inside France, where he founded factories to provide jobs for refugees from Geneva; he lived there till he died.

Lyon, which disputes with Marseille the title of France's "second city", was colonized by the Romans who called it Lugdunum. It has been a key trading center since the Middle Ages, and benefits from a fine position where the Rhône and Saône rivers meet. It is a dignified town, with fine buildings along the quays. It has long been famous for its silk-weaving and it became a major banking center in the 19th century (the great Crédit Lyonnais was founded here), only to be cheated of this role by Parisian centralism. Today chemicals and engineering are foremost among its many industries. Its society once had a reputation for enclosed and stuffy conformism: but recently Lyon has become far more lively and international. It retains its reputation as the center of French gastronomy.

From Lyon the Rhône flows on to the fascinating ancient town of Vienne, which still has relics of its Roman colonization. Farther south, around Tain l'Hermitage, are some of the best of the Côtes-du-Rhône vineyards. The Rhône valley is lushly fertile, but in places heavily industrial too – not only around Lyon but up at Creys-Malville village, where Europe's leading plutonium fast-breeder reactor is located.

There is other and much older industry to the west, around the big town of St-Etienne, which grew prosperous from its coal mines, though these are now exhausted. Some old-fashioned firms that used to make shotguns, bicycles and sewing-machines have closed too. It has not been easy for this former Communist bastion to shake off depression and find new investment. Both around the town and down in the Ardèche department, where the river Ardèche cuts its way through rocky gorges, there is fine hilly scenery. Here the Massif Central slopes to the Rhône.

To the north of Lyon is rich farming country, where the Bresse plain yields high-quality poultry, eggs and dairy products, and where the local cooking mirrors this excellence. Péarouges is a picturesque medieval hilltop village; at Bourg-en-Bresse, the Gothic monastery church of Brou, one of France's finest, has

Rhône-Alpes
The snowy Alps rise on the eastern side of this region, by the Italian border: here Mont Blanc is Europe's highest mountain. To the west, the river Rhône flows from Geneva to the major city of Lyon, on its way to the sea. The region has much modern industry, and also vineyards such as the Beaujolais.

Population: 5.2 million; area 43,700sq km; capital, Lyon pop. 418,000 (with suburbs, 1.2 million), 462km from Paris. Other main towns, St Etienne pop. 206,000, Grenoble pop. 160,000.

Left Sheep in Upper Savoy being prepared to leave their high summer pastures and return to the more temperate valleys for the winter. Seasonal transhumance of this kind is still practiced by farmers in many hilly parts of France.

Below Annecy is a beautiful old town of arcades, narrow streets and quiet canals, but it also has modern industry. It stands on a serene lake, amid the Dauphiné Alps.

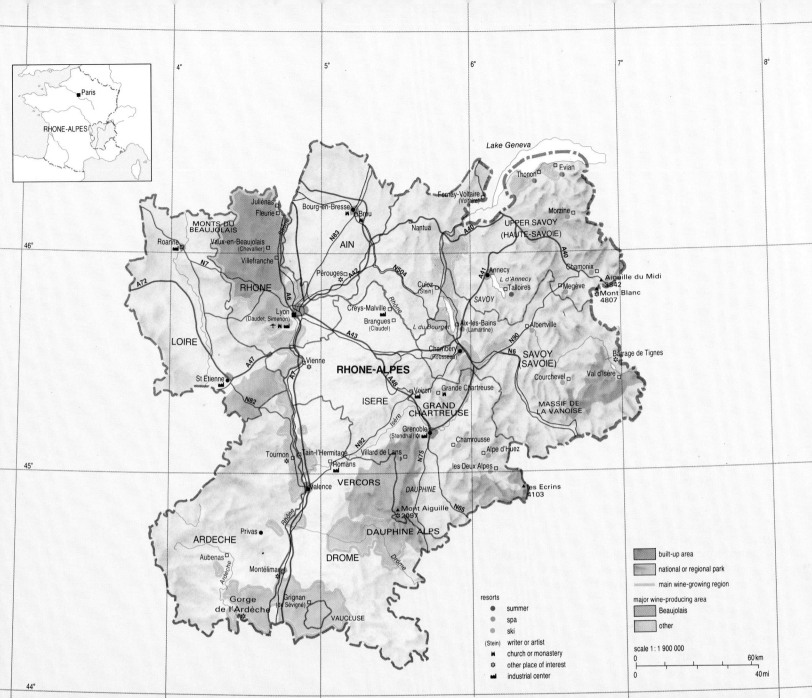

4°
5°
6°
7°
8°

Lake Geneva

46°
45°
44°

MONTS DU
BEAUJOLAIS

Juliénas
Fleurie

Roanne
Vaux-en-Beaujolais
(Chevallier)
Villefranche

RHONE

LOIRE

St Etienne

Bourg-en-Bresse
Brou

Nantua

AIN

Pérouges

Lyon
(Daudet; Simenon)

Creys-Malville

Brangues
(Claudel)

Vienne

N504

Rhône

Évian
Thonon

Fernay-Voltaire
(Voltaire)

UPPER SAVOY
(HAUTE-SAVOIE)

Morzine

Chamonix
Aiguille du Midi
3842
Mont Blanc
4807

Annecy
L d'Annecy
Talloires

Megève

SAVOY

Culoz
(Stein)

L du Bourget
Aix-les-Bains
(Lamartine)

Albertville

Chambéry
(Rousseau)

RHONE-ALPES

Veurey
Grande Chartreuse

ISERE

GRAND
CHARTREUSE

Grenoble
(Stendhal)

Tournon
Tain-l'Hermitage
Villard de Lans

SAVOY
SAVOIE)

Barrage de Tignes

Courchevel
Val d'Isère

MASSIF DE
LA VANOISE

Chamrousse
Alpe d'Huez

Romans
les Deux Alpes

Valence

VERCORS

DAUPHINE

Mont Aiguille
2097

les Ecrins
4103

ARDECHE

Privas

DAUPHINE ALPS

Aubenas

DROME

Montélimar

Gorge
de l'Ardèche

Grignan
(de Sévigné)

VAUCLUSE

Rhône

Drôme

Ardèche

	built-up area
	national or regional park
	main wine-growing region
major wine-producing area	
	Beaujolais
	other

resorts
● summer
● spa
● ski
(Stein) writer or artist
♦ church or monastery
✻ other place of interest
⚒ industrial center

scale 1 : 1 900 000

0 ———— 60 km
0 ———— 40 mi

Left Chamrousse, a popular ski resort only 20km from Grenoble, was a venue for the 1968 Winter Olympics. Skiing did not develop in the French Alps until after 1918, but then grew so fast that Chamonix was chosen for the first-ever Winter Olympics, in 1924. Today Chamonix, below Mont Blanc, is the largest ski resort in the region; Megève and Courchevel are the most fashionable.

Right One of Grenoble's many "firsts" was to build the first funicular in France. Its modern successor now takes tourists up to the high Bastille fortress, for a panorama of the Alps, new skyscrapers and old red-roofed houses. In one of them Stendhal was born in 1783: he wrote savagely about the townsfolk in his memoirs, and has never been forgiven for it locally.

marvelous carved choir-stalls and white marble tombs. West of the broad Saône river, the farmers produce light and fruity red wines in the gentle Monts du Beaujolais. "Three great rivers flow into Lyon", the saying goes, "the Rhône, the Saône and Beaujolais wine." Each of the wine's nine great *crus* relates to a village – Juliénas, Fleurie, Brouilly and so on – and you can drive through them along a signposted route, stopping for tipples at the many *caves* (winecellars) and bistros. Even more than in Burgundy's wine areas, the people of Beaujolais are pleasure-loving and hospitable with an earthy sense of humor – much as described in *Clochemerle*, the satiric novel that the Lyon journalist Gabriel Chevallier based on the village of Vaux-en-Beaujolais.

The Alpine region to the east comprises the former provinces of Dauphiné (capital, Grenoble) and Savoy (capital, Chambéry). The counts of Dauphiné ceded their territory to France in 1349. The dukedom of Savoy held out for far longer: independent until the 16th century, it was then united with the kingdom of Piedmont across the Alps, and only in 1860 did the Savoyards vote to join France. The pride of Savoy are the high snowy Alps, which at Mont Blanc (4807 meters) reach their loftiest point of the entire range: a cable-car, claimed to be the world's highest, takes you up to the Aiguille du Midi (3,843 meters), just below Mont Blanc, for a stunning panoramic view. The Dauphiné Alps, though less high, have scenery of crags and glaciers that is just as dramatic.

The uplands below these peaks used to be among the poorest and most isolated parts of France. Yet though poor, the Savoy villages, with their wooden chalets, had a picturesque Swiss-like charm, whereas the Dauphiné villages with houses made of local stone, looked far more austere. In appearance they remain so today, though the poverty has been largely erased by the advent of mass tourism. The first sporting mountaineers, many English, came in the 18th century.

Huge new hydroelectric schemes have been further changing the local scene, bringing in new jobs and industries. Like the ski resorts, they have helped to end the peasants' hardship and isolation but do little for the scenery. The titanic dam at Tignes provides Grenoble with much of its electricity.

Not all the tourists come for the winter sports. Savoy has some glorious lakes, too, whose shores are crowded in summer. To the north, it borders on the big Lake Geneva, where Evian is one of the most fashionable of French spa resorts. Annecy, a delightful old town, lies on a mountain-girt lake of the same name which is probably France's prettiest (here Rohmer filmed *Claire's Knee*). Aix-les-Bains, another well-known spa, dating from Roman times, stands on the beautiful Lac du Bourget, whose mood changes with the weather, from serenely sparkling to darkly glowering. Here Lamartine went boating with his beloved Julie, and later, as she lay dying, composed his mournful poem, *Le Lac*. Earlier, in the 1730s, Jean-Jacques Rousseau, whose philosophy was inspired by a love of nature, lived in the area with his "patroness" Madame de Warens, in a trim stone house (now a museum) outside Chambéry.

Grenoble, in its splendid mountain setting, has built up a legendary reputation in France as an industrial boom-town and innovative pioneer. "What Grenoble does today, the rest of France will do tomorrow", it has been said. It was a sleepy burg devoted to glove-making until the 1870s, when hydroelectric

power generated in the nearby mountains became available. This spawned industries that have always been at the forefront of research – hydraulics, turbines, and today electronics and nuclear research. Since 1945 the population has quadrupled, to over 400,000, and the university is a pace-setter in science. One reason for the city's success is human: scientists and executives are attracted to its mountain setting, with superb ski-slopes on their doorstep. Since the 1960s Grenoble has pioneered an open, mobile, informal society, untypical of the French provinces.

Near Grenoble, the high rocky Vercors massif was a key Resistance center in 1943–4, and saw some bloody battles. Today, Germans and others visit it for skiing. North of the city, the Chartreuse massif is where hydroelectricity was first pioneered, in the 1870s. It is also the site of a noted Carthusian monastery whose monks still produce their traditional yellow and green Chartreuse liqueurs, made from mountain herbs. Grenoble is known for its creamy potato dish, *gratin dauphinois*, and Savoy for its local fish and its cheeses, notably Gruyère.

Above A 19th-century puppet figure wearing the helmet of the French Revolution – part of a remarkable collection of puppets in the Museum of Old Lyon, at the Hôtel Gadagne, which gives a vivid picture of the city's history. Lyon was critical of the Revolution, and was punished for it by Robespierre during the Terror, when many were guillotined in the Place des Terreaux.

Above The church of St-Jean stands by the Saône in the St-Jean quarter of Vieux-Lyon – a fascinating area of old alleyways lined with stately Renaissance mansions, many of them now tastefully restored. Here the rich silk-merchants lived in the 15th century, while the silkworkers toiled in hovels up the hill. Strange passageways, known as *traboules*, cut right through the courtyards and hallways of many buildings, adding to Vieux-Lyon's aura of mystery. Today it is also the young people's nightlife quarter, with noisy bars and discotheques. But it still houses plenty of the tiny, modest bistros known as *bouchons*, where the food is good, cheap and truly Lyonnais.

Right Lyon's stately town hall has a 17th-century façade designed by Hardouin-Mansart, architect to Louis XIV. It faces a monumental fountain of four rampant horses. Among those who held office in this building was Edouard Herriot, the Radical Party leader. He was mayor of Lyon from 1905 to 1955, save for a break in World War II – the time when Klaus Barbie was Gestapo chief for the Lyon area. Barbie's much-publicized trial was held in 1987 in the Palais de Justice, across the Saône from the town hall.

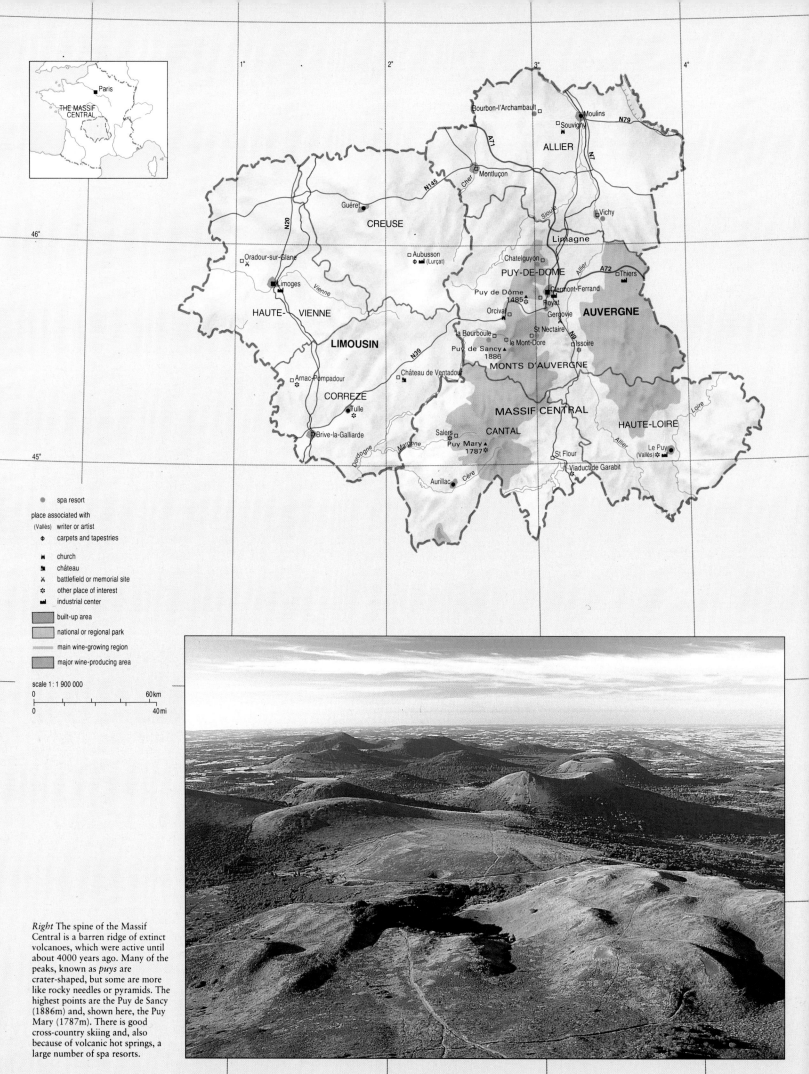

Paris

THE MASSIF
CENTRAL

46°

45°

Bourbon-l'Archambault
Moulins
Souvigny
ALLIER
A71
Montluçon
N79
N7
Cher
N145
Guéret
CREUSE
Sioule
Vichy
Limagne
Oradour-sur-Glane
Aubusson
(Lurçat)
Chatelguyon
Allier
A72
Thiers
PUY-DE-DÔME
Limoges
Puy de Dôme
1485
Clermont-Ferrand
Royat
AUVERGNE
HAUTE- VIENNE
Vienne
Orcival
Gergovie
la Bourboule
St Nectaire
N9
Issoire
LIMOUSIN
N39
le Mont-Dore
Puy de Sancy
1886
MONTS D'AUVERGNE
Arnac-Pompadour
Château de Ventadour
CORRÈZE
MASSIF CENTRAL
Loire
Tulle
Salers
CANTAL
HAUTE-LOIRE
Brive-la-Gaillarde
Puy Mary
1787
Allier
St Flour
Le Puy
(Vallès)
Dordogne
Maronne
Viaduct de Garabit
Aurillac
Cère

spa resort

place associated with
(Vallès) writer or artist
Φ carpets and tapestries
⌂ church
⌂ château
⚔ battlefield or memorial site
✿ other place of interest
⌂ industrial center
built-up area
national or regional park
main wine-growing region
major wine-producing area

scale 1 : 1 900 000
0   60km
0   40mi

Right The spine of the Massif
Central is a barren ridge of extinct
volcanoes, which were active until
about 4000 years ago. Many of the
peaks, known as *puys* are
crater-shaped, but some are more
like rocky needles or pyramids. The
highest points are the Puy de Sancy
(1886m) and, shown here, the Puy
Mary (1787m). There is good
cross-country skiing and, also
because of volcanic hot springs, a
large number of spa resorts.

THE MASSIF CENTRAL

The Auvergne (population 1.3 million) and Limousin (population 730,000) regions comprise within their borders the major part of the Massif Central, a vast granite plateau whose spine is a high ridge of extinct volcanoes, rising to 1886 meters at Puy de Sancy. This is one of the wildest, strangest and least populated parts of France, with varied, beautiful scenery – sweeping forests of oak, pine and chestnut, upland lakes full of trout, bare hills above lush valleys set with orchards. However, before the coming of modern transportation and communications it was also a bitterly isolated area – and this and the often long, hard winters have helped to mold the character of these tough peasant people.

The Auvergnats were long seen as the archetypal French peasants – stocky in build, dour, wary of strangers, and not always very hygienic. Like the Scots, they were also proverbially thrifty, making them the butt of endless jokes. In a way, these traits persist, but modern life has been mellowing these people. The impact of tourism and the building of good roads have relieved their isolation and made them more open and friendly. Neat new villas have appeared everywere, beside the squat and austere traditional houses built of local basalt or granite, with their steep-sloping roofs of dark slate.

Ever since the last century, poverty has obliged people to emigrate heavily from these regions. They went mainly to Paris, which today still has more Auvergnats than the region's own capital, Clermont-Ferrand (population 151,000). In Paris many of them started up little businesses called *bougnats*, selling coal and firewood, which they would combine with running a modest café or bistro. Today the *bougnats* have gone, but Auvergnats remain extraordinarily successful in Paris' catering trade and are said to own or manage some 60 percent of all its cafés. They also retain a vibrant loyalty to the *pays* they have left: in Paris they cling together in their own colony, often intermarrying, and in old age many retire to the Auvergne and are buried in the village of their birth. But the young are still emigrating and Limousin, with only 44 people per square kilometer, has the lowest population density of mainland France.

Folk traditions survive more solidly than in most parts of France, aided by amateur groups who make a conscious effort to revive those that are threatening to die out. The *bourrée* of the Auvergne is an ancient waltz-like dance said to be of local Celtic origin. Most country people can still perform it, and will do so at fêtes or weddings, either in modern or traditional dress – the men in flowery waistcoats, wide-brimmed hats and bright scarves, the women in long, colorful skirts – to the tune of a local *vielle*, a kind of viol, and a *cabrette*, an instrument like bagpipes. Some old rural handicrafts, such as lacemaking and papermaking, are also kept alive and officially sponsored.

Agriculture is still the main economic activity. To the north, around Vichy, the fertile Limagne plain yields cereals, tobacco, sugar beet and fruit, while the hillier areas are given over to breeding sheep and cattle. Here the big spring and autumn cattle markets remain a lively tradition, with the sturdy Limousin strains in great demand for exports. Dairy farming too

Below Although farming has been modernizing fast, many poor smallholdings remain, such as the one shown here, where peasants scratch out a hard living with a patch of vines, a few sheep and other animals. With their legacy of poverty, the Auvergnats despise exterior display, and will seldom

Left A 10th-century Byzantine church, approached by 267 steps, stands atop this high rocky *puy*, in the town of Le Puy, which bears the name of these strange volcanic formations. Another *puy* in the town, the Rocher Corneille, is crowned by a huge red cast-iron statue of Notre-Dame, weighing 110 tonnes. It is less beautiful than Le Puy's fine Romanesque cathedral. Delicate silk and cotton lace-making is still an active local industry.

Right A craftsman at work on enameling in Limoges, France's chief center for the making of enamel and porcelain. The local porcelain industry dates from the discovery of large kaolin deposits in the area in 1768. But enameling had been done for centuries before, and is still more art than industry. Many craftsmen have their own little workshops, which are open to visitors.

pretty up their austere housefronts. Interiors, too, are simple: old peasant homes have just one living room with a huge chimney-piece and no real bedrooms, just alcoves or bed-cupboards.

Below Tobacco is grown on the plains, and here a small producer is sorting out the leaves, but today the process is generally more industrialized than this. The growers sell their produce to the government, which has a monopoly of the French tobacco industry.

Below center Among the rural traditions that are being kept up, even revived, is the *bourrée*, a country dance of courtship and love, with many gestures of coquetry, flirtation and gallantry.

is prolific, and the region produces many cheeses, including the large, fairly hard Cantal, which is a little like Cheddar. The local cuisine is basic but, with a peasant ingenuity, it brings out the tastiness of cheap ingredients. Tripe and black pudddings are popular, as are thick meat soups, stuffed cabbage and even (in Limousin) broiled larks.

The main industrial area is around Clermont Ferrand, biggest town of the Massif. Here a rubber industry started in the 1830s, and in 1886 was taken over by the Michelin family, who built it up into one of the world's leading car-tire firms. Still family-owned, Michelin has its headquarters and main plant in the town, which has also diversified into plastics, chemicals and metalwork. Some other towns retain their traditional activities – tanneries at Le Puy, cutlery at Thiers (a cottage industry, recently modernized). Aubusson, a major tapestry-making center since the 15th century, has seen a remarkable postwar revival thanks to the efforts of a great artist, the late Jean Lurçat, who set up a tapestry studio there. Limousin's capital, Limoges, has been a center of quality porcelain manufacture since the late 18th century, using local kaolin deposits.

Limousin is the poorest of all French regions, and rural Auvergne is not much better off. In a bid to inject new life, and to check the disturbing depopulation of some areas, governments since the 1960s have instigated specially-funded development programs – building new highways, promoting crafts and small industries, and developing tourism and forestry (the Massif has huge forests, but as yet no paper-mills). These initiatives, which have met with sporadic success, have come mainly from right-wing governments, for by coincidence three of France's leading modern right-of-center leaders have had their roots in the Massif Central – Valéry Giscard d'Estaing, Jacques Chirac, and the late Georges Pompidou, who was born in the Cantal and whose shrewd, earthy conservatism seemed typically Auvergnat. The Auvergne still loyally votes for the right, but in 1986 Limousin was one of the only two regions in France to elect a left-wing assembly – a symptom, in part, of frustration at its economic plight.

Tourism embraces cross-country skiing in winter, as well as summer hiking around the high volcanic crests, known as *puys*. This volcanic area is also rich in hot springs, and thus has more spas than any other part of France. Vichy is the biggest, best-known and most fashionable; Royat, la Bourboule and le Mont-Dore are also important. These health resorts are frequented by patients, young and old alike, many of them seeking a cure for their illnesses, and paid for by social security.

The Massif Central has fewer historic buildings than many other regions, but they include the fine Romanesque churches at Orcival and Souvigny, the lovely Renaissance hill-village of Salers and the ruins of the troubadours' château of Ventadour. Also, past wars, ancient and modern, have left their traces. On the plateau of Gergovie, near Clermont, Julius Caesar in 52 BC attacked but failed to defeat the Gauls' leader, Vercingétorix, while at Oradour-sur-Glane, near Limoges, on 10 June 1944 a German SS division murdered 642 villagers, most of them women and children, who were shut up in the church and attacked with smoke-bombs. The charred ruins of the village have been kept as a memorial to this, the most terrible of Nazi massacres in France.

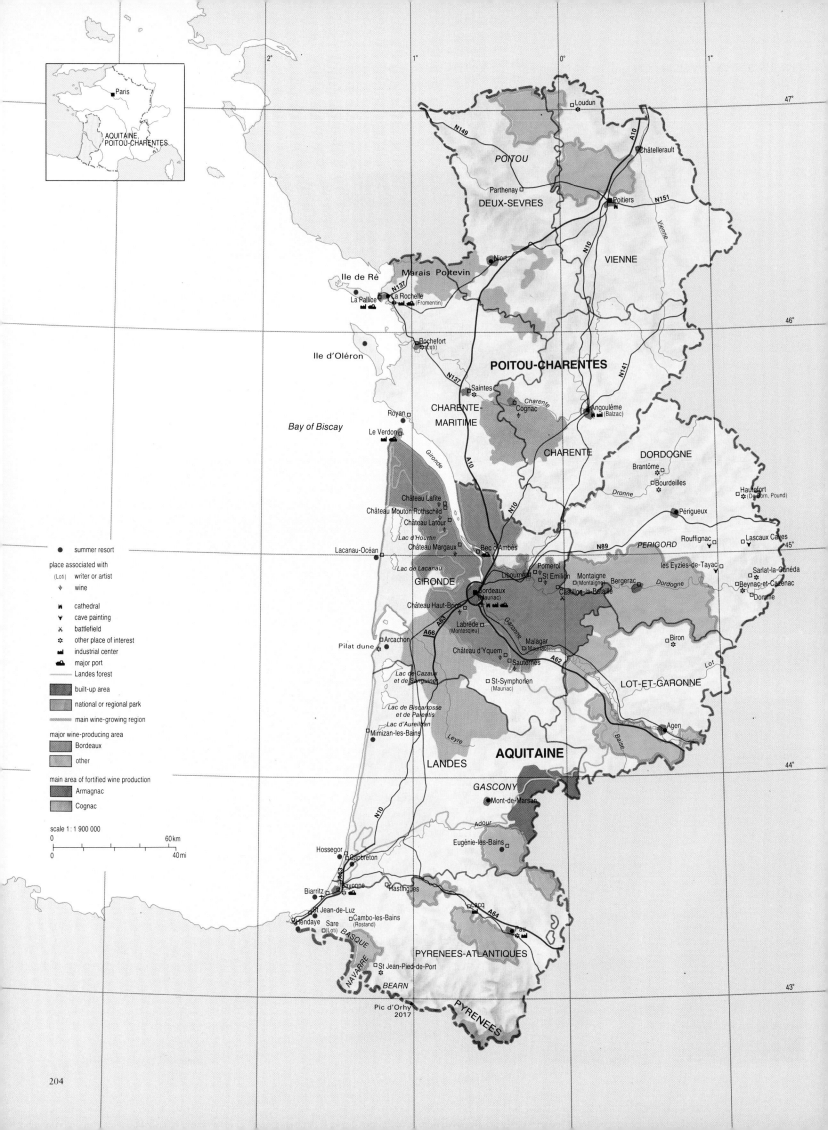

Paris

47°

Loudun

N149

POITOU

A10

Châtellerault

Parthenay

Poitiers

N151

DEUX-SEVRES

VIENNE

N10

Niort

Vienne

Ile de Ré

Marais Poitevin

N137

La Rochelle
(Fromentin)

46°

La Pallice

Rochefort
(Loti)

Ile d'Oléron

N137

POITOU-CHARENTES

N141

Saintes

CHARENTE-
MARITIME

Charente

Cognac

Angoulême
(Balzac)

DORDOGNE

Royan

CHARENTE

Brantôme

Bay of Biscay

Bourdeilles

Hautefort
(De Born, Pound)

Le Verdon

Gironde

N137

Dronne

Château Lafite

N10

Périgueux

Château Mouton Rothschild

Château Latour

PERIGORD

Rouffignac

Lascaux Caves

Lac d'Hourtin

N89

Château Margaux

Lacanau-Océan

Bec d'Ambès

les Eyzies-de-Tayac

Sarlat-la-Canéda

Lac de Lacanau

Pomerol

Beynac-et-Cazenac

GIRONDE

Libourne

St Emilion

Montaigne
(Montaigne)

Bergerac

Dordogne

Domme

Bordeaux
(Mauriac)

Castillon-la-Bataille

Château Haut-Brion

Biron

A63

Labréde
(Montesquieu)

Garonne

Pilat dune

A66

Arcachon

Malagar
(Mauriac)

Biron

Château d'Yquem

Lac de Cazaux
et de Sanguinet

Sauternes

A62

LOT-ET-GARONNE

St-Symphorien
(Mauriac)

Lot

Lac de Biscarrosse
et de Parentis

Lac d'Aureilhan

Agen

Mimizan-les-Bains

Leyre

Baïse

LANDES

AQUITAINE

44°

GASCONY

Mont-de-Marsan

Adour

Hossegor

Eugénie-les-Bains

Capbreton

N10

Bayonne

Hastingues

A63

Lacq

A64

Biarritz

St Jean-de-Luz

Cambo-les-Bains
(Rostand)

Pau

Hendaye

Sare
(Loti)

BASQUE

PYRENEES-ATLANTIQUES

NAVARRE

St Jean-Pied-de-Port

BEARN

43°

Pic d'Orhy
2017

PYRENEES

Legend

• summer resort

place associated with

(Loti) writer or artist

⚘ wine

Ŵ cathedral

Ⅴ cave painting

✕ battlefield

✿ other place of interest

⚒ industrial center

⚓ major port

Landes forest

built-up area

national or regional park

main wine-growing region

major wine-producing area

Bordeaux

other

main area of fortified wine production

Armagnac

Cognac

scale 1 : 1 900 000

0   60 km

0   40 mi

AQUITAINE, POITOU-CHARENTES

Known to the Romans as Aquitania, "land of waters", because of its long seacoast and many rivers, this vast ancient province used to stretch as far north as Poitiers, embracing all of the modern regions of Aquitaine (population 2.7 million) and Poitou-Charentes (population 1.6 million). For 300 years much of it was under English rule, from 1152, when Henry II married Eleanor of Aquitaine, to 1453, when the English were finally defeated at the end of the Hundred Years War. They have left many memorials: for example, a village in Béarn called Hastingues, where John of Hastings built a fortified gate that still stands. But today old animosities are forgotten: Britons are warmly welcomed as visitors or even, in areas such as Pau or the Dordogne, as residents.

Modern Aquitaine is a wealthy and diverse region. The Garonne flows past Bordeaux, the elegant capital, and past its famous vineyards, to a broad estuary where it changes its name to Gironde. From here a long flat sandy coastline runs south past the vast pine forests of the Landes to the fashionable resort of Biarritz, the unusual and appealing Basque country and the high snow-capped Pyrenees on the border

Aquitaine, Poitou-Charentes
Aquitaine, one of the great historic regions of France, has a long, flat Atlantic coastline, stretching north from the high Pyrenees on the Spanish border, to the broad estuary of the Gironde. Its capital, Bordeaux, is a trading center for the famous vineyards all around. To the south are the huge pine forests of the Landes; to the east, the lovely river Dordogne. The climate is mild, and farming is rich; there are also new modern industries, mainly at Bordeaux. Poitou-Charentes, to the north, covers a wide and fertile plain. It includes the brandy-growing district around Cognac, and the stately old seaport and Huguenot stronghold of La Rochelle.

Aquitaine: population 2.7 million; area 41,300sq km; capital, Bordeaux pop. 211,000. Other main town, Pau pop. 85,000.
Poitou-Charentes: pop. 1.6 million; area 25,800sq km; capital, Poitiers pop. 83,000. Other main town, La Rochelle pop. 78,000.

with Spain. Inland lies the gentle Béarn country; also, the western part of the old duchy of Gascony (now mostly in the Midi-Pyrénées region), with the Dordogne to the northeast. Aquitaine is a gentle, sunny land, fanned by Atlantic breezes, less dry and hot than Provence and much greener; it exudes well-being and good living. Its rich agriculture tends toward luxury produce – *foie gras* and truffles, duck and lamb, vintage wines. Farming, forestry and tourism have long been the main activities; but now, in some places, modern industry has come in too, with big new aerospace and electronics firms around Bordeaux and Pau, including Dassault making military aircraft. These have, in part, taken over from declining traditional industries, such as leather goods and furniture-making. Major natural gas deposits found in the 1950s at Lacq, near Pau, prompted major new gas-based industries there, but the deposits are now running low.

Bordeaux, the region's biggest city by far, became a flourishing center under the Romans, who called it Burdigala; then England's Black Prince held court there during the Hundred Years War. Its museums and its Romanesque/Gothic cathedral are remarkable. In the 18th century it acquired the many stately buildings that remain its hallmark today, such as the Grand Théâtre and the Bourse; and since World War II it has known a new era of glory under its forceful, long-ruling Gaullist mayor, Jacques Chaban-Delmas, a former Prime Minister. He used his influence in Paris to attract new industry, and has done much to bring a new vitality to this formerly staid city of wine and timber merchants.

But these trades remain important, especially wine. The vineyards date from Roman times, and already in the Middle Ages had a huge export trade, above all to England. Most of the finest reds come from the Médoc region north of Bordeaux, where the vineyards belong to great patrician estates such as Mouton-Rothschild and Château Lafite. East of the city, other fine reds are produced around Pomerol and St Emilion, where the vinegrowing properties tend to be smaller. Dry white wines come from the Entre-Deux-Mers sector, and sweeter ones from around Sauternes where, Château d'Yquem is France's greatest luxury dessert wine. The Bordeaux wine trade is occasionally affected by scandals of fraudulent labeling, but it remains immensely lucrative: the great vintages, improving with age, reach the top world prices for still wines.

Timber comes mainly from the Landes, the largest pine forest in Western Europe, sweeping for 240 kilometers across a flat plain. As recently as the 19th century this area was all marsh and scrub. The sea gales blew the coastal sands inland, blocking the rivers and thus creating a bog, so that the peasants had to walk around on stilts. Then, engineers cleverly fixed the dunes by planting reeds, broom and pines, and later afforested the whole plain. Today its timber has become less lucrative, and some big landowners have converted areas for cereals and sheep-breeding. But many distinctive old *maisons landaises* remain – timbered farmhouses with long, low-sloping roofs.

This is the *pays* of novelist François Mauriac, who evoked it so vividly and poetically. Born in Bordeaux in 1885, he remained closely involved with the Garonne valley, where he had a home, and with the forest around St-Symphoriem where he spent boyhood summers. In his books, this forest wears contrasting faces: idyllic and sensuous in the

Delicacies of the Southwest

In a land where agriculture and cuisine are both varied and subtle, each region has its special produce which finds its way into local dishes. So it is in the southwest – in Aquitaine, Poitou-Charentes and the western Massif Central. Near the Pyrenees, wood pigeons migrating seasonally are trapped in huge nets (a popular pastime), and then served up in a rich stew. Around Bordeaux, they cook local lampreys in red wine. Salty conserved goose and cepes, a kind of mushroom, are everywhere popular. In the Dordogne, as in much of Aquitaine, the cuisine based on local produce is rich and succulent, if a shade monotonous – sliced breast of duck, *confit* of duck or goose, hot foie gras with grapes in a wine sauce. In Limousin they cook goose stuffed with local chestnuts. Poitou's rolling plain is used for cereal growing and livestock breeding. The rich milk of the local goats is considered ideal for children. The Charente area, more lush and southerly, produces sweet pink melons, figs and big artichokes. Its coast is France's main breeding ground for oysters and mussels. Much of this produce goes into the original local cooking – mussels or eels stewed in white wine, snails in red wine.

Right A foie gras market in the Dordogne, where the force-feeding of geese to make this delicacy is done on an industrial scale by big farms, and by smallholders too. The birds are stuffed with maize, forced down their throat by a tube attached to an electrical pump. The swollen liver may weigh 800g and will fetch maybe $300 a kilo. Farmers claim that the geese enjoy their meals, and there is hardly any anti-goose-stuffing lobby in France.

Below Roquefort, blue-veined, with a uniquely tangy taste, is to other cheeses what champagne is to other wines. Made from the milk of ewes that roam the uplands, it is matured in chalky caves in the Aveyron village of Roquefort. A rare penicillin fungus, which grows in these caves, is added to the young cheese to produce its special aroma.

Above Specially trained pigs are used to hunt out truffles in the Dordogne, the area that produces the best French truffles. These fungi, a superior kind of mushroom, grow on the roots of oaks and some other trees. They sell at high prices, being hard to find, and are prized for their subtle, fragrant flavor. They are used in omelettes, foie gras, and meat or poultry dishes.

Below An expert tastes cognac in a wine cellar. Over 200 firms produce cognac in the town of that name. All cognac is made from grapes of the surrounding Charente area, and its quality depends partly on the soil, partly on the methods of distilling and aging. It matures in special casks, which gives the colorless *eau-de-vie* its glowing amber tint.

Left Harvesting walnuts and then shelling them (*above*) in the Dordogne. So common is the walnut in France that its name is just *noix* (nut), as if there were no other. Besides being eaten raw, the nuts are pressed to produce oil for salads or cooking; walnut bread, spiced with finely chopped nuts, has become fashionable.

autobiographical *Le Mystère Frontenac*, oppressively claustrophobic in his masterwork *Thérèse Desqueyroux*, with its images of forest fires, suffocating summer heat, and the wild moaning of the pines at night. Today the Landes does not seem gloomy. The lofty marine pines and ancient oaks, all well-spaced, the quiet streams and lost lagoons, create a serene and secret world, strange and beautiful. Along the coast are broad sandy beaches backed by high dunes and freshwater lakes, popular with tourists; Arcachon, once a smart winter resort, has some charmingly bizarre neo-baroque villas.

East of the Basque country is Béarn, a lushly pastoral area of green hills where salmon leap in the fast rivers gushing down from the Pyrenees. Its graceful capital, Pau, has a fine castle where the lords of Béarn, Foix and Navarre once ruled over much of southern France: Henri IV, that most popular of kings, was born here. Béarn's mild winters later drew many Britons to settle here, after Wellington's officers discovered it when returning from Spain. By the 1860s a third of Pau's population was British, making it the biggest British colony outside the Empire, with its own tea parties and foxhunts, and the Continent's first golf course. Today most of the British have gone, but the traditions of golf and foxhunting have remained.

Today the area that is the most popular with the British, and also the Dutch and others, is the old province of Périgord, renamed the Dordogne department after the lovely river that winds through it to join the Garonne. This quintessence of French rural tradition has prehistoric cave-paintings, old hilltop castles, walled villages made of golden local stone, forests of oak and chestnut, and much else that draws foreigners in their tens of thousands to buy holiday or retirement homes. The American poet Ezra Pound also loved the Dordogne and wrote about it evocatively. The Dordogne produces truffles, and on an industrial scale some farmers force-feed geese to make *foie gras*.

To the north, Poitou-Charentes' capital is the university city of Poitiers. But its loveliest town is the superb old seaport of La Rochelle, with its 14th-century harbor forts and Renaissance town hall. This former Huguenot stronghold, besieged and starved by Richelieu in 1627, still has a thriving Protestant community. Among other old towns, Saintes has relics of its days as a Roman city, and a fine medieval core; Angoulême, with its 12th-century cathedral, is a former papermaking center whose narrow bourgeoisie was brilliantly satirized by Balzac in *Les Illusions perdues*. Near Niort is the curious Marais Poitevin, an isolated marshy area cut by tree-lined canals, where the peasants carry around everything – even their cows – in punt-like boats.

The region's supreme glory – cognac – comes from the town of that name on the river Charente. Here in the 17th century the local growers, having trouble with the exports of their dullish white wine, began to distill it to a seventh of its volume. Their Dutch and English customers were supposed to dilute it with water; but they found a taste for the firewater itself, which the Dutch dubbed *brandewijn* (burned wine), corrupted by the English into "brandy". Today any distilled wine is a brandy: but cognac comes only from the Cognac area, where it is produced under the strictest rules and matured in special casks of Limousin oak. Over 200 local firms make it, ranging from great names like Rémy Martin down to tiny farms, and over 80 percent is exported.

The Basques

The Basques are a race apart, a people of unknown origin, with a strong and engaging personality. They have their own language, which some still speak, full of "tz's and "x's, unrelated to any other. And they zealously keep up their own traditions – the bounding folk dances, the game of *pelota*, the Basque beret, the red, white and green costumes. While the French Basques, like their Spanish counterparts, enjoy bullfights, they also have a less ferocious sport – the cow race (*course des vaches*). Frisky heifers are baited in a friendly way by mock-toreadors.

In the villages, the neat houses, mostly in chalet style, have red roofs and white walls with criss-cross beams. In the graveyards some tombs bear the Basque cross, an inverted swastika dating from a pre-Christian era. But although their past is mysterious, the Basques are a down-to-earth people, expressing strong emotions through song and dance. At a festival they will exuberantly wave their red-white-and-green national flag, but unlike the Basque separatists in Spain, most French Basques are happy to remain part of France.

Below This funeral dance with a coffin performed by fishermen, is characteristically Basque. Other Basque dances include a comic dance with a stuffed pig, and joyful high-leaping dances, accompanied by the strange whooping cries that Basque peasants use to signal to one another in their mountain valleys.

Right The beech forest of Iraty lies up in the Pyrenees by the frontier. Smuggling has long been traditional in these upland areas, where remote paths lead into Spain. Many villagers used to earn a living from contraband in sheep, cattle and brandy. Today the traffic is mostly in mechanical and electronic goods. But the EC's single market now spells doom to the smuggling industry.

Above The Basques' favorite sport is *pelota*, a fast game rather like squash or fives. It is played on an open-air court against a high wall (the *fronton*) and every village has one. The players, usually three-a-side, strike a hard ball with a thin wicker basket strapped to the wrist (as here), or with a gloved hand or even, despite the blisters, with a bare one. Basque emigrants to the Americas have invented an even faster version of the game, called *cesta punta*.

Below A traditional horse fair, where the dealers are wearing the typical *beret basque*. Farming is the Basques' main activity. Besides horses, the Basques breed sheep and dairy cows, and grow corn and apples. Some cottage crafts still flourish, including the making of the springy rope-soled *espadrilles* (shoes) that Basques still wear. Fishing is also practiced. Tunny fish caught in the stormy Bay of Biscay finds its way into Basque dishes such as *ttoro*, a type of rich fish stew.

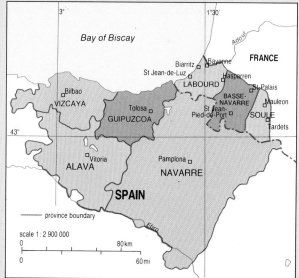

Left A lively dance from Navarre province. Basque folk dancers' costumes are colorful and varied. Some dances, with waving handkerchiefs, stick-beating, and jingling bells on the ankles, recall English Morris-dancing; so does the comic prancing character with a wicker-framed horse round his middle. In the Soule area, dancers perform medieval charades called *mascarades* and *pastorales*.

The Basque regions of France and Spain
Most of the million or so Basques in Europe live in Spain, in and around industrial towns such as Bilbao. Their French cousins across the border are fewer and more rural. The coast around Biarritz is fashionable and in summer crowded with tourists. The true *pays basque* is inland where old villages nestle in the Pyrenean foothills – idyllic, save for the damp, often stormy climate.

LANGUEDOC, MIDI-PYRENEES

Within the borders of Languedoc-Roussillon (population 2.3 million) and Midi–Pyrénées (population 2.11 million) lies the whole of the former historic province of Languedoc. Its capital was Toulouse, on its western edge, but its heartland was the coastal plain toward Montpellier, today called Lower Languedoc. This sun-parched land, covered in vineyards, backed by dry stony foothills of the Cévennes, is the epitome of southern France. This was once the center of a vast but vague medieval area called Occitania, where the *langue d'oc* was spoken; today many older country people (and some idealistic city intellectuals) still speak this ancient tongue, which is akin to Provençal. Some extremists wish to create an Occitan nation.

Lower Languedoc's plain is one of Europe's oldest through-routes for traders and invaders, and today for tourists. In 600 BC it was settled by Phocaeans from Greece, who brought the culture of the vine and olive. Then came the Romans, who made Narbonne the capital of this key province of their empire, called Gallia Narbonnensis. In the Dark Ages the Saracens invaded; they were a warlike but cultured people who were a major formative influence on the civilization that blossomed in the 11th and 12th centuries, when Languedoc was a powerful independent realm ruled by the Counts of Toulouse. But then, in the early 13th century, the Cathar heresy provoked the fury of the pope and the King of France, and it was cruelly suppressed in a campaign that mixed religious crusade with imperial expansion. Some 200 of the Cathars were burned alive at their lonely mountain citadel of Montségur, whose ruins still stand, and in Béziers over 15,000 men, women and children were butchered in 1209. Even today, these events have not been forgotten or forgiven by the people of Languedoc, where tribal memories run deep and resentment against Paris persists.

This resentment has centered on the vineyards, which produce 40 percent of all France's wine and most of its cheaper table wine. So easy was it to produce wine at low cost on these sunny slopes that the region never bothered to industrialize, and the countless small growers would be stirred into action only when their interests seemed threatened. Since the late 1950s, the government has upset them by imposing some major development projects. A wide irrigation canal was dug westward from the Rhône, with the aim of inducing the *vignerons* to uproot some vines and switch to more useful produce. To encourage tourism, a chain of eight huge modern resorts was built along the coast from the Rhône to the Pyrenees. However, the local people were scarcely consulted about these schemes and at first reacted angrily. They rioted against the canal, yet expected to go on being subsidized for their wine surpluses, whenever a bumper harvest sent prices tumbling.

Over the past ten years or so, a new, more realistic generation of local leaders has arisen in Languedoc. The growers are now uprooting their worst vines, and the quality of the wines has been improving: some, such as the Corbières and Costières du Gard, are rather good, yet still quite cheap. Moreover, regional

Left The Cirque de Gavarnie, in the high Pyrenees south of Lourdes, is a vast natural amphitheater set among mountains on the Spanish border that rise to over 3300m. There are dazzling panoramas of snow, ice, rock and waterfalls. One of these falls, the Grande Cascade, is Europe's highest (over 400m). Gavarnie village has a 14th-century pilgrim church.

Right The majestic medieval walls of Aigues-Mortes provide the background for this *course à la cocarde*, a sport popular in the Nimes area: amateur toreadors compete to snatch rosettes from the bulls' horns. It is less lethal than real Spanish-style bullfights, which are held in the Roman arenas at Nimes and Arles.

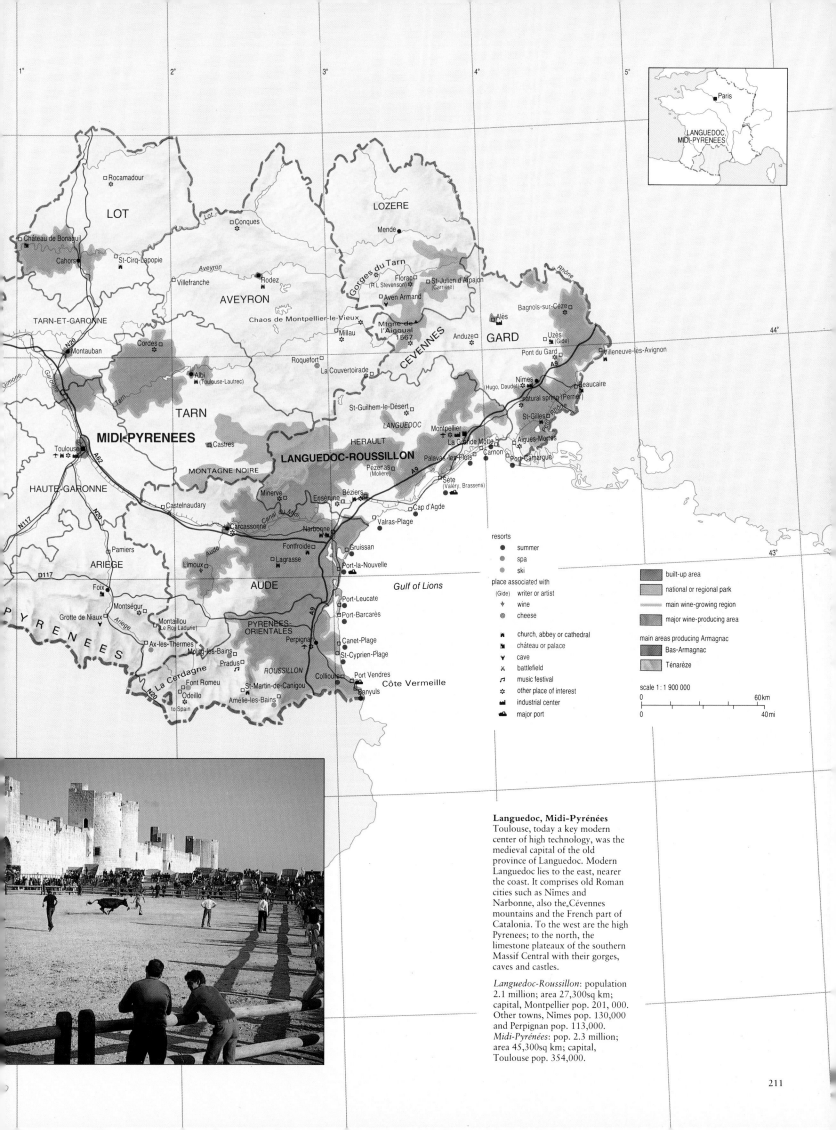

Paris

LANGUEDOC,
MIDI-PYRENEES

□ Rocamadour

LOT

LOZERE

□ Château de Bonaguil

□ Conques

Mende

✿ Cahors

St-Cirq-Lapopie

Aveyron

Gorges du Tarn

Florac
(R L Stevenson)

St-Julien d'Arpajon
(Carrière)

Bagnols-sur-Cèze

□ Villefranche

Rodez

AVEYRON

Aven Armand

Rhône

Alès

Uzès
(Gide)

Villeneuve-lès-Avignon

Chaos de Montpellier-le-Vieux

Mtgne de
l'Aigoual
1567

CEVENNES

Anduze

GARD

44°

□ Montauban

N20

□ Cordes

Millau

Roquefort

La Couvertoirade

Pont du Gard

A9

Beaucaire

Gimone

Garonne

Albi
(Toulouse-Lautrec)

Tarn

St-Guilhem-le-Désert

Nîmes
(Hugo, Daudet)

natural spring (Perrier)

TARN

LANGUEDOC

St-Gilles

MIDI-PYRENEES

HERAULT

Montpellier

Petit Rhône

Aigues-Mortes

Castres

LANGUEDOC-ROUSSILLON

La Grande Motte

Toulouse

A62

MONTAGNE NOIRE

Pézenas
(Molière)

Palavas-les-Flots

Carnon

Port-Camargue

HAUTE-GARONNE

Sète
(Valéry, Brassens)

Castelnaudary

Minerve

Ensérune

Béziers

N117

N20

Canal du Midi

Cap d'Agde

Carcassonne

Narbonne

Valras-Plage

Pamiers

Fontfroide

resorts

Aude

Lagrasse

Gruissan

● summer

ARIEGE

Limoux

Port-la-Nouvelle

● spa

D117

● ski

Foix

AUDE

Gulf of Lions

place associated with

Montségur

(Gide) writer or artist

Grotte de Niaux

Port-Leucate

♈ wine

Ariège

A9

Port-Barcarès

◎ cheese

Montaillou
(Le Roy Ladurie)

PYRENEES-
ORIENTALES

▲ church, abbey or cathedral

Ax-les-Thermes

Perpignan

Canet-Plage

▲ château or palace

PYRENEES

Molitg-les-Bains

St-Cyprien-Plage

♈ cave

Pradus

ROUSSILLON

✕ battlefield

La Cerdagne

Collioure

Port Vendres

♫ music festival

Font Romeu

Côte Vermeille

✿ other place of interest

Odeillo

St-Martin-de-Canigou

▬ industrial center

to Spain

Amélie-les-Bains

Banyuls

⚓ major port

□ built-up area

□ national or regional park

main wine-growing region

major wine-producing area

main areas producing Armagnac

■ Bas-Armagnac

□ Ténarèze

scale 1 : 1 900 000

0   60km

0   40mi

43°

Languedoc, Midi-Pyrénées

Toulouse, today a key modern
center of high technology, was the
medieval capital of the old
province of Languedoc. Modern
Languedoc lies to the east, nearer
the coast. It comprises old Roman
cities such as Nîmes and
Narbonne, also the Cévennes
mountains and the French part of
Catalonia. To the west are the high
Pyrenees; to the north, the
limestone plateaux of the southern
Massif Central with their gorges,
caves and castles.

Languedoc-Roussillon: population
2.1 million; area 27,300sq km;
capital, Montpellier pop. 201, 000.
Other towns, Nîmes pop. 130,000
and Perpignan pop. 113,000.
Midi-Pyrénées: pop. 2.3 million;
area 45,300sq km; capital,
Toulouse pop. 354,000.

reforms have at last given Languedoc some sense of being in charge of its own destiny. For many years after the war this conservative region voted left, less from conviction than from hostility to center-right governments in Paris; many towns were even Communist-ruled. But then in the 1980s it swung to the right: and the main tensions were now not so much Paris-directed as held within the region, between the rightist assembly and Georges Frèche, the assertive Socialist mayor of the capital, Montpellier.

The graceful city of Montpellier has a lovely ancient kernel of narrow traffic-free streets, well restored, and one of Europe's oldest universities, noted for medicine. It used to be a sleepy wine-trade town, but is now rapidly developing as a center of modern high-technology research and industry: IBM's factory is the largest in France, with a staff of 3000. Montpellier has just completed some monumental new building projects designed by the Catalan architect Ricardo Bofil. No other town in France has been growing faster in the past decade.

Nîmes, an old Protestant city, equally mixes medieval core and new industry, along with its grandiose Roman relics; it also invented jeans, "denim" being a corruption of "de Nîmes". The Languedoc plain, in fact, has a whole string of fascinating towns drenched in history. Uzès' massive feudal castle is still the home of a ducal family dating as far back as Charlemagne; nearby is the spectacular Pont du Gard, a three-tier Roman bridge built in 19 BC. Beaucaire's former annual trade fair was once the foremost in Europe; St-Gilles' old church has some of the finest medieval sculpture in France; amid salty marshes by the sea is the tiny medieval walled town of Aigues-Mortes, from where St-Louis sailed for the Seventh and Eighth Crusades. Nearby is an abrupt modern contrast: the huge 1960s resort of La Grande Motte, with its ranks of ziggurat blocks and holiday flats in weird shapes and colors. Another big new resort, Cap d'Agde, built as a pastiche of a local fishing village, contains Europe's largest nudist holiday center, accommodating 20,000.

Also on this coast, the picturesque old port of Sète has Venice-like canals, and a quiet cemetery high above the sea where Paul Valéry, born in the town, set his best-known poem, *Le Cimetière marin* (Graveyard by the sea), and now lies buried. Narbonne, the old Roman capital, has a superb towering Gothic cathedral and episcopal palace. At Carcassonne is the greatest of all medieval fortresses in France, where 500 people still live within the ramparts, while Albi, to the north, with its wonderful pink-brick cathedral, has a museum full of the paintings of its famous local son, Toulouse-Lautrec.

The countryside retains some curious old traditions and festivals. In some villages, people are thrown into heaps of mud, or pelted with eggs, or are rolled in pools of wine. Wild bulls are let loose in the streets, and bullfights are popular. In the Cévennes mountains to the north, the peasant people are more reserved; many are still Protestant, and their past persecution is vividly related in the Musée du Désert, near Anduze. The Cévennes, a great block of schist and granite, has splendidly varied scenery – wild in places, green in others, where deep valleys are filled with woods of pine and chestnut. Here Robert Louis Stevenson made his famous *Travels with a Donkey* in 1878. To the north, the high limestone plateau of the *causses* is cut by the deep and spectacular Tarn gorge, and the

Above The 15th-century château of Champs lies amid the wild and lovely uplands of the Lozère department, which is the least densely populated in France (14 people per sq km): it has more sheep than humans, and only one set of traffic lights.

Overleaf The ruined medieval castle of Castlebou has a dramatic setting deep in the Tarn gorge.

Right An old bridge spanning the river Garonne at Toulouse. Behind it is one of the city's old churches, in the heart of the medieval quarter of stately mansions built of mellow rose-pink brick. They stand tight-packed along narrow streets, and many are still inhabited by descendants of the great patrician families who ruled Toulouse in its golden age.

Below An outdoor antique market in Collioure, best-known and most picturesque of the resorts along the Côte Vermeille, named after its russet rocks. This old fishing village drew Matisse, Dufy, Picasso and others to work there, and the Fauvist movement was born there in 1905. It is crowned by a 12th-century castle of the Knights Templar.

Above Medieval sculptures of mythical chimeras adorn the graceful 14th-century cloister of the Augustins' monastery in Toulouse, which now houses one of the best museums in France.

gigantic Aven Armand cavern has large stalagmites in strange shapes.

Roussillon, to the south of Languedoc, is the French part of Catalonia. Before joining France in 1659, it belonged to the kings of Aragon, and it remains very Catalan – in its dialect, its *sardaña* dances and its arcaded squares. Around Perpignan, the palm-shaded capital, is a fertile plain growing early fruit and vegetables. To the south, the rugged Côte Vermeille has russet rocks. To the west, the Pyrenees rise up to snowy peaks, where can be found the lonely abbey of St-Martin-de-Canigou which nestles in the hills. On the Cerdagne pastoral plateau, Odeillo is the site of Europe's leading solar furnace.

Much farther to the west is Toulouse, a proud historic city that today has found a new vocation as a key center of high technology, especially the aerospace industries. Toulouse in the early Middle Ages was the most important town in France outside Paris, capital of the independent Languedoc. This golden age ended when it was brutally annexed to the French crown in the 13th century; even today, hostility to Paris is stronger here than in most French cities. In the 1914–18 war it became an aircraft-making center when the Government moved some key armaments factories there, to be as far from the Germans as possible. The principal state aircraft factory, today called Aérospatiale, subsequently emerged; it is notable for jet airliners, first the Caravelle, then Concorde (built in conjunction with the British), and today the various versions of the Airbus. Under Government impulsion, Toulouse has also diversified, to become France's leading center for scientific research and higher studies in aeronautics, space and electronics. Once a slow, sleepy old town, it is now very modern and cosmopolitan and is developing dynamic new links with Spain, just across the Pyrenees. Yet it remains also a mellow, very cultured city, with a charming medieval core of old mansions, all built of the local rose-pink brick – *la ville rose*, it calls itself. It has a strong musical tradition, some fine medieval churches and a fierce local pride. But the old local families, their roots deep in history, slow and easygoing in their life styles, do not always get on easily with the clever, thrusting new arrivals from Paris and elsewhere – the engineers and scientists, pilots and professors.

Just west of Toulouse, historic Languedoc gives way to Gascony, a vaguely defined historic area whose chief town was Auch. Gascons had a reputation for shrewdness, bravery and hotheadedness, qualities displayed in fiction by Dumas' d'Artagnan and Rostand's *Cyrano de Bergerac*, both "typical" Gascons. They both enjoyed their armagnac, a brandy subtly different from cognac, and often just as good, produced in the rolling country north of Auch. To the southwest is industrial Tarbes, and the pilgrimage town of Lourdes. There is good skiing up in the mountains here, and dramatic scenery such as the Cirque de Gavarnie, a natural amphitheater with cliffs nearly one and a half kilometers high. North of Toulouse, toward Périgord, the river Lot flows past old castles and hilltop villages, amid some of France's loveliest scenery.

The best-known dish of Languedoc is cassoulet, a heavy white-bean stew with preserved goose, pork, mutton and spicy sausages. Garlic and olive oil are much used in local cooking. The coast, especially at Sète, has a range of spicy fish specialities.

PROVENCE

The region of Provence-Alpes-Côte d'Azur (population 4.1 million) is many people's favorite, and much the most visited region outside Paris. Provence has a density and variety of interest that perhaps has no equal in Europe. It is a land of clear light (which captivated Cézanne and Van Gogh), bold sensuous colors and spicy tastes, of ancient history, vivid folk traditions and modern sophistication.

Provence was first colonized around 600 BC by Phocaean Greeks who founded Massilia (Marseille), Nikaia (Nice) and other places. At the same time Celtic migrants from the north allied and intermarried with the native Ligurian tribes, thus forming the basis of Provence's population. In 125 BC the Romans conquered the region and built arenas, theaters, baths, temples and villas, many still extant. Some 300 years later the Emperor Constantine built a palace at Arles, establishing it as the leading town of Provence, from where early Christianity spread across the region, until the time of the Saracen invasions.

From the 11th century the Counts of Provence established an autonomous realm, with Aix-en-Provence as their capital. Aix-en-Provence knew a golden age under the cultured and fun-loving "Good King René" (who was really a count) of the House of Anjou. But then his successor rashly bequeathed the realm to Louis XI, and so Provence became part of France. However, the Nice area, for centuries under the Italian House of Savoy, did not join France until 1860. Soon afterward this famous coast, known then as the Riviera, now as the Côte d'Azur, became the world's foremost pleasure-haunt of the rich and titled. Today, it caters much more for mass tourism and the lucrative convention trade.

Its main town is Nice, which was founded in 350 BC by Greeks, then colonized by the Romans. It is the oldest resort on this coast. In the late 18th century the English began to come for the winter season, and in the 1820s they financed the building of a coastal road which today is the famous Promenade des Anglais, named after them. Queen Victoria was among the many royalty who wintered in Nice. Today it is not just a tourist center, but also a busy commercial metropolis, rich in contrasts. The plush hotels and boutiques by the promenade coexist with the teeming alleys of the Vieille Ville, Italian in character. Nice is a town of modern art, but also of new high-tech industry. It has long had a reputation for civic corruption and Mafia-linked crime – as denounced by Grahame Greene, who lived nearby, in his book *J'Accuse: The Dark Side of Nice* (1982). The long-serving mayor, Jacques Médecin, resigned and fled the country in 1990, as charges of corruption were finally being prepared against him.

Among the Côte d'Azur's other towns, flowery Menton has a cosily genteel, old-fashioned air, while Cannes is a smart, glittering showcase of modern tourism. West of Cannes, the rugged red rocks of the Esterel coast lead to Roman Fréjus with its amazing 5th-century baptistry and Gothic cathedral.

Farther on is the old fishing port of St Tropez, set in

Above Pleasure boats at anchor off the rugged coast of Porquerolles, largest of the three lovely Iles d'Hyères, whose rocky cliffs contrast with lush subtropical vegetation. Long a haunt of pirates, they are now besieged by tourists. Port-Cros, the second island, is hilly and mysterious. Ile du Levant, the third, is in part a naval base, in part a nudist colony.

Right Women in Arles in local costume, preparing for a festival. This dress is no longer used for daily wear, for it is too much trouble: to prepare the coiffure for an Arlesian bonnet takes over an hour. But Arles remains a lively center of Provençal folk tradition. The women are still famed for their beauty, as in the days when Daudet wrote *l'Arlésienne*.

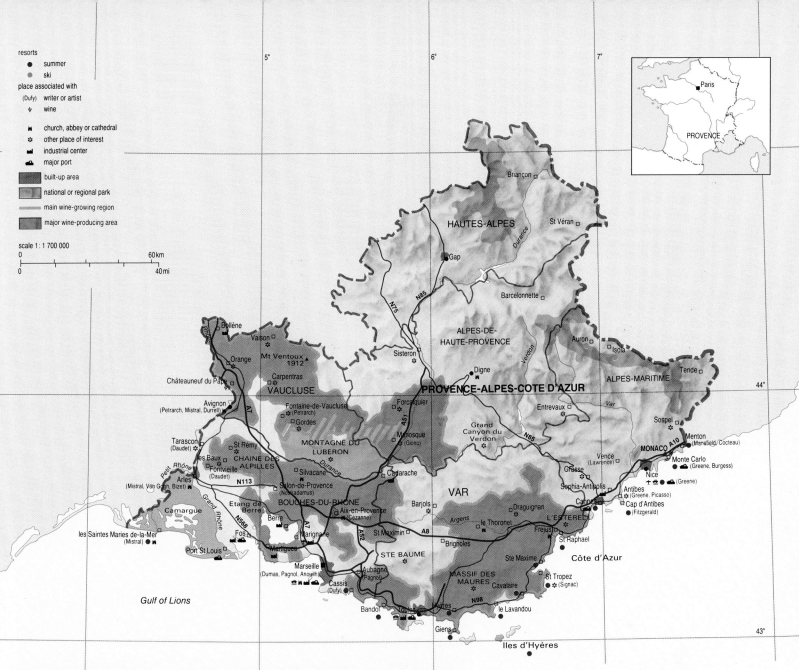

Map legend

resorts
- summer
- ski

place associated with
- (Dufy) writer or artist
- ✿ wine
- ♨ church, abbey or cathedral
- ✿ other place of interest
- industrial center
- major port
- built-up area
- national or regional park
- main wine-growing region
- major wine-producing area

scale 1 : 1 700 000

0 — 60km
0 — 40mi

Inset (France)
Paris
PROVENCE

Map labels

Briançon
HAUTES-ALPES
St Véran
Gap
Barcelonnette
ALPES-DE-HAUTE-PROVENCE
Auron
Isola
Tende
ALPES-MARITIME
Sisteron
Digne
PROVENCE-ALPES-COTE D'AZUR
Bollène
Vaison
Mt Ventoux 1912
Orange
Carpentras
Châteauneuf du Pape
VAUCLUSE
Fontaine-de-Vaucluse (Petrarch)
Gordes
Forcalquier
Entrevaux
Sospel
Avignon (Petrarch, Mistral, Durrell)
Monosque (Giono)
Grand Canyon du Verdon
Vence (Lawrence)
Menton (Mansfield/Cocteau)
Tarascon (Daudet)
St Rémy
MONTAGNE DU LUBERON
MONACO
Monte Carlo (Greene, Burgess)
Les Baux
CHAINE DES ALPILLES
Fontvieille (Daudet)
Silvacane
Cadarache
Grasse
Nice (Greene)
Arles (Mistral, Van Gogh, Bizet)
Salon-de-Provence (Nostradamus)
Sophia-Antipolis
Antibes (Greene, Picasso)
Camargue
Etang de Berre
BOUCHES-DU-RHONE
Barjols
VAR
Cannes
Cap d'Antibes (Fitzgerald)
les Saintes Maries-de-la-Mer (Mistral)
Berre
Aix-en-Provence (Cézanne)
Argens
le Thoronet
Draguignan
L'ESTEREL
Fos
Marignane
St Maximin
A8
Brignoles
Fréjus
St Raphael
Port St Louis
Martigues
STE BAUME
Ste Maxime
Côte d'Azur
Marseille (Dumas, Pagnol, Anouilh)
Aubagne (Pagnol)
MASSIF DES MAURES
St Tropez (Signac)
Cassis (Dufy)
Cavalaire
Bandol
Toulon
Hyères
le Lavandou
Giens
Iles d'Hyères
Gulf of Lions

44°
43°
5°
6°
7°

Left Herds of half-wild white horses roam the salty marshes of the Camargue, a solitary expanse of lagoon and plain within the delta of the Rhône. It is a strangely beautiful region with its own mystique and traditions, and is noted for its wildlife. Part of it is a nature reserve, with many species of birds, including flocks of pink flamingoes which migrate here each summer. The herds of black fighting bulls, and the horses, are tended by cowboy-like ranchers, call *gardians*, who live in isolated thatched cottages out on the marshes.

Provence

The heartland of Provence is its western part, between Marseille and Avignon, where Roman monuments, medieval abbeys and palaces bear witness to its remarkable history. The seaport of Marseille is its modern capital; its old capital was Aix-en-Provence; at Avignon the Popes held court in 1307–77. Here the broad Rhône flows through a fertile plain, broken by barren craggy hills, to reach the sea near the marshy Camargue. To the east, a beautiful indented coastline leads to the Côte d'Azur whose famous resorts – Nice, Cannes and others – still exert their glamor. This coast is very crowded, but its vast hinterland of limestone plateaux, stretching westward from the Alps to the Rhône valley, remains empty and unspoilt.

Provence – Côte d'Azur: population 4.1 million; area 32,400sq km; capital, Marseille pop. 878,000. Other main towns, Nice pop. 338,000, Toulon 181,000, Aix 124,000 and Avignon 91,000.

a lovely wide bay. It has had a curious history: first a Greek trading post, then a self-governing republic, then a center for artists and writers in the early 20th century, before, in 1956, the young director Roger Vadim used it as the location for his film *Et Dieu créa la femme*. His star was his wife, the still little-known Brigitte Bardot, whose father had a villa there. The *succès fou* of this film made St Tropez into the symbol of a new permissive, hedonistic epoch. The cult, now somewhat jaded, still persists. St Tropez attracts a glamorous showbiz high society, as well as show-off Bohemian eccentrics and tourist mobs who come in search of its elusive legend.

Along this glorious coast, the Massif des Maures face the idyllic Iles d'Hyères, and the road leads on to the great naval base of Toulon, where the young Bonaparte first won military distinction and where, many years later, the Vichy fleet scuttled itself. Inland, the strange rocky massif of Ste Baume enshrines early Christian legend: St Mary Magdalene is said to have spent 30 years alone in a cave on these heights, now a pilgrimage center. And near Aubagne, amid the hamlets and wild limestone hills where he spent his boyhood, Marcel Pagnol set his racy stories of Provençal rural life and was buried there.

Marseille, torrid, rough and exciting, is the second city of France (a role it disputes with Lyon) and its main Mediterranean seaport. It has a superb setting around a wide bay, circled by barren limestone hills. Founded by Greeks from Asia Minor in 600 BC, it became the main Greek colony in the west. Always powerful commercially, it knew its true heyday in the later 19th century, after the opening of the Suez Canal and the French conquest of North Africa. Its port has since declined, but several major industries survive, including the making of *pastis*. It famous mayor in 1953–86, Gaston Defferre, was a Socialist leader of great influence. Marseillais today retain much of the hot-blooded, earthily humorous character described by Pagnol in his *Marius* trilogy. Drug-trafficking has declined, but there is still sporadic gangsterism, as well as racial tension between Muslim immigrants and National Front supporters, many of them French repatriates from North Africa.

The spacious hinterland sweeps north – to the handsome Cistercian abbey of le Thoronet, to the Lubéron hills, now popular with the Paris intelligentsia as a holiday retreat, and to the unspoilt upland country of Jean Giono, who lived and died at Manosque, and wrote with such feeling about this landscape and its simple peasants. At Avignon, the majestic Palace of the Popes towers above a fascinating old city that hosts Europe's leading annual drama festival (but the fabled bridge across the Rhône is broken). Aix-en-Provence, in a way Avignon's rival, is full of patrician grace, with an intimate medieval nucleus, a famous shaded avenue, the Cours Mirabeau, a fine cathedral, and a noted university. Arles, is mellow and seductive, has bullfights in the Roman arena, and some of the finest museums in France – among them, the folklore museum established by the great Provençal poet Frédéric Mistral.

The half-ruined village and feudal castle of les Baux, high on a rock in the craggy Chaine des Alpilles, is one of the most haunting sights in France and has a momentous history. To the south is the Camargue, a mysterious flat expanse of lagoon and marsh, where in the seaside town of les Saintes Maries-de-la-Mer, the local gypsies hold a big annual festival. In its strange

Below The Bravade is a famous annual folk festival in St Tropez, dating from the 16th century. An armed guard in the uniform of that time fires salvoes of blank cartridges, amid much mirth and merriment, and the bust of St-Torpes is paraded round the town. Initially a Greek trading-post, St Tropez remained a quiet fising village until it was taken up by artists such as Matisse and Bonnard, and writers like Colette. Brigitte Bardot and her husband Roger Vadim then gave it notoriety with their film *Et Dieu créa la femme*, and it has never looked back.

Above Along the seafront at Cannes, many of the classic luxury hotels – led by the Carlton and the Martinez – have their private beaches, equipped with parasols and sun-loungers. The palm-lined promenade, La Croisette, is the most glamorous in France, and Cannes remains the smartest of the Côte d'Azur resorts. It ws just a fishing-village until 1834 when British aristocrats turned it into a smart winter retreat.

Left High heels and bikini in a chic boutique are all part of Cannes' showy sophistication, which reaches its height during the Film Festival in May. Cannes also retains a faithful clientèle of mainly elderly aristocrats but today its tourist revenue comes mostly from upmarket business congresses.

Above left Lavender is grown on the plateaux of upper Provence around Riez, best seen in July when it is in bloom. Some of the lavender is used by the perfume industry at Grasse, where scent-making was introduced from Italy in the 16th century. Today, however, the factories rely mainly on imported flowers or synthetic essences.

Left The Vieux Port in the heart of Marseille. Once the city's main port, it is now used mainly by pleasure craft and a few fishermen. The modern port is to the north. But the Vieux Port remains central to the mystique of Marseille. Here scores of harborside bistros serve *bouillabaisse*; and here Pagnol set his evocative *Marius* trilogy.

Right Arles, crowned by the cathedral of St-Trophîme, is the quintessence of old Provence, full of fine churches, museums and Roman remains. After Constantine built a palace there in the 4th century, it was briefly the capital of the Roman Empire. Then it became a key focus of early Christianity: St Augustine was consecrated Archbishop of Canterbury there in 597. More recently it was a center for artists, musicians and writers, and the place where Van Gogh cut off his ear.

fortified church the heroine of Mistral's epic *Mireille* died. Another writer who loved his native Provence, Alphonse Daudet, made nearby Tarascon the setting for his *Tartaria* tales, in which he portrays the volatile Provençal character with gentle irony. Tarascon has a superb moated Renaissance castle.

The people of Provence speak French with a sharp accent ("*byeng*" for "*bien*"), harsh and grating in the cities, softer in rural areas. In the olden days everyone spoke Provençal, a mellifluous language similar to Occitan. In the 19th century a group of poets called the Félibrige, led by Mistral (he himself wrote only in Provençal), made strong efforts to revive it: but they, like others since then, had little success outside intellectual circles. Few people speak Provençal today. In rural architecture, tradition has survived much better. Farmsteads and villas mostly have stone walls and sloping roofs of red terracotta tiles; the north wall is often blind, as a defence against the Mistral, the icy north wind that spasmodically sweeps through the region in winter. Many areas now have strict rules whereby new buildings must conform to traditional styles of appearance and construction.

Inevitably, some of the old folk-traditions have been disappearing from daily life. Only rarely do women now wear the old Provençal costumes and head-dresses: but, as in other regions such as Brittany, efforts have been made recently to revive the old customs for festivals and weddings. Many new folk groups have been formed and have learned to dance the *farandole*, to the tune of the *tambourin* (a narrow drum) and *galoubet* (a flute). A few of these instruments are still being made. Also, each village still has its big annual fête, including contests and games, a communal feast, and perhaps a folklore display.

Another tradition that has been preserved is the making of *santons* for Christmas cribs, or simply as secular ornaments. These clay, costumed figurines, invented in Marseille, at first were solely religious but now include stock Provençal characters. Other handicrafts, such as olive-wood sculpture, ceramics, and the weaving of bright Provençal fabrics, have also been revived.

Provence's economy is heavily based on farming and tourism, with modern industry only a little way behind. Agriculture is as varied as the soil and scenery. The lower Rhône valley is France's leading market garden, producing melons, asparagus, peaches, and much besides. Rice is grown in the Camargue. Provence with its chalky soil is also France's major producer of olives and olive oil, and has some good wines, notably in the Rhône area (Châteauneuf-du-Pape, for instance). In the lush valleys around Grasse, roses, jasmine, mimosa and other flowers are cultivated massively, more today for the cut-flower markets than for the traditional Grasse perfume factories. Lemons and oranges are a speciality of the sheltered coast near Menton.

As for industry, the shipbuilding and repairing works at Marseille and Toulon are in decline. But to the west, around the lake of Berre and the new port of Fos, are big new oil refineries, steel and petrochemical works, and Europe's largest helicopter factory, while in the Rhône and Durance valleys are new hydroelectric works and nuclear power stations. Lastly, the Côte d'Azur has found a surprising new vocation as a zone for high technology and research, centering on the new "international scientific park" of Sophia-Antipolis, near Cannes.

Hill Villages of Provence

In Provence, as in some other parts of southern France, scores of old fortified villages are set on hilltops or terraced along mountainsides. Some are spectacularly sited, such as Èze, perched high above the Côte d'Azur. Some lie close to big towns yet seem a world away. Some, built of local stone, appear to be part of the rocks on which they sit, or are crowned by a half-ruined château. Some have alleys so narrow that cars cannot enter; inside is a maze of winding steps, vaulted archways, shady arcades and little squares where fountains play.

The villages were built on high ground for security, against pirates or medieval marauders. The peasants would till their fields by day, then sleep within the ramparts. Only in the more secure 19th century did they move to live in the valleys.

With the rural exodus of recent decades, many villages were threatened with abandonment, and some remote ones today are derelict ruins, eerie and silent. However, other modern trends have brought to many a new lease of life. Some have become busy tourist centers, their houses neatly restored, their alleys lined with bistros and boutiques. Hundreds of others have been taken over by the postwar fashion among middle-class city dwellers for buying a holiday or retirement home in the country. As haunts of the Parisian intelligentsia, they have become quite stylish – an artificial trend, but better than letting them die.

Right An alley in Èze, an old village giddily perched on a rocky outcrop, 400m almost sheer above the sea near Monaco.

Above An old fountain in the main street of St-Paul-de-Vence, a famous hill village near Nice. Its 16th-century ramparts bear witness to the days when it was a French frontier post facing rival Savoy across the Var valley. Now full of tourist boutiques, between the wars it was an artists' colony.

The beautiful gallery of the Fondation Maeght, designed by J.L. Sert, contains works by Chagall, Kandinsky, Miró and others, while the little Colombe d'Or hotel displays works by Picasso, Utrillo and Braque, who were friends of the owner.

Left Only 19km from the bustle of Nice, yet utterly remote on a rocky spur in a deep winding valley, medieval Peillon retains its visual character, even if most of its inhabitants are now Nice commuters, not true locals.

Below Tourette-sur-Loup is a handsome old fortified village on a hill above the Loup valley west of Vence. It remains a lively center of artists and craftworkers, whose studio-boutiques line its circular main street. They sell puppets, woven cloths, fabrics, metal jewelry and much else. Behind the altar in the 15th-century church is a curiosity: a 1st-century pagan Gallo-Roman shrine, with an inscription to the god Mercury.

DOM-TOMS

DOM-TOMs
The Départements d'Outre-Mer (DOMs), integrally part of France, include three in the Caribbean area (Guadeloupe, Martinique and French Guiana) and one in the Indian Ocean (Réunion). The Territoires d'Outre-Mer (TOMs) are mainly in the Pacific (French Polynesia).

Right Pleasure yachts at a holiday resort in Guadeloupe. Tourism, especially from North America, has become an important industry here and in Martinique. As well as the climate, sandy beaches and exotic vegetation, these French-influenced islands also offer a far better cuisine than in the English- speaking Caribbean.

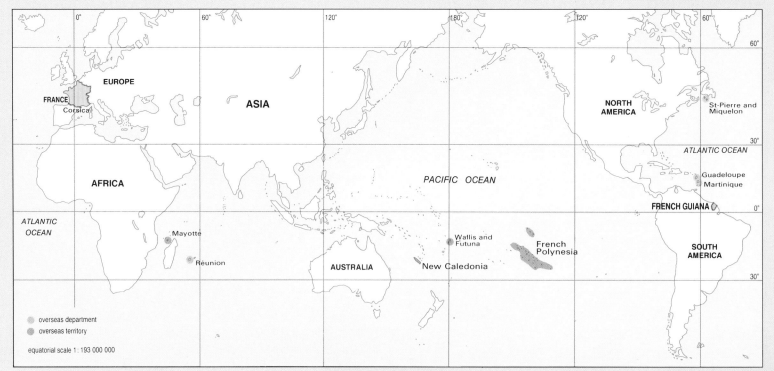

During the 1950s and 1960s France gave full independence to its vast colonial possessions in Africa and Indochina. But it has kept some smaller places, nearly all islands, by integrating them into the Republic, with the support of their populations. These are the DOM-TOMs. The term is an acronym made up of two sets of initials. The Départements d'Outre-Mer (DOMs) mostly in the Caribbean, were made fully part of France in 1946, and their inhabitants full French citizens, who elected representatives to the parliament in Paris, and enjoyed the same local self-government as in France. The Territoires d'Outre-Mer (TOMs), mostly in the Pacific, have much local autonomy and also elect deputies and senators to Paris, but are not so completely integrated. Some other small islands have a somewhat different status.

The Caribbean DOMs (Guadeloupe, Martinique, and French Guiana on the mainland) were colonized in the 17th century by the French, who imported African slaves to work the plantations. Today small separatist movements exist, but most people are content to remain part of France, if only because of the huge economic advantages. France pours subsidies into these DOMs, whose people enjoy full French welfare benefits.

The principal TOM is French Polynesia – five archipelagos whose main island is Tahiti. The French and others have long had a romantic view of these remote, exotic haunts. New Caledonia has a strong independence movement and this has led to unrest. In many ways, these DOM-TOMs are a liability for France – but they have some practical strategic uses, too. The Ariane space rockets are launched from Guiana; French nuclear weapons are tested on Mururoa atoll in the Pacific.

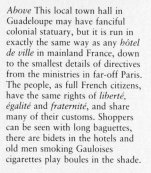

Far left A typical French colonial residence in Réunion, built around 1860. People carry umbrellas – usually brightly colored – against both the hot sun and sudden showers.

Left A wooden colonial residence in Martinique. French settlers to the island built up large fruit and sugarcane plantations, using the sugarcane to make rum. There are still some rich French farmers, and bananas and rum are still Martinique's main exports. Rum, known as *le p'tit punch*, is the staple local apéritif and costs almost nothing. Tourism is important to the economy.

Above Young men at an outdoor party in Réunion. After the island had been settled by the French in the 17th century, African slaves were imported to work on the coffee and sugar plantations. Slavery was abolished in 1848, but many inhabitants today are descended from slaves. The population is of mixed African, French and Asian descent, with much intermarriage. Many young people go to study or work in France, where they tend to be much better accepted than North African Muslims.

Above This local town hall in Guadeloupe may have fanciful colonial statuary, but it is run in exactly the same way as any *hôtel de ville* in mainland France, down to the smallest details of directives from the ministries in far-off Paris. The people, as full French citizens, have the same rights of *liberté*, *égalité* and *fraternité*, and share many of their customs. Shoppers can be seen with long baguettes, there are bidets in the hotels and old men smoking Gauloises cigarettes play boules in the shade.

CORSICA

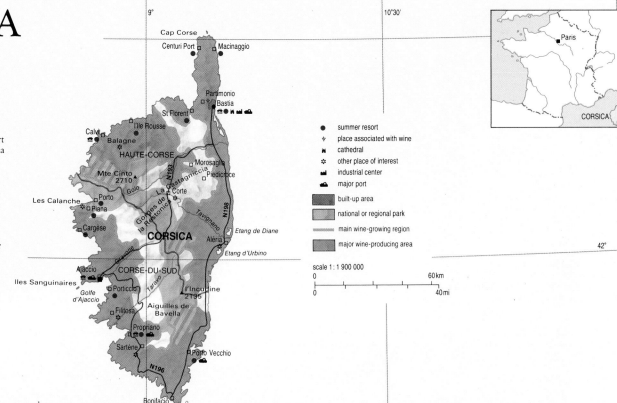

Corsica

Annexed by France in 1768, the island of Corsica is today fully part of the French Republic. Yet it has a stronger sense of its separateness than any other French region. Its people are inward-looking, passionate and sometimes violent. It is also the least populated of French regions. The mountains to the northwest and southeast form two main massifs, and before modern times much of the interior was virtually impassable. Today there is little industry, and not much farming, but plenty of tourism. Bonifacio, Sartène and Corte are the most interesting old towns.

Population: 246,000; area: 8,600sq sq; capital: Ajaccio pop. 55,000. Other main town Bastia pop. 45,000.

A rugged mountain island of great scenic beauty, Corsica remains thinly populated and remarkably unspoilt. Much of the east coast is flat and straight; but along the west coast, sandy bays and coves alternate with sheer cliffs, and with wooded headlands topped by ancient Genoese forts. The wild interior has forests of chestnuts, oak and laricio pine, upland sheep-pastures, gorges with rushing torrents, prickly pear and eucalyptus on the warmer slopes; and everywhere is the rough bush country known as *maquis*, a riot of wild flowers and scented herbs in spring, but parched in summer when fires are frequent.

Among the island's numerous invaders were the ancient Greeks and Romans, who left traces of a town at Aléria, on the east coast; the Pisans, who came in the 11th century and built chapels some of which survive, and the Genoese, who expelled the Pisans and who ruled until 1755. Then, after a popular uprising, Corsica knew 14 brief years of independence, under Pascal Paoli, today revered as its national hero. A better-known Corsican, Napoleon Bonaparte, born in 1769 at Ajaccio, fought for France against his own homeland and so is not too popular locally.

Although Corsicans do not feel French, few of them want outright independence from France; most would settle for autonomy. However, the extremist Liberation Front continues its bomb attacks, directed mainly against "foreign" (i.e. French) investment. The Corsicans are a proud people, with fierce clan loyalties and implacable codes of personal honor, whose violation can lead to violence. The bloody *vendetta* (the word is Corsican) is less common than it used to be but old family feuds still continue across generations. There is still much violence, robbery and gangsterism.

Many Corsicans are concerned that the island should not be ruined by massive development, like so much of the Mediterranean and so they have vetoed many new tourist projects. Therefore, Corsica remains scenically very unspoilt, and modern hotels are few. Apart from tourism, the staple activities are wine

and citrus fruit production. The full-bodied red wines such as Patrimonio go well with the rough but tasty local dishes, for example, bean soup, stuffed piglet, goat stew and wild boar.

Ajaccio and Bastia, both finely situated but dusty and graceless, are the only towns of any size. Calvi is the leading resort, followed by Porticcio and Porto Vecchio; the most striking scenery is around Porto and on the Cap Corse peninsula. The fascinating old port of Bonifacio is theatrically located on a high limestone cliff. Sartène and Corte, the island's ancient capital, are dignified but austere inland towns, prime centers of Corsican tradition.

Above Built by the Genoese in the late 15th century, the massive citadel at Calvi crowns a little town that is now Corsica's major seaside resort, with a long sandy beach that curves round a lovely bay. In 1794 the citadel was besieged and captured by the British, after a bombardment during which Lord Nelson, then a captain, lost his right eye. A walk round the ramparts offers impressive views. The hinterland, the Balagne country, has lush orchards and unspoilt old villages.

BIBLIOGRAPHY

Before the Franks and general history
P. Ariès et al., (eds), *History of Private Life*, 4 vols, London, 1987–90.
M. Bloch, *French Rural History: an Essay on its Basic Characteristics*, London, 1966.
F. Braudel, *The Identity of France,* 2 vols, London, 1988, 1990.
F. Braudel and E. Labrousse (eds), *Histoire économique et sociale de la France*, 4 vols, Paris, 1970–82.
J.L. Brunaux, *The Celtic Gauls: Gods, Rites and Sanctuaries*, London, 1988.
R. Cobb, *A Second Identity: an Essay on France and French History*, Oxford, 1969.
R. Dion, *Le Paysage de la vigne*, Paris, 1990.
J.F. Drinkwater, *Roman Gaul: the Three Provinces 588 BC – AD 260*, Beckenham, 1983.
G. Duby (ed), *Histoire de la France*, 3 vols, Paris, 1982.
G. Duby (ed), *Histoire de la France urbaine*, 5 vols, Paris, 1978–85.
G. Duby and A. Wallon (eds), *Histoire de la France rurale*, 4 vols, Paris, 1975–7.
P. Goubert, *The Course of French History*, Oxford, 1991.
J. Guilaine, *La France d'avant la France: du néolithique à l'âge du fer*, Paris, 1980.
H. Le Bras and E. Todd, *The Explanation of Ideology: Family Structure and Social Systems*, London, 1985.
S. Piggott, G. Daniel and C. McBurnet (eds), *France before the Romans*, London, 1978.
J.R. Pitte, *Histoire de paysage français*, 2 vols, Paris, 1983.
X. de Planhol, *Géographie historique de la France*, Paris, 1988.
A.L.F. Rivet, *Gallia Narbonensis*, Paris, 1988.
N.K. Sandars, *Bronze Age Cultures in France*, Cambridge, UK, 1957.
C. Scarre (ed), *Ancient France. Neolithic Societies and Their Landscapes, 6000–200 BC*, Edinburgh, 1983.
R. Van Dam, *Leadership and Community in Late Antique Gaul*, Berkeley, California, and London, 1985.
E.M. Wightman, *Gallia Belgica*, London, 1985.

The Dark Ages and medieval period
D. Bates, *Normandy before 1066*, London, 1982.
M. Bloch, *Feudal Society*, 2 vols, London, 1965.
D. Bullough, *The Age of Charlemagne*, London, 1965.
P. Contamine, *War in the Middle Ages*, London, 1984.
P. Dixon, *Barbarian Europe*, Oxford, 1976.
G. Duby, *The Chivalrous Society*, London, 1977.
G. Duby, *Rural Economy and Country Life in the Medieval West*, London, 1968.
J. Dunbabin, *France in the Making, 843–1180*, Oxford, 1985.
G. Fourquin, *Lordship and Feudalism in the Middle Ages*, London, 1976.
P.J. Geary, *Before France and Germany: The Creation and Transformation of the Merovingian World*, Oxford, 1982.
E.M. Hallam, *Capetian France, 987–1328*, London, 1980.
E. James, *The Franks*, Oxford, 1988.
E. James, *The Origins of France: from Clovis to the Capetians, 500–1000*, Oxford, 1982.
E. Le Roy Ladurie, *Montaillou*, Paris, 1978.
J. Sumption, *The Albigensian Crusade*, London, 1978.
J.M. Wallace-Hadrill, *The Barbarian West, 300–1000*, London, 1962.

The early modern period
W.J. Beik, *Absolutism and Society in Seventeenth-Century France*, Cambridge, UK, 1985.
P. Benedict (ed), *Cities and Social Change in Early Modern France*, London, 1989.
R. Bonney, *Society and Government in France under Richelieu and Mazarin, 1624–61*, London, 1988.
R. Briggs, *Early Modern France*, Oxford, 1977.
K. Cameron (ed), *From Valois to Bourbon: Dynasty, State and Society in Early Modern France*, Exeter, 1989.
P. Goubert, *The Ancien Régime. French Society, 1600–1750*, London, 1974.
M. Greengrass, *France in the Age of Henri IV*, London, 1984.
N. Hampson, *The Enlightenment*, London, 1990.
R.J. Knecht, *Francis I*, Cambridge, UK, 1982.

E. Le Roy Ladurie, *The French Peasantry, 1450–1660*, Aldershot, 1987.
J. McManners, *Death and the Enlightenment*, Oxford, 1981.
R. Mettam, *Government and Society in Louis XIV's France*, London, 1977.
D. Roche, *The People of Paris: an Essay in Popular Culture in the Eighteenth Century*, Leamington Spa, 1986.

From the French Revolution to 1945
J.P. Azéma, *From Munich to the Liberation, 1938–44*, Cambridge, UK, 1984.
K. Baker, C. Lucas and F. Furet (eds), *The French Revolution and the Creation of Modern Political Culture*, 3 vols, Oxford, 1988–90.
J. Becker, *The Great War and the French People*, Leamington Spa, 1985.
P. Bernard and H. Dubief, *The Decline of the Third Republic, 1914–38*, Cambridge, UK, 1985.
A. Cobban, *A History of Modern France*, 3 vols, London, 1990.
W. Doyle, *The Oxford History of the French Revolution*, Oxford, 1989.
G. Dupeux, *French Society, 1789–1970*, London, 1976.
C. Jones, *The Longman Companion to the French Revolution*, London, 1988.
R. Kedward, *Occupied France: Collaboration and Resistance, 1940–4*, London, 1985.
M. Larkin, *France since the Popular Front*, London, 1988.
R. Magraw, *France, 1815–1914. The Bourgeois Century*, London, 1983.
J. McMillan, *Dreyfus to de Gaulle*, London, 1985.
A. Plessis, *The Rise and Fall of the Second Empire, 1852–71*, Cambridge, UK, 1985.
R. Price, *A Social History of Nineteenth-Century France*, London, 1987.
R. Price, *The French Second Republic. A Social History*, London, 1972.
D. Sutherland, *France, 1789–1815: Revolution and Counterrevolution*, London, 1985.
D. Thompson, *Democracy in France since 1870*, Oxford, 1969.
J. Tulard, *Napoleon. The Myth of the Saviour*, London, 1984.
E. Weber, *France, fin de siècle*, Cambridge, Mass., London, 1986.
E. Weber, *Peasants into Frenchmen: The Modernization of Rural France, 1870–1914*, Oxford, 1977.
T. Zeldin, *France 1848–1945*, 2 vols, Oxford, 1973, 1977.

From 1945 to the present
P. Alexandre, *Le Duel de Gaulle–Pompidou*, Paris, 1970.
P. Favier and M. Martin-Roland, *La Décennie Mitterand, vol 1, Les Ruptures*, Paris, 1990.
J.R. Frears, *France under the Giscard Presidency*, London, 1981.
F. Giles, *The Locust Years: the Story of the Fourth French Republic*, London, 1991.
R.W. Johnson, *The Long March of the French Left*, London, 1981.
S. July, *Les Années Mitterrand*, Paris, 1986.
H. Luthy, *The State of France*, London, 1953.
J. Monnet, *Memoirs*, London, 1978.
P. Seale and M. McConville, *French Revolution 1968*, London, 1968.
A. Touraine, *The May Movement: Revolt and Reform*, New York, 1971.
P. Viannson-Ponte, *Histoire de la République Gaullienne*, 2 vols, Paris, 1970–1.
P. Williams and M. Harrison, *De Gaulle's Republic*, Harlow, 1960.

Society and general
J. Ardagh, *France Today*, London, 1988.
S. de Beauvoir, *The Second Sex*, London, 1953.
M. Bernard, *Sarcellopolis*, Paris, 1964.
R. Bernstein, *Fragile Glory: a Portrait of France and the French*, New York, 1991.
B. Cathelat, *Les Styles de vie des Français, 1978–98*, Paris, 1977.
D.G. Charlton (ed), *France: A Companion to French*

Studies, London, 1979.
F. de Closets, *Toujours plus!*, Paris, 1982.
M. Crozier, *Etat modeste, Etat moderne*, Paris, 1987.
M. Crozier, *On ne change pas la société par décret*, Paris, 1979.
M. Crozier, *The Bureaucratic Phenomenon*, London, 1964.
J.B. Duroselle, F. Goguel, S. Hoffmann *et al.*, *France, Change and Tradition*, Cambridge, Mass., 1963.
Etiemble, *Parlez-vous Franglais?*, Paris, 1964.
M. Gallant, *The Affair of Gabrielle Russier*, New York, 1971.
M. Gregoire, *Le Metier de femme*, Paris, 1965.
J.-A. Kosciusko-Morizet, *La "Mafia" polytechicienne*, Paris, 1973.
D. Leger and B. Hervieu, *Le Retour a la nature*, Paris, 1979.
A. Minc, *La Machine égalitaire*, Paris, 1987.
A. Peyrefitte, *Le Mal français*, Paris, 1976.
P. Rambali, *French Blues*, London, 1989.
A. Rouède, *Le Lycée impossible*, Paris, 1967.
A. Sampson, *The New Europeans*, Sevenoaks, 1968.
P. Simon, *Rapport sur le comportement sexuel des Français*, Paris, 1972.
C. Sinclair-Stevenson, *That Sweet Enemy*, London, 1987.
P. Thody and H. Evans, *Faux Amis and Key Words*, London, 1985.
G. Vincent, *Les Français, 1946–75*, Paris, 1977.
F. de Virieu, *La Fin d'une agriculture*, Paris, 1967.
G. Wright, *Rural Revolution in France*, Oxford, 1964.
V. Wright, *Conflict and Consensus in France*, London, 1979.
T. Zeldin, *The French*, London, 1983.

Cultural and intellectual life
R. Barthes, *Critique et vérite*, Paris, 1966.
A. Cohen-Solal, *Sartre, a Life*, London, 1987.
R. Debray, *Le Pouvoir intellectuel en France*, Paris, 1979.
M. Foucault, *Les Mots et les choses*, Paris, 1966.
A. Glucksmann, *Les Maîtres penseurs*, Paris, 1977.
R. Hayman, *Proust, a Biography*, London, 1990.
R. Hayman, *Writing Against: a Biography of Sartre*, London, 1986.
B.-H. Lévy, *La Barbarie a visage humain*, Paris, 1977.
P. Ory, J.-F. Sirinelli, *Les Intellectuels en France, de l'Affaire Dreyfus a nos jours*, Paris, 1986.
G. Painter, *Marcel Proust*, London, 1983.

The regions
J. Ardagh, *Provence, Languedoc and Cote d'Azur*, London, 1990.
J. Ardagh, *Writers' France*, London, 1989.
J. Ardagh (ed), *The Collins Guide to France*, London, 1985.
J. Ardagh, *Rural France*, London, 1983.
P. Frappat, *Grenoble, le mythe blesse*, Paris, 1979.
J.F. Gravier, *Paris et le désert français*, Paris, 1972.
G. Greene, *J'Accuse*, London, 1982.
R. Grizell, *South-West France*, London, 1990.
P.-J. Hélias, *Le Cheval d'orqueil*, Paris, 1975.
P. Mayle, *Toujours Provence*, London, 1991.
P. Mayle, *A Year in Provence*, London, 1989.
V. Menkes-Ivry, *Alsace*, London, 1991.
P. Mérindol, *Lyon, le sang et l'argent*, Paris, 1978.
Michelin Green Guides to France, Paris, London, New York.
E. Morin, *Plodémet*, London, 1971.
L. Wylie, *Village in the Vaucluse*, London, 1961.

GLOSSARY

Académie Française Founded in the 17th century, France's leading and very prestigious literary academy. It's 40 self-electing members are mostly writers, but include some scientists, diplomats, clerics, etc. Women are rarely admitted.

Action Française A right-wing, nationalist and anti-Semitic political group, which was founded in 1899 and survived until 1944. It ran a newspaper of the same name, edited by the writer Charles Maurras.

Albigensian heresy A form of catharist heresy and Manicheanism (qv) spread, apparently from Bulgaria, into southern France between 1145 and 1155. Particularly strong in the area around Albi (hence the name), the heresy spread throughout the feudal county of Toulouse and beyond. Pope Innocent VIII launched a crusade against it in 1209, and Simon de Montfort led northern knights on cruel repressive campaigns. The "Albigens Crusade" ended in 1229, and the heresy's last stronghold at Montseġur fell in 1245.

Ancien Régime "Former" (rather than "Old") regime. The name given by the French Revolutionaries of 1789 to the absolutist régime they had just overthrown. The term covered social and economic arrangements (eg feudalism) as well as the political system of absolutism. The term is now generally used to describe the French system of government from the 16th century to 1789.

anticlericalism Opposition to organized religion had been known in the Middle Ages, but it was especially in the 18th century that it became intellectually respectable and socially widespread. It became a major political force in the French Revolution, when the Catholic church became over-identified with counter-revolution.

Ariane The name for a series of space rockets, launched in French Guiana in recent years by the European Space Agency, under French technical management.

armagnac A brandy (wine-based spirit) produced in the Gers department of southwest France, and rivaling cognac in quality.

autoroutes The French name for freeways (motorways). France has a network of some 7,000 km; most of them bear heavy toll charges.

baccalauréat The high school leaving examination, taken usually at age 18 or 19, which must be passed by those seeking university entrance, but equally guaranteeing them a university place.

baguette (literally, rod or stick) A long, thin loaf of crispy, French bread, made with white flour.

Bastille The massive fortress, built in the 14th century as part of Paris's city walls. Its storming by the Parisian crowd on 14 July 1789 has become part of the legend of the Revolution. The assailants captured it for military purposes, mainly to help defend the city against royal troops. It immediately, however, became a symbol of the overthrown Ancien Régime (qv) and was demolished forthwith.

belle époque, la (literally, beautiful era) The period, roughly 1880–1914, that in Paris was a relatively carefree age of artistic flowering and exuberant social sophistication.

bistro(t) Originally meaning a quick-service bar for cab-drivers (the word is Russian, meaning "quick"), it later came to denote any simple bar or café, and today has been extended to mean also a small atmospheric restaurant, often quite smart.

bocage A Norman word meaning pastoral countryside broken up into smallish fields lined with hedges or trees, of the kind found in northwest France.

"boite" (literally, box) A colloquial term for a nightclub.

"bon chic bon genre" ("BCBG") Almost untranslatable,

a modern colloquial term denoting members of moneyed, conventional upper class and upper middle class society, roughly the equivalent of "Preppy" or "Sloane Ranger".

bougnats Small traditional stores, mostly run by Auvergnats in Paris, selling coal and firewood and combined with a café. Few still exist.

bouillabaisse A pungent garlic-flavored fish stew, originating in the Marseille area. It is expensive, and often considered the queen of French classic dishes.

boules A variant of *pétanque* (qv).

bourgeoisie, grande, bonne, petite Terms denoting some of the complex strata of the French middle class. *Grande* are very grand and powerful, almost aristocratic; *bonne* are the "upper" or "middle" middle class (liberal professions, etc); *petite* are lower middle class (tradesmen, artisans, clerical workers, etc).

bourrée A country folk dance from Auvergne, and the music that goes with it.

calvados An apple-based alcoholic spirit, named after the Normandy department where it is mainly produced.

Canard Enchaîné, Le A Paris satirical weekly newspaper, with a great influence and reputation in political circles.

cassoulet A rich stew of white beans, pork sausages, preserved goose, etc, originating from the Toulouse area.

castellan Governor of a castle, or tenant holding it for an overlord. Castellans based in fortified, well-supplied castles were a thorn in the flesh of the centralizing medieval monarchy, since they could hold out a long time against seige.

Celtic Gauls The Celts were Indo-European peoples who inhabited Europe from the second millenium BC. These groupings had occupied present-day France, as well as parts of Belgium, western Germany and northern Italy, by the first millenium BC. From the second century BC, the Romans colonized this area, and named it "Gaul", hence the population became known as Celtic Gauls.

chanson (literally, song) A peculiarly French genre of poetic ballad, dating from the Middle Ages, made popular in modern times by singers such as Edith Piaf, Charles Trenet and Jaques Brel.

charcuterie Processed pork meat sold in the form of cold sausages, terrines, etc.

chasse, la Hunting of wild game, pheasants, rabbits, etc, which is very popular and usually practiced on foot with rifles.

civitas (plural *civitates*) A politico-geographical unit of administration in the Roman Empire. Many of the *civitates* of Gaul corresponded to pre-colonization tribal units, and they were accorded privileges and exemptions from taxes.

cognac The world's most distinguished brandy (wine-based spirit), made in and around the town of Cognac, in southwest France, from grapes grown in local vineyards.

"cohabitation" The term used to denote the period in 1986–8 when President Mitterrand, a Socialist, had no choice but to share power (ie "cohabit") with a Right-of-center Prime Minister, Jacques Chirac.

Comédie Française France's leading State theater company, founded in 1680.

Committee of Public Safety The emergency war cabinet, selected from among members of the Convention (qv), which ran the war effort from April 1793 to 1795. In its most heroic, yet terrible, phase in 1793–4, when dominated by Robespierre, it inaugurated the Terror (qv) which saved France from almost certain military defeat.

communes The basic unit of French local government, ranging in size from small villages to big cities such as Paris. There are some 36,500 *communes*, each with an elected council.

Concordat of 1801 The formal agreement on 16 July 1801 between First Consul Napoleon Bonaparte and Pope Pius VII. It permitted the unhindered reestablishment of the Catholic faith following the anticlerical (qv) extremes of the 1790s. Catholicism became the faith of the "majority of the French people" (not the state) and religious toleration was maintained. The Concordat was a powerful factor in stabilizing the Napoleonic regime.

Confédération Française Démocratique du Travail One of the two leading pro-Socialist, non-Communist trade unions in France.

Confédération Général du Travail The largest French trade union, allied to the Communist Party.

Convention The National Assembly, 1792–5, which was created on the overthrow of Louis XVI to establish a new, republican constitution. It was elected on the basis of universal male suffrage.

Cordeliers A radical political club in Paris, 1790–4. More democratic in membership and aims than the Jacobins (qv), it preached radical republicanism and social leveling. It derived its name from the monastery of the Fransiscans (known as Cordeliers) where it held its sessions.

courses des vaches Mock bull-fights using heifers; these are popular in the Landes and Basque regions of southwest France.

couture, la Sewing and dressmaking: the term *haute couture* means the world of fashion.

Crédit Lyonnais One of the largest French banks, founded in Lyon, but now based in Paris.

cru The term used to denote a particular production of wine.

cubism An influential trend in modern art, pioneered in Paris in the period 1907–14 by Picasso, Braque and others as a reaction against Impressionism (qv). It aimed to analyze forms in geometric terms or reorganize them in various contexts; color remained secondary to form.

cuisine bourgeoise The kind of classic French cooking practiced in many middle-price restaurants and middle-class homes.

cuisine paysanne A simple but robust and tasty style of cooking with peasant origins, found in many cheaper rural restaurants.

Declaration of the Rights of Man Decree of the National Assembly of 26 August 1789 laying down the basis of the new, liberal constitution. Rights of Man listed included: equality before the law, religious tolerance, freedom of expression and the press, fiscal equality, etc.

départements A unit of local government: metropolitan France is divided into 96 *départements*, which are grouped into 22 *régions*.

Directory The Republican regime that governed France between the dissolution of the Convention (qv) and the advent of Napoleon Bonaparte in 1799. By attempting to provide checks against a strong executive, it proved to be a weak regime whose history was punctuated by coups d'etat.

drugstore, le Borrowing an American name, but bearing little relation to its homonym, *le drugstore* is a modern brasserie/restaurant with multiple boutiques attached, all staying open very late. They are found widely in many larger townsand cities.

druids A learned, priestly class of Celtic Gaul (qv), known to exist from the 3rd century BC. They were suppressed under the Emperor Tiberius from AD 9 in favor of the imperial cult.

Ecole Nationale d'Administration France's prestigious postgraduate civil service college, set up in Paris in 1946. Its graduates occupy many key posts of power and influence.

Ecole Normale Supérieure A traditional elitist college in Paris, whose role is to educate future university and *lycée* (high school) teachers.

Edict of Nantes The royal proclamation of Henry IV, 13 April, 1598, allowing French Huguenots (qv) a degree of toleration, civil liberties and security. The Edict signaled the end of the Wars of Religion (qv), allowing France the chance to recover. Huguenots had their rights progressively eroded over the course of the 17th century, and on 18 October 1685, Louis XIV formally revoked the Edict, outlawing protestantism within France. Over 200,000 Huguenots fled France under the provisions of this measure.

Enlightenment Name given to the movement of ideas in the 18th century, characterized by a more questioning attitude toward revealed truth and a scientific approach to natural and social phenomena. It was embodied in the writings of the *philosophes* (philosophers) such as Voltaire, Montesquieu, Diderot and Rousseau. It was more than an intellectual movement, moreover, and had fundamental importance in art, literature, and music, and fostered a more rational, secularized, view of the world.

Entente Cordiale of 1904 Treaty of 8 April 1904 between England and France resolving a number of important colonial issues between the two powers, and providing the basis for later political and military cooperation. France's alliance with Russia in 1907 lined up the three so called "Entente powers" against Austria, Germany and Italy in the run-up to World War I.

Estates General France's national representative assembly before the French Revolution, composed of representatives of the clergy, ("First Estate"), the nobility ("Second Estate") and the remainder of the population ("Third Estate"). Originating in the 14th century, its last meeting was in 1789, when it was transformed into the National Assembly.

European Coal and Steel Community Set up in 1951 by France, Germany and some other countries, in order to coordinate their coal and steel industries, the ECSC was a precursor of the so-called "Common Market" (today the European Community).

existentialism A philosophical system, originating in Germany, that was espoused by Jean-Paul Sartre and others in the 1940s and 1950s and had much intellectual influence at that time.

"faire le pont" The phrase for taking a four-day weekend break, when a public holiday falls on a Tuesday or Friday.

fauvism An influential new style of painting developed by Henri Matisse and others in the period 1898–1910.

Figaro, Le A leading Paris daily newspaper, with mainly conservative views.

film d'auteur The concept, common in France, of cinema as personal creative expression: the director is "author" of a *film d'auteur*, as much as a novelist is of a novel.

Force Ouvriere One of the two leading non-Communist trade unions, which is fairly close to the Socialist Party.

franglais The vogue in post-war France for appropriating English and American words and expressions into French daily speech (and quite often using them incorrectly).

Franks Confederation of a number of formerly independent tribes (including the Salians and the Ripuarians) massed on the lower Rhine from the 3rd century AD. They harassed Roman Gaul for over one century before the Romans started to cooperate with

them, enlisting their support, for example, to repel Attila the Hun in 451. Clovis of the Salian Franks was the founder of the Merovingian dynasty from 481.

Free French *Forces françaises libres (FFL)* A force led by General de Gaulle who refused to accept Vichy France's capitulation to Germany and fought on after July 1940. At first only in exile, the Free French become more militarily ambitious as time went on and linked increasingly effectively with the *Forces Françaises de l'Interieur (FLL)* who led the resistance inside France.

Galéries Lafayette One of the largest and oldest of Paris department stores.

garrique Stony, hilly, shrub-covered country found near the Mediterranean coast, notably in Languedoc and Provence.

Gauls see Celts.

Girondins A parliamentary grouping in the National Assembly from 1791 to 1793, many of whose members were from the department of the Gironde – hence the name. The group came to represent a more federal and moderate system of government than the centralized, authoritarian regime advocated by their arch-opponents, the Jacobins (qv), who had them proscribed in mid 1793.

gite (literally, lodging) A term used today for farm buildings or rural cottages adapted for holiday rental purposes.

Grandes Ecoles A number of exclusive colleges that exist parallel to the university system, and whose diplomas tend to have much more value than an ordinary degree. *Ecole Polytechnique* is the most influential.

Grands Corps de l'Etat, les Comprised mainly of alumni of the elitist colleges, a group of influential State bodies (such as the Conseil d'Etat and Corps des Mines) that have a club-like role as exclusive reservoirs of top talent, as well as performing specific technical functions.

guillotine A method of execution by beheading originated by the Parisian surgeon Antoine Louis, but to which the Parisian physician and member of the National Assembly J.I. Guillotine gave his name. Despite its subsequent notoriety, the guillotine was viewed as a more egalitarian and more humane method of execution than those that had obtained under the Ancien Régime.

haute cuisine A refined, calorie-rich and expensive style of cooking developed mainly in the 19th century by great chefs such as Escoffier; today it has been pushed out of fashion by *nouvelle cuisine* (qv).

Huguenots Name of uncertain origin given to French Calvinists from the middle of the 16th century.

Humanité, l' The Paris daily newspaper of the Communist Party.

Immortel (literally, immortal) Popular name for a member of the Académie Française (qv).

Impressionists A highly innovative and influential group of French painters, notably Renoir, Monet and Pissarro, who emerged in Paris in the 1870s. They were linked by their common interest in capturing immediate visual impressions, with an emphasis on light and color.

Jacobins Members of the Jacobin clubs meeting throughout France in the 1790s. They derived their name from the fact that the Parisian club held its meetings in the former monastery of the Dominicans (known in Paris as "Jacobins"). At the height of the Terror (qv), the Jacobins stood for strong, centralized authority emanating from Paris.

"King's Evil" A name for scrofula – a tuberculous swelling of the lymph glands, for example, in the neck. From the late 13th century, the kings of England and France were both reputed to have the miraculous power

of curing scrofula by their touch which hence became known as the "King's Evil". This alleged power became an important ingredient in the theory and propaganda of divine right monarchy. Kings of England practiced the rite until 1714, the kings of France until 1830.

langue d'oc, langue d'oil Terms for the two main languages of medieval France, where the word "yes" was "oc" in the south and "oil" (today "oiu") in the north. The former, more commonly known as Occitan, gave its name to the province of Languedoc.

Left Bank *Rive Gauche* The left bank of the Seine (actually on the south side) in central Paris. It contains the main university and publishing districts, and the term is used to denote "intellectual" and "student" Paris, as opposed to the more commercial or bourgeois districts of the Right Bank.

légion d'honneur An order of merit founded by Napoleon. The decoration is awarded for military or civilian services, and is sometimes given to foreigners.

Libération A Paris daily newspaper, with radical views.

limes The military frontier of Roman Gaul, separating the Roman province from Germany. It became increasingly permeable from the 3rd century AD as Germanic tribes penetrated into Gaul.

lycée State-run high school (grammar school).

Maginot line System of defensive bunkers and fortifications built along the Franco-German frontier on the orders of War Minister André Maginot after 1931. The line did not, however, extend along the Franco-Belgian frontier, through which the German army entered France in 1940, thus completely outflanking troops along the Maginot line.

Maisons de la Culture A network of large multipurpose arts centers, built in some French cities in the 1960s, on the initiative of André Malraux, then de Gaulle's Minister of Culture.

maisons landaises Traditional low-roofed farmhouses and other rural dwellings, found in the Landes forest, southwest France.

Manicheanism A dualistic system of thought held by, for example, the Albigensians (qv) which maintained that the Devil was the creator of matter and was a kind of second God.

maquis A Corsican word for wild scrubland and woodland, which in 1940–4 was applied to those members of the armed Resistance in France itself who took to hiding in this rough country.

massif A broad upland area that is semi-mountainous, eg the Massif Central.

Minitel A home videotex service introduced into French homes and offices since 1984.

Monde, Le The most prestigious French daily paper, published in Paris each weekday afternoon.

Monnet Plan Instituted by Jean Monnet in 1946, a central planning agency with a series of five-year national plans, which has done much to promote French economic development, especially in the earlier post-war years. Moulin Rouge A cabaret and dance-hall in Montmartre, Paris, famous since the late 19th century for its cancan dancing. Toulouse-Lautrec was an *habitué*.

National Front (Front National) Extreme-right political party with strong racist overtones, which developed during the 1980s under the leadership of the demagogue Jean-Marie Le Pen.

naturalism A theory of fiction promoted by Emile Zola in the period 1865–95, which he sought to exemplify in his own novels. The theory emphasizes scientific observation of life, whether attractive or otherwise.

nouveau roman An avant-garde literary trend of the 1950s and 1960s, led by the novelist Alain Robbe-Grillet.

nouveaux philosophes A dominant trend in intellectual Paris since the late 1970s, led by a group of young writers in noisy rebellion against the Marxist ideology in which they had been brought up.

nouvelle cuisine A light, modern and inventive style of cooking, introduced in the 1970s by a few star French chefs such as Paul Bocuse; it has since become fashionable worldwide in expensive restaurants.

Nouvelle Droite A right-wing intellectual movement that was briefly fashionable in Paris in the late 1970s and early 1980s.

nouvelle vague The name given to the heterogeneous "new wave" of talented young film directors (Godard, Truffaut, Resnais and others) who rejuvenated the French cinema in the years after 1956 and promoted the *film d'auteur* (qv).

pagus See pays.

pardon A traditional Catholic outdoor festival special to Brittany.

Paris Commune The Revolutionary municipal council organized in Paris from March to May 1871. The Commune modeled itself on Paris's radical government of the Terror (qv) of 1792–4, attacked the national assembly's acceptance of peace with Germany following military defeat in the Franco-Prussian War, and called for radical transformation. The Commune was brutally crushed by the Third Republic, with over 20,000 deaths in street fighting and reprisals.

Paris-Match A Paris weekly magazine noted for its photojournalism.

pastis An aniseed-based alcoholic drink taken usually as an apéritif, and very popular in Provence, where it originated.

pâté de foie gras A delicacy made from the swollen livers of geese, specially force-fed.

pays A vague term denoting a "natural region" and its inhabitants, who share some sort of common identity, set of traditions and community of interests. The term derives from the latin *pagus* (plural *pagi*), which denoted such a region below the level of the more formal *civitas* (qv), the base unit of administration in Roman Gaul.

pelota A fast outdoor game very popular in the Basque country, not unlike a mixture of fives and squash.

pétanque Better known by the name of its variant, *boules*, a slow game played with metal balls on a rough outdoor pitch, and especially popular in Provence. The game of bowls developed from it.

pied noirs (literally, black feet) Nickname for former French settlers in Algeria, now nearly all repatriated to France.

Pompidou Center Large cultural center of striking modernistic design, opened in central Paris in 1987; more generally known as the Centre Beaubourg.

Popular Front The left-wing alliance between socialists and communists formed in opposition to the rise of right-wing ideologies and movements. The two parties formed an electoral pact in 1934 and this bore fruit in May 1936 when, with Communist support, Léon Blum became the first socialist prime minister and introduced an important social program. Blum fell in 1937 and, although he attempted to resuscitate a Popular Front government in 1938, he failed to surmount the formidable domestic and international problems facing France.

puy Hill of volcanic origin, either crater-shaped or spiky-shaped, found in the Massif Central.

Resistance Term most commonly applied to those inside France who fought the German occupiers in 1940–44.

Saint Bartholomew's Eve Massacre The slaughter of approximately 2,000 leading Huguenots (qv) in Paris on 24 August 1572. Allegedly aimed at forestalling a Huguenot coup d'etat, the massacre led to the death of numerous Huguenot dignitaries who were present in the capital for the marriage of the daughter of Regent Catherine de Medici to the Huguenot Henry de Navarre (the future Henry IV). The incident was the worst atrocity of the Wars of Religion (qv) and worsened interdenominational strife; it was echoed in a number of provincial cities.

sans culottes Literally those who were "without breeches" – that is individuals who wore workmen's trousers rather than outward signs of gentility. The term was used to describe the politically radical small property-owners and artisans active in Parisian politics and street militancy, especially during the Terror (qv).

Sarcelles The best-known of a number of new high-rise estates of cheap housing that were built hurriedly in the Paris region in the 1950s and 1960s, to meet the grave housing shortage.

SNCF Société Nationale des Chemins de Fer Français – the State-owned company that operates France's railroads.

Stavisky Affair Political and financial scandal in 1934 centering on political corruption, and involving the Russian Jewish businessman, Sergei Alexandre Stavisky and prominent Radical politicians. Anti-Semitic right-wing militants utilized the affair (including the mysterious death of Stavisky) to attack the parliamentary and democratic basis of the Third Republic, which was also tarnished in the eyes of the Left.

structuralism Not so much a philosophy as a new intellectual method that attracted much attention in French academic and literary milieux in the 1970s. Roland Barthes and Claude Lévi-Strauss were among its leading lights. It had some influence outside France too, but its impact has since waned.

"Sun King" The "Roi Soleil" (Louis XIV) who was associated with the emblem of the sun from his youth. It became a symbol of his power in royal propaganda and was a recurrent theme in the design and decoration of Versailles.

"systeme D, le" Colloquial term for the common French habit of solving problems by improvisation and finding ingenious short-cuts.

Terror The policy of draconian repression instituted in the war emergency of 1792–4, and directed by the Committee of Public Safety (qv). The Terror prevented France disintegrating under allied military attack, but at a high cost: 40,000 individuals were executed by guillotine or firing squad, and perhaps several hundreds of thousands more died in the bloody repression of counter-revolutionary insurrections, notably in western France.

théâtre du boulevard Common term for the middlebrow commercial theater in Paris, as opposed to the more serious State-subsidized or fringe theaters.

Three Estates See **Estates General**

Treaty of Verdun Treaty of 843 between three sons of Louis the Pious (and the grandsons of Charlemagne) which divided the Carolingian empire into three blocs, and was fundamental in the historical formation of both France and Germany. An eastern bloc (ruled by Louis the German) was separated from a western bloc (in the hands of Charles the Bald), by a strip of territory running from the North Sea to the Mediteranean (under Lothar).

"Trois Glorieuses" (les) (i) Name given to the three days of Parisian streetfighting on the 27–29th July 1830, which overthrew the Restoration monarchy of Charles X and led to the institution of the July Monarchy of Louis Philippe.
(ii) The name given to the three lavish banquets held in Burgundy in November, at the time of the annual wine auctions.

vendetta Corsican term for a bitter long-lasting feud between rival families: although less common and less lethal than they used to be, vendettas still exist on the island.

Vercingetorix Chief of the Arveni tribe who mobilized Gaulish resistance to Roman invasion in 52 BC. He was beseiged and captured by Julius Caesar at Alésia, taken to Rome for Caesar's triumph, and executed.

Vichy Provincial spa town where, following France's defeat by Germany in 1940 and the overthrow of the Third Republic, the collaborationist *Etat Français*, or Vichy regime was based until its own overthrow in 1944.

vie associative, la Current French term for the clubs, societies and associations of a local community; this form of social life is less developed in France than in English-speaking countries.

Wars of Religion The series of civil wars that wracked France between 1560 and 1598. Religious strife between Catholics and Huguenots (qv) often overlay important dynastic tensions and internal power politics between the high aristocracy. Henry IV's accession in 1589, followed by military successes down to 1594 and the introduction of the Edict of Nantes (qv) ended the disturbances.

LIST OF ILLUSTRATIONS

Abbreviations: t=top, tl=top left, tr=top right,
c=center, b=bottom etc.

BAL = Bridgeman Art Library, London, DF =
Documentation Français, Paris, DHG = Denis
Hughes-Gilbey, Alton, Hants, DP = Daniel Philippe,
Brussels, E = Explorer, Paris, J-LC = Jean-Loup
Charmet, Paris, M = Magnum, London and Paris, RH =
Robert Harding Picture Library, London, RMN =
Réunion des Musées Nationaux, Paris, RV =
Roger-Viollet Collection, Paris

Maps drafted by Euromap, Pangbourne; Lovell Johns,
Oxford; Alan Mais, Hornchurch.

Endpapers: Map of France from the *Atlas of Blaeu*,
Amsterdam, 1647.

GAZETTEER

An entry that is not in France includes its country name and a descriptive term if a physical feature, eg Sardinia (*isl*), (*Italy*). An entry followed by an asterisk indicates a small territorial unit, eg county, province or region.

Aachen (Aix), (*Germany*), 50°46′N 6°06′E, 88
Aballo *see* Avallon
Abbeville, 50°06′N 1°51′E, 48, 58, 184
Acadia*, 72
Adda (*r*), 15
Adige (*r*), 32
Adour (*r*), 14, 25, 204, 209
Agathe *see* Agde
Agde (Agathe), 43°19′N 3°29′E, 25
Agedincum *see* Sens
Agen (Aginnum), 44°12′N 0°38′E, 14, 25, 32, 37, 48, 165, 204
Agincourt, 50°28′N 2°08′E, 45
Aginnum *see* Agen
Aigoual, Mtgne de l′, 44°08′N 3°35′E, 211
Aigues-Mortes, 43°34′N 4°11E, 211
Aiguille, Mont, 44°50′N 5°30′E, 197
Aiguille du Midi (*mt*), 45°52′N 6°53′E, 197
Aiguilles de Bavella (*mts*), 41°47′N 9°10′E, 224
Aime (Axima), 45°33′N 6°40′E, 25
Ain (*r*), 192
Ain*, 165, 197
Aisne (*r*), 25, 85, 184, 189
Aisne*, 165, 184
Aix *see* Aachen
Aix-en-Provence (Aquae Sextiae), 43°31′N 5°27′E, 25, 32, 45, 48, 55, 100, 110, 217
Aix-les-Bains, 45°41′N 5°55′E, 197
Ajaccio, 41°55′N 8°43′E, 15, 63, 100, 102, 104, 165, 224
Alamannia*, 32
Alava*, 209
Alba (Alba Augusta), 44°56′N 4°32′E, 25
Alba *see* Apt
Alba Augusta *see* Alba
Albertville, 45°50′N 6°24′E, 102, 197
Albi, 43°56′N 2°08′E, 37, 45, 48, 51, 58, 165, 211
Albitimilium *see* Ventimiglia
Alderney (*isl*), (*UK*), 49°43′N 2°12′E, 14
Alençon, 48°25′N 0°05′E, 48, 55, 88, 165, 178
Aléria, 42°05′N 9°30′E, 224
Alès, 44°08′N 4°05′E, 51, 211
Alesia *see* Alise Ste Reine
Alise Ste Reine (Alesia), 47°33′N 4°30′E, 25, 192
Alléans, 47°26′N 2°37′E, 25
Allier (*r*), 14, 25, 100, 102, 104, 110, 121, 175, 200
Allier*, 165, 200
Alpe d'Huez, 45°05′N 6°05′E, 197
Alpes-de-Haute-Provence*, 165, 217
Alpes-Maritime*, 165, 217
Alps (*mts*), (*France/Switzerland*), 45°30′N 10°00′E, 12, 15
Alsace*, 55, 73, 85, 88, 165, 189
Altaich (*Germany*), 49°02′N 13°06′E, 32
Amboise, 47°25′N 1°01′E, 174
Amélie-les-Bains, 42°27′N 2°39′E, 211
Amiens (Samarobriva), 49°54′N 2°18′E, 25, 32, 45, 48, 55, 58, 73, 85, 88, 100, 104, 110, 165, 184
Amsterdam I, 37°55′S 77°40′E, 72
Ancenis, 47°23′N 1°10′W, 174
Ancona (*Italy*), 43°37′N 13°31′E, 88
Ancy-le Franc, 47°47′N 4°10′E, 192
Andematunnum *see* Langres
Anderitum *see* Javols
Andernach (Antunnacum), (*Germany*), 50°26′N 7°24′E, 25
Anduze, 44°03′N 3°59′E, 211
Aneto Peak (*mt*), (*Spain*), 42°37′N 0°40′E, 14
Angers (Iuliomagus), 47°29′N 0°32′W, 14, 25, 29, 32, 37, 45, 48, 51, 58, 63, 73, 88, 100, 102, 110, 165, 174
Angoulême (Iculisma), 45°40′N 0°10′E, 14, 25, 32, 48, 102, 165, 204
Aniane, 43°41′N 3°35′E, 32
Anjou*, 174
Annecy (Boutae), 45°54′N 6°07′E, 25, 48, 102, 165, 197
Antibes (Antipolis), 43°35′N 7°07′E, 25, 217
Antibes, Cap d′, 43°33′N 7°08′E, 217
Antipolis *see* Antibes
Antunnacum *see* Andernach
Antwerp (*Belgium*), 51°13′N 4°25′E, 45, 85
Anzin, 50°22′N 3°30′E, 184
Anzio (*Italy*), 41°27′N 12°38′E, 88
Aosta (Augusta Praetoria), (*Italy*), 45°43′N 7°19′E, 25
Apennines (*mts*), (*Italy*), 43°50′N 12°00′E, 15
Apt (Alba), 44°15′N 4°30′E, 25
Aquae *see* Baden-Baden
Aquae Convenarum *see* Bagnères-de-Bigorre
Aquae Mattiacae *see* Wiesbaden
Aquae Neri *see* Néris-les-Bains
Aquae Sextiae *see* Aix-en-Provence
Aquae Tarbellicae *see* Dax
Aquileia (*Italy*), 45°47′N 13°22′E, 32
Aquitaine*, 29, 32, 45, 165, 204
Arae Flaviae *see* Rottweil
Arausio *see* Orange
Arc, 47°02′N 5°06′E, 45
Arcachon, 44°40′N 1°11′W, 204
Arcole (*Italy*), 45°22′N 11°17′E, 66
Ardèche (*r*), 197
Ardèche*, 165, 197
Ardennes*, 165, 189
Areines, 47°54′N 1°16′E, 25
Arelate *see* Arles
Argens (*r*), 217
Argentan, 48°45′N 0°01′W, 88, 178
Argenteuil, 48°57′N 2°15′E, 181
Argentomagus *see* Argenton
Argenton (Argentomagus), 46°36′N 1°30′E, 25
Argentorate *see* Strasbourg
Argonne, Fôret d′, 49°10′N 5°00′E, 189
Argues, 49°57′N 1°10′E, 51
Arguin (*Mauritania*), 20°30′N 16°32′W, 72
Ariege (*r*), 211
Ariège*, 165, 211
Arles (Arelate), 43°41′N 4°38′E, 25, 32, 37, 45, 217
Arleuf, 47°03′N 4°01′E, 25
Arlon (Orolaunum), (*Belgium*), 49°41′N 5°49′E, 25, 29
Armagnac*, 45
Armorican Massif, 48°06′N 3°00′W, 14
Arnac-Pompadour, 45°24′N 1°28′E, 200
Arnay-le-Duc, 47°08′N 4°30′E, 51
Arnhem (*Netherlands*), 52°00′N 5°53′E, 88
Arnières, 49°00′N 1°07′E, 25
Arno (*r*), 15
Arras (Nemetacum), 50°17′N 2°46′E, 25, 32, 37, 45, 48, 63, 85, 165, 184
Arrats (*r*), 211
Arrée, Mt d′, 48°30′N 3°40′W, 170
Arromanches, 49°20′N 0°38′W, 178
Artois*, 45, 55
Arz (*r*), 170
Aspern (*Austria*), 48°36′N 16°35′E, 66
Assini (*Ivory Coast*), 5°08′N 3°30′W, 72
Attigny, 49°28′N 4°35′E, 32
Atuatuca *see* Tongeren
Aubagne, 43°17′N 5°35′E, 217
Aube (*r*), 189
Aube*, 165, 189
Aubenas, 44°37′N 4°24′E, 197
Aubigné, 47°41′N 0°16′E, 25
Aubusson, 45°58′N 2°10′E, 104, 200
Auch (Elimberris), 43°40′N 0°36′E, 25, 32, 37, 45, 55, 165, 210
Aude (*r*), 211
Aude*, 165, 211
Auerstädt (*Germany*), 51°16′N 11°30′E, 66
Auga *see* Eu
Augst (Augusta Rauricorum), (*Switzerland*), 47°32′N 7°44′E, 25
Augusta Praetoria *see* Aosta
Augusta Rauricorum *see* Augst
Augusta Taurinorum *see* Turin
Augusta Treverorum *see* Trier
Augusta Viromanduorum *see* Vermand
Augustobona *see* Troyes
Augustodunum *see* Autun
Augustodurum *see* Bayeux
Augustomagus *see* Senlis
Augustonemetum *see* Clermont-Ferrand
Augustoritum *see* Limoges
Aulnay-sous-Bois, 48°57′N 2°31′E, 181
Aulne (*r*), 170
Aurillac, 44°56′N 2°26′E, 58, 165, 200
Auron, 44°13′N 6°57′E, 217
Auschwitz (*Poland*), 50°02′N 19°11′E, 89
Austerlitz (*Czechoslovakia*), 49°10′N 16°53′E, 66
Austrasia*, 29, 32
Austrian Netherlands*, 63
Autessiodurum *see* Auxerre
Autricum *see* Chartres
Autun (Augustodunum), 46°58′N 4°18′E, 25, 32, 58, 192
Auvergne, Monts d′, 45°28′N 3°00′E, 200
Auvergne*, 45, 165, 200
Auvers-sur-Oise, 49°05′N 2°10′E, 181
Auxerre (Autessiodurum), 47°48′N 3°35′E, 25, 32, 45, 48, 58, 85, 165, 192
Avallon (Aballo), 47°30′N 3°54′E, 25, 192
Avaricum *see* Bourges
Aven Armand, 44°14′N 3°22′E, 211
Avenches (Aventicum), (*Switzerland*), 46°53′N 7°03′E, 25
Avennio *see* Avignon
Aventicum *see* Avenches
Aveyron (*r*), 211
Aveyron*, 165, 211
Avignon (Avennio), 43°56′N 4°48′E, 25, 37, 45, 48, 55, 58, 63, 73, 88, 100, 102, 110, 165, 217
Avignon and Comtat Venaissin*, 48, 63
Avranches (Legedia), 48°42′N 1°21′W, 25, 178
Ax-les-Thermes, 42°43′N 1°49′E, 211
Axima *see* Aime
Azay-le-Rideau, 47°16′N 0°28′E, 174

Baccarat, 48°27′N 6°45′E, 189
Bad Kreuznach (*Germany*), 49°51′N 7°52′E, 29
Baden-Baden (Aquae), (*Germany*), 48°45′N 8°15′E, 25
Baeterrae *see* Bèziers
Bagacum *see* Bavai
Bagnères-de-Bigorre (Aquae Convenarum), 43°04′N 0°09′E, 25, 210
Bagnères-de-Luchon, 42°48′N 0°35′E, 210
Bagnoles-de-l'Orne, 48°33′N 0°25′W, 178
Bagnols-sur-Cèze, 44°10′N 4°36′E, 211
Bailén (*Spain*), 38°06′N 3°46′W, 66
Bailleul, 50°44′N 2°44′E, 184
Baise (*r*), 204, 211
Balagne (*mts*), 42°35′N 8°50′E, 224
Ballon d'Alsace (*mt*), 47°49′N 6°52′E, 189
Bandol, 43°08′N 5°45′E, 217
Banyuls, 42°29′N 3°08′E, 211
Bar-le-Duc, 48°46′N 5°10′E, 165, 189
Barbizon, 48°26′N 2°36′E, 181
Barcelona (*Spain*), 41°25′N 2°10′E, 32, 66
Barcelonnette, 44°24′N 6°40′E, 55, 217
Barjols, 43°33′N 6°01′E, 217
Barr, 48°25′N 7°27′E, 189
Barrage de Tignes, 45°30′N 6°51′E, 197
Bas-Rhin*, 165, 189
Basle (*Switzerland*), 47°33′N 7°36′E, 58
Basque*, 204
Bassano (*Italy*), 45°46′N 11°44′E, 66
Basse-Navarre*, 209
Bastia, 42°41′N 9°26′E, 15, 55, 63, 102, 104, 165, 224
Bastogne (*Belgium*), 50°01′N 5°43′E, 88
Batavian Republic*, 63
Bautzen (*Germany*), 51°11′N 14°29′E, 66
Bavai (Bagacum), 50°12′N 3°36′E, 25
Bavaria*, 32
Bayeux (Augustodurum), 49°16′N 0°42′W, 25, 37, 178
Bayonne (Lapuridum), 43°30′N 1°28′W, 14, 25, 37, 45, 48, 55, 58, 63, 102, 204, 209
Bazas (Vasates), 44°26′N 0°12′W, 25, 45
Bearn*, 204
Beaucaire, 43°48′N 4°37′E, 211
Beauce*, 174
Beaugency, 47°47′N 1°38′E, 174
Beaujolais, Monts du, 46°12′N 4°15′E, 197
Beaumont Hamel Park, 50°06′N 2°34′E, 184
Beaune, 47°02′N 4°50′E, 192
Beauvais (Caesaromagus), 49°26′N 2°05′E, 25, 32, 37, 165, 184
Bec d'Ambès, 45°02′N 0°35′W, 204
Beg-Meil, 47°52′N 3°59′W, 170
Belfort, 47°38′N 6°52′E, 85, 165, 192
Belle Ile, 47°25′N 3°10′W, 14, 170
Benevento (*Italy*), 41°08′N 14°46′E, 33
Bénodet, 47°53′N 4°06′W, 170
Berchtesgaden (*Germany*), 47°38′N 13°00′E, 88
Berek-Plage, 50°24′N 1°34′E, 184
Bergen-Belsen (*Germany*), 52°40′N 9°57′E, 88
Bergerac, 44°50′N 0°29′E, 45, 204
Berlin (*Germany*), 52°32′N 13°25′E, 88
Bern (*Switzerland*), 46°57′N 7°26′E, 15
Berre, 43°28′N 5°10′E, 217
Berry*, 45, 174
Besançon (Besontio), 47°14′N 6°02′E, 25, 29, 32, 45, 48, 55, 58, 73, 100, 102, 110, 165, 192
Besontio *see* Besançon
Béthune, 50°32′N 2°38′E, 18, 184
Beuvray (Bibracte), 46°55′N 4°06′E, 25
Beynac-et-Cazenac, 44°51′N 1°08′E, 204
Béziers (Baeterrae), 43°21′N 3°13′E, 25, 37, 102, 211
Biarritz, 43°29′N 1°33′W, 204, 209
Bibracte *see* Beuvray
Bilbao (*Spain*), 43°15′N 2°56′W, 209
Bingen (Bingium), (*Germany*), 49°58′N 7°55′E, 25
Bingium *see* Bingen
Biron, 44°40′N 0°40′E, 204
Blanc, Mont, (*France/Italy*), 45°50′N 6°52′E, 12, 15, 197
Blanzée, 49°11′N 6°09′E, 32
Blavet (*r*), 170
Blavia *see* Blaye
Blaye (Blavia), 45°08′N 0°40′W, 25
Blois, 47°36′N 1°20′E, 45, 48, 165, 174
Bobbio (*Italy*), 44°46′N 9°23′E, 32
Bobigny, 48°55′N 2°27′E, 165, 181
Bohemia*, 32
Bois de Compierre, 47°05′N 3°42′E, 25
Bollène, 44°16′N 4°45′E, 217
Bologna (*Italy*), 44°30′N 11°20′E, 88
Bon de Guebwiller (Grand Ballon), (*mt*), 47°53′N 7°06′E, 189
Bonifacio, 41°23′N 9°10′E, 224
Bonn (Bonna), (*Germany*), 50°44′N 7°06′E, 25, 29
Bonna *see* Bonn
Bonnée, 47°55′N 2°32′E, 25
Borbetomagus *see* Worms
Bordeaux (Burdigala), 44°50′N 0°34′W, 14, 18, 25, 29, 32, 37, 45, 48, 51, 55, 58, 63, 73, 88, 100, 102, 104, 110, 165, 204
Borodino (*USSR*), 55°01′N 37°19′E, 66
Bosnia*, 33
Bouches-du-Rhône*, 165, 217
Bougival, 48°52′N 2°09′E, 181
Boulogne (Gesoriacum), 50°43′N 1°37′E, 12, 25, 32, 58, 73, 85, 88, 102, 184
Boulogne-Billancourt, 48°50′N 2°14′E, 181
Bourbon*, 45
Bourbon-l'Archambault, 46°36′N 3°03′E, 200
Bourdeilles, 45°19′N 0°35′E, 204
Bourg-en-Bresse, 46°12′N 5°17′E, 58, 165, 197
Bourges (Avaricum), 47°05′N 2°23′E, 25, 29, 32, 37, 45, 48, 51, 55, 58, 63, 73, 100, 165, 174
Boutae *see* Annecy
Bouzy, 47°50′N 2°07′E, 25
Brabant*, 45
Bram, 43°14′N 2°07′E, 25
Brangues, 45°43′N 5°30′E, 197
Brantôme, 45°22′N 0°40′E, 204
Bremen (*Germany*), 53°05′N 8°48′E, 88
Bressuire (Segora), 46°50′N 0°29′W, 25
Brest, 48°23′N 4°30′W, 12, 14, 45, 55, 58, 73, 88, 100, 102, 104, 110, 170
Brétigny, 48°37′N 2°19′E, 45
Breton March*, 32
Briançon (Brigantio), 44°53′N 6°39′E, 25, 217
Briare (Brivodurum), 47°38′N 2°44′E, 25
Brie*, 181
Brigantio *see* Briançon
Brignoles, 43°25′N 6°03′E, 217
Brinon-sur-Sauldre, 47°34′N 2°15′E, 174
Briord, 45°32′N 5°42′E, 25
Brittany*, 29, 32, 45, 51, 165, 170
Brive-la-Galliarde, 45°09′N 1°32′E, 200
Brivodurum *see* Briare
Brou, 46°10′N 5°18′E, 197
Brouage, 45°51′N 1°04′W, 58
Bruges (*Belgium*), 51°13′N 3°14′E, 37, 45
Brumath, 48°44′N 7°43′E, 32
Brussels (*Belgium*), 50°50′N 4°21′E, 14, 37, 58, 85, 88
Buchenwald (*Germany*), 51°03′N 11°15′E, 88
Budapest (*Hungary*), 47°30′N 19°03′E, 89
Bugey, 45°50′N 5°20′E, 104
Burdigala *see* Bordeaux
Burgundy*, 29, 32, 45, 165, 192
Bussy-Rabutin, 47°34′N 4°32′E, 192
Buzenol (*Belgium*), 49°38′N 5°36′E, 25

Cabellio *see* Cavaillon
Cabourg, 49°17′N 0°07′W, 178
Cadarache, 43°40′N 5°44′E, 217
Cadayrac, 44°25′N 2°30′E, 25
Caen, 49°11′N 0°22′W, 37, 48, 55, 58, 63, 73, 88, 100, 104, 110, 165, 178
Caen-Ouistreham, 49°18′N 0°15′W, 102
Caesarodunum *see* Tours
Caesaromagus *see* Beauvais
Cahors (Divona), 44°28′N 0°26′E, 25, 32, 37, 45, 48, 165, 211
Calais, 50°57′N 1°52′E, 14, 45, 48, 55, 58, 73, 85, 88, 100, 102, 184
Calvados*, 165, 178
Calvi, 42°34′N 8°44′E, 224
Camaracum *see* Cambrai
Camargue (*marsh*), 43°30′N 4°37′E, 14, 217
Cambo-les-Bains, 43°22′N 1°24′W, 204
Cambrai (Camaracum), 50°10′N 3°14′E, 25, 32, 48, 85, 184
Camembert, 48°52′N 0°10′E, 178
Cancale, 48°41′N 1°51′W, 170
Canche (*r*), 184
Canet-Plage, 42°40′N 3°01′E, 211
Cannes, 43°33′N 6°59′E, 15, 18, 100, 217
Cantal*, 165, 200
Capbreton, 43°38′N 1°25′W, 204
Cape Breton I (*Canada*), 45°50′N 62°30′W, 72
Carantec, 48°40′N 3°55′W, 170
Carcaso *see* Carcassonne
Carcassonne (Carcaso), 43°13′N 2°21′E, 25, 37, 165, 211
Cargèse, 42°08′N 8°36′E, 224
Carinthia*, 32
Carnac, 47°35′N 3°05′W, 170
Carniola*, 32
Carnon, 43°32′N 3°58′E, 211
Carpentorate *see* Carpentras
Carpentras (Carpentorate), 44°03′N 5°03′E, 25, 217
Carteret, 49°22′N 1°48′W, 178
Casinomagus *see* Chassenon
Cassel (Castellum Nenapiorum), 50°48′N 2°29′E, 25, 184
Cassino (*Italy*), 43°21′N 13°26′E, 88
Cassis, 43°13′N 5°32′E, 217
Castellum Nenapiorum *see* Cassel
Castelnaudary, 43°18′N 1°57′E, 211
Castelnau-Montratier, 44°17′N 1°21′E, 25
Castel Roussillon (Ruscino), 42°36′N 2°44′E, 25
Castiglione (*Italy*), 45°23′N 10°29′E, 66
Castillon, 45°02′N 0°05′W, 45
Castillon-la-Bataille, 44°51′N 0°02′W, 204
Castres, 43°36′N 2°14′E, 51, 211
Catalonia*, 66
Cauterets, 42°53′N 0°06′W, 210
Cavaillon (Cabellio), 43°50′N 5°02′E, 25
Cavalaire, 43°10′N 6°35′E, 217
Cavillonum *see* Chalon-sur-Saône
Cemenelum *see* Cimiez
Cenabum *see* Orléans
Centre*, 165, 174
Centuri Port, 42°57′N 9°20′E, 224
Cère (*r*), 200
Cergy-Pontoise, 49°03′N 2°05′E, 165, 181
Cévennes (*mts*), 44°02′N 3°35′E, 14, 211
Chablis, 47°49′N 3°48′E, 192
Chagny, 46°55′N 4°45′E, 192
Chaine des Alpilles (*mts*), 43°45′N 5°00′E, 217
Châlons-sur-Marne (Durocatalauni), 48°58′N 4°22′E, 25, 32, 37, 48, 58, 85, 165, 189
Chalon-sur-Saône (Cavillonum), 46°47′N 4°51′E, 25, 45, 102, 192
Chambéry, 45°34′N 5°55′E, 48, 102, 110, 165, 197
Chambord, 47°37′N 1°32′E, 174
Chamonix, 45°55′N 6°52′E, 197
Champagne*, 45
Champagne-Ardenne*, 165, 189
Champellement, 47°19′N 3°47′E, 25
Champigneulles, 48°44′N 6°10′E, 189
Champs, 48°52′N 2°37′E, 181
Chamrousse, 45°08′N 5°53′E, 197
Chandernagore (*India*), 22°23′N 87°22′E, 72
Channel Islands, (*UK*), 49°27′N 2°51′W, 14
Chantilly, 49°12′N 2°28′E, 184
Chaos de Montpellier-le-Vieux (*mts*), 44°09′N 3°11′E, 211
Charente (*r*), 204
Charente*, 165, 204
Charente-Maritime*, 165, 204
Charleroi (*Belgium*), 50°25′N 4°27′E, 85
Charles-de-Gaulle, 48°59′N 2°34′E, 181
Charleville-Mézières, 49°46′N 4°43′E, 165, 189
Charolais*, 48, 55
Chartres (Autricum), 48°27′N 1°30′E, 25, 29, 32, 37, 48, 58, 165, 174
Chassenon (Casinomagus), 45°51′N 0°45′E, 25
Châteaubleau, 48°59′N 2°32′E, 25
Château-Chinon, 47°04′N 3°56′E, 192
Château de Bonaguil, 44°32′N 1°01′E, 211
Château de Ventadour, 45°25′N 2°05′E, 200
Chateau du Haut-Barr, 48°42′N 7°20′E, 189
Châteaudun, 48°04′N 1°20′E, 174
Château d'Yquem, 44°33′N 0°25′W, 204
Château Haut-Brion, 44°45′N 0°39′W, 204
Château Lafite, 45°14′N 0°48′W, 204
Château Latour, 45°10′N 0°44′W, 204
Château Margaux, 45°02′N 0°41′W, 204
Château Mouton Rothschild, 45°13′N 0°47′W, 204
Châteauneuf du Pape, 44°04′N 4°50′E, 217
Châteauroux, 46°49′N 1°41′E, 58, 165, 174
Château Thierry, 49°03′N 3°24′E, 85, 184
Chatelguyon, 45°55′N 3°04′E, 200

Lisbon (*Portugal*), 38°44'N 9°08'W, 66
Lisieux (Noviomagus), 49°09'N 0°14'E, 25, 32, 178
l'Isle Adam, 49°07'N 2°14'E, 181
Livarot, 49°01'N 0°10'E, 178
Livorno (*Italy*), 43°33'N 10°18'E, 88
Loches, 47°08'N 0°58'W, 174
Locmariaquier, 47°34'N 2°57'W, 25
Locronan, 48°06N 4°13'W, 170
Lodève (Luteva), 43°44'N 3°19'E, 25
Lodz (*Poland*), 51°49'N 19°28'E, 89
Loing (*r*), 181, 192
Loir (*r*), 174
Loire (*r*), 12, 14, 25, 29, 32, 37, 45, 48, 51, 55, 58, 63, 73, 85, 88, 100, 102, 104, 110, 121, 165, 174, 192, 200
Loire*, 165, 197
Loire-Atlantique*, 165, 174
Loiret*, 165, 174
Loir-et-Cher*, 165, 174
Lombardy*, 32
Lonato (*Italy*), 45°28'N 10°29'E, 66
London (*UK*), 51°30'N 0°10'W, 51
Longuer, 49°56'N 5°31'E, 32
Longwy, 49°32'N 5°46'E, 55, 85, 189
Lons-le-Saunier, 46°41'N 5°33'E, 165, 192
Loos, 50°31'N 2°52'E, 85
Lopodunum *see* Ladenburg
Lorient, 47°45'N 3°21'W, 12, 55, 58, 73, 88, 102, 170
Lorraine*, 55, 73, 85, 88, 165, 189
Lorsch (*Germany*), 49°39'N 8°35'E, 32
Lot (*r*), 14, 25, 37, 45, 55, 100, 102, 104, 110, 121, 165, 211
Lot*, 165, 211
Lot-et-Garonne*, 165, 204
Loudun, 47°01'N 0°05'E, 204
Louisiana*, 72
Lourdes, 43°06'N 0°02'W, 37, 210
Louviers, 49°13'N 1°11'E, 178
Lower Normandy*, 165, 178
Lozère*, 165, 211
Lübbecke (*Germany*), 52°19'N 8°37'E, 32
Lübeck (*Germany*), 53°52'N 10°40'E, 88
Luberon, Mtgne du, 43°49'N 5°26'E, 217
Lucca*, 63
Lugdunum *see* Lyon
Lugdunum Batavorum *see* Valkenburg
Lugdunum Convenarum *see* St Bertrand de Commingues
Lunéville, 48°35'N 6°30'E, 189
Lutetia *see* Paris
Luteva *see* Lodève
Luxembourg (*Luxembourg*), 49°37'N 6°08'E, 14, 85, 88
Luxeuil, 47°49'N 6°24E, 32, 192
Luz, 42°47'N 0°01'E, 58
Lyon (Lugdunum), 45°46'N 4°50'E, 14, 18, 25, 29, 32, 37, 45, 48, 51, 55, 58, 63, 73, 88, 100, 104, 110, 120, 165, 197
Lyons-la-Fôret, 49°24'N 1°28'E, 25

Maastricht (*Netherlands*), 50°51'N 5°42'E, 29, 32
Macinaggio, 42°56'N 9°26'E, 224
Mâcon, 46°18'N 4°50'E, 48, 58, 165, 192
Madagascar (*isl*), 25°00'S 45°00'E, 72
Madras (*India*), 13°05'N 80°18'E, 72
Madrid (*Spain*), 40°25'N 3°43'W, 66
Mahé (*India*), 11°41'N 75°31'E, 72
Main (*r*), 25
Maine*, 45
Maine-et-Loire*, 165, 174
Mainz (Moguntiacum), (*Germany*), 50°00'N 8°16'E, 25, 29, 32
Maison Laffitte, 48°56'N 2°13'E, 181
Malagar, 44°35'N 0°17'W, 204
Malmaison, 48°53'N 2°11'E, 181
Malo-les-Bains, 51°03'N 2°25'E, 184
Malta (*isl*), 35°20'N 16°20'E, 72
Malvae *see* Mauves
Manche*, 165, 178
Mandeure (Epomanduodurum), 47°27'N 6°48'E, 25
Manosque, 43°50'N 5°47'E, 217
Mantes, 48°59'N 1°43'E, 181
Marais Poitevin (*marsh*), 46°24'N 1°15'W, 174, 204
Marans, 45°13'N 5°43'E, 51
March of Friuli*, 33
Marengo (*Italy*), 44°12'N 7°52'E, 66
Marennes, 45°50'N 1°06'W, 12
Marie-Galante (*isl*), 15°57'N 61°54'W, 72
Marignane, 43°25'N 5°12'E, 217
Maritime Alps (*mts*), 44°10'N 7°30'E, 15
Marne (*r*), 12, 14, 25, 32, 45, 85, 88, 100, 102, 104, 110, 121, 165, 181, 184, 189
Marne*, 165, 189
Marne-la-Vallée, 48°51'N 2°39'E, 181
Maronne (*r*), 200
Marquesas Is, 9°50'S 139°57'W, 72
Marseille (Massilia), 43°18'N 5°22'E, 14, 18, 25, 32, 48, 58, 63, 73, 88, 100, 102, 104, 165, 217
Martigny (Octodurum), (*Switzerland*), 46°06'N 7°04'E, 25
Martigues, 43°24'N 5°03'E, 217
Martinique (*isl*), 15°00'N 61°50'W, 72, 222
Massif Central (*mts*), 45°20'N 3°00'E, 12, 14, 200
Massilia *see* Marseille
Matterhorn (*mt*), (*Switzerland*), 45°59'N 7°39'E, 15
Maubeuge, 50°17'N 3°58'E, 85, 184
Mauleon, 43°14'N 0°53'W, 209
Maures, Massif des, 43°20'N 6°20'E, 217
Mauritius (*isl*), 21°20'S 50°51'E, 72
Mauthausen (*Austria*), 48°15'N 14°31'E, 88
Mauves (Malvae), 47°13'N 1°32'W, 25
Mayenne (*r*), 14, 174, 178
Mayenne*, 165, 174
Mayotte (*isl*), 14°37'S 42°50'E, 72, 222
Meaux (Melororium Civitas), 48°58'N 2°54'E, 25, 45, 51, 181
Medan, 48°57'N 1°59'E, 181
Mediolanum *see* Evreux
Mediolanum *see* Milan
Mediolanum *see* Saintes
Megève, 45°51'N 6°37'E, 197
Meillant, 46°47'N 2°30'E, 175
Melle-sur-Béronne, 46°12'N 0°08'W, 51
Melororum Civitas *see* Meaux
Melun, 48°32'N 2°40'E, 45, 48, 85, 165, 181
Mende, 44°32'N 3°30'E, 165, 211
Menton, 43°47'N 7°30'E, 217
Messines (*Belgium*), 50°46'N 2°54'E, 85
Metz (Divodurum), 49°07'N 6°11'E, 25, 29, 32, 48, 55, 58, 63, 85, 88, 100, 104, 110, 165, 189
Metz*, 55
Meursault, 46°59'N 4°47'E, 192
Meurthe-et-Moselle*, 189
Meuse (*r*), 14, 25, 32, 45, 58, 85, 88, 189
Meuse*, 165, 189
Midi-Pyrenees*, 165, 211
Milan (Mediolanum), (*Italy*), 45°28'N 9°12'E, 25, 32, 88
Millau, 44°06'N 3°05'E, 51, 211
Milly, 46°22'N 4°40'E, 192
Mimizan-les-Bains, 44°13'N 1°18'W, 204
Minatiacum *see* Nizy
Minerve, 43°21'N 2°41'E, 211
Minorca (*isl*), (*Spain*), 39°48'N 4°49'E, 72
Mirande, 43°31'N 0°25'E, 210
Mittelbau-Dora (*Germany*), 51°35'N 11°01'E, 88
Moguntiacum *see* Mainz
Moignt, 34°20'N 3°58'E, 25
Moissac, 44°07'N 1°05'E, 37
Molitg-les-Bains, 42°39'N 2°23'E, 211
Molsheim, 48°33'N 7°30'N, 189
Monaco (*Monaco*), 43°46'N 7°23'E, 73
Mondovi (*Italy*), 44°23'N 7°49'E, 66
Monfalcone (*Italy*), 45°49'N 13°32'E, 88
Mons (*Belgium*), 50°28'N 3°58'E, 85
Monségur, 44°39'N 0°06'E, 51
Montaigne, 44°52'N 0°05'E, 204
Montaillou, 42°42'N 1°54'E, 211
Montauban, 44°01'N 1°20'E, 48, 51, 55, 63, 165, 211
Montbard, 47°38'N 4°20'E, 192
Montbéliard, 47°31'N 6°48'E, 48, 104, 192
Montbéliard*, 63
Montceau-les-Mines, 46°40'N 4°23'E, 192
Mont Dauphine, 44°40'N 6°38'E, 55
Mont-de-Marsan, 43°54'N 0°30'W, 165, 204
Monte Carlo (*Monaco*), 43°44'N 7°25'E, 217
Monte Cassino (*Italy*), 43°20'N 13°24'E, 32
Montélimar, 44°33'N 4°45'E, 197
Montenegro*, 66
Monte Rosa (*mt*), (*Switzerland*), 45°57'N 7°53'E, 15
Montfort-l'Amaury, 48°47'N 1°49'E, 181
Monthermé, 49°53'N 4°44'E, 189
Montjouer, 45°58'N 1°28'E, 25
Montlouis, 42°30'N 2°08'E, 55
Montluçon, 46°20'N 2°36'E, 104, 200
Montmorency, 48°59'N 2°19'E, 181
Montoir, 47°20'N 2°08'W, 174
Montpellier, 43°36'N 3°53'E, 14, 18, 37, 48, 55, 63, 100, 104, 110, 165, 211
Montreuil, 50°28'N 1°46'E, 184
Mont Royal, 48°29'N 7°25'E, 55
Mont-St-Michel, 48°38'N 1°30'W, 37, 178
Mont-Ste-Odile, 48°27'N 7°27'E, 189
Montségur, 42°51'N 1°49'E, 211
Mont Valérien, 48°54'N 2°15'E, 181
Morbihan*, 165, 170
Moret, 48°22'N 2°49'E, 181
Morhange, 48°56'N 6°38'E, 85
Morlaix, 48°35'N 3°50'W, 48, 170
Morosaglia, 42°26'N 9°18'E, 224
Morvan (*mts*), 47°12'N 4°00'E, 192
Morzine, 46°11'N 6°43'E, 197
Moscow (*USSR*), 55°45'N 37°42'E, 66
Moselle (*r*), 15, 25, 32, 45, 58, 85, 88, 189
Moselle*, 165, 189
Moulins, 46°34'N 3°20'E, 55, 165, 200
Moutiers (Darantasia), 45°29'N 6°32'E, 25
Mulhouse, 47°45'N 7°21'E, 15, 18, 85, 88, 100, 102, 104, 110, 189
Munich (*Germany*), 48°08'N 11°35'E, 88

Naix (Nasium), 48°43'N 5°16'E, 25
Namur (*Belgium*), 50°28'N 4°52'E, 85
Nancy, 48°42'N 6°12'E, 15, 18, 48, 55, 58, 63, 73, 85, 88, 100, 102, 104, 110, 165, 189
Nanterre, 48°53'N 2°13'E, 100, 165, 181
Nantes (Portus Namnetum), 47°14'N 1°35'W, 14, 18, 25, 32, 37, 48, 51, 55, 58, 63, 73, 88, 100, 102, 104, 110, 165, 174
Nantua, 46°09'N 5°36'E, 197
Naples (*Italy*), 40°50'N 14°15'E, 89
Naples*, 66
Narbo *see* Narbonne
Narbonne (Narbo), 43°11'N 3°00'E, 25, 29, 32, 37, 45, 48, 58, 211
Nasium *see* Naix
Natzweiler, 48°22'N 7°26'E, 88
Navarre*, 204, 209
Neckar (*r*), 25
Neerwinden (*Belgium*), 51°58'N 4°56'E, 63
Nemausus *see* Nîmes
Nemetacum *see* Arras
Nemours, 48°16'N 2°41'E, 181
Nérac, 44°08'N 0°21'E, 51
Néris-les-Bains (Aquae Neri), 46°18'N 2°38'E, 25
Neuchâtel (*Switzerland*), 46°59'N 6°55'E, 51
Neuengamme (*Germany*), 53°31'N 10°07'E, 88
Neuf Brisach, 48°01'N 7°33'E, 55
Neumagen (Noviomagus), (*Germany*), 49°51'N 6°55'E, 25
Neuss (Novaesium), (*Germany*), 51°12'N 6°42'E, 25
Neustria*, 29, 32
Neuve-Chapelle, 50°35'N 2°47'E, 85
Nevers, 47°00'N 3°09'E, 45, 48, 58, 165, 192
Nevers*, 45
New Caledonia (*isl*), 22°50'S 143°40'E, 73, 222
Newfoundland (*isl*), 49°20'N 56°40'W, 72
Nicaea *see* Nice
Nice (Nicaea), 43°42'N 7°16'E, 15, 18, 25, 55, 58, 63, 73, 100, 102, 104, 110, 165, 217
Nice*, 63, 73
Nièvre*, 165, 192
Nijmegen (Noviomagus), (*Netherlands*), 51°50'N 5°52'E, 25, 32
Nijon (Noviomagus), 48°03'N 5°31'E, 25
Nîmes (Nemausus), 43°50'N 4°21'E, 25, 48, 51, 58, 63, 73, 100, 165, 211
Niort, 46°19'N 0°27'W, 48, 58, 73, 165, 204
Nizampatam (*India*), 15°56'N 80°44'E, 72
Nizy (Minatiacum), 49°35'N 4°04'E, 25
Nogent, 48°19'N 0°50'E, 174
Nohant, 46°38'N 1°58'E, 174
Noire, Mtgne, 43°29'N 2°25'E, 211
Noirmoutier, 47°01'N 2°15'W, 174
Noirmoutier, Ile de, 47°00'N 2°15'W, 14, 174
Nord*, 165, 184
Nordalbingia*, 32
Nordgau*, 32
Nord-Pas-de-Calais*, 165, 184
Normandy*, 45
Northern Circars*, 72
Nôtre-Dame-de-Lorette, 50°26'N 2°43'E, 184
Novaesium *see* Neuss
Novempopulana*, 29
Novi (*Italy*), 44°46'N 8°47'E, 66
Noviodunum *see* Jublains
Noviodunum *see* Nyons
Noviodunum *see* Soissons
Noviomagus *see* Lisieux
Noviomagus *see* Neumagen
Noviomagus *see* Nijmegen
Noviomagus *see* Nijon
Noviomagus *see* Speyer
Noviorigum *see* Royan
Noyers-sur-Andelys (Nuceriae), 49°13'N 1°24'E, 25
Noyon, 49°35'N 3°00'E, 32
Nuceriae *see* Noyers-sur-Andelys
Nuits-St-Georges, 47°08'N 4°57'E, 192
Nuremberg (*Germany*), 49°27'N 11°05'E, 88
Nyons (Noviodunum), (*Switzerland*), 46°23'N 6°15'E, 25

Obernai, 48°28'N 7°30'E, 189
Octodurum *see* Martigny
Odeillo, 42°29'N 2°02'E, 211
Odet (*r*), 170
Ognon (*r*), 192
Oise (*r*), 14, 45, 85, 88, 181, 184
Oise*, 165, 184
Oléron, Ile d', 45°55'N 1°16'W, 14, 204
Oloron, 43°12'N 0°35'W, 51
Omaha Beach, 49°22'N 0°53'W, 88, 178
Oppenheim (*Germany*), 49°52'N 8°22'E, 88
Oradour-sur-Glane, 45°56'N 1°03'E, 200
Orange (Arausio), 44°08'N 4°48'E, 25, 48, 55, 63, 217
Orange*, 55
Orcival, 45°48'N 2°50'E, 200
Orhy, Pic d' (*mt*), 42°59'N 1°01'W, 204
Orléans (Cenabum), 47°54'N 1°54'E, 14, 18, 25, 32, 37, 45, 48, 51, 55, 58, 63, 73, 85, 88, 100, 110, 165, 174
Orly, 48°45'N 2°24'E, 181
Ornans, 47°07'N 6°08'E, 192
Orne (*r*), 178
Orne*, 165, 178
Orolaunum *see* Arlon
Orthez, 43°29'N 0°46'W, 48
Ortles (*mt*), (*Italy*), 46°31'N 10°33'E, 15
Ostend (*Belgium*), 51°13'N 2°55'E, 85
Ottoman Empire*, 66
Ouistreham, 49°16'N 0°15'W, 178
Oust (*r*), 170

Paderborn (*Germany*), 51°43'N 8°44'E, 32
Paimpol, 48°47'N 3°03'W, 170
Paimpont Forest, 48°05'N 2°15'W, 170
Palavas-les-Flots, 43°31'N 3°56'E, 211
Paluel, 49°48'N 0°46'E, 104
Pamiers, 43°07'N 1°36'E, 104, 211
Pamplona (*Spain*), 42°29'N 1°39'W, 209
Pannonia*, 33
Papal States*, 66
Paris (Lutetia), 48°52'N 2°20'E, 14, 16, 17, 18, 25, 29, 32, 37, 45, 48, 51, 55, 58, 63, 66, 73, 85, 88, 100, 102, 104, 110, 116, 165, 181
Paris*, 165, 181
Parma*, 63
Parnay-le-Monial, 46°27'N 4°07'E, 192
Parthenay, 46°39'N 0°14'W, 204
Parthenopean Republic*, 63
Partimonio, 42°43'N 9°22'E, 224
Pas-de-Calais*, 165, 184
Passchendaele (*Belgium*), 50°54'N 3°01'E, 85
Patay, 48°03'N 1°42'E, 45
Pau, 43°18'N 0°22'W, 14, 55, 100, 102, 110, 165, 204
Pavia (*Italy*), 45°12'N 9°09'E, 32
Pays d'Auge*, 178
Pays-de-la-Loire*, 165, 174
Perigord*, 204
Périgueux (Vesunna), 45°12'N 0°44'E, 14, 25, 32, 48, 165, 204
Pérouges, 45°55'N 5°15'E, 197
Perpignan, 42°42'N 2°54'E, 48, 55, 100, 110, 165, 211
Perros-Guirec, 48°49'N 3°27'W, 170
Petit-Mars, 47°23'N 1°27'W, 25
Petit Morin (*r*), 181
Petit Rhône (*r*), 211, 217
Pézenas, 43°28'N 3°25'E, 211
Phalsbourg, 48°47'N 7°16'E, 189
Piana, 42°14'N 8°39'E, 224
Picardy*, 45, 165, 184
Picquigny, 49°57'N 2°09'E, 45
Piedicroce, 42°22'N 9°22'E, 224
Piedmont*, 63
Pilat dune, 44°37'N 1°12'W, 204
Pilsen (*Czechoslovakia*), 49°45'N 13°25'E, 88
Piombino (*Italy*), 42°56'N 10°32'E, 63
Piombino*, 66
Pistae *see* Pîtres
Pîtres (Pistae), 47°39'N 1°11'E, 25
Plombières-les-Bains, 47°58'N 6°28'E, 189
Plozévet, 47°59'N 4°26'W, 170
Po (*r*), 15, 32, 88
Poissy, 48°56'N 2°02'E, 181
Poitiers (Limonum), 46°35'N 0°20'E, 14, 25, 29, 32, 37, 45, 48, 55, 58, 73, 100, 102, 110, 165, 204
Poitou*, 45, 204
Poitou-Charentes*, 165, 204
Poligny, 46°50'N 5°42'E, 192
Pomerol, 44°56'N 0°12'W, 204
Pondicherry (*India*), 11°59'N 79°50'E, 72
Pons, 45°35'N 0°32'W, 48
Pont-à-Mousson, 48°55'N 6°03'E, 189
Pontarlier, 46°55'N 6°24'E, 192
Pont Aven, 47°51'N 3°44'W, 170
Pont de Tancarville, 49°29'N 0°28'E, 178
Pont du Gard, 43°57'N 4°32'E, 211
Ponthiru, 48°54'N 4°32'E, 32
Pont-l'Evêque, 49°17'N 0°11'E, 178
Pontvallain, 47°45'N 0°11'E, 45
Port-Barcarès, 42°44'N 3°02'E, 211
Port-Camargue, 43°30'N 4°09'E, 211
Port-en-Bessin, 49°21'N 0°45'W, 12
Porticcio, 41°51'N 8°45'E, 224
Port-la-Nouvelle, 43°02'N 3°02'E, 102, 211
Port-Leucate, 42°49'N 3°02'E, 211
Porto, 42°17'N 8°42'E, 224
Porto Vecchio, 41°35'N 9°16'E, 224
Port St Louis, 43°23'N 4°48'E, 217
Port-Royal-des-Champs, 48°46'N 2°02'E, 181
Portus Namnetum *see* Nantes
Port Vendres, 42°31'N 3°06'E, 211
Pouldreuzic, 7°57'N 4°21'W, 170
Pouzauges, 46°47'N 0°51'W, 174
Pradus, 42°36'N 2°25'E, 211
Privas, 44°44'N 4°36'E, 165, 197
Propriano, 41°40'N 8°54'E, 224
Provence*, 29, 32, 45, 51
Provence-Alpes-Côte d'Azur*, 165, 217
Provins, 48°34'N 3°18'E, 48, 181
Prum (*Germany*), 50°12'N 6°25'E, 32
Prussia*, 66
Puy de Dôme (*mt*), 45°46'N 2°56'E, 12, 14, 200
Puy-de-Dôme*, 165, 200
Puy de Sancy (*mt*), 45°32'N 2°48'E, 12, 14, 200
Puy d'Issolu (Uxellodunum), 44°53'N 1°29'E, 25
Puy-du-Fou, 46°55'N 0°58'W, 174
Puy Mary (*mt*), 45°05'N 2°38'E, 200
Pyrenees (*mts*), (*France/Spain*), 42°56'N 0°12'E, 12, 14, 25, 204, 211
Pyrenees-Atlantiques*, 165, 204
Pyrenees-Orientales*, 165, 211

Quiberon, 47°29'N 3°07'W, 63, 170
Quierzy, 49°33'N 3°05'E, 32
Quimper, 48°01'N 4°06'W, 102, 165, 170

Raetia*, 32
Rambouillet, 48°39'N 1°50'E, 181
Rance (*r*), 170
Rauranum *see* Rom
Ravenna (*Italy*), 44°25'N 12°12'E, 32
Ravensbruck (*Germany*), 53°12'N 13°10'E, 88
Ré, Ile de, 46°10'N 1°26'W, 14, 204
Regensburg (*Germany*), 49°01'N 12°07'E, 32, 66
Rehme (*Germany*), 52°13'N 8°49'E, 32
Reichenau (*Germany*), 47°42'N 9°05'E, 32
Reims (Durocortorum), 49°15'N 4°02'E, 14, 25, 29, 32, 37, 45, 48, 58, 63, 73, 85, 88, 100, 110, 189
Reims, Mt de, 49°10'N 4°03'E, 189
Remagen (Rigomagus), (*Germany*), 50°34'N 7°14'E, 25, 88
Remiremont, 48°01'N 6°35'E, 32, 189
Rennes (Condate), 48°06'N 1°40'W, 14, 18, 25, 32, 45, 48, 58, 63, 73, 100, 102, 104, 110, 165, 170
Rethel, 49°31'N 4°22'E, 45, 189
Réunion (*isl*), 20°22'S 55°10'E, 72, 222
Rheinzabern (Tabernae), (*Germany*), 49°07'N 8°18'E, 25
Rhine (*r*), 12, 15, 25, 29, 32, 45, 48, 51, 58, 73, 85, 88, 100, 102, 110, 121
Rhône (r), 12, 14, 25, 29, 32, 37, 45, 48, 51, 55, 58, 63, 73, 88, 100, 102, 104, 110, 121, 165, 197, 211, 217
Rhône*, 165, 197
Rhône-Alpes*, 165, 197
Ribeauvillé, 48°12'N 7°20'E, 189
Ribemont (Ribodi Mons), 49°48'N 3°28'E, 25
Ribemont-sur-Ancre, 50°02'N 2°37'E, 25
Ribodi Mons *see* Ribemont
Richelieu, 47°01'N 0°20'E, 55
Rigomagus *see* Remagen
Riom, 45°54'N 3°07'E, 55
Riquewihr, 48°09'N 7°17'E, 189
Risle (*r*), 178
Rivoli (*Italy*), 45°04'N 7°31'E, 66
Roanne, 46°02'N 4°05'E, 48, 58, 104, 197
Rocamadour, 44°48'N 1°36'E, 211
Rochefort, 45°57'N 0°58'W, 55, 58, 204
Rodez (Segodunum), 44°21'N 2°34'E, 25, 32, 58, 165, 211
Rom (Rauranum), 46°18'N 0°06'E, 25
Romans, 45°03'N 5°03'E, 197
Rome (*Italy*), 41°53'N 12°30'E, 15, 32, 63, 88
Romilly, 47°58'N 1°14'E, 174
Romorantin-Lanthenay, 47°22'N 1°44'E, 174
Roncesvalles (*Spain*), 43°00'N 1°19'W, 32
Roosebeke (*Belgium*), 50°50'N 2°36'E, 45
Roquefort, 43°59'N 2°58'E, 211
Roscoff, 48°43'N 3°59'W, 170
Rotomagus *see* Rouen
Rottenburg (Sumelocenna), (*Germany*), 48°28'N 8°55'E, 25
Rottweil (Arae Flaviae), (*Germany*), 48°10'N 8°38'E, 25
Roubaix, 50°42'N 3°11'E, 184
Rouen (Rotomagus), 49°26'N 1°05'E, 14, 18, 25, 29, 32, 37, 45, 48, 51, 55, 58, 63, 73, 88, 100, 102, 104, 110, 165, 178
Rouffignac, 45°02'N 0°59'E, 204
Roussillon*, 55, 211
Royan (Noviorigum), 45°38'N 1°02'W, 25, 204
Royat, 45°45'N 3°03'E, 200
Royaumont Abbey, 49°10'N 2°24'E, 181
Rungis, 48°48'N 2°23'E, 181
Ruscino *see* Castel Roussillon
Ry, 49°24'N 1°24'E, 178

Saarwerden*, 63
Sables-d'Or, 48°39'N 2°24'W, 170
Saché, 47°15'N 0°30'E, 174
Sachsenhausen (*Germany*), 52°37'N 12°58'E, 88
St André-sur-Cailly, 49°26'N 1°28'E, 25
St Armand les-Eaux, 50°31'N 3°28'E, 184
St Avold, 49°06'N 6°43'E, 189
St Barthélemy (*isl*), 17°55'N 62°50'W, 72

INDEX

OCEANVS BRITANNICVS

Sorlinges

Tintagel cast · Pleymouth

Port laud · Nieuport · De So...

The landes end · Dartmouth

Lezard point · Start point

Alderney · Oderville · Sussaye · Cherborg · Capleny · Esterfal

Garnesey · S. Marten · Dielete · Bail · Valanques · Quarin · Berneville · Honsleur

I. Jarsey · Trinita · CONSTAN · ...ieux · ...S.L. · AUGE · Caen · Belem

S. Malo · M.S. Michel · Auranches · NORMAN · Alençon

Plampol · Roscou · S. Landeloy · Triguer · Pontrion · Lavolin · S. Brieux · Drian · Dol · Pleguuen · Plemate · LE · MAINE · Mans

P. Busel · Obruaz · Lion · Morlaix · Guingant · Moncentour · Jugon · Fougeres · Argentre

Brsal · Blancsablon · Lesneven · Peacoat · Quintin · Rohan · BRE · Vitre · Mayenne · Pontoron

Le four · Conquet · Libaarnee · Landernau · La Saille · TAIGNE · HAVLTE B. · Breal · Renes · S. Sulpice · Chemire · Pierre

Heysant · S. Matheu · Landevenet · Landevillian · Chenge · Novialle · La Guille · Ch. Giron · Rue · Chateaudun · Durtail · TOVRA

La Baza frede · S. Pol David · Asuen flu · Castleaulm · Brasser · Ceral · Mesac · Bellar · Craon · La Flèche · Tours

Fontenau · BASSE BRETAIGNE · Jecelin · S. Michiel · Baugy · Angiers · ANIOV

Audierne · Le Favoet · Granchamp P. Corbin · Roch Bernard · Cha Briant · Segre · Caude · ANIOV · IOV

Painmark · Quimpereuren · Gemene · Landerai · Chastelparret · Redon · Mesguer · Nantes · S. Fleurant · Chantenceaux · Vihiry · Ports

Pou(te) · Quimperlay · Blavet · Blanct · Lacot · Auzay · Villaine flu · Loire flu · Tessanges · Moutagne · Moncotour · Aigault · Chastellery

Chons · Lopezzian · Groye · Vannes · Prieres · La Maux · Crosie · Romoville · Bremi · Bour neuf · Montagu · Maudeurien · Chasteaumur · Tour Landri · Mirebeau · Calan

Belle Ille · Cant · Aberat · Peners · Armetier · Bonges · Pouzauge · Partenay · Poictiers

AQVI TANICVS

I. Nermenstier alis Keys · Beamont · Aprement · La Chataignera · Lussignan · POICTOV · Lussac · Vivone · Persac

Talmont S. Michiel · Roche sur Ion · Fontenay · Contye · S. Maxent · Pamprou · Chouhe · Sivray · Charo

Isle de Rez · S. Martin · Luçon · Seure flu · Niort · Chizay · PICTONES · Ruffec

S. Denis · Rochelle · Chateillon · Tanay boutonne · Maillezay · Dompierre · Reoffec

Isle d'Oleron · S. Andrien · Oleron · Cherante · Taillebourg · Matha · Champaigne · Angoules me · Rochefoucaut

La Tramblae · Nazare · XAN · S. Lan d'Angely · Pons · TOIN · Secoufac · Roche Beaucourt · S. Privat

Soubize · Bruage · Angoumois · GE · S. Aulaye · PER · Perigeux

Marennes · Soubson · Iumesan · Archac · Cognac · Chasteau nuf · Bourdeilla

OCEANVS

Guaronne flu · Constan · Soulac · Les parre tillou · Royan · Talemont · Coniak · Blais · Auchelaure · Mussidan · Vesersin

Citron · Macau · Bourg · Libonna · Mortaigne · Langeal · Lisle flu · Sarlate

Anchises · MEDOC · Bordeaux · Miferrant · Geuisac · Dordogne flu · Bergerac · Castelnaus · QVER

Barp · Aubares · Bodensac · Cadillac · Macaire · Dural · Ville neufue · P. S. Marie

Araxon · Lospital · Langen · La Rol · D'agen · Agen · Mirande

Les Lanes · Capsieux · Buser · Tonins · Guaronne flu · Lisle

EN · NE · sols · GVII · Belin · BAZAS · ALBRET · Verac · Beaumont · Mirande

Caberton · Mont · La faye · M. de Marsan · Monreal · Castel rusin

La fave · Tartas · Millas · Nogeret · S. Sever · La tour · Fronfac

Bayonne · La Doure · Aire · ARMIGNAC · Aux · Grenade · Thoulou

Gatura · Dais · Tolozete · S. Martin

BISCAIAE · Fuenten · an de Luz · Causalion · Salson · BIGORRE · Orson · Comingeois

Vitoria · Deuis · S. Pelasquet · Nichat · Pau · Moclus · Neseron · Rieux · Cazeres

PARS · Pampelona · Roncevalles · Pais de Bearn · Oleron · Castellm · Puymory

Logronno · Saltoterre · Orthes · Tarbe · Montes · HISPANIAE · Morogsat · Aretraf

GALLIA

LE ROYAVME DE FRANCE.

Amsterodami · Excudebat Guilielmus

Miliaria Gallica communia

5 · 10 · 15 · 20

Miliaria Germanica communia